Classroom Assessment
for Student Learning

Doing It Right—Using It Well

Richard J. Stiggins, Judith A. Arter,
Jan Chappuis, and Stephen Chappuis

Boston Columbus Indianapolis New York San Francisco Upper Saddle River
Amsterdam Cape Town Dubai London Madrid Milan Munich Paris Montreal Toronto
Delhi Mexico City Sao Paulo Sydney Hong Kong Seoul Singapore Taipei Tokyo

Cover design: Kaija Juszak

Book design and typesetting: Heidi Bay, Grey Sky Design

Editing: Robert L. Marcum, editorbob.com

Project coordination: Barbara Fankhauser

ISBN-10: 0-13-254876-3

ISBN-13: 978-0-13-254876-2

10 9 8 7 6 5

Acknowledgments

This program, including all components (book, CD, DVD, and interactive videos), is the result of a team effort, and that team extends far beyond us four authors. First and foremost, we wish to acknowledge our teachers—those from whom we have learned the most over the years: Anne Davies of British Columbia, Carol Commodore of Wisconsin, Ken O'Connor from Toronto, Donna Snodgrass of Cleveland, Ohio Schools, Vicki Spandel of Sisters, Oregon, and Ruth Sutton of Manchester, United Kingdom. Each has made unique and important contributions to our collective understanding of sound classroom assessment practice. In this same sense, we wish to express appreciation to the Assessment Reform Group of the United Kingdom, and particularly to professors Paul Black and Dylan Wiliam for connecting us to a world of exciting new ideas about assessment *for* learning.

Several teachers, and in some cases their students, were gracious enough to share their ideas on camera for the benefit of others. Each has contributed to the specificity and practicality of our presentation. To begin with, we thank Tia Wulff, who has made our ideas come alive in her classroom so completely and effectively and who has been a most articulate advocate for assessment *for* learning. Thanks also to the following teachers from the Beaverton, Oregon schools: Jesse Scott, Penny Tateoka, and Jim Zaworski; from Bloomington, Illinois: Superintendent Bob Nielsen and his team, Cindy Helmers, Marcia Hirst, Cheryl Jackson, Julie Riley, and Susan Silvey; from the Central Kitsap schools in the state of Washington: Cheryl Junt, Tim McNett, Lemelle Stiles, Paulette Thomas, and Shannon Thompson.

Our team also included the very patient and capable students of Jackson Park Elementary School in Bremerton, Washington and of Cleveland High School, Portland, Oregon.

On the inhouse production and details side, special thanks to ETS team members, Barbara Fankhauser, Mindy Dotson, Laura Camacho, and Sharon Lippert. Also, our special awards for patience, good humor, and outstanding technical advice go to freelancers production editor, Robert L. Marcum, and design consultant, Heidi Bay.

Finally, over the years, we have shared our ideas with many thousands of teachers across the land. Often, we have benefited immensely as those ideas are transformed by these outstanding educators and come marching back to us in refined forms. Thus, we learn as much about assessment *for* learning from our "students" as they learn from us. For this, we thank you.

Rick Stiggins

Judy Arter

Jan Chappuis

Steve Chappuis

Table of Contents

Principles of Assessment *for* Learning and Assessment Quality

CHAPTER

Classroom Assessment: Every Student a Winner!

[T] he teaching profession is a calling, a calling with the potential to do enormous good for students. Although we haven't traditionally seen it in this light, assessment plays an indispensable role in fulfilling our calling. Used with skill, assessment can motivate the unmotivated, restore the desire to learn, and encourage students to keep learning, and it can actually create—not simply measure—increased achievement.

None of this happens if assessment functions solely as an accountability measure, as it does in the case of standardized testing and in determining grades. Because we now understand that assessment can work in positive ways to benefit learning, the time is right to add to our definition of good teaching *the skillful use of assessment—doing it right and using it well.*

Four authors will speak to you in this book—Rick, Judy, Jan, and Steve—collectively representing years of experience with educational measurement, classroom assessment, teaching, staff development, and administration. You may hear our individual voices as you read, but we have a single message throughout: The paramount assessment responsibility we share as educators is to protect students' well-being through use of sound practices. In this program of study, we offer the tools needed to ensure that the good you do in your teaching is joined with and made more powerful by the good you do in assessing.

DEEPEN UNDERSTANDING

Activity 1.1   Program Introduction

For a brief introduction to the book and accompanying resources, please watch the accompanying DVD segment entitled "Program Introduction."

Keys To Quality Classroom Assessment

To begin our examination of student-involved classroom assessment, we present three descriptions of students' assessment experiences.

A Good Example: Emily

As you read the first example, keep this guiding question in mind: What did this teacher do to enhance student motivation and learning?[1]

At a district school board meeting, a high school English faculty is presenting the results of their evaluation of the new writing instruction program they have implemented over the past year. The audience includes a young woman named Emily, a junior at the high school, sitting in the back of the room with her parents.

As part of their preparation for this program, the English faculty attended a summer institute on assessing writing proficiency and integrating such assessments into teaching and learning. The English department expected this approach to produce much higher levels of writing proficiency.

As the first step in presenting program evaluation results, the English chair, Ms. Weathersby, who also happens to be Emily's English teacher, distributes an anonymous sample of student writing to the board members, asking them to read and evaluate the writing. They do so, expressing their dismay quietly as they go. They are less than complimentary in their commentary on the work sample. One board member reports with some frustration that, if this represents the results of that new writing program, then it clearly is not working. The board member is right. This is, in fact, a pretty weak piece of work.

Ms. Weathersby asks the board members to be very specific in stating what they don't like about this writing. As the board registers its responses, a faculty member records the criticisms on chart paper. The list is long, including everything from repetitiveness and disorganization to short, choppy sentences and disconnected ideas.

Next, Ms. Weathersby distributes another sample of student writing, asking the board to read and evaluate it. Now this, they report, is more like it. This work is much better. Again, Ms. Weathersby asks them to be specific: "What do you like about this work?" They list positive aspects: good choice of words, sound sentence structure, clever ideas, and so on.

Emily and her parents have been watching intently, registering every comment, and right now, Emily is feeling confident, happy, and proud. This has been a special year for her and her classmates. For the first time ever, they became partners with their English teachers in managing their own improvement as writers.

Ms. Weathersby started the year by working with students to implement new state writing standards, including understanding quality performance in content, voice, word choice, sentence fluency, organization, and conventions, and by sharing new analytical scoring guides written just for students. Each scoring guide explained the differences between good and poor-quality writing in understandable terms. When Emily and her teacher evaluated her first two pieces of writing using these standards, she received very low ratings. Not very good. . . .

But the class also began to study samples of writing that Emily could see were very good. By practicing evaluating them with the new scoring guides, she began to understand *why* they were good. The differences between these and her work started to become clear. Ms. Weathersby began to share examples and strategies that would help her writing improve one step at a time. As she practiced and time passed, Emily and her classmates kept samples of their old writing to compare to their new writing, and they began to build portfolios. Thus, she watched her own writing skills improve. At midyear, her parents were invited in for a conference at which Emily, not Ms. Weathersby, shared the contents of her portfolio and discussed her emerging writing skills. Emily remembers sharing thoughts about some aspects of her writing that had become very strong and some examples of things she still needed to work on. Now, the year was at an end and here she sat waiting for her turn to speak to the school board about all of this.

Having set the board up by having them analyze, evaluate, and compare these two samples of student work, Ms. Weathersby tells them the two pieces of writing they had just evaluated, one of relatively poor quality and one of outstanding quality, were produced by the same writer at the beginning and at the end of the school year. This, she reports, is evidence of the kind of impact the new writing program is having on student writing proficiency.

Needless to say, all are impressed. One board member wonders aloud, "Have all your students improved in this way?" Having anticipated the question, the rest of the English faculty joins the presentation and produces carefully prepared charts depicting changes in typical student performance over time on rating scales for each of six dimensions of good writing. They accompany their description of student performance on each scale with actual samples of student work illustrating various levels of proficiency.

Further, Ms. Weathersby informs the board that the student whose improvement has been so dramatically illustrated with the work they have just analyzed is present at this school board meeting, along with her parents. Emily is ready to talk with the board about the nature of her learning experience.

Interest among the board members runs high. Emily explains how she has come to understand the important differences between strong and weak writing. She refers to differences she had not understood before, how she has learned to assess her own writing and to fix it when it doesn't "work well," and how she and her classmates have learned to talk with her teacher and each other about what it means to write well. Ms. Weathersby talks about the improved focus of writing instruction, increase in student motivation, and important positive changes in the nature of the student–teacher relationship.

A board member asks Emily if she likes to write, and she answers, "I do now!" This board member turns to Emily's parents and asks their impression of all of this. They report with pride that they had never seen so much evidence before of Emily's achievement and most of it came from Emily herself. Emily had never been called on to lead the parent-teacher conference before. They had no idea she was so articulate. They loved it. Their daughter's pride in and accountability for achievement had skyrocketed in the past year.

As the meeting ends, it is clear to all in attendance that evening that this application of student-involved classroom assessment has contributed to important learning. The English faculty accepted responsibility for student learning, shared that responsibility with their students, and everybody won. There are good feelings all around. One of the accountability demands of the community was satisfied with the presentation of credible evidence of student success, and the new writing program was the reason for improved student achievement. Obviously, this story has a happy ending.

DEEPEN UNDERSTANDING

Activity 1.2 Emily's Interview

1. To see and hear an interview with Emily conducted the morning after the board meeting, go to the segment of the accompanying DVD entitled, "Interview with Emily." Her writing samples appear in Figure 1.1.

2. Think back to the guiding question at the opening of the scenario: What did this teacher do to enhance student motivation and learning?

Figure 1.1   Emily's Papers

Beginning of the Year Writing Sample

Computers are a thing of the future. They help us in thousands of ways. Computers are a help to our lives. They make things easier. They help us to keep track of information.

Computers are simple to use. Anyone can learn how. You do not have to be a computer expert to operate a computer. You just need to know a few basic things.

Computers can be robots that will change our lives. Robots are really computers! Robots do a lot of the work that humans used to do. This makes our lives much easier. Robots build cars and do many other tasks that humans used to do. When robots learn to do more, they will take over most of our work. This will free humans to do other kinds of things. You can also communicate on computers. It is much faster than mail! You can look up information, too. You can find information on anything at all on a computer.

Computers are changing the work and changing the way we work and communicate. In many ways, computers are changing our lives and making our lives better and easier.

End of the Year Writing Sample

So there I was, my face aglow with the reflection on my computer screen, trying to come up with the next line for my essay. Writing it was akin to Chinese water torture, as I could never seem to end it. It dragged on and on, a never-ending babble of stuff.

Suddenly, unexpectedly—I felt an ending coming on. I could wrap this thing up in four or five sentences, and this dreadful assignment would be over. I'd be free.

I had not saved yet, and decided I would do so now. I clasped the slick, white mouse in my hand, slid it over the mouse pad, and watched as the black arrow progressed toward the "File" menu. By accident, I clicked the mouse button just to the left of paragraph 66. I saw a flash and the next thing I knew, I was back to square one. I stared at the blank screen for a moment in disbelief. Where was my essay? My ten-billion-page masterpiece? Gone?! No—that couldn't be! Not after all the work I had done! Would a computer be that unforgiving? That unfeeling? Didn't it care about me at all?

I decided not to give up hope just yet. The secret was to remain calm. After all, my file had to be somewhere—right? That's what all the manuals say—"It's in there somewhere." I went back to the "File" menu, much more carefully this time. First, I tried a friendly sounding category called "Find File." No luck there; I hadn't given the file a name.

Ah, then I had a brainstorm. I could simply go up to "Undo." Yes, that would be my savior! A simple click of a button and my problem would be solved! I went to Undo, but it looked a bit fuzzy. Not a good sign. That means there is nothing to undo. Don't panic . . . don't panic . . .

I decided to try to exit the program, not really knowing what I would accomplish by this but feeling more than a little desperate. Next, I clicked on the icon that would allow me back in to word processing. A small sign appeared, telling me that my program was being used by another user. Another user? What's it talking about? I'm the only user, you idiot! Or at least I'm trying to be a user! Give me my paper back! Right now!

I clicked on the icon again and again—to no avail. Click . . . click . . . clickclickclickCLICKCLICKCLICK!!!! Without warning, a thick cloud of smoke began to rise from the back of the computer. I didn't know whether to laugh or cry. Sighing, I opened my desk drawer, and pulled out a tablet and pen. It was going to be a long day.

Source: Personal writing by Nikki Spandel. Reprinted by permission.

Some Students Aren't So Lucky

Here is another story of classroom assessment as retold by Krissy's parents. As you read it, consider this question: What did this teacher do that made it difficult for the student to achieve the learning goals?[2]

Third-grade Krissy arrived home one afternoon full of gloom. She said she knew we were going to be angry with her. She presented us with a sheet of paper—the third-grade size with the wide lines. On it, she had written a story. Her assignment was to write about someone or something she cares deeply about. She wrote of Tiger, a small kitten that had come to be part of our family, but who had to return to the farm after two weeks because of allergies. Tiger's departure had been like the loss of a family member. Krissy cried for the kitten and we shed a few tears for Krissy.

On the sheet of paper was an emergent writer's version of this story—not sophisticated, but poignant. Krissy's recounting of events was accurate and her story captured her very strong sadness and disappointment at losing her new little friend. She did a pretty darn good job of portraying the event and her feelings.

At the bottom of the page, below the story, was a big red circled "F". We asked her why, and she told us that the teacher said she had better improve or she would fail. Questioning further, we found that her teacher had said that students were to fill the page with writing. Krissy had used only three-quarters of the page, so she hadn't followed directions and so deserved an F.

When she had finished telling us this story, Krissy put the sheet of paper down on the kitchen table and, with a discouraged look, said in a small voice, "I'll never be a good writer anyway." My recollection of that moment remains vivid after many years.

In fact, she had *succeeded* at hitting the achievement target. She produced a clear and compelling narrative. But her confidence in herself as a writer was deeply shaken because her teacher failed to disentangle her expectation that students comply with directions with her expectation that they demonstrate the ability to write well. As a result, both the assessment and the feedback had a destructive impact on this student. Without question, it's quite easy to see if the page is full. But is that the point of writing instruction?

DEEPEN UNDERSTANDING

Activity 1.3 Case Comparison: Emily and Krissy

1. What problems do you see in Krissy's case?

2. What are the essential differences between Emily's and Krissy's experiences? Why did one work when the other did not?

Another Story of Student Success

Here is a third classroom assessment scenario. Ms. Weathersby engaged Emily and her classmates in developing and using performance assessments; this teacher uses a traditional selected response and extended response test to achieve the same result. Once again, as you read, think of what this teacher is doing well in using classroom assessment as a learning tool for students.

Mr. Heim, a middle school science teacher, plans a 3-week unit of instruction on the environmental effects of pollution. Students are to know (1) how to calculate the concentrations of pollutants in the most commonly reported units, (2) the effects of several common pollutants at various concentrations on plants, animals, and humans, and (3) several proposals for reducing pollution and the arguments of various stakeholders. In addition, Mr. Heim wants his students to use their content knowledge to compare proposals for mitigating pollution, and to evaluate the arguments that different groups of stakeholders are likely to make. These learning targets align with the following science and mathematics state academic achievement standards for middle schoolers in Florida (Florida Department of Education, n.d.):

- *Science:* Extends and refines knowledge of ways that human activities may deliberately or inadvertently alter the equilibrium in the ecosystem. Knows possible causes for a species to become threatened, endangered, or extinct. Knows some of the functions of some types of cells, tissues, organs, and systems in advanced organisms.

- *Mathematics:* Knows the relationships among fractions, decimals, and percents given a real-world context. Knows equivalent forms of large and small numbers in scientific and standard notation. Solves real-world problems involving integers, ratios, proportions, numbers expressed as percents, decimals, and fractions in two- or three-step problems.

To clarify his goals, Mr. Heim develops a plan for a 50-point final exam before beginning instruction. This plan is shown in Table 1.1.

Table 1.1   Mr. Heim's Sample Test Blueprint

		PATTERN OF REASONING		
	Know	**Compare**	**Evaluate**	**Total**
Concentrations	10	0	0	10
Effects of Pollutants	7	8	0	15
How to Reduce Pollution	6	10	9	25
Total	23	18	9	50

The plan says that the final exam will ask students 10 knowledge questions about concentrations—define and convert among parts per million, parts per billion, and percent concentrations. The exam will allot 7 points to questions covering knowledge about acceptable levels of various pollutants and the effects of various levels on plants, animals, and humans. The exam also will allot 8 points to questions that require students to compare effects. Finally, the text will allot 6 points to knowledge questions about proposals for reducing pollution, 10 points to questions that require comparing various proposals and arguments, and 9 points to questions that ask students to evaluate the effect on pollution of various solutions.

Mr. Heim uses the plan in various ways. He makes sure that the priorities in the assessment align with those in his instruction. He gives each student a copy of the final exam plan on the first day of the unit, to help them understand the learning priorities. He writes four or five test questions every day as the unit unfolds, connecting his questions directly to the focus of instruction. He creates a practice version of the exam, which he can use as a pretest or a practice test a few days before the actual final to help students identify remaining weaknesses for last-minute study. He engages his students in writing some of the questions for the practice test, thus helping them focus on and practice with important content and valued patterns of reasoning.

> **DEEPEN UNDERSTANDING**
>
> ### Activity 1.4 Case Comparison: Emily and Mr. Heim's Class
>
> What do this case and the case of Emily's writing have in common as keys to the effective and productive use of classroom assessment as a teaching and learning tool? List the similarities and compare your list to those keys we describe in the following section.

What Are the Keys to Quality Classroom Assessment?

These scenarios highlight a variety of sound and unsound classroom assessment practices that are the focus of this professional development program. Sound and productive classroom assessments are built on a foundation of the following five key dimensions:

- Arise from and be designed to serve the *specific information needs of intended user(s)*

- Arise from clearly articulated and appropriate *achievement targets*

- *Accurately reflect* student achievement

- Yield results that are *effectively communicated* to their intended users

- *Involve students* in classroom assessment, record keeping, and communication

These keys are illustrated in Figure 1.2. Notice that the assessment context—*intended users and uses* and *learning targets*—combines to help determine a proper *assessment design*, from which the best mode of *communication* is derived. *Students are involved* at all steps. High-quality classroom assessment equals accurate information—clear purposes, clear learning targets, and an appropriate design—used effectively to help students learn.

Figure 1.2   Keys to Quality Classroom Assessment

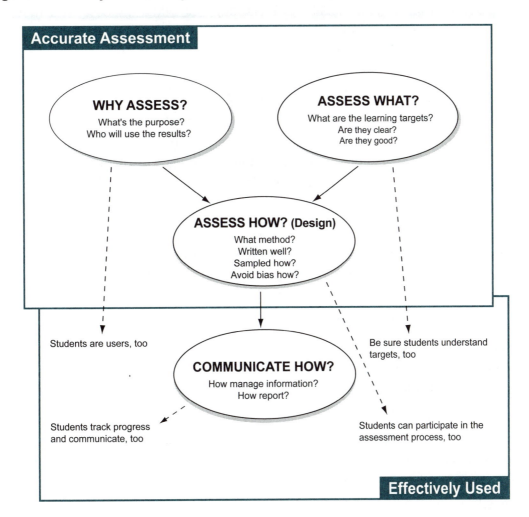

This is it in a nutshell. This entire professional development program is built around two driving themes: *assess accurately* and use assessment to *benefit students*, not merely to grade and sort them. The succeeding chapters of this book proceed systematically through the various elements of Figure 1.2.

Our goal is to enable you to internalize this line of development to select, create, and/or use assessments that are of high quality and that support student success. Further, our goal is to ensure that you understand why it is essential to adhere to these standards of good practice any time student achievement is assessed.

Why Assess? To Serve Users' Information Needs

We assess to gather evidence of student learning that will inform instructional decisions in ways that maximize that learning. Both Ms. Weathersby and Emily used evidence from writing assessments to decide how to improve Emily's writing. Mr. Heim and his students used assessment to decide where to concentrate their studies. As learning progresses, we and our students need regular information about what they have and have not yet learned. This permits us and them to make instructional decisions that keep them growing.

We make some decisions frequently, such as when we decide what comes next in student learning within lessons or when we try to discover what's blocking student learning. Typically, these decisions are made day to day in the classroom based on evidence derived from classroom activities and assessments.

We make other decisions periodically, such as when we assign report card grades or identify students for special services. Here we also rely on classroom assessment evidence accumulated over time and for different purposes. In this case, we want to determine how much learning has occurred up to a point in time.

Other instructional decisions are made less frequently, such as when school districts make adjustments in instructional programs or purchase curriculum materials. Often these decisions turn on results of once-a-year standardized tests reflecting very broad content domains.

It is therefore apparent that different assessments serve a variety of users and uses, centering on achievement defined at a variety of levels, and requiring a variety of kinds of assessment information delivered at different times. All resulting information must be accurate and used effectively.

In any assessment context, whether supporting learning while it is happening or checking for it after it has happened, we must start by understanding the information needs of the intended users. Then we build our assessment to meet those needs. These assessment purposes (users and uses) influence the form and frequency of assessment, as well as the level and type of detail required in communicating results.

In this program, we will use the phrases, "assessment purposes," "assessment users and uses," and "serve the user's information needs" interchangeably to refer to the reasons *why* we are conducting any given assessment. To assess well, we must begin by knowing our purpose—who will use results to inform what decisions.

Chapter 2 expands on the various purposes—users and uses—for assessment, including the essential distinction between assessment *for* and *of* learning.

Assess What? Clear Targets

In addition to beginning with a purpose in mind, we must also have a clear sense of the achievement expectations we wish our students to master. Obviously, these achievement expectations are what we will be assessing. We can't develop multiple-choice test items, extended response exercises and scoring procedures, or performance assessments of learning targets that we ourselves have not clearly and completely defined. Ms. Weathersby and her colleagues began their work with a clear and comprehensive vision of good writing. Mr. Heim knows and understands the nuances of the effects of pollution and is a confident, competent master of the patterns of reasoning he wants his students to learn to apply. Understanding the important learning targets is the essential foundation of sound assessment, and of good teaching too. Only when we understand the academic subjects we teach will the achievement targets our students are to master be clear.

When these crucial classroom learning targets are clear, the next step is to transform them into student-friendly language. This represents an important insight into how to use assessment to increase student learning. We know that students' chances of success grow markedly when they start their learning with a clear sense of where they are headed and when they play a role in tracking and communicating about their own progress along the way. We help them succeed, therefore, by providing an understandable vision of success with examples of what success will look like when they get there.

Chapter 3 explores learning targets—knowledge, reasoning, performance skills, and creating products—and how to make them clear to students.

Assess How? Assessment Design to Promote Accuracy

Assessments can produce accurate or inaccurate information about student achievement. They can correctly represent or misrepresent learning. Obviously, our goal is accurate assessment in any context.

The previous two sections lay a foundation for accuracy. If we start assessment development with a clear sense of the intended user's information needs, we have hope of serving them well. If we start with a clear sense of the achievement targets to measure, we lay a foundation from which to accurately assess them. An assessment devised without clear purpose or focus is extremely unlikely to produce accurate information.

Accuracy requires selecting a proper assessment method for each context. Chapter 4 introduces the methods and provides practice in matching assessment methods to learning targets. Each assessment method has unique strengths and limitations, and works well in some contexts (purposes and learning targets) but not in others. Assessment methods are not interchangeable. Our task always is to choose a proper method for the particular situation—the quality of our assessments hinges on our ability to do so.

Once we have chosen a method, we must develop and use it well. That means creating high-quality assessment exercises (test questions, extended written response questions, or performance tasks). It means including enough exercises to lead to confident conclusions about student achievement without wasting time gathering more evidence than the context requires. In Chapters 5–8 we expand on these topics for each individual assessment method: selected response (Chapter 5), extended written response (Chapter 6), performance assessment (Chapter 7), and personal communication (Chapter 8).

Finally, every assessment situation brings with it its own list of things that can go wrong and that can render results inaccurate. For instance, a score on any assessment can misrepresent the student's real achievement if the test questions are poorly written, the directions are misleading, the student suffers from extreme test anxiety, or subjective scoring procedures for extended response or performance assessments are conducted carelessly. It is our responsibility to anticipate what can go wrong in various assessment contexts and prevent those problems when possible.

Thus, to assure accuracy, over and above starting with clear targets and information needs, we must do the following:

- Rely on proper assessment methods for each particular context.

- Sample student achievement appropriately.

- Rely only on quality exercises and scoring procedures to avoid all potential sources of bias.

Communicate Results How? In a Timely and Understandable Manner

Even if learning targets and information needs are clear and the information gathered is precisely accurate, an assessment can fail to achieve its learning ends if the results are not communicated effectively to the intended user(s). If we use test scores to convey results and the users don't understand how the score connects to learning or if we use symbols such as letter grades on a report card when users have a different idea what those symbols mean, we communicate ineffectively and poor-quality decisions, decisions harmful to students, can result.

To prevent such problems, we recommend these guidelines for good communication:

- Everyone must understand the meaning of the achievement target.

- The information underpinning the communication must be accurate.

- Everyone must understand the symbols being used to convey information.

- The communication must be tailored to the intended audience, e.g., level of detail, timing, and format.

Chapter 9 discusses these guidelines more fully; Chapters 10–13 apply them to various communication options—grading, portfolios, conferences, and standardized tests.

Involve Students—Make Assessment Instruction

Student involvement is a critically important shift in our traditional or conventional perspectives regarding the role of assessment in promoting effective schools: the most important instructional decisions (that is, the decisions that contribute the most to student learning) are made, not by the adults working in the system, but by students themselves. Students decide whether the learning is worth the effort required to attain it. Students decide whether they believe they are capable of reaching the learning targets. It is only after our students make these decisions in the affirmative that we, their teachers, can impact their learning lives. So part of our classroom assessment job is to keep students believing in themselves as learners through the effective use of classroom assessment.

The point is not that we adults don't contribute immensely to student learning. We do. We are critical players in teaching, learning, and assessment. It's just that we are second in the rank order of importance as instructional decision makers.

Each chapter includes concrete examples of how to involve students in classroom assessment, record keeping, and communication. Chapter 2 describes the research that supports student-involvement. Chapter 3 provides specific ways to make learning targets clear to students. Chapters 5–8 include step-by-step ways to involve students in every form of assessment, from selected response to performance assessment. Chapters 9–13 explore how to involve students in communicating about their own learning.

Therefore, Our Mission Together

In this program, we will assist educators to achieve the following:

- Become comfortable differentiating among the information needs of the various users of classroom assessment, especially students.

- Understand the importance of and know how to frame learning targets to underpin sound classroom assessments, including developing student-friendly versions of achievement standards.

- Assess student achievement accurately on all occasions by knowing how to select and develop classroom assessments that fit each unique context, involving students in self-assessment when appropriate.

- Understand how to manage and communicate assessment results, again, involving students when appropriate and in ways that promote learning.

We do not assume these topics are entirely new. You may already know a considerable amount about sound classroom assessment practice. Rather, this list of important learnings is intended to frame standards of good practice in their totality, provide a cognitive structure for developing classroom assessment practices, and permit you to extend your repertoire of sound practices.

What sets apart the lessons we teach herein are (1) emphasis on the need for accurate classroom assessment and (2) deep student involvement in classroom assessment as a motivator and a teaching/learning tool.

DEEPEN UNDERSTANDING

Activity 1.5   Evaluating Assessment Quality

1. Return to and read the three opening examples again. Evaluate how you think these teachers did in meeting the requirements described: clear sense of purpose, clear targets, accurate assessment, and effective communication. In addition, did they involve their students in classroom assessment? If so, how and with what result?

2. Reflect on your experience as a student and think of an assessment in which you participated that was a distinctly negative experience for you. As you think about that specific experience, which requirements in our five domains of sound practice did your teacher violate?

3. Finally, think of an assessment experience in your past that represented a distinctly positive experience for you. How did your teacher address each of the dimensions of sound practice?

DEEPEN UNDERSTANDING

Activity 1.6   Watch Video, *Assessment for Student Motivation*

To understand more about productive and counterproductive relationships between assessment and student motivation, please watch the ETS video, *Assessment for Student Motivation*.

To Get the Most from This Program, Form a Learning Team

Although you can certainly learn what you need to know about sound classroom assessment by progressing through this program alone, your learning experience will be deeper if you gather together a few colleagues for periodic discussion of the text and what you've been trying in the classroom. The field of staff development has long been concerned with how to optimize learning for teachers, and much research has focused on answering the question, "What kind of learning environments and experiences are most conducive to adult learning?" The results of numerous studies converge on these key ingredients: access to effective new ideas and strategies, opportunities to try ideas and strategies in the classroom, ability to exercise control over your own learning, and collaboration. As Putnam & Borko (2000, p. 10) state, "For teachers to be successful in constructing new roles, they need opportunities to participate in a professional community that discusses new teacher materials and strategies and that supports the risk-taking and struggle entailed in transforming practice." DuFour (2001, p. 15) amplifies this thought: "Professional development moves from the workshop to the workplace. Emphasis shifts from finding the right speaker to creating opportunities for staff to work together, engage in collective inquiry, and learn from one another. . . . The single most effective way in which principals can function as professional development leaders is in providing a school context that fosters job-embedded professional development."

Why Workshops Are Not Enough

Attending workshops, reading journals and books, and observing in others' classrooms all provide access to new ideas and strategies. However, if our professional development actions stop there, research and experience tell us the new information has little chance of changing our classroom practice. We also need opportunities and support for experimentation in the classroom, coupled with the time to reflect on the results of what we tried. At this point, the workshop model of staff development falls short—all responsibility for figuring out how to apply new information to our classrooms, all experimentation, critiquing, and revision—are left up to the individual, with no time or support for implementation provided. This is where a collaborative learning model of professional development weighs in strongly. Individual teachers are still responsible for trying new ideas out in the classroom, but the model provides time for small groups of teachers to help each other refine implementation.

We have structured this program to maximize its effectiveness in a collaborative learning situation, which we call a *learning team* approach. In this professional development model, the text of the book and the accompanying resources furnish new ideas and strategies. Specific activities offer step-by-step guidance and resources for strategies to try in the classroom. Regular meetings with a group of colleagues provide a forum for discussion and problem solving. In addition, participants in learning teams have opportunity to control which aspects of study they will focus on, the pace of study, and the meeting schedule.

What Is a Learning Team?

Through our experiences with effective adult learning, we have come to the following definition of a *learning team*: "a group of three to six individuals who have committed to meet regularly for an agreed amount of time guided by a common purpose." Because learning along with others who bring different areas of expertise to the table is a central feature of learning teams, we recommend having *three to six participants* on a given team. This structure provides diversity of experience, interpretation, and viewpoint while still allowing time for each member to participate actively in meetings.

The second phrase of our definition, "*who have committed to meeting regularly for an agreed amount of time*," reflects the promise team members make to each other: "You can count on me to be there, because we together create the environment and the expertise necessary for peak learning." If any team member is not committed and present, the team loses the richness of that person's perspective, arguments, and insights.

The last phrase, "*guided by a common purpose*," is the reason team members make the commitment: "Our common purpose in this study is to make classroom assessment work better for our students and ourselves. We know that we won't contribute as productively toward that end if we don't do the agreed reading, viewing, or experimentation between team meetings." Thus, the learning team's goal is to *help all members become assessment literate through collaboration during team meetings and individual study and action between meetings.* To be *assessment literate* means to be skilled both in gathering accurate information about students learning and in using it effectively to promote further learning.

A learning team is not a book group. As pleasant an experience as book groups are, they do not share our goals. While we hope you will find at least portions of this book a pleasure to read, we are fairly certain you are not reading purely for enjoyment and to engage in lively conversation. "What is happening differently *in our classrooms* as a result of what we are doing and learning in our study teams?" Carlene Murphy (2001, p. 12), a leader in the field of learning teams, raises this question when she helps others establish study teams, and it puts the emphasis where, in our opinion, it belongs. The discussion that occurs during team meetings is a means to the end, *and not the end itself.* If we don't commit to trying things out between team meetings, nothing different will be happening in our classrooms, and if that's the case, what's the purpose of our study?

The Learning Team Process

As structured within these materials, the learning team process consists of the following steps:

- Thinking about classroom assessment

- Reading and reflecting on new classroom assessment strategies

- Shaping the strategies into applications

- Trying out applications, observing, and drawing inferences about what does and doesn't work

- Reflecting on and summarizing learning and conclusions from that experience

- Sharing and problem solving with team members

You will notice that the bulk of time is spent in activities between team meetings—acquiring new ideas and applying them in the classroom. Team meetings themselves constitute a small but powerful portion of your learning time. Figure 1.3 apportions the time commitments to each ingredient in our learning team program.

Finding Time

The problem of time is always with us, yet when learning is a priority, school districts, buildings, and groups of teachers have found ways to secure the time needed, both for the individual work required and for team meetings. Options commonly employed include paying a stipend for a set number of hours, offering college and salary-advancement credit, and setting aside contract time. (To help get credit, we've prepared a sample course credit form. It appears on the CD.)

Additional Resources

To view teachers and administrators talking about the effects of learning teams on instructional practices, please watch the accompanying DVD segment entitled "Learning Teams."

Detailed information about how to set up and conduct learning teams is also presented on the CD.

Figure 1.3   Division of Learning Time

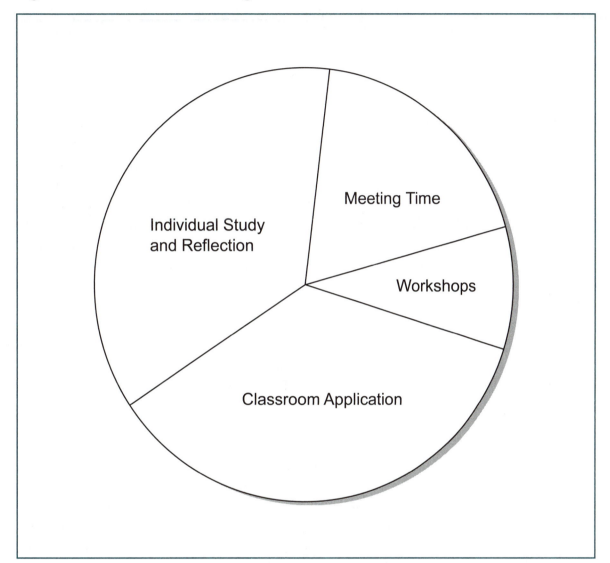

Overview of This Learning Experience

Structure of the Chapters

This book is organized into three parts. Part 1, Chapters 1 through 3, lays out both the principles of assessment quality—"doing it right"—and the principles of assessment *for* learning—"using it well." In Part 2, Chapters 4 through 8, we describe in depth how to "do it right and use it well" within the context of each assessment method: selected response, extended written response, performance assessment, and personal communication. Part 3, Chapters 9 through 13, explains our communication challenge and options—report card grades, portfolios, conferences, and standardized tests—with emphasis on using each in support of student learning.

Features of the Text

Activities to Advance Your Understanding

As you have already experienced, we have included activities to assist your learning as a part of the text. As you read, you will encounter more activities, each of which has one of three purposes: "I get it," "I can use it," or "I know what I know." "I get it" activities (called "Deepen Understanding") will ask you to reflect on a given situation or to create a product, for the purpose of enhancing your sense of the concepts presented. "I can use it" activities (called "Try This") will offer hands-on classroom experience with the concepts. "I know what I know" activities (called "Reflect on Your Learning") will ask you to think further on your learning, giving you a platform from which to make the information your own. You are in control of what and how much you learn; it is our job to offer you the most productive experience available. We believe that if you take advantage of the activities—complete them and reflect on your thinking—you will learn the material at a faster rate and will retain it longer. The ideas herein will have maximum impact on the students you teach. Therefore, we encourage you to throw yourself into this learning experience with vigor *and do the activities.*

A Growth Portfolio

Periodically, we will ask you to prepare a portfolio entry demonstrating your learning about classroom assessment. In doing so, we will follow our guidelines for portfolios as set out in Chapter 11. We encourage you to keep track of, reflect on, and share your learning for the same reasons we encourage you to use portfolios with students: Engaging in these processes deepens your commitment to what you are learning, pushes you to learn more, and offers intrinsic reward for the work you are about to do. On the CD you will find specific information about how to set up and manage your portfolio, along with suggestions for sharing it with others.

The CD and DVD

In the pocket inside the back cover, you will find a DVD, entitled *Classroom Assessment* for *Student Learning: Supplementary DVD*, and a CD, entitled *Classroom Assessment* for *Student Learning: Supplementary CD*. At this point, we hope you have had experience with both. The contents of each disc are organized by this book's chapters, and the discs are designed to support your learning as you proceed. We frequently refer in the text to these discs, asking you to watch a video clip from the DVD or guiding you to further activities and classroom applications on the CD. Also on the CD is a table of contents for the DVD video clips, accompanied by a short description of each segment. None of these resources—the text, the CD, or the DVD—is designed to stand alone; the program of learning requires all three components.

Interactive Program Videos

Should you want to go more deeply into topics discussed in the book, we offer a series of interactive training videos (available on VHS videocassette or DVD), each associated with a particular chapter and offering additional insights and hands-on practice. They can be used as the focus for one or more learning team meetings, as an exploration of a topic of choice for a whole faculty, or for your individual learning experience. These presentations are listed in Figure 1.4.

Figure 1.4   Program Videos

Title	Aligns with Chapter...
Assessment for Student Motivation	1
Evaluating Assessment Quality: Hands-on Practice	2, 3, & 4
Assessing Reasoning in the Classroom	3
Commonsense Paper and Pencil Assessment	5
Designing Performance Assessments for Learning	7
Grading & Reporting in Standards-Based Schools	10
Student-Involved Conferences	12

Other Resources

We at ETS also publish two related books aimed at audiences other than classroom teachers. *Assessment FOR Learning: An Action Guide for School Leaders* is designed to guide administrators through a series of decision points to ensure that the assessment system you are working in is supportive of sound assessment practices. *Understanding School Assessment: A Parent and Community Guide to Helping Students Learn* is a commonsense explanation of what good assessment looks like, how parents can support the development of such a system, and what they can do to help their children at home.

For more detailed information about our videos and books, visit our website at **www.ets.org/ati**.

Summary

Quality classroom assessment produces accurate information that is used effectively to maximize student learning. Accurate information comes from clearly defining learning targets for students, clearly understanding the purpose(s) for which information about student learning is being gathered, using a variety of assessment methods well, and designing assessments that cover important aspects of a learning target and that avoid circumstances that might bias results.

Effective use includes using assessment results to plan instruction, using assessment information and materials to involve students in their own assessment, and communicating assessment results clearly and in a way tailored to the user's needs.

These two aspects of quality form the focus of the professional development experience in *Classroom Assessment* for *Student Learning: Doing It Right—Using It Well*. Every chapter will be cross-referenced to these topics using Figure 1.2. The specific learning targets for the program are listed in Table 1.2.

The program is designed for use in collaborative learning teams. This form of professional development has an extensive foundation in research on effectiveness. The best way to ensure change in the classroom is to try out things in the classroom and discuss experiences in teams. The CD accompanying this program provides extensive assistance with setting up and conducting learning teams.

■ *Tracking Your Learning—Possible Portfolio Entries*

Should you choose to assemble a professional growth portfolio, you may use as entries any of the activities from this chapter. The learning targets for this book, as outlined in Table 1.2 and described in this chapter, will form the basis for evidence of learning you collect. The portfolio entry cover sheet provided on the CD in the file, "Portfolio Entry Cover Sheet," will prompt you to think about how each item you select reflects your learning with respect to one or more of these learning targets.

Table 1.2   Indicators of Sound Classroom Assessment Practice*

1. Why Assess? **Assessment Processes and Results Serve Clear and Appropriate Purposes**	a. Teachers understand who the users and uses of classroom assessment information are and know their information needs. b. Teachers understand the relationship between assessment and student motivation and craft assessment experiences to maximize motivation. c. Teachers use classroom assessment processes and results formatively (assessment *for* learning). d. Teachers use classroom assessment results summatively (assessment *of* learning) to inform someone beyond the classroom about students' achievement as of a particular point in time. e. Teachers have a comprehensive plan over time for integrating assessment *for* and *of* learning in the classroom.
2. Assess What? **Assessments Reflect Clear and Valued Student Learning Targets**	a. Teachers have clear learning targets for students; they know how to turn broad statements of content standards into classroom-level targets. b. Teachers understand the various types of learning targets they hold for students. c. Teachers select learning targets focused on the most important things students need to know and be able to do. d. Teachers have a comprehensive plan over time for assessing learning targets.
3. Assess How? **Learning Targets Are Translated into Assessments That Yield Accurate Results**	a. Teachers understand what the various assessment methods are. b. Teachers choose assessment methods that match intended learning targets. c. Teachers design assessments that serve intended purposes. d. Teachers sample learning appropriately in their assessments. e. Teachers write assessment questions of all types well. f. Teachers avoid sources of bias that distort results.
4. Communicate How? **Assessment Results Are Managed Well and Communicated Effectively**	a. Teachers record assessment information accurately, keep it confidential, and appropriately combine and summarize it for reporting (including grades). Such summary accurately reflects current level of student learning. b. Teachers select the best reporting option (grades, narratives, portfolios, conferences) for each context (learning targets and users). c. Teachers interpret and use standardized test results correctly. d. Teachers effectively communicate assessment results to students. e. Teachers effectively communicate assessment results to a variety of audiences outside the classroom, including parents, colleagues, and other stakeholders.
5. Involve Students How? **Students Are Involved in Their Own Assessment**	a. Teachers make learning targets clear to students. b. Teachers involve students in assessing, tracking, and setting goals for their own learning. c. Teachers involve students in communicating about their own learning.

*Sound classroom assessment practice = Skill in gathering accurate information + effective use of information and procedures

REFLECT ON YOUR LEARNING

Activity 1.7 Classroom Assessment Confidence Questionnaire

To provide a baseline of your current understanding of classroom assessment for learning, find the file, "Confidence Questionnaire," on the CD and answer the survey questions it contains. Consider using this as one of your first entries in a professional growth portfolio. You may wish to answer the questions again at the conclusion of your study, which will provide you with an opportunity to reflect on your learning as a whole.

Notes

1. Adapted from pp. 6–8 of R. J. Stiggins, *Student-Involved Assessment* for *Learning*, 4th ed., 2005, Upper Saddle River, NJ: Merrill/Prentice Hall. Copyright © 2005 by Pearson Education, Inc. Reprinted and adapted by permission of Pearson Education, Inc.

2. Adapted from pp. 12–13 of R. J. Stiggins, *Student-Involved Assessment* for *Learning*, 4th ed., 2005, Upper Saddle River, NJ: Merrill/Prentice Hall. Copyright © 2005 by Pearson Education, Inc. Reprinted and adapted by permission of Pearson Education, Inc.

Assessment *for* and *of* Learning

Self-assessment by pupils, far from being a luxury, is in fact an essential component of formative assessment. (Black & Wiliam, 1998)

[M]any people want to use assessment information, and they want to use it in many ways. Some wish to help students learn more, as when Ms. Weathersby uses writing rubrics in her English classes. Others wish to track student progress toward important learning outcomes, to decide where to allocate resources, to check which adoptions are most effective, to provide accountability information to the public, or to refer students for special services.

We can think of all assessment uses as falling into one of two general categories—assessments *FOR* learning and assessments *OF* learning. Both categories have their place in education and in the classroom—you've been doing both for years. What is perhaps new is an expanded understanding of the roles each should play to maximize student achievement while minimizing unintended negative consequences and side effects for students.

The goal of this chapter is to elaborate the differences and similarities between assessment *for* and *of* learning, relate them to student motivation and learning, and provide an organizing framework for assessment *for* learning in the classroom. In our discussion, we will concentrate on the shaded portions of Figure 2.1.

Figure 2.1   Keys to Quality Classroom Assessment

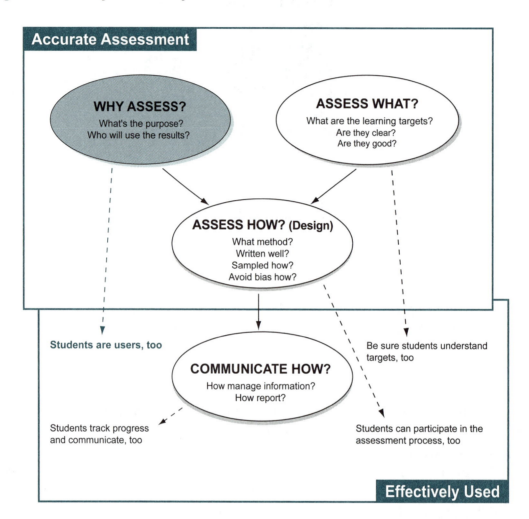

What We Mean by Assessment *for* and *of* Learning

Table 2.2 shows *our* summary of the key differences between assessment *for* and *of* learning. Assessments *of* learning are those assessments that happen after learning is supposed to have occurred to determine if it did. They are used to make statements of student learning status at a point in time to those outside the classroom, as when making student referrals or making decisions about programs. State assessments, local standardized tests, and college admissions tests represent external examinations that do this. But we also conduct assessments *of* learning within the classroom when we gather evidence to determine a student's report card grade. Unit final exams and important projects often serve this purpose.

Assessments *for* learning happen while learning is still underway. These are the assessments that we conduct throughout teaching and learning to diagnose student needs, plan our next steps in instruction, provide students with feedback they can use to improve the quality of their work, and help students see and feel in control of their journey to success. Each one reveals to students increments of achievement and how to do better the next time. On these occasions, the grading function is laid aside. This is not about accountability—those are assessments *of* learning. This is about getting better.

DEEPEN UNDERSTANDING

Activity 2.1 Introduction to Assessment *for* Learning

Please watch the video clip on the accompanying DVD entitled "Assessment OF/ FOR Learning: A Hopeful Vision of the Future." This clip shows Rick explaining the important distinctions between assessment *for* and *of* learning. While you are listening, please complete the form in Table 2.1 to track the differences. A printable version of Table 2.1 appears on the CD.

Table 2.1   Assessment *for* and *of* Learning: Selected Key Differences

	Assessment *for* Learning	Assessment *of* Learning
Reasons for Assessing		
Audience for Results		
Focus of Assessment— Learning Targets		
Place in Time		
Primary Users		
Typical Uses		
Teacher's Role		
Student's Role		
Primary Motivator for Students		
Example(s)		

State in your own words why the distinction between assessment *for* and *of* learning is important:

_____

_____

Table *2.2*   Comparing Assessment *for* and *of* Learning: Overview of Key Differences

	Assessment *for* Learning	**Assessment *of* Learning**
Reasons for Assessing	Promote increases in achievement to help students meet more standards; support ongoing student growth; improvement	Document individual or group achievement or mastery of standards; measure achievement status at a point in time for purposes of reporting; accountability
Audience	Students about themselves	Others about students
Focus of Assessment	Specific achievement targets selected by teachers that enable students to build toward standards	Achievement standards for which schools, teachers, and students are held accountable
Place in Time	A process during learning	An event after learning
Primary Users	Students, teachers, parents	Policy makers, program planners, supervisors, teachers, students, parents
Typical Uses	Provide students with insight to improve achievement; help teachers diagnose and respond to student needs; help parents see progress over time; help parents support learning	Certify student competence; sort students according to achievement; promotion and graduation decisions; grading
Teacher's Role	Transform standards into classroom targets; inform students of targets; build assessments; adjust instruction based on results; offer descriptive feedback to students; involve students in assessment	Administer the test carefully to ensure accuracy and comparability of results; use results to help students meet standards; interpret results for parents; build assessments for report card grading
Student's Role	Self-assess and keep track of progress; contribute to setting goals; act on classroom assessment results to be able to do better next time	Study to meet standards; take the test; strive for the highest possible score; avoid failure
Primary Motivator	Belief that success in learning is achievable	Threat of punishment, promise of rewards
Examples	Using rubrics with students; student self-assessment; descriptive feedback to students	Achievement tests; final exams; placement tests; short cycle assessments

Source: Adapted from *Understanding School Assessment* (pp. 17–18), by J. Chappuis & S. Chappuis, 2002, Portland, OR: Assessment Training Institute. Copyright © 2006, 2002 Educational Testing Service. Adapted by permission.

A useful way to think practically about assessment *for* learning strategies that transform the assessment environment in the classroom comes from Royce Sadler, an Australian researcher:

> *A key premise is that for students to be able to improve, they must have the capacity to monitor the quality of their own work during actual production. This in turn requires that students:*
>
> * *Know what high quality work looks like*
> * *Be able to objectively compare their work to the standard*
> * *Have a store of tactics to make work better based on their observations (Sadler, 1989, p. 119)*

In other words, if we want to use assessment as a tool for learning, students need to

* Know where they're going

* Know where they are now

* Know how to close the gap

As you'll recall, in Chapter 1 we mentioned that many different decision makers count on the availability of accurate information about student achievement to do their jobs to help students learn. We talked about teachers, students, parents, and district staff. Many of these users of assessment are shown in Table 2.3, categorized by major purpose: assessment *for* or *of* learning. As you look through Table 2.3, what do you notice?

Here's what we notice:

* Inside the classroom, assessment *for* and *of* learning are more balanced. For teachers, students, and parents, assessments *of* learning are not enough. This is especially true if the assessment *of* learning is from a once-a-year standardized test. These kinds of assessments don't provide the day-to-day information needed in the classroom. Yet much of our national assessment energy is expended on once-a-year tests.

* Those outside the classroom make almost purely assessment *of* learning decisions, many of which can be made from a once-a-year standardized test.

* Although assessment *of* learning is important, it is not sufficient. Once-a-year assessment meets only the needs of some of those who use assessment information. If the needs of all decision makers are not met, we are out of balance in our assessment systems.

Table 2.3   Purposes for (Users and Uses of) Assessment

Assessment User	Assessment *for* Learning	Assessment *of* Learning
Students	Am I improving over time? Do I know what it means to succeed? What should I do next? What help do I need?	Am I succeeding at the level that I should be? Am I capable of success? How am I doing in relationship to my classmates? Is the learning worth the effort?
Teachers	What does this student need? What do these students need? What are student strengths to build on? How should I group my students? Am I going too fast? Too slow? Too far? Not far enough?	What grade do I put on the report card? What students need to be referred for special service? What will I tell parents?
Parents	What can we do at home to support learning? Is my child learning new things?	Is my child keeping up? Is this teacher doing a good job? Is this a good school? District?
Principal		Is instruction producing results? Are our students ready for the workplace or the next step in learning? How shall we allocate building resources to achieve success?
Superintendent		Are our programs of instruction producing desired results? Is each building producing results? Which schools need additional resources? How shall we allocate district resources to achieve success?

Table 2.3   (Continued)

Assessment User	Assessment *for* Learning	Assessment *of* Learning
State Department of Education		Are programs across the state producing results? Are individual districts producing results? Who is making adequate yearly progress and is not? How shall we allocate district resources to achieve success?
Citizens		Are our students achieving in ways that prepare them to become productive workers and citizens?

Source: Adapted from *Student-Involved Assessment* for *Learning*, 4th ed. (p. 22), by R. J. Stiggins, 2005, Upper Saddle River, NJ: Merrill/Prentice Hall. Copyright © 2005 by Pearson Education, Inc. Adapted by permission of Pearson Education, Inc.

- Students are very important users of assessment information, making critical decisions about themselves as learners. These decisions can have important motivational consequences.

- Individuals make very important decisions about students based on assessment information. Therefore, all our assessments—standardized as well as classroom; assessments *of* learning as well as assessments *for* learning—must be of high quality, yielding accurate results.

You might be thinking assessment *for* and *of* learning sound like formative and summative assessment. If you are, you are correct. Assessment *for* learning is also called "formative" assessment. Assessment *of* learning is also called "summative" assessment. We use here the words *for* and *of* because they are more sprightly and catchy. But, more importantly, the term *assessment* for *learning* has a broader meaning than formative assessment. The traditional way to think of formative uses of assessment is teachers assessing frequently and using the results to plan the next steps in instruction. Assessment *for* learning goes beyond that. It involves teachers providing descriptive rather than evaluative feedback to students. It also includes students—from clarifying targets to self-assessing to communicating with others about their own progress. It's this descriptive feedback and student-involvement aspect of assessment *for* learning that results in the remarkable achievement gains we'll describe in the next section.

If you like the terms "formative" and "summative" better, use them. Just remember to add *descriptive feedback to students* and *student involvement in assessment* to the formative side. For simplicity's sake, we'll occasionally use the words "formative" and "summative." When we do, we mean "formative" in its broadest sense.

Why the Distinction Is Important

And now the kicker: As it turns out, the distinction between assessment *for* and *of* learning is pivotal to understanding the most effective uses of assessment in the classroom.

Impact of Assessment *for* Learning

Research evidence gathered around the world shows what happens to student achievement when the principles of assessment *for* learning permeate the classroom environment. Dozens of studies conducted at all levels of instruction offer evidence of strong achievement gains in student performance as measured by standardized tests (Bloom, 1984; Black & Wiliam, 1998; Black, 2003; Meisels, Atkins-Burnett, Xue, Bickel, & Hon, 2003; Rodriguiz, 2004). The effect of assessment *for* learning on student achievement is some four to five times greater than the effect of reduced class size (Ehrenberg, Brewer, Gamoran, & Willms, 2001). Few interventions in education come close to having the same level of impact as assessment *for* learning.

But the most intriguing result is that, while all students show achievement gains, the largest gains accrue to the lowest achievers. Everyone wins, with those who have the most to win, winning the most.

We're used to thinking about assessment as the measurer of impact of instructional interventions; we implement a new program or teaching strategy and then use assessment to see how effective it was. *In the case of assessment* for *learning, assessment becomes not only the measurer of impact, but also the innovation that causes change in student achievement*; assessment is not just the index of change, it *is* the change.

Black and Wiliam (1998) identify the classroom assessment features that bring about these large achievement gains:

- Assessments that result in accurate information

- Descriptive rather than evaluative feedback to students

- Student involvement in assessment

And so, as you might guess, these are the assessment practices we emphasize in this book. *Accuracy + descriptive feedback + student involvement = achievement gains.*

Assessment and Student Motivation

The reason assessment *for* learning practices yield large achievement gains can best be explained by examining their critical link to student motivation.

How do we use assessment to help students *want* to learn? Our traditional way has been to use assessments *of* learning (for example, grades) to reward behavior we feel leads to learning—doing homework and getting it in on time, preparing for class discussions, participating in class discussions, trying hard, and so on—and punish behavior we feel doesn't lead to learning—not doing homework or getting it in on time, not being prepared for class, not participating in class discussions, not trying. We have factored behavior into grades to motivate students to act in academically responsible ways.

Reflect for a moment on this procedure. Can you identify students for whom promising As and threatening Fs works? It causes them to work hard, get assignments in on time, and learn well? Of course you can. By the same token, can you identify students who are impervious to the threat of failure? For whom grades have ceased to be a motivator at all? Again, you may know one or many such students. Our traditional ways of using assessment to motivate students to want to keep trying—the rewards and punishments of grades—often don't work as we hope they will.

Recent thinking reconfigures ways in which assessment can motivate students to want to learn. According to those who study the human brain (see, for example, Caine & Caine, 1997; Jensen, 1998), we all have an innate desire to learn; we are born with intrinsic motivation. Learning is required for survival. The brain is built to seek information, integrate it with other information, interpret it, remember it, and bring it to bear at the appropriate times. According to these researchers, this intrinsic motivation to learn is supported when the learner meets the following criteria:

- Has a sense of control and choice

- Gets frequent and specific feedback on performance

- Encounters tasks that are challenging, but not threatening

- Is able to self-assess accurately

- Encounters learning tasks related to everyday life

The following conditions tend to drive out intrinsic motivation:

- Coercion

- Intimidation

- Rewards or punishments linked to evaluative judgments

- Comparing one student to another

- Infrequent or vague feedback

- Limitation of personal control

- Responsibility without authority

We seek out learning situations where the items in the first list are true, and avoid learning situations where those in the second list occur.

So, what do you think? Does our traditional use of assessment and grading set up learning environments more like list 1 or list 2?

We believe that traditional assessment procedures look like list 2—in our current system, assessments and grades are used to engineer compliance, deliver evaluative feedback (grades, which many students receive as a judgment of themselves and their worth as people), and compare students to each other (engendering negative competition and thus reinforcing a judgment of self-worth). Students also receive single grades on work without indication of what they did well or what might be their next steps in learning (reducing student control), and feedback pointing out only what they can't do yet instead of describing what they can do (emphasizing negatives instead of positives). Students are thus responsible for work but do not have the knowledge they need to improve.

The Research on Feedback

Black and Wiliam (1998) and other motivational research (Assessment Reform Group, 2002; Butler, 1988; Dweck, 2001; Sadler, 1989) clearly show that the type of feedback given to students affects their motivation to learn:

- It's the *quality* of the feedback rather than its existence or absence that determines its power. Specifically what makes the difference is the use of *descriptive, criterion-based* feedback as opposed to numerical scoring or letter grades.

- Feedback *emphasizing that it's the learning that's important* leads to greater learning than feedback *implying that what is important is looking good or how you compare to others*.

- Descriptive feedback can *focus on strengths or weaknesses*; feedback is most effective when it points out strengths in the work as well as areas needing improvement.

The Goal with Assessment *for* Learning

Assessment *for* learning practices use what is known about how the brain works, how we learn, and how we are motivated to maximize learning. Sadler's (1989) set of three requirements—students know where they are going, where they are now, and how to close the gap between the two—establishes the conditions for students to feel in control of their environment. Under these circumstances students can be challenged without being threatened.

For example, we have a colleague who was teaching a class for teachers on portfolios. A special education teacher in this class wanted to try student self-assessment in writing, but she was afraid that if students actually knew how low they were performing it would damage their self-concepts and cause them to give up. The instructor convinced her to try it anyway. She had her students keep selected samples of writing in a folder, learning to assess it accurately using a well-known writing scoring guide and describing their progress over time.

She reported that her students scored themselves very low at the beginning using the scoring guide—mostly "1s". However, at the end, they were higher, giving themselves more "2s." She also reported that far from being discouraged, her students were very excited because for the first time in their school lives they felt they understood the conditions of their success—they knew that they had made progress, they knew why they made progress, and they knew what they had to do next to improve their writing (L. Paulson, personal communication, September 1985).

The teacher succeeded because students learned how to take control over their own learning, received frequent and descriptive feedback on progress, were challenged without being threatened, and engaged in self-assessment. According to Sadler, the students knew where they were going, they knew where they were at any given time, and they learned what to do to close the gap.

Classroom assessments sometimes slip into deficit mode: the assessment shows students only what they don't know yet or what they need to work on. When we attend to the motivational effects assessment can have, we use it to show students both what they *have* learned and what they need to learn next. Students are where they are. The shift in type of feedback neither changes their level of achievement nor masks it.

DEEPEN UNDERSTANDING

Activity 2.2   Assessment, Achievement, and Motivation

Pause a moment and reconsider one of the classroom examples described in Chapter 1—Emily's writing, Krissy's paper, or Mr. Heim's science class. Go to the accompanying DVD segment entitled "Impact of Student-Involved Assessment" for clips of students and teachers discussing the impact of assessment *for* learning on achievement and motivation. How do their comments compare to your observations about productive connections between assessment and motivation?

What Does Assessment *for* Learning Look Like?

Assessment *for* learning is an interplay between teacher and student. Students are active, not just as test takers, but in thinking about their learning. We all want students to engage in and take active responsibility for their learning, and we can take specific steps to help students answer assessment *for* learning's three questions: (1) "Where am I going?"; (2) "Where am I now?"; and (3) "How can I close the gap?" We call these steps the "Seven Strategies of Assessment *for* Learning." Together, they comprise an organizing framework for assessment *for* learning in the classroom. We explain the strategies briefly here and then go into depth with each in the chapters that follow. The Seven Strategies are shown in Figure 2.2.

Figure 2.2   Seven Strategies of Assessment *for* Learning

Where am I going?

1. Provide a clear and understandable vision of the learning target.

2. Use examples and models of strong and weak work.

Where am I now?

3. Offer regular descriptive feedback.

4. Teach students to self-assess and set goals.

How can I close the gap?

5. Design lessons to focus on one aspect of quality at a time.

6. Teach students focused revision.

7. Engage students in self-reflection, and let them keep track of and share their learning.

Where Am I Going?

Strategy 1: Provide a Clear and Understandable Vision of the Learning Target

Share with your students the learning target(s), objective(s), or goal(s) in advance of teaching the lesson, giving the assignment, or doing the activity. Use language students understand, and check to make sure they understand. Ask, "Why are we doing this activity? What are we learning?" Convert learning targets into student-friendly language by defining key words in terms students understand. Ask students what they think constitutes quality in a product or performance learning target, then show how their thoughts match with the scoring guide or rubric you will use to define quality. Provide students with scoring guides written so they can understand them. Develop scoring criteria with them.

Strategy 2: Use Examples and Models of Strong and Weak Work

Use models of strong and weak work—anonymous student work, work from life beyond school, and your own work. Begin with work that demonstrates strengths and weaknesses related to problems students commonly experience, especially the problems that most concern you. Ask students to analyze these samples for quality and then to justify their judgments. Use *only* anonymous work. If you have been engaging students in analyzing examples or models, they will be developing a vision of what the product or performance looks like when it's done well.

Model creating a product or performance yourself. Show students the true beginnings, the problems you run into, and how you think through decisions along the way. Don't hide the development and revision part, or students will think they are doing it wrong when it is messy for them at the beginning, and they won't know how to work through the rough patches.

Where Am I Now?

Strategy 3: Offer Regular Descriptive Feedback

Offer descriptive feedback instead of grades on work that is for practice. Descriptive feedback should reflect student strengths and weaknesses with respect to the specific learning target(s) they are trying to hit in a given assignment. Feedback is most effective when it identifies what students are doing right, as well as what they need to work on next. One way to think of this is "stars and stairs"—What did the learner accomplish? What are the next steps? All learners, especially struggling ones, need to know that they did something right, and our job as teachers is to find it and label it for them, before launching into what they need to improve.

Remember that learners don't need to know everything that needs correcting, all at once. Narrow your comments to the specific knowledge and skills emphasized in the current assignment and pay attention to how much feedback learners can act on at one time. Don't worry that students will be harmed if you don't point out all of their problems. Identify as many issues as students can successfully act on at one time, independently, and then figure out what to teach next based on the other problems in their work.

Providing students with descriptive feedback is a crucial part of increasing achievement. Feedback helps students answer the question, "Where am I now?" with respect to "Where do I need to be?" You are also modeling the kind of thinking you want students to engage in when they self-assess.

Strategy 4: Teach Students to Self-Assess and Set Goals

Teaching students to self-assess and set goals for learning is the second half of helping students answer the question, "Where am I now?" Self-assessment is a necessary part of learning, not an add-on that we do if we have the time or the "right" students. Struggling students *are* the right students, as much as any others. The research described previously tells us it is they who gain the most. Self-assessment includes having students do the following:

- Identify their own strengths and areas for improvement. You can ask them to do this before they show their work to you for feedback, giving them prior thoughts of their own to "hang" it on—your feedback will be more meaningful and will make more sense.

- Write in a response log at the end of class, recording key points they have learned and questions they still have.

- Using established criteria, select a work sample for their portfolio that proves a certain level of proficiency, explaining why the piece qualifies.

- Offer descriptive feedback to classmates.

- Use your feedback, feedback from other students, or their own self-assessment to identify what they need to work on and set goals for future learning.

How Can I Close the Gap?

Strategy 5: Design Lessons to Focus on One Aspect of Quality at a Time

If you are working on a learning target having more than one aspect of quality, we recommend that you build competence one block at a time. For example, mathematics problem solving requires choosing the right strategy as one component. A science experiment lab report requires a statement of the hypothesis as one component. Writing requires an introduction as one component. Look at the components of quality and then teach them one part at a time, making sure that students understand that all of the parts ultimately must come together. You can then offer feedback focused on the component you just taught, which narrows the volume of feedback students need to act on at a given time and raises their chances of success in doing so, again, especially for struggling learners. This is a time saver for you, and more instructionally powerful for students.

Strategy 6: Teach Students Focused Revision

Show students how you would revise an answer, product, or performance, and then let them revise a similar example. Begin by choosing work that needs revision on a single aspect of quality. Ask students to brainstorm advice for the (anonymous) author on how to improve the work. Then ask students, in pairs, to revise the work using their own advice. Or ask students to write a letter to the creator of the sample, suggesting how to make it stronger for the aspect of quality discussed. Ask students to analyze your own work for quality and make suggestions for improvement. Revise your work using their advice. Ask them to again review it for quality. These exercises will prepare students to work on a current product or performance of their own, revising for the aspect of quality being studied. You can then give feedback on just that aspect.

Strategy 7: Engage Students in Self-Reflection, and Let Them Keep Track of and Share Their Learning

Engage students in tracking, reflecting on, and communicating about their own progress. Any activity that requires students to reflect on what they are learning and to share their progress both reinforces the learning and helps them develop insights into themselves as learners. These kinds of activities give students the opportunity to notice their own strengths, to see how far they have come, and to feel in control of the conditions of their success. By reflecting on their learning, they deepen their understanding, and will remember it longer. In addition, it is the learner, not the teacher, who is doing the work.

Here are some things you can have students do:

- Write a process paper, detailing how they solved a problem or created a product or performance. This analysis encourages them to think like professionals in your discipline.

- Write a letter to their parents about a piece of work, explaining where they are now with it and what they are trying to do next.

- Reflect on their growth. "I have become a better reader this year. I used to . . . , but now I . . . "

- Help plan and participate in conferences with parents and/or teachers to share their learning.

These Strategies as a Progression

The strategies reflect a progression that unfolds in the classroom over time. Students have trouble engaging in later steps (such as self-assessment) if they have not had experience with earlier steps (understanding learning targets and reliably assessing work). Likewise, it is much harder for students to communicate their progress if the learning targets are not clear, if they are not adept at assessing their work, and if they don't know what they need to do to improve.

All assessment *for* learning ideas in the rest of this book will go into the seven strategies in detail. Each application will address one or more of the three questions: *Where am I going? Where am I now?* and *How can I close the gap?*

Summary

In this chapter we have elaborated the differences and similarities between assessment *for* and *of* learning, cited the research linking assessment *for* learning to higher student motivation and achievement, and provided an overview of how to implement assessment *for* learning in the classroom.

Assessment *of* learning occurs to sum up achievement at a particular point in time. It occurs after learning has happened. Assessment *for* learning occurs to regularly inform teachers and students about the progress of learning while that learning is taking place. Its purpose is to improve learning while there is still time to act—before the graded event.

Assessment *for* learning can have a major motivational and achievement impact on students. It enables students to take control of their own learning by providing a clear vision of the learning targets they are to attain, teaching them to assess where they are with respect to the target, and offering strategies they can use to close the gap between where they are and where they need to be. The research on motivation, how we learn, and feedback come together to support assessment *for* learning as the best use of assessment in the service of student learning and well-being.

■ *Tracking Your Learning—Possible Portfolio Entries*

Any of the activities included in Chapter 2 can be used as portfolio entries. Remember, the learning targets for this book are outlined in Figure 2.1, listed in Table 1.2, and described in detail in Chapter 1. The portfolio entry cover sheet provided on the CD in the file, "Portfolio Entry Cover Sheet," will prompt you to think about how each item you choose for your portfolio reflects your learning with respect to one or more of these learning targets.

Specific recommendations for portfolio content follow.

TRY THIS

Activity 2.3   Critique an Assessment for Clear Purposes

The ultimate question we need to ask ourselves is, "Do I know the difference between sound and unsound classroom assessment practices and can I identify strong and weak examples and explain what makes them strong or weak?" To aid you we have developed rubrics for critiquing the quality of classroom assessments. You will find these on the CD, titled "Assessment Quality Rubrics." There is a rubric for each of the keys in Figure 2.1—Clear Purpose, Clear Targets, Sound Assessment Design, Good Communication, and Student Involvement. (When referring to the rubric, we will call these keys *traits*.)

We invite you and/or your learning team to begin your examination of these rubrics by applying the rubric for Clear Purposes to a sample of assessments you use in your state, district, school, or classroom. Every assessment used with students needs to have a clear purpose. Is it an assessment *for* learning? An assessment *of* learning? Are the users and uses inside or outside of the classroom? We recommend that you identify how

---

Activity 2.3   (Continued)

good each of your selected assessments is on the quality trait of Clear Purposes using the following procedure:

1. Individually, read the strong level of the Clear Purposes rubric first—"fast tracked." Then read the beginning level—"side tracked"—and finally the middle level—"on track." Mark the words and phrases that jump out at you as those really describing each level of quality.

2. Discuss any questions you have about the rubric with your colleagues.

3. Individually, look at your first sample assessment. If you think it is strong for the trait of Clear Purposes, begin reading the rubric at the "fast tracked" level. If you think it is weak, begin reading at the "side tracked" level. If you think it is strong, but "fast tracked" doesn't quite match what you see in the assessment, read "on track." Conversely, if you think it is weak, but what you read in "side tracked" doesn't quite describe it, read "on track."

4. There is no such thing as a "right" score, only a "justifiable" score. Justify your score using the words and phrases from the rubric that you think describes the assessment.

5. Compare your "scores" to those of your colleagues. Discuss discrepancies and attempt to come to a resolution.

Since we also introduced student involvement concepts in this chapter, you might want to analyze each of your sample assessments as well for the trait of Student Involvement.

We have several sample assessments on the CD that you may wish to critique, either independently or with your learning team. See the file, "Assessments to Evaluate." Our analyses of each of these samples are also on the CD in the file, "Assessment Critiques."

We don't necessarily expect you to feel comfortable using these rubrics right off the starting block. But, we guarantee that practicing with them over time will serve to help you internalize the features of quality so that you can bring them to bear when you develop or select assessments. Also, as you gain familiarity, the depth of your analyses will increase. So, keeping samples of your critiques in a portfolio over time enables you to easily track your own proficiency.

Activity 2.3   (Continued)

At the end of Chapter 3, we will again ask you to critique some assessments, this time for the trait of Clear Targets. Likewise, at the end of Chapter 4, we'll ask you to take a look at the trait of Sound Assessment Design. We address Good Communication in Chapter 9, and Student Involvement all along.

TRY THIS

Activity 2.4   Student Survey

In Great Britain teachers are expected to inform children of learning targets. In school visits, inspectors ask students to describe what they are learning and whether they know what to do to make their work better (Clarke, 2001; Ruth Sutton, personal communication, July 2001). Asking students this type of question really gets at the extent to which principles of assessment *for* learning are trickling down to students and enabling them to take control of their own learning.

On the CD, in the file entitled "Student Surveys," we include two student surveys that you can ask your students to respond to, to help determine the extent to which your attempts to implement assessment *for* learning practices have influenced your students' ability to be responsible for their own learning. You can use this survey at the beginning, in the middle, and at the end of the year to track change in the assessment environment in your classroom. You can also use the survey as a discussion starter in your learning team or as a thought provoker for yourself.

REFLECT ON YOUR LEARNING

Activity 2.5   Where Am I Now? Self-Assessment

According to Sadler (1989), learning increases when learners know where they are going, know where they are now, and know how to close the gap. In these materials we are assisting you to implement high quality, student-involved assessment *for* learning. These learning targets are displayed in Figure 2.1 and Table 1.2 and described in detail in Chapters 1 and 2.

Figure 2.3 is a self-assessment to be used as one way for you to see where you are now with respect to these learning targets and to track progress over time. You can also use the survey as a discussion starter in your learning team or as a thought provoker for yourself. Figure 2.3 is available in printable form in the CD file, "Determining Where I Am Now."

Figure 2.3 Determining Where I Am Now: Assessment *for* Learning and Assessment Quality Self-Checklist

Directions:

- On a separate sheet of paper, number from 1 to 9.

- Evaluate the classroom practice of yourself, your building, district, or clients for each of the nine statements below, according to the following scale:

  1 = I don't do this, or this doesn't happen in my classroom.

  2 = I do this infrequently, or this happens infrequently in my classroom.

  3 = I do this sometimes, or this sometimes happens in my classroom.

  4 = I do this frequently, or this happens frequently in my classroom.

  5 = I do this on an ongoing basis, or this happens all the time in my classroom.

Survey Statement
1. I understand the relationship between assessment and student motivation and use assessment to build student confidence rather than failure and defeat.
2. I articulate, in advance of teaching, the achievement targets my students are to hit.
3. I inform my students regularly, in terms they can understand, about those achievement targets, in part through the study of the criteria by which their work will be evaluated and samples of high-quality work.
4. My students describe what targets they are to hit and what comes next in their learning.
5. I transform these learning targets into dependable assessments that yield accurate information.
6. I consistently use classroom assessment information to revise and guide teaching and learning.
7. My feedback to students is frequent, descriptive, constructive, and immediate, helping students know how to plan and improve.
8. My students are actively, consistently, and effectively involved in assessment, including learning to manage their own learning through the skills of self-assessment.
9. My students actively, consistently, and effectively communicate with others about their achievement status and improvement.

Source: Adapted from *Assessment* FOR *Learning: An Action Guide for School Leaders* (pp. 176–178), by S. Chappuis, R. J. Stiggins, J. Arter, and J. Chappuis, 2004, Portland, OR: Assessment Training Institute. Copyright © 2006, 2004 Educational Testing Service. Adapted by permission.

CHAPTER

Assess What?
Clear Targets

 ne day in third grade, Claire brought home a math test with a smiley face, a "–3," and an "M" (for "Meets the standard") at the top. Wanting to help her develop as a reflective thinker, Claire's mother engaged her in the following conversation.

Mom: "Honey, this looks good. What does this tell you that you know?"

Claire, looking puzzled: "Math?"

Mom: "What about math?"

Claire: "I don't know. Just math."

So Claire's mother did what any good parent would do. She went to the National Council of Teachers of Mathematics website to look up the math standards. She identified which standard each problem represented, and then wrote the seven standards tested in child-friendly language so Claire could identify what specific math learning she was doing well on and what she needed to work on.

What if Claire had brought home a paper with a frowny face, a "–8," and an "N" (for "Does not meet the standard")? How might that conversation have gone?

Mom: "Honey, what happened here?"

Claire: "I don't know. I don't get it."

Mom: "What parts don't you get?"

Claire: "I don't know."

If Claire's mother doesn't know how to identify the standards, or learning targets, represented on this test (as, in truth, most parents don't), she will be unable to help her daughter see, for example, that two of the seven standards gave her trouble, and that she did fine on five of them. Claire will be unable to see where she has had success in learning or to identify where her difficulties lie.

In this chapter we address the importance of learning targets to teaching, learning, and assessing. We will explain the different kinds of learning targets, how to make them clear to everyone, including students, and the connection to assessment quality. This chapter focuses on the "Assess What" portion of Figure 3.1, including its associated student-involvement considerations.

The Importance of Beginning with Targets

What is the intended learning? That one question should drive all planning and assessment in schools today. Label these learning statements "content standards," "benchmarks," "grade level indicators," "grade level expectations," "essential learnings," "learning outcomes," "lesson objectives," "learning intentions," or whatever you like; they all represent *learning targets*, or *statements of intended learning*. If we don't begin with clear statements of the intended learning, we won't end with sound assessments.

Benefits to Teachers

Know What to Assess

Beginning with clear statements of the intended learning benefits our teaching first of all. Let's say as a part of our curriculum we have the following reading learning target: "Students will comprehend fictional, informational, and task-oriented text." To plan lessons we will need to further define "comprehend" and we will probably want to identify the kinds of fictional, informational, and task-oriented texts we will work with this year. If our local curriculum breaks "comprehend" down into a set of subtargets such as *identifies main idea and supporting details, summarizes text, makes inferences and predic-*

tions, and *uses context clues to determine the meaning of unfamiliar words*, we are much better prepared to select appropriate assessments. We won't, for example, make the mistake of assigning a project, such as "create a diorama," and then using the grade as evidence of comprehension. We will know that we need evidence of students' ability to identify the main idea, identify supporting details, summarize, and so forth to determine their level of comprehension.

Figure 3.1   Keys to Quality Classroom Assessment

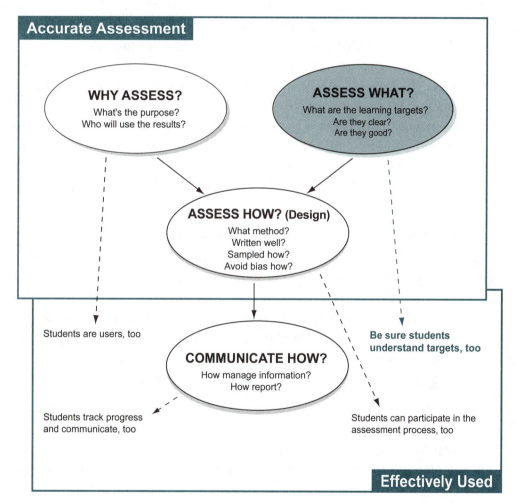

Clarity on What Instructional Activities to Plan

Once we know what our learning targets are and have defined how we will assess them, we are able to think clearly about what combination of instruction and experiences will prepare students both to know what they need to know and to demonstrate their learning. This is often referred to as *intentional* teaching—all instruction and classroom activities are aimed at specified learning targets.

Ability to Balance "In Depth" with "Coverage"

It's April, just after spring break. You look at what is left to teach and the number of days left in the year and wonder how you got into this predicament again. If it's world history, twentieth-century study may boil down to three quick wars. If it's math, geometry may be reduced to a few constructions, or statistics and probability to a few games of chance. If it's language arts, poetry may get the boot. To avoid cramming large amounts of content into short periods of time, or "teaching by mentioning it" (Wiggins & McTighe, 1998, p. 21), teachers have to make hard choices regarding what to leave in and what to take out. A well-designed curriculum offers direction for those choices. You can use it to map out the year in advance, maximizing the chances that you will teach important concepts in depth throughout the year and get students where they need to be by the end of the year.

Know What Your Assessments Reflect at a Finer Grain

When you begin with well-defined learning targets, you are able to plan an assessment that reflects exactly what you will teach and what you expect students to learn. You will also be able to use assessments to further learning, by disaggregating the information on any assessment, learning target by learning target or standard by standard, to show areas of growth and areas needing further work. In addition, when you know which learning targets each assessment measures, you can be sure you're teaching and assessing what you, your colleagues, and your community have determined is most important for students to learn.

Accountability

Is there any reason to *not* include learning targets tested for accountability purposes in your curriculum or in your teaching? We can't think of any, and we can think of a number of reasons why this is a good idea. For one, you won't need to hire outside consultants to help you know what to focus on to improve learning for all students. You'll have that information, because with grade-level or subject learning targets aligned to the standards tested for accountability, you are able to identify from your test results which learning targets—already a part of your curriculum—will need more emphasis or a different approach. This organization of the curriculum allows you as a building or department to be in control of your plan for maximizing student achievement, and not rely on someone else to tell you what to do.

Ability to Work Collaboratively with Other Teachers

Perhaps the most powerful benefit to teachers of having an agreed curriculum and teaching to it is the common ground it offers in working with other teachers. Schmoker (2002, p. 2) suggests the following:

> *The most enormous but peculiarly unsung benefit of common standards is that they provide the rich common context essential to focused, productive teacher collaboration, a sine qua non for improvement (Fullan 2000; Sparks 1998). Stated simply: If we want schools to improve, instruction—teaching lessons themselves —must improve (Stigler and Hiebert 1999). But there also must be a common set of standards. And there must be a commitment to reaching measurable achieve-ment goals by making real adjustments to how we teach these common standards. There is no other way (Glickman 2002, 4–5).*

Benefits to Students

The benefits of clear targets to students are indisputable. When we have a clear vision of where we're headed with students, we can communicate that vision to them. If you think back to the research on the effects of assessment *for* learning on student achievement, you will recall that a key feature to student success is students knowing where they are going, that is, understanding what they are to learn. As author Rick Stiggins likes to say, "Students can hit any target they can see that holds still for them." However, as in the example of Claire's math, if students have no idea what they are supposed to learn, if the only information they have is that we are doing "science" or "social studies," few of them are likely to know how to monitor their own progress and keep themselves on track.

Imagine it is the beginning of math time for a group of elementary students. Listen to this teacher:

"Okay class, take out your math books. Who remembers what we're studying? Yes, decimals. Please turn to page 145. Check your partner's book. Make sure your partner knows where we are. Everybody ready? Today we're going on a decimal hunt. Read the directions on page 145, and then when you know what you're supposed to do, come up to the front to get your materials."

When these students go home tonight and their parents ask them what they learned in school today, they will be justified in answering, "I don't know." Their teacher has given them the subject (math), the topic (decimals), the resource (page 145) and the activity (going on a decimal hunt). What is missing? The intended learning: "We are learning to read decimals to the thousandths place and put them in order." Explaining the intended learning in student-friendly terms at the outset of a lesson is the crucial first step in helping students know where they are going.

Let us say we want students to learn to summarize text. How might we explain to fourth graders what that means? Here is a process you can use:

1. Define the word. The dictionary works well as a starting point, e.g., "*Summarize*: To give a brief statement of the main points, main events, or important ideas."

2. Rewrite the definition as an "I can" (or an "I am learning to") statement, in terms that fourth graders will understand, e.g., "I can summarize text. This means I can make a short statement of the main points or the important ideas of what I read."

3. Try it out on students or a colleague and refine as needed.

4. Have students try this process for subsequent learning goals.

Suppose we are preparing to teach seventh-grade students how to make good inferences. Our process might yield these results:

1. Word to be defined: *Inference*: A conclusion drawn from the information available.

2. Student-friendly language: "I can make good inferences. This means I can use information from what I read to draw a reasonable conclusion."

If, however, we are working with second-graders, our student-friendly language might look like this: "I can make good inferences. This means I can make a guess that is based on clues."

Shirley Clarke (2001), a British teacher and author, describes these "I can" statements as statements of the intended learning. In addition, she recommends that success criteria—statements that describe how we will know that we have learned it—be devised with students, and that they be posted, not just shared verbally. Figure 3.2 illustrates what that might look like for second graders learning to make good inferences. When teachers

TRY THIS

Activity 3.1   Turning Learning Targets into Student-Friendly Statements

Use the process described to create a student-friendly version of this learning target: *Students will compare and contrast elements of text.*

If you are working with a learning team, compare your results. How might you use "I can" statements in the classroom?

she was working with displayed learning intentions and success criteria in poster form, Clarke recounts the following anecdotal results:

> *All children, across the ability range, talked about the 'learning intention', explaining how their teacher wrote it up on a board and even giving me examples of learning intentions from that day. Brighter children said that it helped them focus on the aspect at hand and not get distracted by other things. Less able children said that they looked up at the learning intention—and especially the success criteria—to remind themselves of what they were supposed to be doing! So it has different benefits for different abilities. (Clarke, 2001, pp. 25–26)*

Thinking back to the research discussed in Chapter 2, we recognize that students cannot assess their own learning or set goals to work toward without a clear vision of the intended learning. When they do try to assess their own achievement without understanding the learning targets they have been working toward, their conclusions are vague and unhelpful: "I think it was pretty good." "I need to work harder on math." Making targets clear to students at the outset of learning is *the* fundamental underpinning to any assessment *for* learning practices we will implement.

Again, think back to Claire—a good math student with only a vague idea of what she is learning. Try to interpret the feedback she has received, through her eyes: a smiley face means "this is good," an M means "I met the standard," and –3 means "I got three problems wrong." "Three problems wrong, meets the standard, this is good," but no information about what she knows or doesn't know. Research and common sense both tell us that she could learn more with knowledge of what learning targets she is being held accountable for,

Figure 3.2   Learning Intentions

We are learning to ———▶ Make good inferences

We are looking for ———▶ Guesses based on clues

Source: Adapted from *Unlocking Formative Assessment* (p. 24) by S. Clarke, 2001, London, UK: Hodder & Stoughton.

which ones she has succeeded with, and which ones she needs to keep working on. Were she a struggling learner receiving a summary grade such as an "N" ("Does not meet the standard"), she would have no information to help her see what she has learned and what she needs to work on. Her judgment of "where am I right now?" will likely be answered with one damning word: "failing." When students know which achievement targets they are accountable for learning, our assessments can begin to provide them with specific information about where they have succeeded and where, exactly, they have missed the mark.

Benefits to Parents

Knowing your targets at the outset of teaching also benefits parents. Sending home or posting on your website a list of learning targets written in parent-friendly language can help communicate the depth and breadth of the academic work their children are engaged in. Understanding what the intended learning is helps parents focus their assistance in productive ways. For instance, if you are teaching students how to edit their own papers and you communicate that to parents, you can ask that they not do the editing for their children. If you are working on map-reading skills, you can suggest that parents have their children practice using a map to give directions on a car trip. However, if you are asking students to complete a "Pet Project," and that title alone is all the information parents receive, they will be unlikely to know what they can (and shouldn't) do to support the intended learning.

Additionally, being clear about the intended learning helps parents understand what grades mean in terms of what their children have and have not learned. When grades come home, parents can talk specifically with their children about their strengths and areas for improvement, and help them avoid damaging generalizations, such as, "I'm no good at reading."

Clear Targets

All of these benefits are predicated on the existence of statements of learning that are clear and usable. One way you will know that you have clear and usable targets is if you can determine what kind of learning target is being called for. We offer a categorization framework that identifies five kinds of learning targets: knowledge, reasoning, skills, products, and dispositions. These categories will become especially useful in Chapter 4 when we determine which method we should use to assess intended learning.

Knowledge Targets

Knowledge targets represent the factual underpinnings in each discipline. They are often stated using verbs such as *knows*, *lists*, *names*, *identifies*, and *recalls*. Examples include, "identifies antonyms, synonyms, and common homonyms," "knows multiplication facts to 10," "recalls details from a story," "capitalizes book titles, abbreviations, and proper nouns correctly," "knows the nutritional value of different foods" (Kendall & Marzano, 1997, p. 552). Knowledge targets also call for procedural knowledge, knowing how to do something. They often begin with the phrase *knows how to* or the word *uses*, such as "uses scientific notation to represent very large and very small numbers."

Beyond knowing things outright, there is another way of knowing—knowing via reference. Not everything that we need to know needs to be "by heart." What, of the information students need, will we require they memorize, and what will we teach them to find? Will they memorize the list of prepositions (above, aboard, about . . .)? Addition, subtraction, multiplication, and division facts? The table of periodic elements? The capitals of the 50 U.S. states? As we know, there is not enough time to teach (or for students to learn) everything of importance—we can easily fill the year's teaching time with important things students need to know, thereby losing instructional time for learning targets beyond the knowledge level. Where is the balance? One way to address this problem in part is to determine which knowledge learning targets students will be required to know outright and which they will be required to know via reference. It is an exercise in professional judgment, best conducted with a group of colleagues.

We have to exercise common sense and discernment when classifying learning targets. Just because a target begins with the word *knows* does not mean it is a knowledge target. For example, are "knows how healthy practices enhance the ability to dance" and "knows folk dances from various cultures" (Kendall & Marzano, 1997, pp. 387, 386) both knowledge targets? The first one may be, but what learning is intended by the second? Perhaps it is that students will recognize and be able to name a few dances, or maybe it is that they learn these dances so that they can perform them. We do not know what kind of target we have, and we won't know how to teach to it, unless we can say for sure how the learning is to be demonstrated. Until we can do that, the target is not clear.

TRY THIS

Activity 3.2   Identifying Knowledge Targets

Identify five to seven statements in your local curriculum document (or whatever document you use to guide teaching) that represent knowledge learning targets. Refer to Tables 3.1 and 3.2 for examples.

Reasoning Targets

What does the *use* of knowledge in your discipline look like in life beyond school? Gathering knowledge without the ability to apply it in context is not the aim of schooling today; rather, we strive for our students' developing skillful use, or *application*, of that knowledge. So it is that we find the majority of learning targets in curriculum documents today fall into the reasoning category. Reasoning targets represent mental processes such as *predicts*, *infers*, *classifies*, *hypothesizes*, *compares*, *concludes*, *summarizes*, *analyzes*, *evaluates*, and *generalizes*.

Patterns of Reasoning

At this point, we will benefit from thinking closely about the specific patterns of reasoning we expect our students to master. Those we discuss here represent the kinds of reasoning occurring in life beyond school and also those that different reasoning taxonomies have in common.

Table 3.1   Examples of Learning Targets

	Knowledge	**Reasoning**	**Skill**	**Product**	**Disposition**
Mathematics	Recognize and describe patterns (NRC, p. 219)	Use statistical methods to describe, analyze, evaluate, and make decisions (NRC, p. 219)	Measures length in metric and US units (CKSD Gr. K–6 Math, p. 36)	Constructs bar graphs (CKSD Gr. K–6 Math, p. 38)	Likes mathematics
Language Arts (reading/ literature)	Recognizes similes, metaphors, and analogies (CKSD Gr. 7–10 Lang., p. 10)	Formulates questions, makes predictions, verifies and revises understanding while reading (CKSD Gr. 7–10 Lang., p. 41)	Reads aloud with fluency and expression (CKSD Gr. K–6 Lang., p. 32)	None	Chooses to read for enjoyment
Physical Education	Understands long-term physiological benefits of regular participation in physical activity (CKSD PE, p. 46)	Analyze fitness assessments to set personal fitness goals; strategize ways to reach goals; evaluate activities (CKSD PE, p. 54)	Dribbles to keep the ball away from an opponent; passes and receives on the move (CKSD PE, p. 44)	Develops a personal health-related fitness plan (CKSD PE, p. 47)	Plays basketball for fun
Social Studies	Explains the important characteristics of U.S. citizenship (WA EALR: Civics)	Distinguishes between historical fact and opinion; compares and contrasts points of view from an historical event (CKSD Soc. St., p. 83)	Participates in civic discussions with the aim of solving current problems (WA EALR: Civics)	Creates a product that uses social studies content to support a thesis (WA EALR: Soc. St. Skills)	Intends to vote in every election
Science	Knows that energy can be transformed between various forms (CKSD Sci., p. 7)	Examines data/results and proposes meaningful interpretation (CKSD Sci., p. 20)	Uses simple equipment and tools to gather data (CKSD Sci., p. 19)	Constructs physical models of familiar objects (CKSD Sci., p. 21)	Looks forward to science class
Theater	Identifies elements of design in a given play (NT Gr. 6)	Compares and contrasts theater performances from various cultures and times using appropriate arts vocabulary (NT Gr. 5)	Demonstrates relationship and interactive responsibilities of the artist/performer and audience (WA EALR: Arts)	Creates a scripted scene based on improvised work (NT Gr. 5)	Wants to participate in community theater
Spanish	Comprehends vocabulary (CKSD World Lang., p. 13)	Compare and contrast cultural features from the USA and the Spanish-speaking world (CKSD World Lang., p. 13)	Pronounces correctly: vowel/consonant sounds; dipthongs(CKSD World Lang., p. 13)	Writes simple descriptions and narratives (CKSD World Lang., p. 13)	Enjoys opportunities to converse in Spanish

Source: Items are taken from the following sources. See the References for full citations: CKSD = Central Kitsap School District (1999–2002); NRC = National Research Council (1996); NT = North Thurston Public Schools (2001); WA EALR = *Washington State Essential Academic Learning Requirements* (2004).

Table 3.2   Content Standards—Key Words

Target Type	Explanation	Content Standards Key Words	Examples
Knowledge/ Understanding	Some knowledge/facts/ concepts to be learned outright; some to be retrieved using reference materials	Explain, understand, describe, identify, tell, name, list, define, label, match, choose, recall, recognize, select, know	Vocabulary Measurement concepts U.S. government structure Patterns of growth and development
Reasoning	Thinking proficiencies— using knowledge to solve a problem, make a decision, plan, etc.	*Analyze:* components, parts, ingredients, logical sequence, steps, main idea, supporting details, determine, dissect, examine, order *Compare/contrast:* discriminate between alike and different, distinguish between similarities and differences, juxtapose *Synthesize:* combine into, blend, formulate, organize, adapt, modify *Classify:* categorize, sort, group, give examples *Infer/deduce:* interpret, implications, draw conclusions, predict, hypothesize, generalize *Evaluate:* justify, support opinion, think critically, appraise, critique, debate, defend, dispute, evaluate, judge, prove	Think critically Analyze authors' use of language Solve problems Compare forms of government Self-evaluation Analyze health information
Skills	Behavioral demonstrations; where the doing is what is important; using knowledge and reasoning to perform skillfully	Observe, focus attention, listen, perform, do, question, conduct, work, read, speak, assemble, operate, use, demonstrate, measure, investigate, model, collect, dramatize, explore	Read fluently Oral presentations Play an instrument Use laboratory equipment Conduct investigations
Products	Where the characteristics of the final product are important; using knowledge, reasoning, and skills to produce a final product	Design, produce, create, develop, make, write, draw, represent, display, model, construct	Writing Artistic products Research reports Make a map Personal fitness plan Make a model that represents a scientific principle

DEEPEN UNDERSTANDING

Activity 3.3 Identifying Reasoning Verbs

What kinds of reasoning do you want your students to be able to do? Make a list of all reasoning verbs that come to mind.

Inductive and Deductive Reasoning

Induction and deduction both require inference, and to understand them, we need to be clear about what it means to infer. The *New Oxford American Dictionary* defines *infer* in this way: "deduce or conclude (information) from evidence and reasoning, rather than from explicit statements" (Jewell & Abate, 2001 p. 896). An inference, therefore, is a reasonable guess based on information, sometimes called, "reading between the lines."

When we reason *inductively*, we use particular facts or evidence to infer a general rule or principle. Sound inductive reasoning requires that we select relevant facts or evidence, interpret them accurately, and then draw careful conclusions based on them.

When we reason *deductively*, we begin with a general rule or principle and from that we infer a specific conclusion or solution. Sound deductive reasoning requires that we apply what the general rule tells us to a specific case and draw a plausible conclusion about that specific case. For example, consider the general rule, "All people get mad sometimes." We can therefore conclude, "Mom is a person; therefore, Mom gets mad sometimes."

Analytical Reasoning

When we reason analytically, we examine the components or structure of something. Analysis often requires that we investigate how the component parts relate to each other or how they come together to form a whole. We might ask students to analyze a controversial decision, wherein they identify the arguments for and against a particular action. We might ask them to conduct an experiment to analyze a compound to determine its component chemicals. Students engage in analysis when they determine the meaning of unknown words by breaking them into prefixes, suffixes, and root words. We undertake analysis to understand something more deeply or to provide an interpretation of it. For students to be successful at such tasks, they must be able to identify the parts of something and then have practice at describing relationships among those parts, or between the part and the whole.

DEEPEN UNDERSTANDING

Activity 3.4 Identifying Inductive and Deductive Reasoning

Which of these questions require an inductive inference and which call for a deductive inference?

- Given the evidence provided in the reading (an article about the stock market), what is the relationship between interest rates and stock values?

- Given what you know about the role geography plays in the growth of cities, describe the ideal location for a new city.

- If the chemical test yields this result, what element is it?

- Given what you know about the physical characteristics of insects, is this creature an insect?

(*Answers:* inductive, deductive, inductive, deductive)

Comparative Reasoning

Describing the similarities and differences between two or more items is at the heart of comparative reasoning. Notice that in this definition, comparative reasoning encompasses both *compare*—to find similarities, and *contrast*—to find differences. We begin with simple tasks such as asking students to say how two things are alike or different. But comparative reasoning in its more complex form requires that students select appropriate items to compare, and then select salient features to base their comparison on, before performing the actual comparison (Marzano, Pickering, & McTighe, 1993). The act of contrasting can be defined as identifying differences, or it can extend to the concept of *juxtaposition*, whereby we place two very different objects, emotions, thoughts, melodies, arguments, people, side by side to define each in sharp relief or to cause the differences between them to stand out distinctly. *Contrast*, used in this sense, is a device we manipulate for effect in areas such as writing, music, art, and drama. Venn diagrams and T-charts are two common graphic organizers used to help students understand the structure of comparative reasoning.

Classifying

Classification can be thought of as sorting things into categories based on certain characteristics. At its least complex application, classification consists of sorting objects into predetermined, clearly defined categories. To sort well at this basic level, students need practice at identifying and observing for the pertinent charactistics.

However, a more rigorous application of this pattern of reasoning requires students to select or create the categories. Playing the game "Twenty Questions" is an example of this aspect of classifying: the goal of each question is to find out what category the object fits into and to narrow the categories sequentially so as to deduce the correct answer. For example, a player might first ask, "Is it an animal?" to classify the object according to general type. Next, she might ask, "Is it bigger than a bread box?" to classify the object according to size. The third question might be, "Does it live around here?" to narrow the possibilities according to habitat, and so forth. The trick in Twenty Questions, as in all classification exercises, is to identify relevant categories that will provide the maximum information about the objects or concepts under consideration.

Another in-depth mental process we engage in during classification is refining categories as we sort to make them more precise, for the categories need to be as comprehensively defined as possible to allow for accurate sorting. We encounter new information or phenomena that don't quite fit the distinctions as they stand, so we revise the definition of our categories, or create new ones. For example, Richard is sorting a year's worth of photos to put them into albums. He starts by sorting them by season—winter pictures in this pile, spring pictures in this pile, and so on. Pretty soon he notices that he needs a more detailed ordering scheme if he is to create a chronological album, so he refines the categories to represent months. All is well until May, the month with three family birthdays, an anniversary, and Mother's Day—too many pictures. He decides to categorize May further by event. So it is that classification requires us to test our categories, notice when they don't quite fit, and carefully refine them to accommodate the new evidence.

We classify to count and compare (as in creating a bar graph to show relationships among things), to clarify (as in determining whether a sowbug is an insect), to differentiate (as in determining whether a statement is a main idea or a supporting detail), to draw conclusions (all people get mad sometimes; my mother is a person; my mother gets mad sometimes), to make decisions (as in categorizing household expenses to determine how to save money), or to organize information or concepts (as in outlining a paper to make sure information is in the right place). In its grandest application, classification is about the organizational schemes we impose on the world around us to understand it better. How we identify those categories controls how we view the world.

Evaluative Reasoning

Evaluative reasoning involves expressing and defending an opinion, a point of view, a judgment, or a decision. It can be thought of as having three facets: an assertion, criteria the assertion is based on, and evidence that supports the assertion. When engaging in evaluative thinking, students generally are able to begin with an assertion, but are often unable to articulate the other two components, criteria and evidence; in many cases, students express an opinion and then support it with further opinions.

We cannot call this *evaluative* thinking until students are able to identify criteria for making their assertion and are able to provide credible evidence that matches the criteria. For example, let's say we ask students to take a position on whether a literary character should or shouldn't have done something. Either position is defensible, but to demonstrate evaluative thinking, students will have to select and defend evaluative criteria. (How do we judge an action? On what basis? Such criteria might include one or more of the following: the action's effect on others, a moral or ethical stance towards the action, its effect on the character, the potential for long-term benefit vs. short-term gain, and so on.) Then, to defend their judgment, students will have to produce credible evidence and show how it fulfills their criteria. Similarly, when we ask students to evaluate the quality of their own work, they will need to use criteria describing levels of quality and then match their observations about their work to the criteria. In mathematics problem solving, students choose a strategy by evaluating the options, and they also must evaluate how well the strategy they selected is working along the way. In science, students evaluate the validity of their conclusions based on what they know about experimental design. In social studies, we ask students to evaluate the quality of the arguments a politician makes against a set of criteria.

Synthesis

Synthesis is the process of combining discrete elements to create something new. Cookies are an example of synthesis; when we combine the ingredients—eggs, milk, flour, sugar, salt, and vanilla—we get something new, cookie dough, which some people bake before eating. The process of synthesizing involves identifying the relevant ingredients to combine and then assembling them in such a way so as to create a new whole. Writing a report is an act of synthesis; we want our students to create something new (in their own words) from separate ingredients through a specific process. To do that they must locate and understand various bits of relevant information, sort through them, think about how they fit together, and assemble and present them in a way that does not copy any of the original sources.

Assembling differs according to the context. The color green can be synthesized by mixing blue and yellow pigment with a little water. To make the nylon used in women's stockings the ingredients, 1,6-hexanediamine and adipic acid, are mixed and then heated using steam under pressure. The act of interpreting data to draw a conclusion requires that we take discrete bits of information, look for patterns, and create new information— the conclusion. To write a story, we try out various combinations of setting, characters, problem, and resolution until we are satisfied with the mix.

The accompanying CD includes resources for teaching various patterns of reasoning in the file entitled "Graphic Organizers."

Concluding Thoughts About Patterns of Reasoning

These categories of reasoning will help you think through the learning targets you hold for students and to identify which ones call for which type of reasoning. A plethora of classification systems for reasoning exists, each a synthesis of its author's thought. We have chosen these six patterns (inductive and deductive inference, analysis, comparison, classification, evaluation, and synthesis) to represent those most commonly found among various taxonomies and systems. We also wanted to define reasoning targets in terms of patterns commonly represented in standards documents, and in terms you and your students could relate to. You may find other patterns or definitions that fit your needs more closely. Before you adopt them, be sure they are based on the best current understanding of reasoning in your subject area, and be sure you can explain them clearly in student-friendly terms. Table 3.3 shows examples of language arts and science reasoning targets representing each of these six patterns.

TRY THIS

Activity 3.5 Identifying Reasoning Targets

Identify five to seven statements in your local curriculum document (or whatever document you use to guide teaching) that represent reasoning learning targets. Categorize them according to the pattern of reasoning called for. Refer to Tables 3.1 and 3.2 for examples.

Table 3.3   Reasoning Learning Targets in Language Arts and Science

Pattern of Reasoning	Language Arts	Science
Inductive and Deductive Inference	Inference: What does this story suggest about ____? Inductive inference: Now that you have read this story, what do you think is its general theme or message? Deductive inference: Given what you know about the role of a tragic hero in classic literature, if *this* character is a tragic hero, what do you think will happen next?	Inference: Draw a conclusion based on inquiry. Inductive inference: Plot the locations of volcanoes and earthquakes to make a generalization about plate motions. Deductive inference: Use characteristic properties of liquids to distinguish one substance from another.
Analysis	Write a paper detailing the process you used in writing your term paper.	Conduct an investigation to determine the active ingredient in an herbal medicine.
Comparison	Identify similarities and differences between an Egyptian version of *Cinderella* and a Chinese version.	Make a chart showing ways in which the natural environment and the constructed environment differ.
Classification	Given a selection of words, sort them into categories representing parts of speech.	Sort and order objects by hardness.
Evaluation	Evaluate accuracy of information from a variety of sources.	Evaluate conclusions drawn from an experiment for legitimacy.
Synthesis	Write a fictional narrative.	Write a lab report.

Knowledge or Reasoning?

Determining whether a target is in the knowledge or reasoning category sometimes can be tricky. "Compares and contrasts main characters in a novel." Knowledge or reasoning? It presents itself as a reasoning target, but if the teacher compares and contrasts the main characters in a novel, and then tests students' ability to replicate her reasoning about the same characters, she is not testing their reasoning; she is testing *recall* of the information she shared with them. If it was intended to be a reasoning target, it no longer is—it has devolved to a knowledge target. To test a reasoning proficiency, we must provide students with a novel application of the specific pattern of reasoning. The key to making the determination here lies in asking, "Who is doing the reasoning?" Are the students doing something more than remembering the reasoning the teacher previously demonstrated?

Teaching for Understanding

And, what about the word *understands*? Many, many standards begin with it. Although *understands* may imply more depth of learning than *knows*, to be sure that it does we must be specific about whether we are expecting recall of information or something more. If we intend something more, we must define it before we can teach or assess it. In all cases we know of, the "something more" is defined in terms of reasoning targets. It is our view that by engaging in specific reasoning processes that can be learned and refined, students develop and deepen conceptual understanding.

The Balance Between Knowledge and Reasoning

In finding the balance between knowledge and reasoning learning targets, we must emphasize our belief that knowledge targets *are* important; there is information in *each* subject we teach that is important to know. The trick, of course, is to identify it. Where we sometimes err is in continuing to attempt to teach more fact-level content than can be learned in the time we have. We need to acknowledge this and fix it by selecting the fact-level content that will give us the most bang for our buck and still leave enough time in the year to teach students to use the content in ways that mirror what practitioners in our discipline do. Chances are, you did not choose to become an expert in your content area because you loved memorizing facts. What do social studiers do in life beyond school? Generally, they do not function as walking almanacs. They are lawyers, politicians, demographers, economists, social scientists, anthropologists, and voters, among other things. What do people who study math do? Practitioners in each field we teach in school have a body of knowledge at instant recall, and they also know how to exercise specific patterns of reasoning, perform skillfully with knowledge, and create quality products. Therefore, our learning targets in each subject must reflect the balance of kinds of knowledge and application required of us in life beyond school, which leads us directly to our next category of learning targets.

DEEPEN UNDERSTANDING

Activity 3.6 Watch Video, *Assessing Reasoning in the Classroom*

To understand more about patterns of reasoning and how to assess them, please watch ETS's video, *Assessing Reasoning in the Classroom.*

Performance Skill Targets

For our purposes—to categorize learning targets in order to know how to teach and assess them—when we speak of skill targets, we are referring to those performances that must be demonstrated and observed—heard or seen—to be assessed. Examples include oral fluency in reading, driving with skill, serving a volleyball, conversing in a second language, giving an oral presentation, directing scenes and productions, demonstrating movement skills in dance, and playing a musical instrument. Knowledge targets *always* underlie skill targets; in many cases reasoning targets do also. In the case of oral fluency in reading, prerequisite knowledge includes the sounds each letter is capable of making, the sounds letters can make when blended, what happens to the sound of a medial vowel in a word with a final *e*, and so forth. In the case of driving with skill, prerequisite knowledge, such as knowing the rules of the road, is necessary but not sufficient; reasoning is also required, for example when analyzing a situation for danger.

TRY THIS

Activity 3.7 Identifying Skill Targets

Identify five to seven statements in your local curriculum document (or whatever document you use to guide teaching) that represent performance skill targets. Categorize them according to the type of skill called for. Refer to Tables 3.1 and 3.2 for examples.

Product Targets

We also include products among our valued achievement targets. Certain of our learning targets call for students to create a product, such as "creates tables, graphs, scatter plots, and box plots to display data," "notates music," "uses desktop publishing software to create a variety of publications," (Kendall & Marzano, 1997, p. 582) or "creates a personal wellness plan." Curricula generally include far fewer product targets than knowledge and reasoning targets.

TRY THIS

Activity 3.8 Identifying Product Targets

Identify five to seven statements in your local curriculum document (or whatever document you use to guide teaching) that represent product targets. Note your observations about the balance of knowledge, reasoning, skill, and product targets represented in your curriculum. If you are a member of a learning team, consider discussing the observed balance or imbalance at your next meeting. Again, refer to Tables 3.1 and 3.2 for examples.

Task or Target?

The ability to distinguish between the task, the activity students will engage in, and the learning target, what they are to learn by engaging in the activity, is crucial to creating an accurate assessment. For example, "Make a desk" is not a product target generally represented in Principles of Technology curricula. Skillful use of machinery, knowing how to join pieces of wood, how to finish surfaces (knowledge, reasoning, and skill targets), *are* likely to be part of the curriculum. The product, the desk, may be the artifact we use to judge the student's achievement of the knowledge, reasoning, and skill targets, but the purpose of the class is not to teach students how to make desks. Similarly, "Create a diorama" does not generally surface as a product learning target. Instead, it is a product we would ask students to create if it would demonstrate attainment of specific learning targets. The key question, as always, is, "What is the intended learning?" "Create a diorama" is a task we give students as evidence they have attained . . . what? On the other hand, written products such as term papers, research reports, and lab reports often appear in curricula as product targets. They are not only the vehicle by which we judge knowledge and reasoning proficiencies; such products themselves are the focus of the lesson.

Dispositional Targets

Our last category of valued targets for students, dispositional targets, is not one that usually surfaces in state standards. Targets in this realm reflect attitudes and feeling states, such as, "I look forward to coming to school each day," "Music is worth studying," or "I like math." They represent important *affective* goals we hold for students as a byproduct of their educational experience, and as such, are not assessed for the purpose of grading. We do not hold students accountable for these targets in the same way that we hold them accountable for mastery of knowledge, reasoning, skill, and product targets, but that does not mean they are unimportant or that we would never assess for them. Understanding students' dispositions provides valuable insights into who they are as learners, insights that help us work more effectively with them as individuals and as a group.

We can think about dispositional targets in terms of three characteristics (Stiggins, 2005). They have (1) a specific object as their focus, (2) a positive or negative direction, and (3) varied levels of intensity, from strong to weak. When we assess them, we are looking for information about both the direction and level of intensity of feeling toward the specific focus. For example, we might offer a series of statements such as, "I am good at reading," I like reading," and "I read for enjoyment in my spare time." After each statement, students would mark one answer choice from the following options: "strongly agree," "somewhat agree," "neutral or no opinion," "somewhat disagree," or "strongly disagree." In this case, the students' attitude about reading is the focus; they are asked whether they feel positively or negatively about each statement, and how strongly. Examples of dispositional learning targets are given in Table 3.1

Summary of Learning Targets

Table 3.4 summarizes kinds of learning targets.

Table 3.4   Kinds of Learning Targets

- **Knowledge**—The facts and concepts we want students to know

- **Reasoning**—Students use what they know to reason and solve problems

- **Skills**—Students use their knowledge and reasoning to act skillfully

- **Products**—Students use their knowledge, reasoning, and skills to create a concrete product

- **Dispositions**—Students' attitudes about school and learning

Learning Targets, State Standards, and Curriculum

What's in a Name, or, Kinds of Learning Targets out There

Content standards, benchmarks, goals, outcomes, enduring understandings, essential learnings, essential questions, developmental continua: each district has its own vocabulary to describe the collection of statements of achievement expectations for students. You will be best served by understanding how your state and district organizes such statements, and which terminology they use. At this writing, there is no national curriculum or one nationally agreed structure for curriculum.

Where Do Targets Come From?

National subject area organizations, such as the following, publish statements of intended learning, often by grade or course levels:

- American Association for the Advancement of Science

- American Council on the Teaching of Foreign Languages

- Center for Civic Education

- Consortium of National Arts Education Associations

- International Reading Association

- International Technology Education Association

- National Association for Sport and Physical Education

- National Center for History in the Schools

- National Center for Research in Vocational Education

- National Council for the Social Studies

- National Council on Economic Education

- National Council of Teachers of English

- National Council of Teachers of Mathematics

- National Research Council (for Science standards)

- National Science Teachers Association

Curricular frameworks and statements of intended learning are also published in various disciplines by national committees convened for that purpose. For more information on the standards movement and organizations publishing standards, we refer you to *Content Knowledge: A Compendium of Standards and Benchmarks for K–12 Education*, 2nd edition (Kendall & Marzano, 1997).

Individual states publish standards, most often informed by one or more content-area organizations' standards. At this writing, 49 of the 50 states have some version of academic standards in place. In some states, the academic standards serve as the curriculum; in others, the state standards function as a guide to the development of local district curriculum.

When school districts develop their own curriculum, they often rely on both the state standards and the work of the national organizations.

How Are Targets Organized?

As different states, districts, and schools identify learning targets, they adopt differing organizational structures. Your curriculum may be set up so that it is easy or difficult to understand what to teach and how to assess it. Whatever the case, it is important to understand your own document's organizational framework. We outline a few common patterns here. Because their intent is to guide teaching and learning, most curricular documents begin with broad goals and then progress to smaller units of learning. Some curricula begin with broad statements of intended learning by the end of high school. Some start with broad statements in a given subject. The broad statements, sometimes known as goals or exit outcomes, are often translated into benchmarks, which are generally set at multiyear intervals and used as signposts along the way toward a culminating outcome or standard. From there, some curricula define grade level or course outcomes, or statements of intended learning. At this point, some schools and districts determine enduring understandings and essential questions (Wiggins & McTighe, 1998). Others plan a concept-based curriculum (Erickson, 2001). Still others detail unit-level learning targets. In the primary grades, some districts design or adopt developmental continua to represent the stages of learning students are to progress through in areas such as reading and writing.

We Need Good Curriculum Guides

We believe every teacher should have access to a practical curriculum guide, one that provides a clear vision of the intended learning and points the way for teaching and assessing. A good curriculum will link each year's learning targets to the previous and following year's targets, providing continuity among grade levels. The benefits of this to students and teachers are obvious: If we know that every student has had plenty of exposure to learning how to put a capital letter at the beginning of a sentence and a punctuation mark at the end in grades kindergarten through two, it would be reasonable to expect that knowledge in grade three, and to hold students accountable for demonstrating it. If we have no clear knowledge of what previous teachers have taught, we may spend valuable teaching time covering things that students have learned before. Or, we may expect them to come to us having learned certain important concepts, only to find that they were not in their previous teacher's plan for the year.

Additionally, a good curriculum will make the links to state or provincial standards (or to whatever standards form the basis for your accountability testing) clear. It will help you answer the question, "What specifically will the state (or province) hold my students accountable for having learned?" A curriculum that has been aligned to state or provincial standards allows you to use accountability test data to identify which portions of your curriculum students do well on and which portions students do not do well on, and to adjust teaching and resources accordingly.

Articulation between grade levels and alignment with accountability measures are only part of the picture. Another crucial aspect is amount. Does your curriculum take into account the "180-day rule?" That is, does it acknowledge how much time you have to teach? It is not possible to teach everything that is important to learn, yet many curricula are designed to reflect everything that could be taught at that grade level in a particular subject, thus turning a blind eye to the pace of learning. A good curriculum guide will limit your responsibility for what to teach of all that could be taught. What are the "we agrees" at each grade level—the knowledge, reasoning, skill, and product targets *most* important for these students to master? What do we promise our colleagues—our teammates in this endeavor—we will help students learn?

Lastly, we recommend that the learning targets in your curriculum be stated so that everyone who teaches a subject interprets them the same way. Is it clear what to teach from the statements in your curriculum?

What Happens When the Curriculum Has Problems?

Your curriculum is your first assessment guide. A curriculum with problems is a curriculum that sits on the shelf. Teachers often substitute the textbook, a list of units or activities, or a series of projects for a curriculum. Let's take a look at what happens in each of these cases.

When we base our teaching on a series of units, activities, or projects, we know what to teach, but we may not know what to assess. Our classrooms may be filled with busy, excited, motivated students. However, if activities are not consciously designed or selected with learning targets in mind, if we are not clear about the intended learning *in advance*, assessments cannot be counted on to provide accurate information about particular learning targets. In addition, without the unifying thread of underlying learning targets, we will not be able to build intentionally on previous learning, either from our own teaching or from the teaching in prior grades. Neither will subsequent teachers be able to build intentionally on what we have done with students. In essence, we are each in private practice, our own little teaching universe, unaware of what our students bring with them and unable to articulate what we send them off to the next grade with. As teachers come and go from a building, the instructional program meanders. Our scores on accountability measures are up or down, and we may have to rely on an outside program to straighten us out, imposing a "drop-in" remedial mini-curriculum. None of this is in the best interest of students.

If we rely on the textbook to stand in as our curriculum, we may think we have solved the problem of articulation between grade levels, and perhaps alignment with state or provincial standards. However, when textbooks serve as the curriculum, we face several problems.

First, many textbooks contain too much content to teach in a year, which is in part due to how they are designed. If you are a member of a district textbook review committee (searching for a new series to purchase), you will generally look for the best match between the text's coverage and your local curriculum. Textbook companies know this; they include in their products as much as could be taught in that grade level in that subject, in order to align with all potential clients' curricular objectives. (Even when companies advertise their texts as aligned with *your* state standards, it does not mean they are aligned with your state standards *alone*.) Therefore, by design, most textbooks address much more content than can be successfully taught in any one class in a year. In order to include so much content, textbooks most often lack in-depth treatment of any one concept. In addition, textbooks provide little or no guidance on which information is of lesser and greater importance, leading teachers to try to cover it all or (absent a curriculum) to choose idiosyncratically what to teach. When we cover material, we teach at a pace that far outstrips learning for most students; when we select what to teach on our own, we negate the benefit for students of experiencing an articulated curriculum.

In "Seven Reasons Why a Textbook Is Not a Curriculum," Shutes and Peterson (1994) assert the following:

> It is . . . time to recognize that in a curriculum vacuum, textbooks have fostered a preoccupation with content that has made content coverage an end in itself, has made didactic treatment of fact-level information the standard teaching method, and has overwhelmed learners with more information than they could possibly handle. Ironically, the teachers' strategies to cope with excess content may have alienated many of their students not only from the content but from school itself. (p. 12)

Note that they begin their statement with the phrase, "in a curriculum vacuum." What is ironic today is that many of us are not operating in a curriculum vacuum, yet textbooks' tables of contents still outline the learning for many classes. Consider these facts as reported by Schmoker and Marzano (1999):

> Although U.S. mathematics textbooks attempt to address 175 percent more topics than do German textbooks and 350 percent more topics than do Japanese textbooks, both German and Japanese students significantly outperform U.S. students in mathematics. Similarly, although U.S. science textbooks attempt to cover 930 percent more topics than do German textbooks, and 433 percent more topics than do Japanese textbooks, both German and Japanese students significantly outperform U.S. students in science achievement as well (Schmidt, McKnight, & Raizen, 1996). (n.p.)

Beyond doubt, it is not the number of topics covered that leads to higher achievement. When teachers adopt a textbook as the curriculum, they must move quickly; they cannot take the time to go deeply into any one concept or topic, and they cannot pace the learning to meet the students' needs. The result is "repetition of unelaborated information, (making) the teacher active and the learners passive; it ensures that almost all the instruction will be direct exposition, and it almost guarantees that most students will be overwhelmed by the information overload and will forget most of the information before the course is over" (Shutes & Peterson, 1994, p. 13).

TRY THIS

Activity 3.9 Curriculum Discussion

Prepare to discuss with your learning team the following questions: Do you have a curriculum? Is it helpful in the ways described here? Do you use it? If not, what do you use? What conclusions can you draw about curriculum from your answers and your thoughts as you are reading this chapter?

What to Do—Deconstructing Standards

Even if your curriculum is in good shape, some learning targets for students are inevitably something less than clear. Have you ever looked at a curriculum guide or list of content standards and asked yourself, "What am I going to teach here?" Or, "How do I explain this to students?" Or, "Will my colleagues interpret this the same way I do?"

In this section we present a technique for clarifying learning targets—whether for content standards that just need a little fine tuning, or for situations in which you have to translate state or provincial standards on your own—called "deconstructing standards." This is the process of taking a broad and/or unclear standard, goal, or benchmark and breaking it into smaller, more explicit learning targets that can be incorporated into daily classroom teaching.

When we deconstruct a statement of intended learning, we break it into its component parts. (This will sound familiar to those of you who practiced Madeline Hunter's [1982] task analysis, an aspect of lesson design that came into use in the 1970s.) We ask a series of questions:

- What knowledge will students need to demonstrate the intended learning?

- What patterns of reasoning will they need to master?

- What skills are required, if any?

- What product development capabilities must they acquire, if any?

For example, let's say that you are a driver's education teacher and you want students to be able to drive a car with skill. What does this mean? What would you teach? In Table 3.5 we've broken "Will drive a car with skill" into the knowledge that students need to drive a car well, the reasoning proficiencies students need, and the skills they need. Note that in this case, driving with skill requires creation of no products. It is a *skill*-level learning target that requires *knowledge* and *reasoning* underpinnings.

As another example consider the learning goal, "understands the binomial theorem." This goal might be interpreted one of several ways: "knows it by sight—can identify it from a list," "can reproduce it when asked," "can use it to solve a problem," "can select problems best solved by using it," or "can write a problem that would require the binomial theorem to solve." Each of these interpretations would have different implications for instruction. How will we define "understands?" In this case, it has at least one knowledge component: "knows what the binomial theorem is." It may have reasoning components as well, such as, "knows when to use the binomial theorem," "uses the binomial theorem to solve problems," and "identifies problems best solved using it." As the learning goal is stated, it does not have any skill or product components.

In general, if a target is at the knowledge level, it will have no reasoning, skill, or product components. Reasoning targets do have knowledge components, but they do not require skill or product components. Skill targets require underlying knowledge and reasoning, but not products. Product targets will require knowledge and reasoning, and might be underpinned by skill targets as well.

Going through the process of deconstructing a standard with colleagues is a good way to get clear about the intended learning, so that everyone is riding the horse in the same direction. Then, if the process continues on to translating the deconstructed learning targets into student-friendly language, as in the example in Table 3.5, we have clear targets for both teachers and students.

When deconstructing standards, remember you are looking at what the content standard requires students to know and be able to do, not how you will assess it. Because the significance of this statement might not be immediately obvious, consider the standard, "compare and contrast democracies with other forms of government," which is a reasoning target.

Table 3.5   Deconstructing an Everyday Learning Objective: "Will drive a car with skill"

Deconstructed Learning Objective	
Knowledge/ Understanding	Know the law Understand informal rules of the road, e.g., courtesy Understand what different parts of the car do Read signs and understand what they mean Understand what "creating a danger" means Understand what "creating a hazard" means
Reasoning	Analyze road conditions, vehicle performance, and other driver's actions; compare/contrast this information with knowledge and past experience; synthesize information; and evaluate options to make decisions on what to do next Evaluate "am I safe" and synthesize information to take action if needed
Skills	Steering, shifting, parallel parking, looking, signaling, backing up, etc. Fluidity/automaticity in performing driving actions
Products	None

Student-Friendly Learning Target Statements	
Knowledge/ Understanding	I can explain the laws about driving—speed limits, stopping, how to take turns with other drivers, when to signal, when to use my lights, etc. I can describe what different parts of the car do—steering wheel, gear shift, lights, brakes, gas pedal, mirrors, gauges, etc. I can read traffic signs and I can describe what they mean—yield, stop, merge, etc. I can describe several ways that drivers can "create a danger" and list ways to prevent or avoid such dangers.
Reasoning	I can decide what to do next based on my understanding of how cars work, what other drivers are doing, and road conditions. I can figure out when I am safe and when I am in danger. When I am in danger I can figure out what to do to reduce my danger.
Skills	I can keep the car going the direction I want using the steering wheel. I can shift gears smoothly and at the right time. I can parallel park within one foot of the curb without hitting anything. I can drive the car well without having to think about it every minute, etc.
Products	None

This standard requires knowledge of what a democracy is and knowledge of other types of government—purposes and how power is acquired, used and justified; and how government can affect people. It also requires practice in comparing and contrasting—a reasoning proficiency—using the knowledge of different forms of government. So, there are two, and only two, parts to the content standard—knowledge and reasoning.

Now, you might assess these knowledge and reasoning portions through an oral presentation (a skill), or a report (a product). These oral presentations or reports require a lot of other proficiencies, such as writing and delivery. Because of the other proficiencies needed in an oral presentation, or a written product, you might be tempted to list them all as you deconstruct the standard, *but don't*. The standard only requires knowledge and reasoning. *Deconstruct only the content standard, rather than all possible ways to assess it or all possible ways to teach it.*

We must be vigilant in distinguishing between learning targets—statements of what we want students to know and be able to do—and the manner in which we'll teach or assess them—the tasks and assignments we'll give students to do.

TRY THIS

Activity 3.10   Deconstructing Standards

Either with colleagues or alone, select a content standard, benchmark, or grade-level learning expectation that is unclear, or that teachers might interpret differently. Deconstruct it into its component learning targets by asking these questions:

- What knowledge will students need to know to be successful?

- What patterns of reasoning, if any, will students need to master to be successful?

- What skills, if any, will students need to master to be successful?

- What products, if any, will students need to practice creating to be successful?

A worksheet for deconstructing standards is provided on the CD in the file, "Deconstructing Standards."

Concluding Thoughts

It is not our purpose in this book to guide curriculum development, but to make as strong a case as we can for the necessity of framing clear and specific learning targets at the outset of teaching as an imperative to sound assessment. Most pointedly, we emphasize the practical and moral imperative of each teacher understanding each learning target clearly, in agreement with others who teach the same subjects, and in agreement with those who create the external assessments designed to measure student achievement for accountability purposes.

Absent a strong curricular framework, long-term student achievement is at risk. Of all the things that can be taught in a given discipline, we are accountable to our students to select that which has most lasting benefit, that which is most central to the practice of our discipline in life beyond school, that which will best prepare them for the learning they will encounter in the next grade or course, and that which they will be held accountable for having learned. We urge you not to reject your curriculum, but to work to fix it. As we have seen, no one benefits in the long run when each of us goes into private practice in our classrooms.

Summary

Clear learning targets are essential for sound assessment. We can't assess what is not clear. But beyond this, clear targets benefit teachers, students, and parents by clarifying in the following ways what to assess and what instructional activities to plan:

- Help to avoid the problem of too much to teach and too little time.

- Provide a foundation for collaborative planning among teachers.

- Facilitate assessment for learning—when students understand the intended learning they are set up for productive self-assessment and goal setting.

- Facilitate communication with parents.

We separated learning targets into five categories and presented examples of each type, as summarized in Table 3.4.

We presented this classification scheme in preparation for determining the most appropriate assessment methods for each type of target, which is explained in Chapter 4.

Finally, we focused on different organizational schema for collections of learning targets and offered suggestions for what to do if your curriculum or content standards are not yet clear. Specifically, we described how to "deconstruct" standards to make the prerequisite knowledge, reasoning, skill, and/or product targets clear.

■ *Tracking Your Learning—Possible Portfolio Entries*

Any of the activities included in Chapter 3 can be used as portfolio entries. Remember, the learning targets for this book are outlined in Figure 3.1, and listed in Table 1.2 and described in detail in Chapter 1. The portfolio entry cover sheet provided on the CD in the file, "Portfolio Entry Cover Sheet," will prompt you to think about how each item you choose for your portfolio reflects your learning with respect to one or more of these learning targets.

Specific recommendations for portfolio content follow.

TRY THIS

Activity 3.11   Critique an Assessment for Clear Targets

In Chapter 2 we introduced you to the rubrics for analyzing and improving the quality of classroom assessments. In that chapter we suggested it would be worthwhile to look at some sample assessments for clear purposes and student involvement. The ultimate goal of Chapter 3 is to ensure that each and every assessment has a foundation of clear and important learning targets—we know exactly what learning targets are addressed on every single assessment. So, in this chapter, we're asking you to get out the assessment samples again for another look; this time for clear and important learning targets.

You will find the classroom assessment quality rubrics on the CD, entitled "Assessment Quality Rubrics." There is a rubric for each of the keys in Figure 3.1— Clear Purpose, Clear Targets, Sound Assessment Design, Good Communication, and Student Involvement. Using the rubric for the trait Clear Targets, proceed through the following steps:

1. Individually, read the strong level of the rubric first—"fast tracked." Then read the beginning level—"side tracked"—and finally the middle level—"on track." Mark the words and phrases that jump out at you as those really describing each level of quality.

2. Discuss any questions you have about the rubric with your colleagues.

Activity 3.11   (Continued)

3. Individually, look at your first sample assessment. If you think it is strong for the trait of Clear Targets, begin reading the rubric at the "fast tracked" level. If you think it is weak, begin reading at the "side tracked" level. If you think it is strong, but "fast tracked" doesn't quite match what you see in the assessment, read "on track." Conversely, if you think it is weak, but what you read in "side tracked" doesn't quite describe it, read "on track."

4. There is no such thing as a "right" score, only a justifiable score. Justify your score using the words and phrases from the rubric that your felt described the assessment.

5. Compare your scores to those of your colleagues. Discuss discrepancies and attempt to come to a resolution.

We have several sample assessments on the CD to use for practice in the file, "Assessments to Evaluate." Our analyses of each of these samples are also on the CD in the file, "Assessment Critiques."

When you finish analyzing your assessments discuss your comfort level using the rubrics. Was it easier than last time? How easy was it to match the sample assessments to the rubrics? What questions does this process raise for you?

PART

2

Assessment Methods

Assess How?
Designing Assessments
to Do What *You* Want

[S] o far, we have examined two keys to assessment quality. The first key is to know at the outset how we intend to use assessment results. Sometimes we can use them to promote learning (assessment *for* learning) and other times to check to see if learning has occurred—that is, for purposes of accountability (assessment *of* learning). As the second key to quality, we have established that assessments must be designed to reflect the variety of achievement targets that underpin standards: mastery of content knowledge, the ability to use knowledge to reason, demonstration of performance skills and product development capabilities. Now we consider the third key to classroom assessment quality—how to design assessments that cover our targets and serve our purposes (the shaded portion of Figure 4.1).

In this chapter we describe four assessment methods representing the range of assessment options, explain how to choose which method to use for any given learning target, and outline the steps in assessment planning and development. We treat each of the four assessment methods in depth in Chapters 5 through 8; here we offer an overview with an emphasis on selecting the proper method and on thoughtful assessment planning.

Figure 4.1   Keys to Quality Classroom Assessment

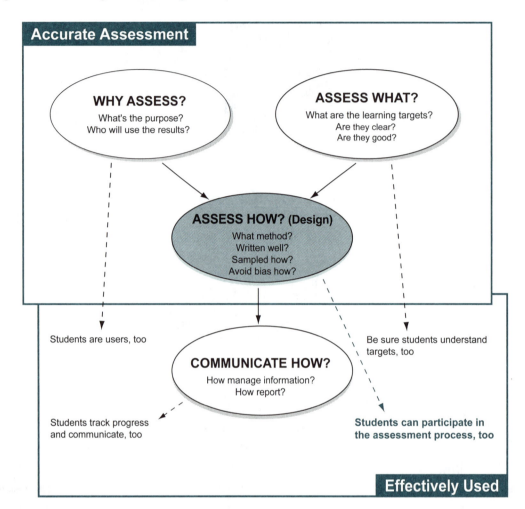

Assessment Methods—A Menu of Options

Throughout our school careers, both as students and as teachers, we have encountered thousands of different assessments. Although the variations are endless, all of the assessments we have experienced and give today fall into one of four basic categories of methods:

1. Selected response and short answer

2. Extended written response

3. Performance assessment

4. Personal communication

All four methods are legitimate options when their use correlates highly with the learning target and the intended use of the information. (Portions of the following discussion are adapted from Stiggins, 2005.)

Selected Response

Selected response and short answer methods consist of those in which students select the correct or best response from a list provided. Formats include multiple choice, true/false, matching, short answer, and fill-in questions. (Although short answer and fill-in-the-blank do require students to generate an answer, they call for a very brief answer that is counted right or wrong, so we include these options in the selected response category.) For all selected response assessments, students' scores are figured as the number or proportion of questions answered correctly.

Extended Written Response

Extended written response assessment requires students to construct a written answer in response to a question or task rather than to select one from a list. An *extended* written response is one that is at least several sentences in length. Examples include the following:

- Compare pieces of literature, solutions to environmental problems, or economic events.

- Analyze artwork, forms of government, or solutions to problems.

- Interpret music, scientific information, or polling data.

- Solve a mathematics problem and show and explain all work.

- Describe in detail a scientific, mathematical, or economics process or principle, such as how supply and demand works.

We judge correctness of extended written responses by applying one of two types of predetermined scoring criteria. One type gives points for specific pieces of information that are present. For example, when students in a biology class are asked to describe the Krebs cycle, points might be awarded for noting that the cycle describes the sequence of reactions by which cells generate energy, takes place in the mitochondria, consumes oxygen, produces carbon dioxide and water as waste products, and converts ADP to energy-rich ATP. The second type of criteria can take the form of a rubric, such as a general rubric for making comparisons, which can be applied to any exercise calling for comparison.

Scores therefore also take one of two forms: number or percentage of points attained, or rubric scores.

Performance Assessment

Performance assessment is assessment based on observation and judgment; we look at a performance or product and make a judgment as to its quality. Examples include the following:

- Complex performances such as playing a musical instrument, carrying out the steps in a scientific experiment, speaking a foreign language, reading aloud with fluency, repairing an engine, or working productively in a group. In these cases it is the doing—the process—that is important.

- Creating complex products such as a term paper, a lab report, or a work of art. In these cases what counts is not so much the process of creation (although that may be evaluated, too), but the level of quality of the product itself.

As with extended written response assessments, performance assessments have two parts: a performance task or exercise and a scoring guide. Again, the scoring guide can award points for specific features of a performance or product that are present, or it can take the form of a rubric, in which levels of quality are described. For example, to assess the ability to do a simple process, such as threading a sewing machine, doing long division, or safely operating a band saw, points might be awarded for each step done in the correct order. Or, for more complex processes or products, you might have a rubric for judging quality that has several dimensions, such as ideas, organization, voice, word choice, sentence fluency and conventions in writing, or content, organization, presentation, and use of language in an oral presentation. Again, scores could be reported in number or percent of points earned, or in terms of a rubric score.

Personal Communication

Gathering information about students through personal communication is just what it sounds like—we find out what students have learned through interacting with them. Examples include the following:

- Looking at and responding to students' comments in journals and logs

- Asking questions during instruction

- Interviewing students in conferences

- Listening to students as they participate in class

- Giving examinations orally

We usually think of this as informal, rather than formal assessment (in which results are recorded for later use). Often it is. However, as long as the learning target and criteria for judging response quality are clear, information gathered via personal communication can be used to provide descriptive feedback to students, for instructional planning, and for student self-reflection and goal setting. If planned well and recorded systematically, information from personal communication can be used as the basis for assessments *of* learning.

Student responses are evaluated in one of two ways. Sometimes the questions we ask require students to provide a simple, short answer, and all we're looking for is whether the answer is correct or incorrect. This is parallel to scoring for written selected response questions. Questions during instruction usually call for these short answer oral responses.

Other times, student oral responses are longer and more complex, parallel to extended written response questions. Just as with extended written response, we evaluate the quality of oral responses using a rubric or scoring guide. Longer, more complicated responses would occur, for example, during oral examination or oral presentations.

Misconceptions About Assessment Methods

Much "lore" exists about assessment methods, and we address a few of the most common misconceptions here.

1. *Shouldn't we only be using "authentic" assessments—performance assessments—to judge student progress?* None of these methods is inherently superior to any other, and all are viable if used well. Good assessment means clearly knowing what it is you want to assess and then choosing the best method to get the job done, which, as we will show, depends on the purpose and the learning targets being assessed.

2. *I can see how to involve students in assessment when using a performance assessment, but how do you do it with other methods? Doesn't student involvement require performance assessment?* Although many of our strongest examples of student involvement in the past have come from performance assessment applications, there is a vast, untapped reservoir of student-involvement practices leading to higher learning within each assessment method. You will find extended examples in Chapters 5 through 8.

3. *What about portfolios? I notice they aren't listed as a method. Where do they fit in?* Portfolios are a wonderful idea and we devote an entire chapter to their use later in the book. However, they are not an assessment method, but a vehicle for collecting evidence of, tracking, and communicating about student learning. Portfolios offer a way to involve students deeply in the overall process—self-assessment, tracking progress, reflecting on work, goal setting, and communicating about learning. In this sense, portfolios play a valuable role in creating assessment *for* learning in the classroom.

4. *What about presentations, group projects, worksheets, observations, exhibitions of mastery, posters, and the other ways that teachers gather information?* All of these artifacts and procedures can be classified within the four basic assessment methods described. Presentations and observations are examples of performance assessment. Exhibitions of mastery and group projects can take the form of extended written response, performance assessment, or personal communication depending on how they are carried out. Worksheets are not a method at all because they can contain various types of questions. (Usually worksheets consist of selected response or extended written response questions.) Likewise, posters can be considered either extended written response or performance assessment depending on the assignment and the learning targets being assessed.

Target–Method Match

One of the values in classifying assessments according to method is that we can think clearly about how to assess what we are teaching. The heart of accuracy in classroom assessment revolves around matching different kinds of achievement targets, with all the forms and nuances of each, to the appropriate assessment method. This is easily done and can save time in the long run.

To begin thinking about the match between kind of learning target and assessment method, please complete the following two activities. You may want to discuss possible answers with colleagues.

DEEPEN UNDERSTANDING

Activity 4.1   Which Method?

Let's say you need to assess student achievement on each of the following learning targets. Which assessment method—selected response/short answer, extended written response, performance assessment, or personal communication—would you choose? Please jot down your answers and save them for later reference.

1.   Ability to write clearly and coherently

2.   Group discussion proficiency

3.   Reading comprehension

4.   Proficiency using specified mathematical procedures

5.   Proficiency conducting investigations in science

DEEPEN UNDERSTANDING

Activity 4.2 Target–Method Match

For this activity, you will determine which assessment method is the best match for each of the four kinds of learning targets: knowledge, reasoning, skill, and product targets. To do this you will need to read through the following four scenarios and record your answer to each question by marking an "X" in the appropriate box on Figure 4.2 when your answer is "Yes." (A printable version of the figure is on the accompanying CD in the file, "Target–Method Match Chart.") You can put an "X" in more than one box. You can use capital "X" to denote really good matches, and a checkmark to denote an acceptable match under certain conditions (or whatever easily distinguishable marks you wish). On a separate sheet of paper, write your justifications for each answer, as requested. To make your choices, think about accuracy and efficiency: which methods will provide the most accurate information with the highest degree of efficiency? If you are working with a learning team, consider discussing your responses as a group.

Scenario 1: Assessing Student Mastery of Content Knowledge

Scenario: You want your students to master specific subject matter knowledge because it represents an important foundation for later work. You plan a series of instructional activities to help your students reach this goal. Now you want to assess to be sure they've got it. In this particular case, you want them to know the material outright, not through the use of reference materials.

Question 1: Should you assess mastery of this material using selected response or short answer modes of assessment, such as multiple choice, true/false, or matching exercises? Briefly explain your response.

Question 2: Should you assess your students' mastery of this material using an extended written response form of assessment? Defend your answer.

Question 3: Should you use a performance assessment to assess students' mastery of this content knowledge? Defend your answer.

Question 4: Do you think the personal oral communication form of assessment—by oral exam, interview, conference, or discussion—could viably assess your students' mastery of this content knowledge? Why or why not?

Activity 4.2 (Continued)

Scenario 2: Assessing Reasoning Proficiency

Scenario: You are a teacher who has seen to it that your students are able to access important knowledge when required. Now you want to see if they can use that knowledge productively to solve relevant problems. You want to see if they can reason analytically (think about the parts of things) and comparatively (think in terms of similarities and differences), draw inferences, and think critically (take and defend a position on an issue, for example).

Question 1: Can you get at these things with selected response or short answer assessments? Why or why not?

Question 2: Does extended written response assessment work in contexts where we seek to assess reasoning proficiency? Why or why not?

Question 3: Is performance assessment a viable alternative? Why or why not?

Question 4: Can we use personal oral communication as an assessment method to probe a student's ability to reason effectively and solve problems? Defend your response.

Scenario 3: Assessing Mastery of Skills

Scenario: You teach French and wish to assess your students' skill at communicating in that language in a conversational situation. So the skill of *oral language proficiency* is your target.

Question 1: Can you assess oral language proficiency in a conversational context using a selected response or short answer mode of assessment? Defend your answer.

Question 2: Can you assess these skills using extended written response assessment? Why or why not?

Question 3: Will performance assessment work as a basis for assessing the foreign language speaking proficiency of your students? Why or why not?

Question 4: Can you use personal oral communication as a basis for assessing conversational skill in a second language? Defend your response.

Question 5: Would your responses also apply to other skills such as operating a sewing machine, dribbling a basketball, or reading aloud fluently?

Activity 4.2 (Continued)

Scenario 4: Assessing the Ability to Create Quality Products

Scenario: You want your students to be able to create quality products—products that meet certain specified standards. They might be samples of writing, term papers, technology products, craft products, artistic creations, or others. Your instruction has centered on helping students learn the differences between products that are of high and low quality. You have provided practice in developing products that meet your standards. Now it is time to assess the students' achievement to see if your instruction was effective.

Question 1: Can you assess the ability to create these kinds of products using selected response or short answer modes of assessment? Why or why not?

Question 2: Will extended written response assessment work for evaluating this kind of achievement? Explain.

Question 3: Can performance assessment provide the evidence of proficiency needed to evaluate this kind of achievement target? Defend your response.

Question 4: Is personal oral communication a viable way to assess when creation of a product is the target? Why or why not?

Checking Your Matches

Table 4.1 identifies the strong matches between kinds of achievement targets and assessment methods. Please compare the table to the target–method match choices made by your team. Note and discuss discrepancies.

Figure 4.2   A Plan for Matching Assessment Methods with Achievement Targets

Target to Be Assessed	Assessment Method			
	Selected Response	Extended Written Response	Performance Assessment	Personal Communication
Knowledge Mastery				
Reasoning Proficiency				
Performance Skills				
Ability to Create Products				

Source: Adapted from *Student-Involved Assessment* for *Learning*, 4th ed. (p. 65), by R. J. Stiggins, 2005, Upper Saddle River, NJ: Merrill/Prentice Hall. Copyright © 2005 by Pearson Education, Inc. Adapted by permission of Pearson Education, Inc.

Assessing Knowledge Targets

Selected Response

There is usually no argument about this match. Selected response options do a good job at assessing mastery of discrete elements of knowledge, such as important history facts, spelling words, foreign language vocabulary, and parts of plants. These assessments are efficient in that we can administer large numbers of questions per unit of testing time and so can cover a lot of material relatively quickly. Thus, it is easy to obtain a good sample of student knowledge so that we may infer level of overall knowledge acquisition from the sample on the test.

Table 4.1   Links Among Achievement Targets and Assessment Methods

Target to Be Assessed	Assessment Method			
	Selected response	**Extended Written Response**	**Performance Assessment**	**Personal Communication**
Knowledge Mastery	Good match for assessing mastery of elements of knowledge.	Good match for tapping under-standing of rela-tionships among elements of know-ledge.	Not a good match—too time consuming to cover everything.	Can ask ques-tions, evaluate answers and infer mastery—but a time-consuming option.
Reasoning Proficiency	Good match only for assessing understanding of some patterns of reasoning.	Written descrip-tions of complex problem solutions can provide a window into rea-soning proficiency.	Can watch students solve some problems and infer reasoning proficiency.	Can ask student to "think aloud" or can ask followup questions to probe reasoning.
Skills	Not a good match. Can assess mastery of the knowledge prerequisites to skillful performance, but cannot rely on these to tap the skill itself.		Good match. Can observe and evaluate skills as they are being performed.	Strong match when skill is oral com-munication profi-ciency; not a good match otherwise.
Ability to Create Products	Not a good match. Can assess mastery of knowledge prerequisite to the ability to create quality products, but cannot use to assess the quality of products them-selves.	Strong match when the product is written. Not a good match when the product is not written.	Good match. Can assess the attributes of the product itself.	Not a good match.

Source: Adapted from *Student-Involved Assessment* for *Learning*, 4th ed. (p. 69), by R. J. Stiggins, 2005, Upper Saddle River, NJ: Merrill/Prentice Hall. Copyright © 2005 by Pearson Education, Inc. Adapted by permission of Pearson Education, Inc.

Extended Written Response

Extended written response is useful for assessing blocks of knowledge rather than pieces of information detached from one another—causes of environmental disasters, the carbon cycle in the atmosphere, how one mathematical formula can be derived from another, or the concept of checks and balances in government. Extended written response assessments are not as efficient as selected response assessments because responding to each takes longer, but they can get at deeper levels of knowledge.

Performance Assessment

Performance assessment is usually not a good choice for assessing knowledge targets, for three reasons.

We'll illustrate the first reason with a brief example. Let's say we ask a student to complete a rather complex performance, such as writing and executing a computer program, for the purpose of determining if she has the prerequisite knowledge. If the student successfully executes the program, then we know that she possesses the prerequisite knowledge. The problem comes in when the program does not run successfully. Was it due to lack of knowledge of the programming language, due to the inability to use knowledge to create a program that does what it is intended to do, or merely due to the inability to manipulate the keyboard or to proofread? We can't know the reason for failure unless we follow up the performance assessment with one of the other assessment methods. We must ask some short answer or extended response questions to find out if the prerequisite knowledge was there to start with. But, if our initial objective was to assess mastery of specific knowledge, why go through the extra work? To save time and increase accuracy, we recommend using selected response, short answer, and extended written response assessments to evaluate knowledge targets.

The second reason this is not a good match is because it is inefficient to assess all content knowledge with a performance assessment. A single performance task does require some subset of knowledge, and you can assess its presence with a particular performance task, but how many performance tasks would you have to create to cover all the knowledge you want students to acquire? For example, how many performance assessments would it take to determine if students can spell all the words you want them to spell? Or, how many performance assessments would it take to determine if students can perform all the mathematical operations they have been taught in a semester? Again, we recommend assessing knowledge with a simpler method and reserving performance assessment for those learning targets that really require it.

The third reason that performance assessments are usually not a good match for knowledge learning targets has again to do with practicality. It just isn't practical (or safe) to conduct some performance assessments. For example, let's say that you want to know if students can read schedules, such as bus schedules. It would be most "authentic" to ask students to get around town on the bus, but it would be highly inefficient and perhaps dangerous. Asking students to answer multiple-choice or short answer questions requiring understanding of a bus schedule would be a good compromise for getting the information needed.

Personal Communication

This is a good match with knowledge targets for most students at all grade levels, but tends to be inefficient if a lot of knowledge is to be assessed for lots of students. Personal communication works best for real-time sampling of student understanding during instruction. Also, for some students, such as those with special needs, English language learners, or younger students, it is the best way to gather accurate information.

Assessing Reasoning Proficiency

Selected Response

A common misunderstanding is that selected response questions can't assess reasoning proficiency. Although not a good choice for some patterns of reasoning, other patterns of reasoning can be assessed in selected response format. For example:

- Which of the following statements best describes how dogs in real life are different from the dog in the story? (Comparative reasoning)

- What generalization can you make from this selection about how these plants lure their prey? (Inference—generalizing)

- Which answer best explains the author's purpose in writing this story? (Inference—determining author's purpose)

- Choose the sentence that best tells what the story is about. (Inference—identifying main idea)

There are limits to this format when assessing reasoning. If you want to assess how well students can choose from their store of reasoning proficiencies to solve a problem, solve a problem requiring several steps, explain their choice or reasoning process, or defend an opinion, you must use another assessment method. For example, you might ask students to solve the following problem in mathematics: "Estimate the number of hours of TV advertising the typical U.S. fifth grader watches in a year. Describe your procedure for determining your answer." This is an extended response question. If the learning target you want to assess is student reasoning, a single number as the right answer is not the focus of the assessment—the process itself is.

Extended Written Response

Extended written response is a good choice for assessing reasoning targets. Students can be encouraged to write to examine their own thinking. The trick here is to write good questions, ones that require students to analyze, compare, contrast, synthesize, draw inferences, and evaluate *novel* information. For example, if you want students to be able to determine the type of government present in a country (such as democracy, theocracy, dictatorship, or monarchy), you could teach the characteristics of each and practice identifying them. Then, on the assessment, you would give the characteristics of a particular government in a country they had not studied and ask students to identify its type and to explain their reasons.

Remember that to assess reasoning, the question has to be novel. If students worked on the answer to the question during instruction, then the answer is a piece of remembered knowledge, which does not require reasoning. For example, consider the following science standard: "Recognize and analyze alternative explanations and models" (National Research Council, 1996, p. 175). The intent of this standard is that students will be able to use scientific criteria to determine the most plausible explanation or model. To assess this aspect of scientific inquiry, students must be asked to evaluate an explanation or model different than the ones the teacher has used for demonstration and also different from the ones the students have practiced with.

Performance Assessment

This is a partial match for assessing reasoning. For example, we can observe students carrying out science laboratory procedures and draw conclusions about their reasoning based on our observations. But, there's a hitch that keeps performance assessment from being a great match with reasoning targets: we need to make an inference from what we observe. If students do well on a performance task requiring specific patterns of reasoning, we can assume that reasoning is sound. However, if they don't do well, it could be due to lack of prerequisite knowledge, lack of motivation, or to imprecise reasoning. Without engaging in additional time-consuming assessment, we may not be able to judge level of achievement on reasoning targets.

Personal Communication

For gathering accurate information, personal communication is a strong match to reasoning targets. Teachers can ask students questions to probe more deeply into a response. Or, students can demonstrate their solution to a problem, explaining their reasoning out loud as they go.

The drawbacks with using personal communication to assess reasoning proficiency are, as always, the amount of time it takes and the record-keeping challenge it poses.

Assessing Performance Skills Targets

There is really only one assessment method that adequately covers performance skills targets, and that is performance assessment. We can use other assessment methods to determine if students possess the knowledge required to perform skillfully, but the only way to determine whether students can actually perform skillfully is to watch them do it and then judge their level of achievement. For example, we can ask students to answer selected response or oral questions about how to conduct themselves during a job interview, but the only way to determine how well they can do it is to watch them during a simulated job interview.

Performance assessment overlaps with personal communication when the performance skills in question fall into the category of oral proficiency, such as speaking a foreign language or giving an oral presentation.

Assessing Proficiency in Creating Products

As with performance skills, the only option for determining whether students can create a certain kind of product is performance assessment: have them create the product or performance and then judge its quality. Once again, we can assess the knowledge required for creating a quality product with a less time-consuming method, but the only way to determine students' levels of proficiency in creating the product is to have them create it.

Performance assessment overlaps with extended written response when the product in question requires writing, such as writing a business letter, lab report, research report, or health and fitness plan.

Thinking About Target–Method Match

Take a look back to Activity 4.1. See if you'd like to amend any of your original decisions and explain why. Then read our suggested answers here and see if you agree. You may want to discuss your responses and thoughts with your learning team.

1. *Writing proficiency*

    The act of writing creates a product that is then assessed with a scoring guide describing components of quality, such as: ideas, organization, voice, word choice, sentence fluency, and conventions. We might also look at the process of writing to observe thinking strategies, planning strategies, revision techniques, or editing proficiency, which would also require a performance assessment.

2. *Group discussion proficiency*

    Group discussion is a performance skill—to make a judgment about a student's level of proficiency, we have to observe it. Therefore, a performance assessment is the best option.

3. *Reading comprehension proficiency*

    This situation is more complicated. Reading comprehension is an act of reasoning. While students must have decoding proficiency, knowledge of vocabulary, and so forth to comprehend, these are prerequisites that would be assessed prior to determining level of comprehension. Since comprehension is reasoning, we must first define the kind or kinds of reasoning we want to assess. Then we could choose to assess it with selected response (e.g., which of following is most likely to happen next?), extended written response (e.g., list the main idea and two supporting details, or summarize the passage), or personal communication (e.g., orally retell the story, or orally answer comprehension questions).

    You might be thinking, "Couldn't we also use performance assessment, like having the students create a poster depicting the main sequence of events in a story, or create a picture that depicts the character of the protagonist?" If what you are assessing is comprehension, the poster or artwork is just the context in which we are getting the extended written response so that we can judge comprehension. We don't want to use information about the quality of the poster or picture as a product itself as evidence of reading comprehension.

4. *Proficiency using specified mathematical procedures*

"Using mathematical procedures" might imply knowledge—ability to carry out the steps in a procedure—or it might imply reasoning—understanding when to use a mathematical procedure. You could use selected response, extended written response, or personal communication to assess either a knowledge or reasoning interpretation.

5. *Proficiency conducting labs in science*

Proficiency conducting labs in science is a performance skill—skillfully using equipment—therefore it requires a performance assessment—watching students use the equipment.

TRY THIS

Activity 4.3 Analyze Samples for Target–Method Match

In the CD file, "Assessments to Evaluate," examine the samples entitled "Mathematics Assessment and Instructional Guide," "Fish Tank," and "Emerson Essay Test," and decide the extent to which each has used an appropriate assessment method for the learning targets being assessed. To decide, you'll first need to identify the kind of learning target and the assessment method. Then refer to Table 4.1 to determine the quality of the match.

Now, look at some of the assessments you have used in the past and decide the extent to which each has used an appropriate assessment method for the learning targets being assessed. To decide, you'll first need to identify the kind of learning target and the method of assessment. Then refer to Table 4.1 to determine the quality of the match. The learning targets might not be clear enough to decide whether the method(s) are appropriate. If so, make a note to that effect and decide what to do about the situation if you want to use the assessment again.

Assessment Development Cycle

All assessments, regardless of method selected, go through the same five stages of development: planning, developing, critiquing, administering, and revising (Figure 4.3). So far in the text, we have discussed three of the four steps in the first stage: determine the intended uses of an assessment, identify the learning targets to be assessed, and select

Figure 4.3   Stages in Assessment Development

1. **Plan:** Assess why? Assess what? Assess how? How Important?

2. **Develop:** Determine the sample. Select, create, or modify test items or tasks and scoring mechanisms.

3. **Critique:** Evaluate for quality.

4. **Administer:** Administer the test or assessment.

5. **Revise:** Evaluate test quality based on results and revise as needed.

the proper assessment method. The fourth step, which we address later in this section, is to determine the relative importance of each learning target so that we sample each adequately.

In the second stage we select or create test items or tasks and scoring mechanisms, adhering to the guidelines offered for each method in Chapters 5 through 8.

During the third stage, we check to make sure we have avoided all possible things that might inadvertently cause results to misrepresent student learning, again using information provided for each method in Chapters 5 through 8.

In the fourth stage, we simply administer the assessment to students.

In the fifth and last stage, we note any problems with the questions, tasks, or scoring mechanisms on the assessment and rework them as needed.

The five stages of development we describe here are presented in the context of a teacher-developed assessment for classroom use. However, they also apply to any other type of assessment developed by grade level teams, content area departments, or district subject-area teams for purposes other than individual classroom use. Short-cycle, common, or interim assessments also need to adhere to standards of quality, and the five stages of development should frame that assessment development process, as well. In Chapters 5 through 8 we will describe any variations on the theme applicable for particular assessment methods.

Stage 1: Plan the Assessment

Creating or selecting a test without having a test plan can result in mismatches between instruction and assessment. The assessment probably will not measure what you intend it to measure, which is known as a *validity* problem. From an assessment quality point of view, this is a bad thing. If you have ever faced an exam yourself that did not match what you thought were the most important aspects of the course you were taking, you know what that feels like from the student's point of view. In the following activity, you will analyze a test you have given to determine its match to the intended learning targets.

When we make a plan for an assessment, whether we intend to create the assessment or just copy it, we are making the advance decisions about validity—what the test will cover and how much weight each learning target will get.

TRY THIS

Activity 4.4 Analyze Your Own Assessment for Clear Targets

Find a selected response test or an extended written response test you have given to students in the past or one you plan to give. Then follow these steps to audit it for clear targets.

1. *Analyze your test item by item.* Identify and write down what learning each item assesses. Describe the learning in whatever terms you want. If two or more items address the same learning, use the same terms to describe that learning. Note the number of test points each item is worth.

2. *Organize the learning targets into a test plan.* Transfer the item information to the chart in Table 4.2 (a printable copy of this table appears on the accompanying CD in the file, "Analyze for Clear Targets").

3. *Question your test plan.* Is this a representative sample of what you taught and what you expected students to learn?

   - Does the number of points for each learning target represent its relative importance within the whole? If not, which ones are out of balance?

   - Does the number of points for each learning target represent the amount of time you spent on it relative to the whole? If not, which ones are out of balance?

   - Are any important learning targets you taught left out? If so, which one(s)?

Activity 4.4 (Continued)

4. *Adjust your test plan.* As needed, adjust the numbers in the "Number of Questions" and/or "Points" column on the table to reflect the amount of time you spent teaching each learning target and each target's relative importance to the content as a whole.

   As needed, add or delete learning targets to reflect what you taught and what you deemed most important to learn and assess.

5. *Draw conclusions about your assessment.* What does the data you wrote into Table 4.2 tell you about the matches among what's written in your curriculum, what you taught, and what you assessed?

Table 4.2   Analyze an Assessment for Targets

Learning Target	Number of Items	Points

Examples at the Assessment Planning Stage

We'll examine the planning stage by following two examples: a secondary music teacher planning an assessment for his unit on the bluegrass music and a fourth-grade teacher planning an assessment for a unit on the physics of sound. The music teacher's assessment plan is presented in Table 4.3, and the fourth-grade teacher's assessment plan is presented in Table 4.4. As you read these tables, please note that there is no single correct format for test plans; we simply have shown two possible formats.

Table 4.3   Test Plan—Bluegrass Music

Content	Know	Analyze	Compare	Total
Individual pieces of music	5		5	10
Musical elements/instruments/ expressive devices	5	5		10
Composers/performers	5	5	5	15
TOTAL	15	10	10	35

Assess Why?

As we saw in Chapter 2, assessment results can be used for many purposes. In each of our two examples, the teachers' primary purposes are twofold: to help students understand how much they have learned, and to add information to the gradebook in preparation for calculating a course grade. Because assessment design is influenced by how we intend to use the results and by whom else will also use them, we answer the question, "Assess why?" first of all.

Assess What?

Sound assessments arise from clear, specific, and appropriate achievement targets. Beginning with clear targets is important because different targets require different assessment methods and also because the breadth and depth of a learning target will affect how much coverage it will need on the assessment and in instruction. So at this juncture, you will do the following:

1. List the major learning targets you will be teaching.

2. Identify the prerequisite subtargets by unpacking or clarifying the learning targets, as needed.

3. Classify the targets, subtopics, and/or unpacked learning targets, into knowledge, reasoning, performance skills, products, and/or dispositions.

4. Write the unpacked and/or clarified learning targets into the appropriate spaces in the test plan format you select. Blank forms are on the CD in the file, "Test Planning Forms."

Table 4.4   Test Plan—The Physics of Sound, for Fourth Graders (Selected Targets)

Learning Target	Type of Target	Assessment Method	Percent Importance
Acquire vocabulary associated with the physics of sound	Knowledge	Selected Response	25%
Learn that sound originates from a source that is vibrating and is detected at a receiver such as the human ear	Knowledge	Selected Response	5%
Use knowledge of the physics of sound to solve simple sound challenges	Reasoning	Extended Written Response	20%—Present novel sound challenge; student describes how to solve it
Understand the relationship between the pitch of a sound and the physical properties of the sound source (i.e., length of vibrating object, frequency of vibrations, and tension of vibrating string)	Reasoning	Extended Written Response	10%—Give two novel examples and student compares pitch
Use scientific thinking processes to conduct investigations and build explanations: observing, comparing, and organizing (1) How sound travels through solids, liquids, and air; (2) Methods to amplify sound at the source and at the receiver	Reasoning Skill	Extended Written Response & Performance Assessment	40%—Design an experiment for a given hypothesis; give data/student organizes; set up stations/students conduct an experiment—all novel

Source: From the *FOSSR Physics of Sound Teacher Guide*, © The Regents of the University of California, 2005, developed by Lawrence Hall of Science and published by Delta Education, LLC. Reprinted by permission.

The secondary school music teacher whose test plan is represented in Table 4.3, has planned a 3-week unit of instruction on bluegrass music. He has chosen bluegrass music as the context for the following music standards:

- Classifies selected exemplary works from various historical periods by genre, style, and composer.

- Explains how use of specific musical elements (for example, rhythm, melody, timbre, expressive devices) is characteristic of music from various world cultures.

- Identifies music that represents the history and diverse cultures of our state.

- Identifies important composers and performers who influenced various genres of American music.

Students will need to acquire some knowledge about bluegrass music in three categories—works (famous pieces of music), musical elements (used to give the music the bluegrass feel), and composers/performers. In addition, the teacher will teach students to use the content knowledge in each of these three areas to reason analytically and comparatively. As indicated in the test plan, any single test question either will test knowledge or will be a combination of knowledge and the reasoning that is to be performed using that knowledge.

In the plan for the fourth-grade unit on the physics of sound, the teacher has written selected learning targets down the left-hand column of Table 4.4. The type of learning target is noted in the next column.

These teachers chose content categories based on their state content standards, local curriculum guides, and natural subdivisions of content. They chose reasoning patterns from content standards, local curriculum, and priorities in their teaching.

Assess How?

This is fairly straightforward. Once you have classified learning targets by type it is easy to decide which assessment method to select by referring to the matching guidelines in Table 4.1.

The fourth-grade teacher is emphasizing science process skills as well as knowledge and reasoning so she will be using more than one assessment method. She has chosen the planning format shown in Table 4.4, which allows her to specify how each learning target will be assessed. The music teacher has only knowledge and reasoning learning targets. He has decided that the combination of knowledge and reasoning can be assessed well with a selected response test. Since he has no need for a test plan to show different assessment methods, he has chosen a test plan format that emphasizes how content knowledge crosses with level of thinking.

How Important?

When we define the relative importance of each of the learning targets listed, we are mapping out how we will *sample* student learning. What will be most important on this assessment? How many points will each item be worth? For the most part, this is the call of the individual teacher, taking into account the following:

- *The breadth and depth of the learning target.* For example, in Table 4.4, the learning target "Learn that sound originates from a source that is vibrating and is detected at a receiver such as the human ear" doesn't cover as much territory as "Acquire vocabulary associated with the physics of sound," or "Use scientific thinking processes to conduct investigations and build explanations: observing, comparing, and organizing." Therefore, assessing "learning where sound originates" will carry less weight on the assessment, as reflected by the percentage of total points, and other targets will carry more weight.

   In all cases, the assessment must include enough questions or tasks to provide evidence leading us to a confident conclusion about student achievement, without wasting time gathering too much evidence. The critical question is, How much evidence is enough? How many multiple-choice test items, essay exercises, performance tasks? (Each assessment method brings with it a set of rules of evidence for determining how big a sample of student achievement we need. We explain those guidelines in Chapters 5 through 8.)

- *The importance of each learning target.* For example, in Table 4.4, the teacher has determined that the most important learning target focuses on science processes and skills. Scientific information is important, and there is an expectation that students will learn some content information from this unit of study, but process skills are more important in this case. Therefore, science process targets alone will comprise 40 percent of the assessment points and the other four targets combined will total 60 percent.

- *State standards and local curriculum.* For example, the music teacher is guided by the state standard in his emphasis of knowledge and reasoning targets in the unit. Because the state standards emphasize using information to analyze and classify, the teacher has also emphasized it on his test—two-thirds of the points on the test reflect students' ability to apply knowledge in novel ways.

Although not a hard and fast rule, a good guideline for making decisions regarding percentage of importance for each learning target is that percentage of instructional time and percentage of assessment time should be roughly equal. So, if science processes and skills represent 40 percent of importance, roughly 40 percent of instructional time will be used to teach science processes and skills.

Stage 2: Develop the Assessment—Good Exercises and Sound Scoring Procedures

Having chosen one or more assessment methods, we must adhere to guidelines for developing test questions, extended written response exercises, performance tasks, or questions to elicit evidence of the desired student learning. Further, we need accurate scoring keys for selected response assessments and good scoring guides for extended written response and performance assessment. The development guidelines for each are covered in detail in Chapters 5 through 8.

Stage 3: Critique the Assessment

We've carefully selected and clarified learning targets, determined their relative importance, chosen the best assessment method, and carefully written questions, tasks, and scoring guides adhering to standards of quality. We're finished, right?

Well, no. Regardless of how carefully we plan, things can still go wrong that result in inaccurate estimates of achievement. Witness the pumice that wouldn't float in one state's performance assessment of science process skills, the writing prompt that elicited expository instead of persuasive writing from students, the 10th-grade standardized test administered during rioting by seniors, or asking English language learners to write extended responses to math problems.

A list of problems that can result in inaccurate estimates of student learning is presented in Figure 4.4. Note that some of the problems listed, such as unclear targets, inappropriate assessment method, and improper sampling, would be solved by adhering to the test development process as discussed here. Others are crazy little things that can be hard to anticipate if you haven't experienced them. Problems specific to each method will be discussed more fully in Chapters 5 though 8.

Figure 4.4 Potential Sources of Bias and Distortion

1. **Potential barriers to accurate assessment common to all methods**

   A. **Barriers that can occur within the student**
      - Language barriers
      - Emotional upset
      - Poor health
      - Physical handicap
      - Peer pressure to mislead assessor
      - Lack of motivation at time of assessment
      - Lack of testwiseness (understanding how to take tests)
      - Lack of personal confidence leading to evaluation anxiety

   B. **Barriers that can occur within the assessment context**
      - Noise distractions
      - Poor lighting
      - Discomfort
      - Lack of rapport with assessor
      - Cultural insensitivity in assessor or assessment
      - Lack of proper equipment

   C. **Barriers that arise from the assessment itself (regardless of method)**
      - Directions lacking or vague
      - Poorly worded questions
      - Poor reproduction of test questions
      - Missing information

2. **Potential barriers to accurate assessment unique to each method**

   A. **Barriers with multiple-choice tests**
      - Lack of reading skills
      - More than one correct response choice
      - Incorrect scoring key
      - Incorrect bubbling on answer sheet
      - Clues to the answer in the item or in other items

Figure 4.4   (Continued)

B. Barriers with extended written response assessments

- Lack of reading or writing skills
- No scoring criteria
- Inappropriate scoring criteria
- Evaluator untrained in applying scoring criteria
- Biased scoring due to stereotyping of respondent
- Insufficient time or patience to read and score carefully
- Students don't know the criteria by which they'll be judged

C. Barriers with performance assessment

- Lack of reading skills
- Inappropriate or nonexistent scoring criteria
- Evaluator untrained in applying scoring criteria
- Bias due to stereotypic thinking
- Insufficient time or patience to observe and score carefully
- Student doesn't feel safe
- Unfocused or unclear tasks
- Tasks that don't elicit the correct performance
- Biased tasks
- Students don't know the criteria by which they'll be judged
- Insufficient sampling

D. Barriers when using personal communication

- Sampling enough performance
- Problems with accurate record keeping

Source: Adapted from *Practice with Student-Involved Classroom Assessment* (pp. 194–195), by J. A. Arter & K. U. Busick, 2001, Portland, OR: Assessment Training Institute. Copyright © 2006, 2001 Educational Testing Service. Adapted by permission.

Stage 4: Administer the Assessment

If you have completed the steps in the preceding three stages, administering the test should go smoothly and the test itself will meet the information needs of all parties involved. Unfortunately, administering the test has too often been the starting place and the "cycle" may have looked rather linear: teach, test, report. If we have used textbook tests and relied on the textbook company to take us through stages one through three, we may have high-quality items, but we will not have attended to the need to make the test reflect the balance of importance of what we taught. Because textbook tests are generally designed to meet only the teacher's need to generate a grade, it may be quite cumbersome to use them to provide students with specific information regarding their strengths and areas of need, standard by standard. We recommend that you never begin the assessment development cycle at Stage 4.

Stage 5: Revise the Assessment

At this stage, we come full circle to double check that the test did indeed accomplish what we intended. Were we able to use the results for all the decisions we intended to make? Were students able to use the results to keep in touch with the details of their progress? Did a source of bias or distortion creep in? It is almost impossible to eliminate *all* sources of bias and distortion up front. Some only become apparent when you give students the assessment. So,

1. Do the best you can prior to administering the assessment.

2. Watch for possible sources of error during and after the assessment.

3. If something goes wrong, either (1) don't use the results from the tasks in question, or (2) interpret the results with possible bias in mind.

Consider asking students to help in this. Were parts of the test a surprise to them? Did aspects seem not to match their understanding of what it was most important to learn? Were some questions or tasks confusing—the students knew the material, but didn't know how to respond? Remember that our goal in the classroom is to get accurate information about student achievement, and if we know the information is not accurate, we have an obligation to discard it and to revise the assessment, if needed, before future use.

Assessment *for* Learning Using Assessment Plans

Assessment *for* learning and student involvement activities spin directly off the assessment plan. For example, the plan itself can be shared with students ahead of time to make the learning targets clearer. Students can be involved throughout a unit, by identifying where each day's instruction fits into the plan, or by writing practice test questions periodically for each cell of the plan, as a form of review. More ideas for using test plans as instructional tools will be described in Chapters 5 and 6.

For performance assessment targets, students can be given rubrics for the reasoning and skills outlined in the assessment plan and can practice using the rubrics throughout instruction. For example, in the fourth-grade unit on the physics of sound, the teacher has rubrics for what makes good observation, comparing, and organizing. Students can use these rubrics to guide their activities during the experiments outlined in the unit. Then the same rubrics determine success on a final set of culminating activities. The same set of rubrics could also be used in any other unit emphasizing the same reasoning or skill targets, thus building student understanding and competence over time. These and other procedures for using rubrics as tools for learning are examined in detail in Chapter 7.

Summary

No single assessment method is superior to any other. Selected response, extended written response, performance assessment, and personal communication are all viable options depending on the learning targets to be assessed, the purpose of the assessment, and special student characteristics such as age, English proficiency, or specific learning disabilities.

All assessment development proceeds through the same five stages: (1) identify the purpose, specify the targets, select appropriate methods, decide on relative importance of the targets and sample well; (2) write the questions using guidelines for quality; (3) eliminate as many potential sources of bias and distortion as possible; (4) administer the assessment; and (5) examine the results for areas needing fine tuning. By doing the work at each stage, we can have confidence that our assessments are yielding accurate results.

DEEPEN UNDERSTANDING

Activity 4.5   Video Discussion of *Evaluating Assessment Quality*

ETS's interactive video, *Evaluating Assessment Quality: Hands-On Practice*, provides review and extra practice on characteristics of quality classroom assessments—clear purposes, clear targets, target–method match, sampling, and potential sources of bias and distortion—using workshop-type activities. We recommend working through the video with your learning team.

Tracking Your Learning—Possible Portfolio Entries

Any of the activities included in Chapter 4 can be used as portfolio entries. Remember, the learning targets for this book are outlined in Figure 4.1, listed in Table 1.2, and described in detail in Chapter 1. The portfolio entry cover sheet provided on the CD in the file, "Portfolio Entry Cover Sheet," will prompt you to think about how each item you choose for your portfolio reflects your learning with respect to one or more of these learning targets.

Specific recommendations for portfolio content follow.

Activity 4.6 Critique an Assessment for Good Design

In Chapter 2 we introduced rubrics for analyzing and improving the quality of classroom assessments. The rubrics align with the learning targets in Table 1.2 and Figure 4.1. There is a rubric for each of the keys to quality classroom assessments— Clear Purpose, Clear Targets, Sound Assessment Design, Good Communication, and Student Involvement. In Chapter 2 we suggested it would be worthwhile to look at some sample assessments for the traits of Clear Purpose and Student Involvement. In Chapter 3 we proposed that it would be useful to examine sample assessments for the trait of Clear Targets.

Chapter 4 emphasizes the Sound Assessment Design key to quality classroom assessment. Therefore, once again, we recommend that it would be useful to examine at least one classroom assessment for the quality of the design—target–method match, sampling, and attention to possible sources of bias and distortion.

You will find the classroom assessment quality rubrics on the CD file, "Assessment Quality Rubrics." In this case, we'll be using the one called "Sound Assessment Design."

Go through the same steps as previously:

1. Individually, read the strong level of the rubric first—"fast tracked." Then read the beginning level—"side tracked"—and finally the middle level—"on track." Mark the words and phrases that jump out at you as those really describing each level of quality.

2. Discuss any questions you have about the rubric with your colleagues.

3. Individually, look at your first sample assessment. If you think it is strong for the trait of Sound Assessment Design, begin reading the rubric at the "fast tracked" level. If you think it is weak, begin reading at the "side tracked" level. If you think it is strong, but "fast tracked" doesn't quite match what you see in the assessment, read "on track." Conversely, if you think it is weak, but what you read in "side tracked" doesn't quite describe it, read "on track."

4. There is no such thing as a "right" score, only a justifiable score. Justify your score using the words and phrases from the rubric that you felt described the assessment.

Activity 4.6   (Continued)

5. Compare your scores to those of your colleagues. Discuss discrepancies and attempt to come to a resolution.

We have several sample assessments on the CD to use as defaults. See the file, "Assessments to Evaluate." Our analyses of each of these samples are also on the CD in the file, "Assessment Critiques."

When you finish analyzing your assessments, discuss your comfort level using the rubrics. Was it easier than last time? How easy was it to match the sample assessments to the rubrics? What questions does this process raise for you?

TRY THIS

Activity 4.7   Critique Your Own Assessment

Follow the procedure given in Activity 4.6 to apply the trait of "Sound Assessment Design" in the Classroom Assessment Quality Rubrics to an assessment that you currently use. Revise the assessment as needed based on the results.

CHAPTER

[**5**]

Selected Response
Assessment

[S] elected response assessment has come to signify the traditional, old-fashioned way of testing. As recently as the 1920s and 1930s, however, it was known as the new, scientific assessment method, welcomed by those at the forefront of education innovation because it was considered objective—that is, free of teacher judgment. Although its luster has dimmed over the years, it is still a valuable tool in our assessment repertoire and worthy of regular use as both assessment *for* learning and assessment *of* learning.

Selected response assessments can include one or more of four different item types: multiple choice, true/false, matching and short answer fill in. In this chapter, we will examine the following:

- When to use selected response assessments.

- How to build high-quality tests.

- How to use them as assessments for learning by involving students in their planning, development, and use.

The shaded areas of Figures 5.1 and 5.2 show where we are within our framework of study.

Figure 5.1   Keys to Quality Classroom Assessment

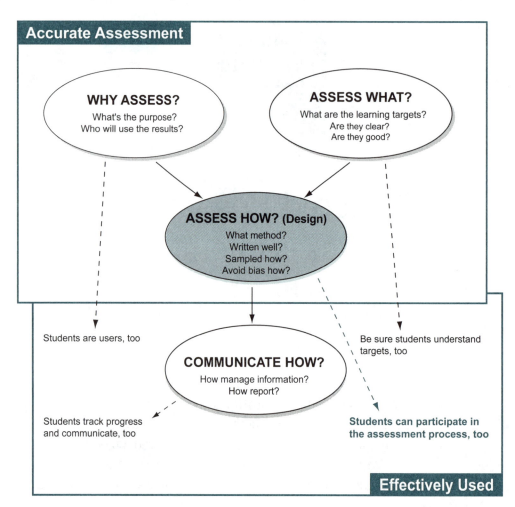

Figure 5.2   A Plan for Matching Assessment Methods with Achievement Targets

Target to Be Assessed	Assessment Method			
	Selected Response	**Extended Written Response**	**Performance Assessment**	**Personal Communication**
Knowledge Mastery				
Reasoning Proficiency				
Performance Skills				
Ability to Create Products				

Source: Adapted from *Student-Involved Assessment* for *Learning,* 4th ed. (p. 84), by R. J. Stiggins, 2005, Upper Saddle River, NJ: Merrill/ Prentice Hall. Copyright © 2005 by Pearson Education, Inc. Reprinted by permission of Pearson Education, Inc.

When to Use Selected Response Assessment

Matching Method to Target

The first condition for using selected response is the type of learning target to be assessed, as described in Activity 4.4, "Target–Method Match," in Chapter 4. Selected response formats are ideal for assessing knowledge-level learning targets and some patterns of reasoning, as shown in Figure 5.2.

> **TRY THIS**
>
> ### Activity 5.1 Learning Targets Best Assessed with Selected Response
>
> To begin applying the content of this chapter to your own context, identify five to seven knowledge and/or reasoning learning targets in the curriculum materials you use. Write them down and save them for further activities.

Other Contextual Conditions

Several other key conditions influence choosing the selected response method of assessment:

- Students can read English well enough to understand what each test item is asking of them.

- The content to be assessed is broad, requiring wide-ranging coverage. Since the response time to one item is so short, we can include lots of items per unit of testing time and thus sample student achievement thoroughly.

- The assessment is to be taken by a large number of students. Electronic or optical scan scoring of response sheets increases scoring efficiency and accuracy.

Developing Selected Response Tests

As we saw in Chapter 4, each individual classroom assessment represents a part of a long-term assessment map that parallels the curriculum map for the reporting period. Each assessment contributes to an accumulating body of evidence of each student's level of achievement. Some assessments will support learning, others will serve to verify that learning has happened. Within this big picture, we plan each individual assessment, some of which may be selected response tests.

We will follow the five stages in the assessment development cycle described in Chapter 4 to develop selected response assessments:

1. Plan the assessment.

2. Develop the assessment.

3. Critique the assessment.

4. Administer the assessment.

5. Revise the assessment.

TRY THIS

Activity 5.2   Create a Quiz

Refer to the learning targets you listed in Activity 5.1. Identify those that you might assess together on one test, and then locate the written material—your textbook or other print material—you use to teach to those learning targets.

- Select a section of that material that is long enough (or extensive enough in its coverage) to permit you to build a 10-item selected response quiz.

- Review the material and build the quiz, being sure to include at least one instance of each selected response format (multiple choice, true/false, matching, and short answer fill in).

Set your new quiz aside for later use and continue reading.

Stage 1: Plan the Assessment

In the planning stage, as presented in Chapter 4, we answer four questions: Assess why? Assess what? Assess how? How important? These decisions are reflected in Figure 5.3. You may want to refer to the CD file, "Test Planning Forms," as you proceed through this first stage.

Figure 5.3   Decisions at the Planning Stage for a Selected Response Assessment

Assess why?

Assessment *for* Learning
> Diagnostic/planning information for teacher
> Diagnostic/planning information for student
> Diagnostic/planning information for others
> Student self-evaluation

Assessment *of* Learning
> Report card grade
> Other accountability decisions

Assess what?

Knowledge and/or reasoning learning targets

Assess how?

Selected response test
> Multiple-choice items
> True/false items
> Matching items
> Short answer fill-in items

How important?

Sample of items to represent the breadth of the learning targets in question and their relative importance in the learning plan

Assess Why?

This first question establishes the purpose for the assessment. It requires that we answer the following questions: How do we want to use the information? Who else will use it? What decisions will they make? For example, if we decide students are one of the intended users of the information, that will drive certain design decisions along the way, as you will see.

Assess What?

This question requires that we list the specific learning targets the test is to measure.

Assess How?

The answer here is, "by means of a selected response test," so we must make sure we have identified only knowledge and reasoning learning targets as the subject of this test. (Although the kinds of selected response items available are listed in Figure 5.3, we need not choose which to use until we develop the test.)

How Important?

This question requires that we assign a relative importance to each learning target. One simple way to do this with selected response questions is to decide how many points the test will be worth and then divide the points according to relative importance of each learning target. The number of points we assign to each learning target outlines our sample. As described in Chapter 4, we select a sample of items to represent the breadth of the learning targets and their importance relative to each other in the instructional period the test is to cover.

Remember, when identifying the relative importance of each learning target, we consciously match our emphasis in assessment to our emphasis in the classroom. If, say, we spend 50 percent of the time learning how to read maps, then roughly 50 percent of the assessment should focus on map reading. If only 5 percent of the course deals with reading maps, then it would be inappropriate to spend 50 percent of the final assessment on map reading.

When using a test developed by someone else—another teacher, a textbook company, or a test publisher—it is crucial to examine it carefully and adjust it as needed for both the learning targets represented and the amount of emphasis each receives prior to deciding to use the test, using the procedure given in Activity 4.4, "Analyze Your Own Assessment for Clear Targets."

Options for Test Plans

As you recall from Chapter 4, in the classroom we propose two useful types of test plans. One is a list of the learning targets and the other is a table representing the learning targets in shortened form. Both are equally effective as test planning instruments.

Table 5.1 shows a plan for a third-grade mathematics test consisting of a list of learning targets.

Table 5.1   Sample Test Plan for a Third-Grade Mathematics Test

Learning Targets	Importance
Number Sense: Identifies place value to thousands Reads, writes, orders, and compares numbers through four digits Reads and writes common fractions to represent models, real-life objects, and diagrams	11 points
Number Operations: Subtracts whole numbers to three digits with borrowing	4 points
Measurement: Reads time to the nearest minute Identifies correct units of measurement for length, capacity, weight, and temperature	5 points

There are times when we may want to frame our test plan in a table format, which is especially useful if we want to ensure that the test covers both recall of important information and reasoning processes we have taught. Figure 5.4 and Table 5.2 show a simple example of a list of learning targets and a test plan for a fifth-grade social studies unit on westward expansion. (Remember that there could be other learning targets taught during the unit—this test plan represents only those covered by the selected response portion of the test.)

Figure 5.4   *Assess What?* Fifth-Grade Social Studies Unit Learning Targets to Be Assessed by a Selected Response Test

- Explain the concept of Manifest Destiny and its contribution to the migration of people in the development of the United States.

- Compare the motives of the different groups who participated in the westward expansion by leaving the eastern United States and heading west.

- Compare the lives of different Native American groups before and after westward expansion.

- Identify significant individuals who took part in the westward expansion.

- Explain how the westward migration led to conflict between Native Americans and settlers and between Mexicans and settlers.

Table 5.2   *How Important?* Selected Response Test Plan for Fifth-Grade Social Studies Unit

Content Category	Know	Compare/Contrast	Totals
Manifest Destiny	2		2
Reasons settlers went west	4	2	6
Life of Native American groups	4	2	6
Significant individuals	4		4
Conflicts caused by westward expansion	10		10
Effects on Native Americans and Mexicans	6		6
TOTALS	30	4	34

In the column labeled *Content Category* on the left of Table 5.2, the learning targets are translated into phrases, or categories, representing the content of each. Each category represents many facts and concepts, some of which will be sufficiently important to test. Table 5.2 also includes columns labeled for the cognitive action to be carried out: know outright and reason comparatively. These patterns will be emphasized during the unit of study. The numbers in each cell represent its relative importance in the unit as planned.

Stage 2: Develop the Assessment

So far, our test plan has yielded a list of learning targets or important concepts and an indication of their relative importance. The steps we take in this next stage are (1) determining specifically what to test, (2) determining what kinds of items to write and writing them, and (3) assembling the test.

TRY THIS

Activity 5.3 Make a Test Plan for Your Quiz

Review the material out of which you built the 10-item quiz in Activity 5.2. If you were to build a test plan reflecting the priorities of that content, what would it look like? Please develop that plan now. You may want to use the form on the CD from Activity 4.4, "Analyze for Clear Targets."

Identifying Important Elements

Even though we have numbers on the test plan to indicate the relative importance of each learning target or content category, we still need to identify what content we will test for each cell. In most cases, we won't test everything students are to have learned. Instead, we will select or create questions that cover as much of the important content as possible, given the amount of testing time available, and that are prudent for the age of our students. We use the results to make an inference: a student who has scored 75 percent on the test has mastered about 75 percent of the material that was intended to be learned. We must carefully select the subset of all possible important aspects of knowledge and reasoning so that our sample allows us to estimate level of achievement accurately.

Even though people often think of selected response tests as objective measures of learning, selecting the content for the test is itself a subjective exercise. The test developer—you yourself, a textbook author, or a test publisher—chooses what will be on the test from a vast array of possibilities. It is a matter of professional judgment, just as is determining how to teach the material in the first place. This element of subjectivity does not compromise the test's validity if we have clearly and accurately identified the learning targets that underpin our content standards.

If we are developing a test in a content area such as social studies or science, we first identify the specific content to include on the test by writing propositions. Propositions are statements of important facts, concepts, or understandings that we will be teaching students to know and understand. They state important elements of content and the kind of reasoning to be carried out, and function as basic units of any kind of selected response item we wish to write.

To write propositions, we begin by reviewing the material we have taught. For every cell in our test plan, we note in writing the most important facts, concepts, or understandings we think every student should have at the end of instruction. We use clearly worded sentences, and write down more propositions than we will need. Additional propositions serve two purposes: (1) they allow the writer to create parallel forms of the test; and (2) because some propositions may not lend themselves to writing clearly focused selected response items, we can decide to assess them with a different method, if needed.

Knowledge Propositions

If, for example, we are writing propositions for the test planned in Table 5.2, we will need a total of 30 knowledge items, 2 of which will relate to Manifest Destiny. As we read through the material, we identify and write down three or four statements that reflect important knowledge about the concept of Manifest Destiny. These are our propositions. They might include the following:

- Manifest Destiny represents a belief that it was natural and right to expand the territory of the United States westward.

- Manifest Destiny represents a mission to impart the government and way of life of United States citizens to people living in the land west of the United States during the 1800s.

- Manifest Destiny was first used as a justification for annexing Texas to the United States.

- Manifest Destiny represents a belief that was used to justify the taking of Native American lands.

The test plan also requires six items in the cell that crosses *Know* with *Effects on Native Americans and Mexicans*. Here are two sample propositions:

- Three effects of westward expansion on Plains Indians were increased disease, removal to reservation lands, and loss of food sources.

- Mexico lost the territory of Texas.

Reasoning Propositions

A reasoning proposition states the result of reasoning applied accurately to the information at hand. To write one, we identify the knowledge to be applied, apply the pattern of reasoning, and state the result as a declarative sentence. Propositions for the cell in Table 5.2 that crosses *Compare/Contrast* with *Reasons settlers went west* might read like this:

- The Mormons went west to practice their religion without persecution, whereas the settlers in Texas went west because land was cheap or free and they wanted a place to start over.

- Both Mormons and settlers in Texas were searching for a better life.

- Settlers were encouraged to move to Texas by the Mexican government, while Mormons were led to settle in Utah by their religious leaders.

Remember that when we intend to evaluate students' ability to reason, we must provide them with a context different than that in which they practiced. If we don't, as we saw in Chapter 3, we will not be capturing real evidence of their reasoning (ability to figure things out). Instead, we will have information about what they remember. If we want to assess the learning target, "Compare the motives of the different groups who participated in the westward expansion by leaving the eastern United States and heading west," we cannot have students practice comparing and contrasting during instruction using the same examples we will use on the test.

TRY THIS

Activity 5.4 Writing Propositions for Your Quiz

Refer to the 10-item test you created in Activity 5.2 and the material that you used as its basis. Identify the 10 propositions that underpin the items on your quiz. Do these adequately represent the most important learnings, in your opinion?

Writing Items

Once you have identified the propositions that reflect important learning, you can write any kind of selected response item you might want to use: multiple choice, true/false, matching, or short answer fill-in. Here's how it works with the following proposition from the Manifest Destiny example:

> *Manifest Destiny represents a mission to impart the government and way of life of United States' citizens to people living in the land west of the United States during the 1800s.*

Multiple-Choice Items

To create a multiple-choice item, begin with a question. Then add a number of answers, only one of which is correct.

> *What was the mission of Manifest Destiny in the United States in the 1800s?*
> a. *To have Lewis and Clark make friends with the Native Americans they met.*
> b. *To move the U.S. form of government and way of life west.*
> c. *To defeat General Santa Anna in the battle of the Alamo.*
> d. *To establish religious freedom for all who lived in the west.*

Figure 5.5 illustrates another example of a proposition from the same social studies unit used to generate each of the different item types.

True/False Items

To create a true/false item that is true, include the proposition on the test as stated. (In this example, for fifth graders, you may want to simplify the proposition so that it reads as follows: Manifest Destiny represents a mission the U.S. had in the 1800s to move its government and way of life westward.)

To create a false true/false item, make one part false:

> *Manifest Destiny represents a mission the United States had in the 1800s to guarantee religious freedom to all settlers.*

Figure 5.5   Turning a Proposition into Different Item Types

Proposition: Three effects of westward expansion on Plains Indians in the 1800s were increased disease, removal to reservation lands, and loss of food sources.
True/False Item: (True) Three effects of westward expansion on Plains Indians were increased disease, removal to reservation lands, and loss of food sources. (False) One effect of westward expansion on Plains Indians was access to better health care.
Fill-in or Short Answer Item: What were three effects of westward expansion on Plains Indians in the 1800s?
Multiple-choice Item: What were three effects of westward expansion on Plains Indians in the 1800s? a. Access to health care, removal to reservation lands, and loss of food sources b. Access to health care, population growth, and opportunities for better jobs c. Increased disease, removal to reservation lands, and loss of food sources d. Loss of their schools, removal to reservation lands, and private ownership of land

Matching Items

A matching exercise is similar to a multiple-choice item, in that the task is to combine the trigger item (or "stem") with its proper match. To identify the content of the trigger item and the match, you simply take a proposition and separate it into to subject and predicate parts. The context where matching items makes sense is where the learning targets can be thought of as a series of closely linked propositions, such as states and their capitals or items to be categorized and their categories. Any individual match (stem and response) would state a single proposition. Matching items generally test knowledge propositions, but they can also be used to assess reasoning propositions.

Fill-in or Short Answer Items

To create a fill-in item, leave out the phrase defining the concept or dealing with the effect and ask a question:

> *What was the mission of Manifest Destiny in the United States in the 1800s?*

Selecting from Among the Formats

Each of the item types has its proper uses. Table 5.3 details strengths and weaknesses of multiple-choice, true/false, matching, and short answer fill-in, test formats.

Table 5.3   Comparison of Selected Response Item Types

ITEM TYPE	USED WHEN	ADVANTAGE	LIMITATIONS
Multiple Choice	There is only one right answer. There are several plausible alternatives to the correct answer.	Can measure a variety of objectives. Easy to score. Can cover lots of material efficiently. Carefully crafted distracters can provide diagnostic information.	Guessing can skew score (up to 33% chance, depending on number of distracters). Can be hard to identify plausible distracters.
True/False	A large domain of content is to be tested, requiring the use of many test items.	Can ask many questions in a short time. Easy to score.	Can be trivial or misleading if not written carefully. Guessing can skew score (50% chance).
Matching	There are many related thoughts or facts; you want to measure association of information.	Can cover lots of material efficiently. Easy to score. Can serve as several multiple-choice items in one (each response is a distracter for the others).	Process of elimination can skew score if not written carefully.
Short Answer or Fill in the Blank	A clear, short answer is required. You want to determine if students know the answer, rather than if they can select it from a list.	Assesses production of a response. Reduces the possibility of getting the right answer by guessing. Can cover lots of material efficiently.	Takes longer to score.

Guidelines for Writing Quality Items

We offer here the commonsense guidelines that test developers use to ensure item quality.[1] The first set of guidelines applies to all item types, and the rest are specific to each particular format. Before reading them, you may want to take the short test in Activity 5.5.

TRY THIS

Activity 5.5 Franzipanics

Imagine you are a student in a class that has just studied the topic of "Franzipanics" and now it's test time. Frankly, this is not your best subject, you don't enjoy it, and you have not studied a lick. However, because you are pretty good at figuring things out, you are prepared to see what you can do on this test without knowing the content. Take the Franzipanics test in Figure 5.6 now. As you do, keep track of how you are figuring out the right answers. After taking the test, go to the file on the CD, "Franzipanics Answers," and compare your answers to those in the answer key. Then read through the guidelines for test and item quality below to see which one or ones each item on the Franzipanics test addresses.

General Guidelines

1. *Keep wording simple and focused. Aim for the lowest possible reading level.* Good item writing represents an exercise in effective written communication.

   Not this:

   > *When scientists rely on magnets in the development of electric motors they need to know about poles, which are?*

   But this:

   > *What are the poles of a magnet called?*
   > *a. Anode and cathode*
   > *b. North and south*
   > *c. Strong and weak*
   > *d. Attract and repel*

Figure 5.6   Test of Franzipanics

Directions: Circle the correct answer for each question.

1. The purpose of the cluss in furmpaling is to remove
   a. cluss-prags
   b. tremalis
   c. cloughs
   d. plumots

2. Trassig is true when
   a. lusp trasses the vom
   b. the viskal flans, if the viskal is donwil or zortil
   c. the belgo frulls
   d. dissles lisk easily

3. The sigla frequently overfesks the trelsum because
   a. all siglas are mellious
   b. siglas are always votial
   c. the trelsum is usually tarious
   d. no trelsa are feskable

4. The fribbled breg will minter best with an
   a. derst
   b. morst
   c. sorter
   d. ignu

5. Among the reasons for tristal doss are
   a. the sabs foped and the foths tinzed
   b. the kredges roted with the orots
   c. few rakobs were accepted in sluth
   d. most of the polats were thonced

6. Which of the following (is, are) always present when trossels are being gruven?
   a. rint and vost
   b. sot and plone
   c. shum and vost
   d. vost

7. The mintering function of the ignu is most effectively carried out in connection with
   a. a raxma tol
   b. the groshing stantol
   c. the fribbled breg
   d. a frally sush

8.
   a.
   b.
   c.
   d.

Source: From *Practice with Student-Involved Classroom Assessment* (p. 126), by J. A. Arter & K. U. Busick, 2001, Portland, OR: Assessment Training Institute. Copyright © 2006, 2001 Educational Testing Service. Reprinted by permission.

2. *Ask a full question in the stem.* This forces you to express a complete thought in the stem or trigger part of the question, which usually promotes students' understanding.

Not this:

> *Between 1950 and 1965*
> a. *Interest rates increased.*
> b. *Interest rates decreased.*
> c. *Interest rates fluctuated greatly.*
> d. *Interest rates did not change.*

But this:

> *What was the trend in interest rates between 1950 and 1965?*
> a. *Increased only*
> b. *Decreased only*
> c. *Increased, then decreased*
> d. *Remained unchanged*

3. *Eliminate clues to the correct answer either within the question or across questions within a test.* When grammatical clues within items or material presented in other items give away the correct answer, students get items right for the wrong reasons.

Not this:

> *All of these are an example of a bird that flies, except an*
> a. *Ostrich*
> b. *Falcon*
> c. *Cormorant*
> d. *Robin*

(The article an at the end of the stem requires a response beginning with a vowel. As only one is offered, it must be correct.)

Not this either:

> *Which of the following are examples of birds that do not fly?*
> a. *Falcon*
> b. *Ostrich and penguin*
> c. *Cormorant*
> d. *Robin*

(The question calls for a plural response. As only one is offered, it must be correct.)

4. *Do not make the correct answer obvious to students who have not studied the material.*

5. *Highlight critical, easily overlooked words* (e.g., NOT, MOST, LEAST, EXCEPT).

6. *Have a qualified colleague read your items to ensure their appropriateness.* This is especially true of relatively more important tests, such as big unit tests and final exams.

7. *Double check the scoring key for accuracy before scoring.*

Guidelines for Multiple-Choice Items

The following guidelines for writing multiple-choice test items allow students to answer questions more quickly without wasting time trying to determine what the question is saying. Here's some multiple-choice lingo. The item "stem" refers to the part of the question that comes before the choices. The "distracters" are the incorrect choices.

1. *Ask a complete question to get the item started, if you can.* This has the effect of placing the item's focus in the stem for clarity, not in the response options.

2. *Don't repeat the same words within each response option; rather, reword the item stem to remove the repetitive material from below.* This will clarify the problem and make it more efficient for respondents to read.

3. *Be sure there is only one correct or best answer.* This is where that colleague's independent review can help. Remember, it is acceptable to ask respondents to select a "best answer" from among a set of correct answers. Just be sure to word the question so as to make it clear that they are to find the best answer.

4. *Word response options as briefly as possible and be sure they are grammatically parallel.* This makes items easier to read and eliminates cues to the right answer.

Not this:

> *Why did colonists come to the United States?*
> a. *To escape heavy taxation by their native governments*
> b. *Religion*
> c. *They sought the adventure of living among native Americans in the new land*
> d. *There was the promise of great wealth in the New World*
> e. *More than one of the above answers*

But this:

> *Why did colonists migrate to the United States?*
> a. *To escape taxation*
> b. *For religious freedom*
> c. *For adventure*
> d. *More than one of the above*

5. *Make all response options the same length.* Testwise students know that the correct answer may be the longest one because writers frequently need to add qualifiers to make it the best choice. If you need to do this, do it to all response options.

6. *Don't use "all of the above" or "none of the above" merely to fill space;* use them only when they fit comfortably into the context of the question. In general, test writers avoid using "all of the above" because if a student can determine that two responses are correct, then the answer must be "all of the above."

7. *Use "always" or "never" in your answer choices with caution.* Rarely are things always or never true. Absolutes are frequently incorrect; a student who knows this but is not sure of the correct answer can automatically eliminate those choices.

8. *It's okay to vary the number of response options presented as appropriate to pose the problem you want your students to solve.* While four or five response options are most common, it is permissible to vary the number of response options offered across items within the same test. It is more important to have plausible distracters than a set number of them.

By the way, here's a simple, yet very effective, multiple-choice test item writing tip: If you compose a multiple-choice item and find that you cannot think of enough plausible distracters, include the item on a test the first time as a fill-in question. As your students respond, those who get it wrong will provide you with a good variety of viable distracters.

Guidelines for True/False Exercises

You have only one simple guideline to follow here: Make the item entirely true or false as stated. Complex "idea salads" including some truth and some falsehood just confuse the issue. Precisely what is the proposition you are testing? State it and move on to the next one.

Not this:

From the Continental Divide, located in the Appalachian Mountains, water flows into either the Pacific Ocean or the Mississippi River.

But this:

The Continental Divide is located in the Appalachian Mountains.

Guidelines for Matching Items

When developing matching exercises, follow all of the multiple-choice guidelines offered previously. In addition, observe the following guidelines:

1. *Provide clear directions for making the match.*

2. *Keep the list of things to be matched short.* The maximum number of options is 10. Shorter is better.

3. *Keep the list of things to be matched homogeneous.* Don't mix events with dates or with names.

Not this:

____	1. Texas	A.	$7,200,000
____	2. Hawaii	B.	Chicago
____	3. New York	C.	Mardi Gras
____	4. Illinois	D.	Austin
____	5. Alaska	E.	50th state

But this:

Directions: New England states are listed in the left-hand column and capital cities in the right-hand column. Place the letter for the capital city in the space next to the state in which it is located. Responses may be used only once.

States	*Capital Cities*
_____ 1. *Rhode Island*	A. *Concord*
_____ 2. *Maine*	B. *Boston*
_____ 3. *Massachusetts*	C. *Providence*
_____ 4. *New Hampshire*	D. *Albany*
_____ 5. *Vermont*	E. *Augusta*
	F. *Montpelier*

4. *Keep the list of response options brief in their wording and parallel in construction.*

5. *Include more response options than stems and permit students to use response options more than once when appropriate.* This has the effect of making it impossible for students to arrive at the correct response purely through a process of elimination.

Guidelines for Fill-in Items

Here are three simple guidelines to follow:

1. *Ask respondents a question and provide space for an answer.* This forces you to express a complete thought.

2. *Try to stick to one blank per item.* Come to the point. Ask one question, get one answer, and move on to the next question.

3. *Don't let the length of the line to be filled in be a clue as to the length or nature of the correct response.* This may seem elementary, but it happens. Again, this can misinform you about students' real levels of achievement.

Not this:

> *In the percussion section of the orchestra are located* _____,
>
> _____, _____, *and* _____.

But this:

> *In what section of the orchestra is the kettle drum found?*
>
> _____.

4. *Put the blank toward the end of the sentence.*

Interpretive Exercises

This is a label used for those instances when we present students with a table of information, a diagram, or some other source of information and then ask them to use that information to figure out answers to reasoning questions. The most common version of this is found in reading comprehension tests, where a passage is accompanied by test items that ask for inferences based on the content of the passage. You might consider using this exercise format when you are not sure that some (or all) of your students have mastered some body of basic knowledge, but nevertheless, you want to assess their reasoning proficiency. Or, you simply want to assess reasoning and don't need to assess content knowledge. Just give the content knowledge and ask them to use it. Table 5.4 shows examples of what such items might look like. For more examples, go to the file on the CD, "Reasoning Item Formulas."

Amount of Testing Time to Allow

Estimate time required to give the test as planned. The typical sitting should be no longer than 45 minutes in grades 3–12. Students can answer anywhere from 25 to 90 questions per sitting depending on their complexity and the students' grade level. Multiple-choice items typically take between 30 and 60 seconds to answer.

Table 5.4   Reasoning Test Item Formulas—Reading Comprehension

Reasoning Learning Target	Item Formula
Make inferences based on the reading	Which sentence tells an idea you can get from this (selection)? a. The correct response is an idea that can reasonably be inferred from the text. b. Incorrect responses are ideas that it seems one might infer from the text but that the selection does not really support.
Make predictions based on the reading	What do you think (character) will do now that (cite circumstances at end of story)? a. The correct response is an outcome that can reasonably be predicted given the information in the text. b. Incorrect responses are not appropriate given the information in the text.
Compare and contrast elements of text	Which sentence tells how (two characters in the story) are alike? a. The correct response identifies an appropriate similarity. b. Incorrect responses do not identify similarities; they may focus on something that is true of one character or the other but not both.
Make connections within texts	Which sentence explains why (event) happened? a. The correct response is a reasonable statement of causation. b. Incorrect responses are events in the story that thoughtful reading reveals are not really the cause.
Make connections among texts	How does (story character's) feelings about (subject) compare to the poet's feeling about (subject)? a. The correct response identifies an appropriate similarity. b. Incorrect responses identify elements that exist in one passage but not in other.

Source: From *Washington Assessment of Student Learning 4th-Grade Reading Test and Item Specifications*, 1998, Olympia, WA: Office of the Superintendent of Public Instruction. Reprinted by permission.

Decide if this amount of testing is acceptable. If the testing time as planned is unreasonable, modify your test by one of the following means:

- Convert some of the more time-consuming item formats to true/false items.

- Test only some of the learning targets—randomly select those to be covered, but be sure to tell students that this is what you will do.

- Combine learning targets and then report results or give descriptive feedback to students by target cluster rather than by learning target.

Assembling the Test

Begin the test with relatively easier items to maximize students' opportunity to start on a note of confidence. Consider arranging the items on your test according to the learning target each represents. If that presents a challenge in direction writing because you would be mixing item formats, consider indicating in some other fashion which learning target each addresses. However, do so only if this information will not give students unfair clues regarding the correct answer. Make sure your students know how many points each question is worth, so they can learn to prioritize their testing time. Put all parts of an item on the same page.

Stage 3: Critique the Assessment

There are two aspects of test quality to evaluate. The first is how well it matches the test plan and the second is how well the items are written.

Matching the Test Plan

To determine how well your actual test matches the test plan, you can use the process and form from Activity 4.4, "Analyze Your Own Assessment for Clear Targets."

Ensuring Item Quality

To evaluate the quality of the items you must do two things: make sure the item itself tests what you intended and check each item for how well it is written.

Item Tests What You Intended

If your items are sound in this respect, you can work backwards to turn them into the propositions you began with. Here's how:

- *Combine the multiple-choice item stem with the correct response.*
- *True true/false items already are propositions.*
- *Make false true/false items true to derive the proposition.*
- *Match up elements in matching exercises.*
- *Fill in the blanks of short answer items. (Stiggins, 2005, p. 109)*

If, by following these steps, you generate a list of the important learning targets or concepts you intended to test, then your items do, indeed test what you intended to test.

Item Is Well Written

You can audit each item using the information summarized in Figure 5.7 to determine if it is well written and to make adjustments as needed.

Stages 4 and 5: Administer the Assessment, Watch for Problems, and Revise as Needed

Even the best planning can't catch all problems with an assessment. Here are two things to watch for as you administer the test:

- Students have enough time to complete all test items. If students don't have the opportunity to attempt each item, their scores will not reflect what they have learned. Watch for students frantically marking items toward the end of the time allowed. Also look for large numbers of incomplete tests.

- Make notes on the questions for which students ask clarifying questions. Consider clarifying the directions or the item itself for the next time you use the test.

Figure 5.7   Test Item Quality Checklist

General guidelines for all formats

_____ Keep wording simple and focused. Aim for lowest possible reading level.

_____ Ask a question.

_____ Avoid providing clues within and between items.

_____ Correct answer should not be obvious without mastering material tested.

_____ Highlight critical words (e.g., most, least, except, not).

Guidelines for multiple-choice items

_____ State whole question in item stem.

_____ Eliminate repetition of material in response options.

_____ Be sure there is only one correct or best answer.

_____ Keep response options brief and parallel.

_____ Make all response options the same length.

_____ Limit use of all or none of the above.

_____ Use "always" and "never" with caution.

Guideline for true/false items

_____ Make them entirely true or entirely false as stated.

Guidelines for matching items

_____ Provide clear directions for the match to be made.

_____ Keep list of trigger items brief (maximum length is 10).

_____ Include only homogeneous items.

_____ Keep wording of response options brief and parallel.

_____ Provide more responses than trigger items.

Guideline for fill-in items

_____ Ask a question.

_____ Provide one blank per item.

_____ Do not make length of blank a clue.

_____ Put blank toward the end.

Figure 5.7   (Continued)

Assembling the test

_____ Arrange items from easy to hard.

_____ Try to group items covering the same targets together, or identify the target each question addresses.

_____ Try to group similar formats together.

_____ Make sure the test is not too long for the time allowed.

Writing directions

_____ Write clear, explicit directions for each item type.

_____ State the point value of each item type.

_____ Indicate how the answer should be expressed (e.g., should the word true or false be written, or T or F? Should numbers be rounded to the nearest tenth? Should units such as months, meters, or grams be included in the answer?)

Formatting test items

_____ Be consistent in the presentation of an item type.

_____ Keep all parts of a test question on one page.

_____ Avoid crowding too many questions on one page.

Source: Adapted from *Student-Involved Assessment* for *Learning*, 4th ed. (p. 107), by R. J. Stiggins, 2005, Upper Saddle River, NJ: Merrill/Prentice Hall. Copyright © 2005 by Pearson Education, Inc. Adapted by permission of Pearson Education, Inc.

TRY THIS

Activity 5.6   Critique the Items in Your Quiz

Now return one final time to the 10-item quiz you developed in Activity 5.2 and evaluate the quality of each test item by working backward to generate the underlying propositions and checking each item against the checklist in Figure 5.7.

Selected Response Assessment *for* Learning

As we saw in Chapter 2, motivation to learn and level of achievement both rise when students are engaged in the assessment process. To see why this might occur, we have only to reflect on what happens to our own understanding of the intended learning when we as teachers engage in activities such as creating a test plan, writing propositions, and developing test items. The following ideas represent ways selected response tests can serve to help students answer the three essential questions at the heart of assessment *for* learning: "Where am I going?"; "Where am I now?"; and "How can I close the gap?" Assessment *for* learning strategies as applied to selected response tests are summarized in Figure 5.8.

Where Am I Going?

Strategy 1: Make Targets Clear

Once you have a test plan, you can use it, not just for test development, but also in service of assessment *for* learning. Give students a list of the learning targets, in terms they understand, at the beginning of the instructional time the test will cover. Let them develop a practice test plan based on their understanding of the relative importance of each learning target and then share your test plan. You can also use a test plan as a way to summarize the day's or week's learning by asking students to identify which cells your instruction has focused on.

Propositions can also play a role in assessment for learning. Explain to students that a proposition is a statement of important learning. Ask them to note what they understand to be the proposition(s) at the center of the day's instruction. Have them keep a list and add to it each day. Help students see how well their lists match your own. Give groups of students your test plan and sample propositions representing the learning thus far. Have them match the propositions to the correct cell in the test plan.

Strategy 2: Use Strong and Weak Models

Give students an item formula, such as the ones in Table 5.4. (For younger students, you will need to translate the item formula into student-friendly language.) Show them a test item created with the formula. Ask them to identify which answers are wrong and which one is right by identifying the response pattern each follows. See Figure 5.9 for an example of how this can work when teaching fourth-grade students to infer.

Figure 5.8 Assessment *for* Learning Strategies: Assessing Knowledge and Reasoning Targets with Selected Response Tests

Where am I going?

1. Make targets clear.

   _____ Write targets in student-friendly language.
   _____ Share test plans at the outset.
   _____ Have students match propositions with test plan cells.
   _____ Have students develop propositions along the way.

2. Use strong and weak models.

   _____ Students identify wrong multiple-choice and fill-in answers and say why.

Where am I now?

3. Provide descriptive feedback.

   _____ Provide feedback target by target on a test.
   _____ Use definition of quality as basis for strengths and focus of improvement.

4. Teach students to self-assess and set goals.

   _____ Students use test plans as a basis for evaluation of strengths and areas for study.
   _____ Students complete self-evaluation and goal-setting form on basis of test or quiz results.

How can I close the gap?

5. Teach focused lessons.

   _____ Students use item formulas to write items.
   _____ Students answer question: *How do you know your answer is correct?*
   _____ Students turn propositions into items and practice answering the items.
   _____ Students create test items for each cell and quiz each other.
   _____ Students use graphic organizers to practice patterns of reasoning.

6. Students practice revising.

   _____ Students answer the question: *How do I make this answer better?*

7. Students reflect on and share what they know.

   _____ Students engage in self-reflection: I have become better at _____.

   I used to _____, but now I _____.

Figure 5.9   Using Item Formulas with Students

Which one of these answers is a good inference, based on the reading selection from *The BFG*? Mark the good inference with a star. The right answer is a good inference because it is a guess based on clues from the story.

a.   The BFG could hear extremely well because he could not see very well.

b.   The author loved his father very much.

c.   The father did not finish high school.

d.   The father had a good imagination.

e.   The father wanted people to think he was a serious man.

f.   The father had a well-developed sense of hearing.

g.   The father was a funny person.

Some of these answers are wrong because they are not inferences at all! They are just facts that the story tells you outright. Write the letters of those wrong answers here:

_____

Some of the answers are wrong because, even though they are guesses, there are no clues in the story to support them. Write the letters of those wrong answers here:

_____

Be careful!!! You might think there is evidence for them, so look closely!!!

Where Am I Now?

Strategy 3: Provide Descriptive Feedback

To offer descriptive feedback, you must know what learning target each item addresses. Then you are able to couch your feedback in terms specific to that target. In the case of an inference test item, if a student chooses the answer that is wrong because, while it is an inference, it is not supported by evidence in the story, you can say, "You have selected an inference, so your answer does represent a guess, but the guess is not supported by evidence (or enough evidence) to be considered a good inference."

Strategy 4: Teach Students to Self-Assess and Set Goals

Hand your test plan out at the beginning of instruction. Have students self-assess on the learning targets or concepts as you teach them, using "traffic light" icons. Students mark the learning target or concept with a large dot—green to indicate confidence in having mastered it ("I've got it"), yellow to indicate a judgment of partial mastery ("I understand part of it, but not all of it"), or red to indicate little or no understanding ("I don't get it at all"). Then let the "greens" and "yellows" partner to fine tune their understanding while you work with the "reds." (Black, Harrison, Lee, Marshall, & William, 2002).

A few days prior to the test, have students self-assess on the learning targets or concepts represented on your test plan. Then have them create a study plan based on what they think they have yet to learn. Or, have students assign themselves to study groups based on their assessment of what they need to learn.

Because students often take tests without knowing what the test measures beyond the most general level ("reading," "social studies," "science"), when they are asked to use test results to share what they know or to set goals for future learning, what they produce is often too general to be of much use: "I am pretty good at math"; "I can read better than I used to"; "I need to study more." Although "take my book home" or "try harder" are noble thoughts, they do not reflect either what students have learned or what they may actually need to learn, and therefore are of limited use. Activity 5.7, beginning on page 158, is designed to help students accurately identify what they know and set goals for their next steps.

How Can I Close the Gap?

Strategy 5: Teach Focused Lessons

Let students create test items using an item formula. See Figure 5.10 for an inference example that would work well as a followup to the activity in Figure 5.9.

After each multiple-choice item on a test, ask students to explain the reason for their selection by including the question, "How do you know your answer is correct?" and providing several lines for a response. Discuss common reasons for right and wrong choices when you pass back the test. Figure 5.11 provides an example with a question asking about an author's purpose.

Assign groups of students to each cell of your test plan. Have them create questions that might be on the test, based on the propositions they generated for each cell during instruction. Have the groups take each others' practice tests.

Teach students to use graphic organizers as a means to understand the specific kind of reasoning called for. After doing activities from Strageties 1 and 2, let students create their own graphic organizer for a specific pattern of reasoning.

Figure 5.10   Student-Generated Inference Questions

How to Write an <u>Inference</u> Question

Here is a recipe that test writers use to create multiple-choice inference questions and answers.

Question:
Which idea does this selection suggest?

Possible responses *(these include the right answer and several wrong answers):*

a. The correct response is a guess that is supported by clues in the text.

b. One incorrect response is a wild guess, because there aren't any clues in the text to support it.

c. Another incorrect response is just a detail from the text recopied. It's not a guess at all.

Now it's your turn!

First, read the assigned passage in the text. Then, work with a partner to create the right and wrong answers to the inference question below.

Here's the inference question:
Which idea does this selection suggest?

You write a correct answer and two incorrect answers. You can mix up the order—the correct answer doesn't have to come first.

a.

b.

c.

Figure 5.11   Example of Followup Question to Probe Reasoning

Which of the following BEST sums up the author's purpose in writing this passage?

a. To show the character of Danny's father.
b. To tell a funny story about a giant.
c. To explain where dreams come from.
d. To keep children from being afraid.

How do you know your answer is correct? _____

_____

_____

Strategy 6: Students Practice Revising

Anything we do to give students practice with applying what they know about quality or correctness to rework their own answers or to offer suggestions on someone else's work causes them to engage in revision. Consider letting them first practice on anonymous responses by answering one or both of the following questions: "What is wrong with this answer?" "What would make this answer better?"

Strategy 7: Students Reflect on and Share What They Know

We may think of this strategy as best suited to performance assessment, but it is equally effective with selected response assessment. Students should be thinking about their achievement with respect to the knowledge and reasoning targets measured by this method, both because they play an important role in their education, and also because it is these fundamental targets that struggling students often have not mastered. As we stated in Chapter 2, any activity that requires students to reflect on what they are learning and to share their progress both reinforces the learning and helps them develop insight into themselves as learners. These are keys to enhancing student motivation.

Some software programs used for reading instruction and assessment harness the power of Strategy 7. They have built-in mechanisms for students to track their progress and communicate their results on reading comprehension learning targets. Students read text varying in length from a passage to a book, answer a variety of questions, and get immediate feedback on how they did. They are able to monitor their own progress and experience the joy of watching themselves grow. For many students, that joy causes them to like the assessment experience, even if they are not wildly successful at first, and it also motivates them to continue reading.

TRY THIS

Activity 5.7 Engaging Students in Self-Reflection and Goal Setting with Selected Response Tests

Choose a selected response test you intend to give to students and complete the following steps. (Blank forms for both an elementary and secondary version of this activity can be found on the CD in the file, "Goal Setting with Tests.")

1. Make a numbered list of the learning targets represented on the test. Figure 5.12 shows an example from a ninth-grade biology class.

2. Transfer that information to the chart in Figure 5.13a by filling out the "Learning Target #" column, which identifies the learning target addressed by each item. Copy the chart for each student and hand it out with the test. Figure 5.13b shows adaptations made for the ninth-grade biology example in Figure 5.12.

3. As students take the test, they note on the chart whether they feel confident or unsure of the correct response to each item. Correct the tests as usual and hand them back, along with the numbered list of learning targets. The students are now ready to identify their own specific strengths and areas for further study by following the steps explained in Figure 5.14.

This activity is most powerful as a learning experience if students have an opportunity to take some version of the test again, as when studying for a retake of the test, or after a quiz or a practice test in preparation for a final exam. In the case of a retake, you may want students to follow up their self-analysis with a specific study plan. Figure 5.15 shows examples of forms used for that purpose.

Figure 5.12   List of Learning Targets Tested—Ninth-Grade Biology Example

Below are **14** Key Learning Targets for Unit 9a. In the student assessment of your achievement of these learning targets, you will identify the areas in which you demonstrated proficiency and the areas in which you need to do additional study and preparation for mastery of the Unit 9 skills and knowledge.

1. Recognize that ecology is the scientific study of the interactions between organisms and their environment

2. Distinguish between a population, community, ecosystem, biome and biosphere

3. Describe how organisms interact with each other in different ways (producers, consumers, predator, prey, scavengers, parasites, decomposers) to transfer energy and matter in an ecosystem

4. Recognize that energy flows from one trophic level (one direction only) to another

5. Recognize 90% of the energy of a trophic level is lost during life processes and as heat in the transfer to the next trophic level

6. Describe how energy relationships can be represented and calculated in food/energy, biomass and numbers pyramids

7. Explain all energy for an ecosystem originates from the sun

8. Diagram the relative amounts of energy in a trophic level using an ecological pyramid

9. Diagram the flow of energy in a food chain or food web

10. Explain why matter is constantly recycled in an ecosystem

11. Recognize each element is cycled in a specific way

12. Express how the recycling of matter is necessary to make it available for organisms to use

13. Distinguish between the four biogeochemical cycles (H_2O, CO_2, O_2, and N_2)

14. Explain the major steps in each of the four biogeochemical cycles (H_2O, CO_2, O_2, and N_2)

Source: Steve Wavra, Sweetwater Union High School District, Chula Vista, CA. Used by permission.

Figure 5.13a   Student Documentation of Selected Response Test Results

Identifying Your Strengths and Focusing Further Study

As you answer each question on the test, decide whether you feel confident in your answer or are unsure about it, and mark the corresponding box.

Problem #	Learning Target #	Confident	Unsure		Right	Wrong	Simple Mistake	Further Study

1. After your test has been corrected, identify which problems you got right and which you got wrong by putting Xs in the "Right" and "Wrong" columns.

2. Of the problems you got wrong, decide which ones were due to simple mistakes and mark the "Simple Mistake" column.

3. For all of the remaining wrong answers, mark the "Further Study" column.

Source: Adapted from *Assessment* FOR *Learning: An Action Guide for School Leaders* (p. 198), by S. Chappuis, R. J. Stiggins, J. Arter, & J. Chappuis, 2004, Portland, OR: Assessment Training Institute. Copyright © 2006, 2004 Educational Testing Service. Adapted by permission.

Figure 5.13b   Student Documentation of Selected Response Test Results— Biology Teacher's Variation

Identifying Your Strengths and Focusing Further Study

As you answer each question on the test, decide whether you feel confident in your answer or are unsure about it, and mark the corresponding box.

Question	Key Learning	Knew It	Wasn't Sure	Guessed		Got It Right	Got It Wrong	Simple Mistake	Misread Question	Need to Re-Study
1	1									
2	2									
3	3									
4	7									
5	3									
6	3									
7	3									
8	3									
9	9									
10	6									
11	2, 9									
12	3									
13	4, 6, 9									
14	3, 4									
15	3, 4									
16	6									
17	6									
18	5									
19	5									
20	6									
21	10, 11, 12									
22	13									
23	5, 11									
24	11, 12, 13									
25	11, 12, 13									
26	11, 13									

Source: Steve Wavra, Sweetwater Union High School District, Chula Vista, CA. Used by permission.

Figure 5.14   Student Analysis of Selected Response Test Results

1. To identify your areas of strength, write down the learning target numbers corresponding to the problems you felt confident about *and* got right. Then write a short description of the target or problem.

MY STRENGTHS:

Learning Target #	Learning Target or Problem Description

2. To determine what you need to study most, write down the learning target numbers corresponding to the marks in the "Further Study" column (problems you got wrong, NOT because of a simple mistake). Then write a short description of the target or problem.

MY HIGHEST PRIORITY FOR STUDYING:

Learning Target #	Learning Target or Problem Description

3. Do the same thing for the problems you were unsure of and for the problems on which you made simple mistakes.

WHAT I NEED TO REVIEW:

Learning Target #	Learning Target or Problem Description

Source: Adapted from *Assessment* FOR *learning: An Action Guide for School Leaders* (p. 199), by S. Chappuis, R. J. Stiggins, J. Arter, & J. Chappuis, 2004, Portland, OR: Assessment Training Institute. Copyright © 2006, 2004 Educational Testing Service. Adapted by permission.

Figure 5.15   Student Goal-Setting Frames

To get better at _____, I could . . .

-
-
-
-
-

Some things I am going to start doing are . . .

-
-
-

I'll start doing this on _____ and work on it until _____.
                                     (date)   (date)

One way I'll know I'm getting better is . . .

_____

_____

Goal	Steps	Evidence
What do I need to get better at?	How do I plan to do this?	What evidence will show I've achieved my goal?

Time Frame: Begin _____   End _____

Date _____   Signed _____

Source: From *Self-Assessment and Goal-Setting*, (p. 45) by K. Gregory, C. Cameron, & A. Davies, 2000, Merville, BC: Connections. Reprinted by permission.

Summary

In this chapter we revisited the idea that selected response items are a good way to measure knowledge and reasoning learning targets, as long as students can read at the needed level to understand the questions. Selected response is an efficient way to cover a lot of content in a short period of time.

Although we reviewed all steps in test development—from planning to critiquing the final product—we focused on creating test plans, generating propositions to identify important content, and adhering to guidelines for writing high-quality selected response items of all types.

Finally, we offered concrete examples of how to involve students in selected response assessment. These strategies focused on how to use these tests to help students answer the three questions that define assessment *for* learning: "Where am I going?"; "Where am I now?"; and "How can I close the gap?"

◼ *Tracking Your Learning—Possible Portfolio Entries*

Any of the activities from this chapter can be used as portfolio entries. Remember, the learning targets for this book are outlined in Figure 5.1, listed in Table 1.2, and described in detail in Chapter 1. The portfolio entry cover sheet provided on the CD in the file, "Portfolio Entry Cover Sheet," will prompt you to think about how each item you select reflects your learning with respect to one or more of these learning targets.

Any of the following activities would make good portfolio entries. Each could also be used as a learning team activity.

TRY THIS

Activity 5.8 Create a Selected Response Assessment

Select an upcoming context (a unit, an area of study, a collection of related learning targets) for which a selected response test would be the appropriate assessment and create that assessment, following the guidelines described in this chapter.

TRY THIS

Activity 5.9   Critique a Selected Response Test You Use

Find a test that came with a text or with the teaching materials you use. Evaluate the test, following the recommendations for critiquing a test. Write a short commentary detailing its strengths and weaknesses. If you plan to use the test, revise it as needed.

DEEPEN UNDERSTANDING

Activity 5.10   Critique "Fish Tank"

Evaluate the test, "Fish Tank," found in the CD file, "Assessments to Evaluate." Follow the recommendations for critiquing a test found in the CD file, "Assessment Quality Rubrics." Our analyses of these samples also appear on the CD in the file, "Assessment Critiques."

DEEPEN UNDERSTANDING

Activity 5.11   Watch Video, *Commonsense Paper and Pencil Assessments*

To review the concepts in Chapter 5, you may want to watch the ETS video, *Commonsense Paper and Pencil Assessments*. The accompanying user's guide also includes reflection and discussion activities appropriate to a small- or large-group setting.

Notes

1. Portions of these writing guidelines have been reprinted and adapted from Chapter 4, pp. 101–106, of R. J. Stiggins, *Student-Involved Assessment* for *Learning*, 4th ed., 2005, Upper Saddle River, NJ: Merrill/Prentice Hall. Copyright © 2005 by Pearson Education, Inc. Reprinted and adapted by permission of Pearson Education, Inc.

Extended Written Response Assessment

We have all experienced extended written response exercises on tests. They may even have provided some of your best horror stories about your own assessment experiences. "Discuss Spain." "Analyze *King Lear.*" "Explain the causes of the Civil War." Extended written response assessment requires students to construct a written answer, at least several sentences in length, in response to a question or task.

How can we write extended written response exercises so that all students have a fair chance of showing what they know? In this chapter, we will address issues of quality and of student involvement with extended written response assessment.[1] We will focus on the following topics:

- When to use the extended written response method.

- How to develop exercises and scoring mechanisms.

- How to involve students in planning, developing, and using extended written response assessment.

In this chapter, we focus on the shaded areas in Figures 6.1 and 6.2.

Figure 6.1   Keys to Quality Classroom Assessment

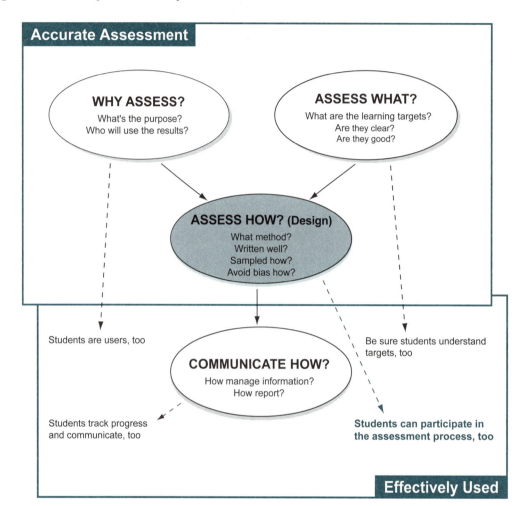

Figure 6.2   A Plan for Matching Assessment Methods with Achievement Targets

Target to Be Assessed	Assessment Method			
	Selected Response	Extended Written Response	Performance Assessment	Personal Communication
Knowledge Mastery				
Reasoning Proficiency				
Performance Skills				
Ability to Create Products				

Source: Adapted from *Student-Involved Assessment* for *Learning*, 4th ed. (p. 116), by R. J. Stiggins, 2005, Upper Saddle River, NJ: Merrill/Prentice Hall. Copyright © 2005 by Pearson Education, Inc. Adapted by permission of Pearson Education, Inc.

When to Use Extended Written Response Assessment

As we saw in Chapter 4, each individual classroom assessment represents a part of a bigger picture represented by a long-term assessment map that parallels the curriculum map. The kinds of learning targets to be assessed, combined with consideration of context factors, will determine whether some of those assessments will take the form of extended written response.

Matching Method to Target

As with all assessment methods, the first condition for using selected response is the type of learning target to be assessed, as described in Activity 4.2, "Target–Method Match," in Chapter 4. Knowledge and reasoning are ideal for extended written response exercises, as shown in Figure 6.2.

As described in Chapter 4, extended written response works well for assessing chunks of knowledge that interrelate, rather than individual pieces of knowledge assessed separately. (Selected response is more efficient for the latter.) For example, in science, we might want students to explain how atoms combine to form other substances, or to describe the Krebs cycle and explain why it is important. In social studies, we might want students to describe the factors that lead to placement of centers of habitation, and why each is important; for example, access to sources of transportation, water, food, and other natural resources.

Extended written response also works well for assessing reasoning. We can't open students' heads to look at their reasoning directly, but we can ask them to write down their thinking or rationale for a response. For example, in mathematics we might ask students to explain how they arrived at an answer. In science, we might ask students to explain their rationale for setting up an experiment. In addition, we can ask students directly to analyze, compare, make inferences about, and/or evaluate information. For example, in a unit on pollution, we might ask students to evaluate which solution to a problem is most likely to have the greatest benefit and to explain the reason for their choice.

TRY THIS

Activity 6.1 Learning Targets Best Assessed with Selected Response

Find three or four knowledge and reasoning learning targets in the curriculum materials you use that could be assessed by means of extended written response. Write them down and save them for later use.

Other Contextual Conditions

Several other conditions influence the selection of the extended written response method of assessment:

- Students need to be proficient in writing English. Extended written response may not work very well for primary students, English language learners, and students with other special needs.

- Extended written response can be time consuming to score well. If you can get the information you need (that is, reflect the target) through the less time-consuming selected response method, then do so.

- Extended written response exercises require consistency in scoring. Use this method only when you know that the scoring guides are of good quality and that scorers will apply them consistently.

- Extended written response is good in assessment *for* learning situations, especially when students are analyzing the quality of reasoning in their own work.

Developing Extended Written Response Assessments

Designing and developing extended written response assessments entail the same five stages, introduced in Chapter 4, that we used with selected response assessment:

1. Plan the assessment.

2. Develop the assessment.

3. Critique the assessment.

4. Administer the assessment.

5. Revise the assessment.

Stage 1: Plan the Assessment

At this first stage, as you remember, we answer four questions: Assess why? Assess what? Assess how? How important? Figure 6.3 presents the range of answers to these questions.

Figure 6.3   The Planning Stage for Extended Response Assessment

Assess why?

Assessment *for* Learning
     Diagnostic/planning information for teacher
     Diagnostic/planning information for student
     Diagnostic/planning information for others
     Student self-evaluation

Assessment *of* Learning
     Report card grade

Assess what?

Knowledge, reasoning, and/or writing learning targets

Assess how?

Extended response exercises and scoring devices

How important?

Sample of items to represent the breadth of the learning targets in question and their relative importance in the learning plan

Assess Why?

As you recall, we build assessments to meet specific user information needs. Thus, in every case, your number one decision is, Will this be an assessment *for* learning or an assessment *of* learning? Who will be using the assessment results and how will they be using them? If it is an assessment *for* learning, is it purely for your use in instructional decision making or is it to serve your students, too? Obviously, this will influence how the assessment relates to your teaching and how you construct, administer, and share the information from the assessment.

Assess What?

For extended written response assessments, we outline the content to be mastered, including the relationships among elements that we expect our students to know and understand. If you wish students to demonstrate mastery of patterns of reasoning, what patterns? Your list of content knowledge, understanding, and reasoning provides the ingredients for exercise development.

Assess How?

Verify one final time that these targets are appropriate for transforming into the extended written response format.

How Important?

Again, it's important to establish priorities at the outset. Which of the learning targets or topics are most important, next most important, and so on? This will serve as the basis for the distribution of points or ratings in the overall assessment plan. The prioritization should parallel the amount of time and emphasis given the various targets or topics in teaching.

As described in Chapter 4, we can create a plan by using either a table or a list of learning targets.

Plans for extended written response tests are similar in their basic framework to those used for selected response assessments, and are different in other ways. Table 6.1 (a repeat of Chapter 1, Table 1.1) is an example of a table of specifications for an extended written response test covering a unit on pollution. Mr. Heim listed the categories of information students are to know on one axis and the patterns of reasoning they are to master on the other. Row and column totals, and therefore entries in the cells of the table, represent the relative emphasis assigned to each.

Unlike tables of specifications for selected response assessments, the cells in the extended written response test plan in Table 6.1 contain the number of points on the test assigned to that content-reasoning combination, not the number of individual test items. Given 50 points for the entire exam, this plan emphasizes how to reduce pollution, requiring that students rely on that understanding to compare and evaluate.

Table 6.1   Mr. Heim's Sample Test Blueprint

		PATTERN OF REASONING		
	Know	**Compare**	**Evaluate**	**Total**
Concentrations	10	0	0	10
Effects of Pollutants	7	8	0	15
How to Reduce Pollution	6	10	9	25
Total	23	18	9	50

TRY THIS

Activity 6.2 Create an Extended Written Response Assessment

Select one of the learning targets you identified in Activity 6.1. Draft an extended written response exercise and a scoring scheme. Put them aside for later use.

Stage 2: Develop the Assessment

One of the advantages often listed for extended written response tests relative to other test formats is that exercises are much easier and less time consuming to develop. Keep in mind, however, that "easier to develop" does not mean they require little thought.

To succeed with this assessment format, we must first write exercises that describe a single, complete, and novel task. Second, we must devise clearly articulated evaluation criteria. If we are not careful at this stage, students who know the material may not perform well, and students who have not mastered the material may be able to look as though they have. Poorly framed extended written response exercises can be a nightmare for students to answer and for teachers to score.

Devising Exercises

Sound extended written response exercises do three things: (1) set a clear and specific context; (2) specify the kind of reasoning to be brought to bear; and (3) point the way to an appropriate response without giving away the store.

Setting the Context

Set the context in the exercise by specifying the knowledge to be brought to bear. For example:

> *During the term, we have discussed both the evolution of Spanish literature and the changing political climate in Spain during the twentieth century.*

Specifying the Reasoning

Specify the kind(s) of reasoning or problem solving, if any, students are to carry out. For example:

> *During the term, we have discussed both the evolution of Spanish literature and the changing political climate in Spain during the twentieth century. Analyze these two dimensions of life in Spain, citing instances where literature and politics may have influenced each other. Describe those influences in specific terms.*

Pointing the Way

Point the direction to an appropriate response by reminding students of the criteria that will be applied in evaluating responses. For example:

> *During the term, we have discussed both the evolution of Spanish literature and the changing political climate in Spain during the twentieth century. Analyze these two dimensions of life in Spain, citing instances where you think literature and politics may have influenced each other. Describe the influences in specific terms. In planning your response, think about what we learned about prominent novelists, political satirists, and prominent political figures of Spain. (5 points per instance, total = 15 points.)*

Let's analyze an extended written response exercise that might arise from a test covering the content of this book on classroom assessment as applied to foreign-language speaking proficiency:

Assume you are a French teacher with many years of teaching experience. You place great value on the development of speaking proficiency as an outcome of your instruction. Therefore, you rely heavily on assessments where you listen to and evaluate performance. But a problem has arisen. Parents of students who attained very high scores on your written tests are complaining that their children are receiving lower grades on their report cards. The principal wants to be sure your judgments of student proficiency are sound and so has asked you to explain and defend your procedures. Describe at least three specific quality standards that your oral proficiency exams would need to meet for you to be confident that your exams truly reflect what students can do; provide the rationale for each. (2 points for each procedure and rationale, total = 6 points.)

Here's the challenge presented to students in a nutshell:

Demonstrate understanding of:	Performance assessment methodology
By using it to figure out:	Proper applications of the method in a specific context
Adhering to these standards:	Include three appropriate procedures and defend them

Offering Choices

We recommend that you don't offer choices. The summative assessment question should always be, "Can you hit the agreed-on target?" It should never be, "Which (or which part of the) target are you most confident that you can hit?" When students select their own sample of performance, it can be a biased one.

Interpretive Exercises

With this format, as with selected response, you don't have to assume that students always have mastered the content around which an exercise is built. If you wish to assess student mastery of specific patterns of reasoning only, you can provide them with a table, chart, or map of background information about a given topic and then ask them to write a response demonstrating that they can figure out relationships between or among things presented. For example, you might present a chart of data, a map, or even a passage of details and ask them to ferret out and depict certain relationships, draw comparisons, conduct analyses,

TRY THIS

Activity 6.3   Revise Your Exercise

Please return now to the extended written response exercise you developed in Activity 6.2. Did you specify the knowledge and kind(s) of reasoning students are to use? Did you remind them of standards by which their work will be judged? Revise your exercise as needed to meet these guidelines.

or create and fill categories. Scoring criteria for essays, then, would reflect the active ingredients of sound reasoning.

Developing Extended Written Response Scoring Procedures

When a student writes a response, we can evaluate whether the student's work demonstrates three different qualities:

- Accurate knowledge and understanding

- Sound reasoning

- Effective written communication

The first two focus on matters of content, while the last treats the response as a product. As we mentioned earlier, in this chapter we focus on how to evaluate the content of the response: accuracy of knowledge and quality of reasoning.

(When the characteristics of effective written communication are evaluated, we would classify the learning target as a product and evaluate it with a performance assessment. A rubric for evaluating writing quality, "6 + 1 Traits," is provided on the CD in the file, "Rubric Sampler.")

Not surprisingly, a key to successful use of extended written response assessment is the clear articulation of appropriate evaluation criteria by which to judge the quality of student responses. We recommend not using "floating standards," in which the evaluator waits to see what responses come in before deciding how to score. Floating standards destroy the validity and reliability of the assessment. Teachers and students alike need to be clear in advance regarding which aspects of the response are important.

Exercise-Specific Scoring

This is the typical procedure. We award points when specific information appears in students' answers. The French teacher example that appeared in the previous section calls for this kind of scoring. Here is the scoring guide:

Give two points if the student's response lists any of these six procedures and defends each as a key to conducting sound performance assessments:

- Specify clear performance criteria
- Sample performance over several exercises
- Apply systematic rating procedures
- Maintain complete and accurate records
- Use published performance assessments to verify results of classroom assessments
- Use multiple observers to corroborate

Also award two points if the response lists any of the following and defends them as attributes of sound assessments:

- Specifies a clear instructional objective
- Relies on a proper assessment method
- Samples performance well
- Controls for sources of rater bias

All other responses receive no points.

Generic Rubrics

Although we often use exercise-specific point-based scoring guides for assessing student understanding of content, they are not our only option. We can use a generic rubric or scoring guide that defines what content understanding looks like, in general, for any body of knowledge. For example, a three-point generic rating scale for "understanding the content" might define three levels of mastery of the required material. Here's an example (a more detailed example of a general rubric for evaluating content understanding, "Essay Scoring Criteria," is provided on the CD in the file, "Rubric Sampler"):

3   The response is clear, focused, and accurate. Relevant points are made with good support. Good connections are drawn and important insights are evident. Vocabulary is used correctly.

2   The response is clear and somewhat focused, but not compelling. Support of points made is limited. Connections are fuzzy, leading to few important insights. Sometimes vocabulary is used correctly, sometimes not.

1   The response misses the point, contains inaccurate information, or otherwise demonstrates lack of mastery of the material. Points are unclear, support is missing, and/or no insights are included. Vocabulary is often used incorrectly.

Notice that such a scoring guide can be used to assign points to student understanding of any body of knowledge. This generic way of evaluating content understanding is especially useful when students are demonstrating their reasoning abilities using different bodies of knowledge. This frequently happens in performance assessments, portfolios, or individual research reports. For the type of understanding we typically assess through extended written response, however, we usually stick with exercise-specific, point-based scoring.

The situation is different if we're also scoring how well students reason with the knowledge given in the exercise. In this case, a generic rubric for the type of reasoning to be demonstrated is required. For example, if the extended written response exercise calls for students to make a generalization based on content, you might use an exercise-specific rubric to assess content understanding, and then a generic rubric to analyze the quality of the generalization, as shown in Figure 6.4.

We recommend generic rubrics for assessing the quality of various patterns of reasoning because they can be shared with students in advance without giving away the answer, used again and again, and overlaid on any body of content. Used this way, they help students come to learn the features of solid reasoning.

Stage 3: Critique the Assessment

An excellent way to check the quality of your exercises is to try to write or outline a high-quality response yourself. If you can, you probably have a properly focused exercise. If you cannot, it needs work.

Remember that there can be sources of bias specific to extended written response assessment. These arise, for example, if students are not yet proficient writers or are English-language learners. Figure 6.5 summarizes the factors to think about when devising extended written response exercises and scoring procedures. Answering these questions assists in constructing effective, high-quality exercises—those that avoid bias and distortion.

Figure 6.4   Rubric for Generalization

Strong

*   Statement is true for evidence presented and extends application logically to a broader array of instances.

Part-way There

*   Statement is true for evidence presented, but application includes too broad an array of instances to be supported by evidence.

*   Statement is true for evidence presented, but application to other instances is based on too little evidence.

Beginning

*   Statement is true for evidence presented, but no extension beyond the evidence is attempted.

*   Statement is true for evidence presented, but application to other instances is not related to evidence.

*   Statement is not true for evidence presented.

TRY THIS

Activity 6.4 Check Your Scoring Criteria

Return to the scoring plan you developed for your exercise in Activity 6.2. Are you clear about what features of the response you will score—content, reasoning, and/or the quality of the writing? Revise your exercise as needed.

Figure 6.5   Quality Guidelines for Extended Written Response Assessments

Quality of the Exercises

- Is extended written response the best assessment method for this learning target?
- Do exercises call for brief, focused responses?
- Is the target knowledge clear?
- Is the reasoning to be done, if any, clear?
- Is the exercise itself written at the lowest possible reading level—will all students understand what they are to do?
- Will students' level of writing proficiency in English be adequate to show you what they know and can do?
- Is there anything in the question that might put a group of students at a disadvantage regardless of their knowledge or reasoning level?
- Are there enough exercises to provide a defendable estimate of student learning on intended targets?

Quality of the Scoring Guide(s)

- Would experts in the field agree with the definition of a quality response?
- For the knowledge aspect of the response, are the criteria clear—would the elements in the scoring plan be obvious to good students without giving away the answer?
- For the reasoning portion of the response (if any), is there a generic rubric that captures the essence of high quality thinking?
- Do the criteria match the exercise?

Scoring Considerations

- Will the number of students to be evaluated be such that the rater(s) can adequately assess each response?
- Is there an adequate amount of person time available to read and evaluate responses?
- Have all scorers been adequately trained to score the essays consistently—will there by a high level of rater agreement?

Source: Adapted from *Student-Involved Assessment* for *Learning*, 4th ed. (pp. 130, 135, 136), by R. J. Stiggins, 2005, Upper Saddle River, NJ: Merrill/Prentice Hall. Copyright © 2005 by Pearson Education, Inc. Adapted by permission of Pearson Education, Inc.

Stages 4 and 5: Administer the Assessment, Watch for Problems, and Revise as Needed

After you conduct, score and interpret the assessment, if it has flaws you will see them very clearly and can then correct them before future use. You also will see if your instruction has fallen short on particular standards, which allows you to fix that both with your current set of students and in future instruction.

DEEPEN UNDERSTANDING

Activity 6.5 Analyze Extended Written Response Assessments for Quality

If you are working with a team, make sure everyone understands the quality guidelines in Figure 6.5 by using those guidelines individually to critique the sample essay questions in Figure 6.6 and then comparing critiques.

Figure 6.6   Sample Extended Written Response Exercises

Essay 1: Label the Graph.[*] This question is intended for grades 3–12. It is one of six exercises using different content to assess problem solving in mathematics. Results are used to track individual student progress toward mastery of state content standards. The scoring criteria have four traits, each scored separately by trained raters—conceptual understanding, mathematical procedures, strategic reasoning, and communication in mathematics. Students may or may not see the criteria depending on the teacher.

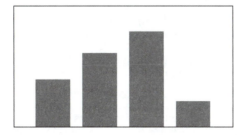

1.   What might this be the graph of? Put titles and numbers on the graph to show what you mean.

2.   Write down everything you know from your graph.

Essay 2: Assembly Line. Intended for grade 6. No scoring mechanism, uses, or targets are described.

"Describe the effect of the development of the assembly line on American society."

[*]Used in several assessments, for example the Oregon state mathematics assessment in 1996.

Figure 6.6   (Continued)

Essay 3: Day and Night. The authors provide examples of several different types of assessment tasks in science—short response to assess knowledge, extended response to assess conceptual understanding, and performance assessments to assess "science knowledge in context," integration of knowledge, practical skills, and reporting skills. The authors use all the sample questions as examples to illustrate methods and when to use them; they specifically state "the assessment tasks provided. . . are not exhaustive, but exemplary. . . ." The sample questions are not meant to be a complete test of any targets.

The following task is intended for grade 2 to assess science understanding.

"Everyone knows about day and night. Write what you think makes day and night. (Four primary lines are given for the response.) Draw a picture to show what you think. (5"x 5" box given for response.)"

The scoring criteria are shown in the following table. Students don't see the criteria.

Score	Label	Description	Examples
2	Scientific Conception	The response indicates that the Earth turns so that the same face is not always facing the Sun.	"The Earth turns every 24 hours and for 12 hours we are facing the Sun."
1	Opposite Sides	The response indicates that the Moon and Sun are on different sides of the Earth and the Earth rotates facing one and then the other. There is no implication that the Sun moves.	"In the day we face the Sun and in the night we turn to face the Moon."
0	Sun Moves	The response indicates that the Sun moves to cause night and day (possibly across the sky).	"The Sun moves and makes way for the Moon."

Additional Notes: Some responses may have mixed the elements of the last two categories. If so, give the score for the lower response. An indication that the Sun moves should take precedence in determining the lower category.

Figure 6.6 (Continued)

Essay 4: Emerson Quiz. This quiz is intended for grades 10–12 to assess mastery of content knowledge (knowledge of Emerson) and reasoning in literature. Results will be used as 10 percent of the final grade in a literature class. Two of the ten essay questions are provided below. Students get 1 point for their answer and 1 point for their rationale.

"Read each of the statements below and put a check if Emerson would most likely complete the activity or put an X if he would disagree or not do the listed activity. For each answer, write your rationale. Include a statement from Emerson's work to support your check or X. Be sure to quote the statement directly and give the page number in parentheses. Use the introduction to Emerson, Nature, and 'Self-Reliance.'

2. _____ look to the past for guidance.
5. _____ join a popular civic organization."

Source: Adapted from *Practice with Student-Involved Classroom Assessment* (pp. 142–143), by J. A. Arter & K. U. Busick, 2001, Portland, OR: Assessment Training Institute. Copyright © 2006, 2001 Educational Testing Service. Exercise "Day and Night" reprinted from *Exemplary Assessment Materials—Science* (p. 15), by Australian Council for Educational Research Ltd., 1996, Victoria, NSW, Australia. Exercise "Emerson Quiz" reprinted from Thomas Mavor, 1999, Brother Martin High School, New Orleans, LA. Reprinted and adapted by permission.

Extended Written Response Assessment *for* Learning

Remember, student motivation and achievement both improve when we use the assessment process to help students answer the following three questions: "Where am I going?"; "Where am I now?"; and "How can I close the gap?" The same strategies we use with selected response tests, as summarized in Figure 5.8, also work with extended written response assessments.

For example, we can engage students in devising practice exercises like those that will appear on a future examination. This will help them learn to center on important content and will require that they become sufficiently comfortable with our valued patterns of reasoning that they can build them into practice exercises. If they write practice exercises, trade with classmates, and write practice responses, both we and they gain access to useful information on what parts of the standards they are and are not mastering.

For a simpler application of this idea, provide students with practice exercises and see if they can place them in the proper cells of the test plan. Then have them defend their placement.

Additionally, we can make use of some scoring guides as instructional tools. Exercise-specific scoring guides cannot function as teaching tools; students cannot use them to practice scoring because these guides outline the specifics of acceptable responses to one exercise. However, you can involve students with developing sample scoring guides for those practice exercises they have created. Or, you can provide sample exercises and have students practice developing scoring guides for them. Further, they can practice scoring each other's responses to those exercises. By repeating this process as students proceed through a unit of study, you can provide them with opportunities to watch themselves improve. Chapter 7 contains more detailed examples of how generic rubrics can be used as instructional tools.

Summary

Extended written response assessments are excellent for assessing extended bodies of knowledge and reasoning learning targets. We followed the creation of these assessments through five stages, with an in-depth focus on the development stage. Exercises need to specify what knowledge and patterns of reasoning, if any, students are to use in crafting their response. They also need to indicate what features of performance will count, by pointing the way to the correct answer without giving away the store. Exercises must avoid other potential sources of bias and distortion such as unclearly written instructions, instructions at too high a reading level, and features that might disadvantage any group. Scoring procedures and guides must be developed along with the exercises. We explored two options: the exercise-specific scoring guide and the generic rubric. The first is most typically used to call out content knowledge that must be present in a correct response, while the second is useful for evaluating patterns of reasoning. We shared a generic rubric for content knowledge, as well.

We concluded with some suggestions for strategies that use extended written response items as assessment *for* learning, where students share the exercise development and scoring responsibility. These strategies connect assessment to teaching and learning in ways that can maximize both students' motivation to learn and their actual achievement.

Tracking Your Learning—Possible Portfolio Entries

Any of the activities included in Chapter 6 can be used as portfolio entries. Remember, the learning targets for this book are outlined in Figure 6.1, listed in Table 1.2, and described in detail in Chapter 1. The portfolio entry cover sheet provided on the CD in the file, "Portfolio Entry Cover Sheet," will prompt you to think about how each item you select reflects your learning with respect to one or more of these learning targets.

Either of the following activities would also make good portfolio entries. Each could also be used as a learning team activity.

TRY THIS

Activity 6.6 Analyze Your Own Extended Written Response Assessments for Quality

Find an extended written response assessment that came with a text or with the teaching materials you use. Evaluate the test, following the recommendations given in this chapter for critiquing an assessment. Write a short commentary detailing its strengths and weaknesses. If you plan to use the test, revise it as needed.

TRY THIS

Activity 6.7 Develop an Extended Written Response Assessment

Select an upcoming context (a unit, an area of study, a collection of related learning targets) for which an extended written response assessment would be the appropriate assessment. Create that assessment, following the guidelines described in this chapter.

Notes

1. Portions of this chapter have been reprinted and adapted from Chapter 5, pp. 115–139, of R. J. Stiggins, *Student-Involved Assessment* for *Learning*, 4th ed., 2005, Upper Saddle River, NJ: Merrill/Prentice Hall. Copyright © 2005 by Pearson Education, Inc. Reprinted and adapted by permission of Pearson Education, Inc.

CHAPTER

Performance
Assessment

[P] erformance assessment, once described as the most authentic of assessment methods, now is seen just as it should be—one valuable way to collect information about student achievement and to involve students in learning. As with any other assessment method, it can be constructed and used well or poorly. This chapter focuses on the following:

- What performance assessment is.

- Which learning targets can be assessed well through performance assessment.

- How to develop the two parts to a performance assessment—tasks and criteria.

- How to determine the quality of tasks and criteria.

- Strategies for using performance criteria as assessment *for* learning.

This chapter demonstrates how one assessment method, performance assessment, fits into each of the keys in Figure 7.1, and delves into the highlighted portion of the target–method match shown in Figure 7.2.

Figure 7.1   Keys to Quality Classroom Assessment

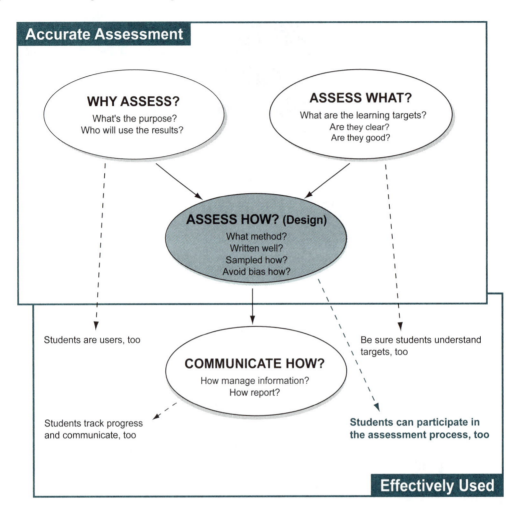

Figure 7.2   A Plan for Matching Assessment Methods with Achievement Targets

Target to Be Assessed	Assessment Method			
	Selected Response	Extended Written Response	Performance Assessment	Personal Communication
Knowledge Mastery				
Reasoning Proficiency				
Performance Skills				
Ability to Create Products				

Source: Adapted from *Student-Involved Assessment* for *Learning*, 4th ed. (p. 141), by R. J. Stiggins, 2005, Upper Saddle River, NJ: Merrill/Prentice Hall. Copyright © 2005 by Pearson Education, Inc. Adapted by permission of Pearson Education, Inc.

Assessment Based on Observation and Judgment

Definition of Performance Assessment

Performance assessment is assessment based on observation and judgment. Students engage in an activity that requires them to apply a performance skill or create a product and we judge its quality. Examples appear in Table 7.1.

Humans have been using performance assessment for at least 3,000 years. To obtain a government position in ancient China, applicants had to demonstrate their skill at writing poetry and shooting with a bow and arrow. Although performance assessment is not a recent innovation, the following aspects of it are more recent developments.

Table 7.1 Examples of Performance Tasks and Performance Criteria

Example	Task(s)	Performance Criteria
Selection onto the wrestling team	Timed run, sit-ups, pull-ups, exhibition matches	Physical fitness; knowledge of the moves; motivation
Old-time fiddle competition	Play three songs—hoe-down, waltz, and tune of choice—total not to exceed three minutes	Quality of intonation, phrasing, and creativity; precision of playing; avoidance of certain bowing patterns
Judging art	Paint a picture, make a sculpture	Quality of theme, composition, use of color
Reading comprehension	Read the story *Stone Fox* and respond to prompts such as, "Record your thoughts, feelings, and questions about what you are reading"; "Select a line or lines from the story that interest you or make you think and tell why you chose these lines."	Score the quality of the responses on a 6-point scale where 6 is an "exemplary" reading performance characterized by insight, constructing and reflecting on meaning in a text, developing connections within and among tests, taking risks, and challenging the text.
Science process skills	Students circulate to six different stations to do hands-on science activities such as analyzing seeds to judge how they might be dispersed. The purpose is to see how well students can make observations, draw inferences from those observations, and use this information to predict what will happen with other plants.	Responses are scored on a scale of 1–4 in two areas: *problem solving/inquiry* and *communication*. A "4" performance on problem solving means that the student analyzed and readily understood the task, developed an efficient and workable strategy, effectively implemented the strategy, and appropriately applied critical knowledge.
Reasoning and persuasive writing	"Imagine that it is 1858 and you make a special trip to hear Abraham Lincoln and Stephen Douglas debating during their campaigns for the Senate. Write an essay in which you explain the most important ideas and issues."*	Students receive scores in content, use of relevant previous knowledge, use of general social studies concepts, quality of the argumentation, appropriate reference to reading materials supplied, and number of historical misconceptions.

* Performance assessment task developed by the National Center for Research on Evaluation, Standards, and Student Testing, UCLA, 300 Charles E. Young Dr. N, mailbox 951522, Los Angeles, CA, phone 310-206-1532; website http://www.cse.ucla.edu.

- *Systematization.* Performance assessment is essentially subjective. Our challenge is to make this subjective form of assessment as objective (free of bias and distortion) as possible by making it more systematic. A lot of the work of making performance assessment systematic is in the area of creating high-caliber mechanisms for rating the quality of performance and teaching human raters to use the criteria to judge performances consistently.

- *Large-scale uses.* The work on consistency has enabled performance assessment to be used more formally outside the classroom as part of standardized, high-stakes tests.

- *Assessment* for *learning.* The work on consistency, oddly enough, has also led to performance assessment's preeminence in involving students in assessment by directing them to the features of work that constitute a quality performance and enabling them to judge levels of quality for themselves.

The Two Parts of a Performance Assessment

Tasks

Tasks are the activities or exercises in which students engage while the teacher observes and judges quality. For example:

- The tasks when being assessed for a driver's license consist of controlling the car under various conditions—driving on the freeway, driving on one- and two-way streets, stopping at stop signs, negotiating turn lanes, backing around a corner, parallel parking, and so on.

- The tasks for Olympic diving consist of a certain number of prescribed dives and a certain number of elective dives.

- The task for judging oral presentation skills is to give an oral presentation.

- The task for ability to work in a group is to have students work in a group.

- The task for judging the ability to cook is to have students cook a variety of dishes.

- The task for judging the ability to carry out experiments in science is to have students conduct a variety of experiments.

A *task* is any activity that we use as a context to observe a skill or a product—a naturally occurring event or a separate event, at the end of instruction or during instruction. The only requirement is that the task elicits the desired skill or product so that it is capable of being judged.

Performance Criteria

What words come to mind when you think of "criteria?" Standards for comparison? Benchmarks? What counts? What you're looking for in work? These are all terms associated with the word. *We define performance criteria as the basis for judging the quality of the performance on the task.* Here are some examples:

- The criteria for the driver's test are the extent to which candidates obey the law, do not cause congestion, and do not cause a danger.

- The criteria for Olympic diving include difficulty of the dive, form, and amount of splash when the diver enters the water.

- The criteria for an oral presentation include the content of what is presented, how the presentation is organized, the appropriateness of the language used for the audience, and the delivery.

- The criteria for group work could include respect for others, degree of participation, and quality of the ideas contributed.

- The criteria for cooking a variety of dishes include taste, texture, scent, and presentation.

- The criteria for scientific experimentation might involve such things as reasoning through the variables that must be controlled, setting up the equipment in the needed configuration, collecting the information needed in an accurate manner, accurately recording data, and drawing a sound conclusion from the information collected.

We will use the words *performance criteria, rubrics, assessment lists,* and *scoring guides* interchangeably in this chapter. Just be aware that not everyone who writes about performance assessment uses these words to mean the same thing. For our purposes here and in the classroom, criteria can be cast in the form of points assigned for specific features of a response, a checklist of important features, or a rating scale. What's important is that the criteria, whatever we call them, present a clear and accurate picture of what constitutes quality.

When to Use Performance Assessment

In Chapter 4 we made the case for reserving performance assessment for those learning targets that really need it: some forms of reasoning, performance skills, and products. Table 7.2 lists concrete examples of such targets for various grade levels from the content standards of several states. Clearly, the most important indicator for use of performance assessment is the nature of the learning target, but other factors may argue for its use as well:

- *The age of students*. About the only ways to determine what younger primary students know and can do are either to ask them about it orally (personal communication) or to watch them do something (performance assessment).

- *Reading and writing proficiency*. Other assessment methods might not provide accurate information in certain contexts, such as with English language learners, or students who don't read or write sufficiently well to answer test questions.

Developing Performance Assessments

The stages in developing performance assessments are those described in Chapter 4 for all assessment methods:

1. Plan the assessment.

2. Develop the assessment.

3. Critique the assessment.

4. Administer the assessment.

5. Revise the assessment.

Table 7.2 Examples of Learning Targets Assessable Using Performance Assessment

Reading	**Reasoning:** Evaluate the validity of what is read. **Skill:** Read at a rate of 110 words per minute by the end of grade 2.
Writing	**Product:** Vary form, detail, and structure of writing in accordance with intended audience and purpose. **Product:** Use language that is precise, engaging, and well suited to the topic and audience.
Communication	**Skill:** Communicate using different forms of oral presentation. **Skill:** Use effective listening and speaking behaviors.
Mathematics	**Reasoning:** Recognize when an approach is unproductive and try a new approach. **Skill:** Accurately measure temperature, distance, weight, and height. **Reasoning/Skill:** Support a conclusion or prediction orally and in writing, using information in a table or graph. **Product:** Create three-dimensional objects.
Physical Science	**Skill:** Choose and use laboratory equipment properly to design and carry out an experiment.
History	**Product:** Organize and record information.
Geography	**Product:** Use data and a variety of symbols and colors to create thematic maps and graphs (e.g., patterns of population, rainfall, or economic features).
Social Studies	**Reasoning and Skills:** Give examples of and exhibit the behavior of good classroom citizens, including respect, kindness, self-control, cooperation, sharing common resources, and good manners. **Skill:** Use maps and globes to locate places referenced in stories and real-life situations.
The Arts	**Reasoning:** Compare and contrast artwork in terms of elements of design. **Product:** Organize art elements to develop a composition and to change the impact of a composition.
Health/Fitness	**Skill:** Wrestle. **Product:** Create and implement a health and fitness plan.
Shop	**Reasoning:** Diagnose car engine problems. **Product:** Make a functional object out of wood or metal.

TRY THIS

Activity 7.1 Learning Targets Best Assessed with Performance Assessment

List several specific learning targets from your current assignment that should be assessed using performance assessment. (Don't list everything that could be assessed this way, just those that are of the highest priority.) Save this list for future use.

Stage 1: Plan the Assessment

Plan the assessment by answering four questions: Assess why? Assess what? Assess how? How important?

Assess Why?

Again, we begin with consideration of how the results of the assessment are to be used and by whom. What decisions will the information drive? How will the assessment be used to meet students' information needs? Specific design choices we make are guided by answers to these questions.

For example, rubrics for use with students will look different than those used on a large-scale, standardized assessment. Assessments developed to provide descriptive feedback may look different from those designed to provide an overall picture of student achievement status.

Assess What?

This question requires that we specify the learning target or targets the assessment is to measure. Although this step may seem simple, it becomes important to have done it when we get to selecting or creating criteria, so don't skip it.

Assess How?

At this step in planning, we double check that performance assessment is the best choice for our purpose and our targets.

How Important?

Have you ever had the feeling that the single state writing sample didn't accurately represent a student's true ability to write? Perhaps the topic was familiar to the student and she performed better than usual, or the task was worded in such a manner that the student might not have understood it and done worse than usual. Or, maybe you noticed that a single event, such as having a student read out loud, didn't really capture the student's true oral reading fluency?

These are issues of sampling. Sampling is extremely important with performance assessment. Because there are so many extraneous factors that can contribute to a student's performance on any single performance task, students need to complete a number of tasks to serve as the basis for a stable estimate of performance (Shavelson, Baxter, & Pine, 1992; Shavelson, Baxter, & Gao, 1993; Gao, 1996).

There aren't any hard and fast rules regarding sampling. A single, good culminating activity that relates directly to skills and products students have been developing all along may be enough. Or a simple, straightforward learning target, such as demonstrating how to use a band saw, might only require a single instance of performance.

However, we often need to gather several samples to get a stable view of student achievement because the behaviors we are assessing are complex. For example, to determine how good students are at solving math problems we would have students use various problem-solving strategies superimposed over a range of content. Or, to determine reading fluency, we might choose several passages from books with different content and purposes—narrative, expository, or persuasive text. As another example, using the writing assessments from the *Work Keys Assessment*, Gao (1996) found that six prompts and two raters were needed to substantially increase ability to generalize about student ability to write.

In situations outside the classroom, such as statewide testing, it can be very expensive and time consuming to collect enough samples of student performance to make stable judgments about individual students.

Enter the portfolio. Although Chapter 11 focuses on portfolios, it is appropriate to mention them here, as well. One way to increase the number of samples that show student progress and status is to have them collect work in a portfolio. If we carefully outline for students the types of entries to use, we can get a good sample. We might require that a writing portfolio have X number of samples of narrative, expository, and persuasive writing. Or, we might require that a math problem-solving portfolio have X samples of work demonstrating different problem-solving strategies using different content.

Several states have attempted to implement portfolios to supplement statewide testing. For example, in Oregon, teachers are supposed to make sure that students have a portfolio to corroborate evidence from the statewide assessment.

Performance assessments don't all have to be given at the end of instruction. We can gather evidence over time, as with a portfolio, to make the sample adequately reflect the breadth and depth of the learning target being assessed. In fact, the types of learning targets covered by performance assessment—reasoning, skills, and products—fit nicely into tracking progress over time using a portfolio.

Portfolios, however, are not just a way to increase the sample of student work so that we obtain more reliable evidence of student performance; they are also a way to involve students in their own assessment to assist them to take control of their learning. They offer so many benefits to student motivation and learning that we would never recommend using portfolios for the sole purpose of increasing sample size. Chapter 11 will offer more information regarding the student-involvement aspects of portfolios.

One final thought about sampling: As with other methods of assessment, we need to consider the importance of the decision to be made from the information to plan sample size. For important decisions, such as placement in a special program or graduation from high school, we need a bigger sample because the decisions can seriously affect a student's life and we want to make sure we are correct. But other decisions we can reconsider easily. For example, if we don't get an accurate picture of student ability to give an oral presentation due to some temporary interfering condition, such as the student being overtired, we may easily retest and replace the erroneous information.

TRY THIS

Activity 7.2 Determining Sample Size

Choose one of the learning targets you listed in Activity 7.1. Consider the breadth and depth of this target. How many samples of student performance might you need to be sure your inference about student proficiency is accurate? Write that number down and save it, noting how you might have to vary the tasks to cover the breadth and depth of the target.

Stage 2: Develop the Assessment—Rubrics

In the case of performance assessment, we need to develop both tasks and scoring guides. In this section we will examine what good rubrics look like and outline how to develop such rubrics.

Rubrics—Distinguishing the Gems from the Duds

Although there is no single "good" rubric, scoring guide, or performance criteria list, there are lots of bad ones out there. Simply type the word *rubric* into any search engine and you'll be confronted with hundreds of hits. How do you select those that are strong? We have developed a rubric for rubrics, a "Metarubric" if you will, to answer that question. Here are the steps we completed to develop the Metarubric, and the results at each step. (To work through these steps for yourself to understand better where the metarubric came from, we recommend completing Segments 2–5 of the ETS video, *Student-Involved Performance Assessment.*)

We brainstormed what we want performance criteria (rubrics, scoring guides) to do for us in the classroom, because uses for the rubric influence design. Here is the list that we generated:

- Define quality for ourselves.

- Describe quality for students.

- Make judgments more objective, consistent, and accurate.

- Improve grading consistency.

- Guide instruction.

- Provide a common language.

- Promote descriptive feedback to students.

- Promote student self-assessment and goal setting.

- Describe quality to parents.

- Make expectations for students explicit.

- Eliminate bias.

- Focus teaching.

- Track student learning.

Notice that the list contains both assessment *for* and assessment *of* learning purposes. In the classroom we want rubrics that can help us with both.

Next, we identified the features that rubrics need to have to serve these purposes. We read what others had to say, made our own lists, and looked at hundreds of sample rubrics to identify everything of importance. Here is our list of what makes a good rubric:

- Focus on what is important.

- Be clear enough for everyone to understand.

- Define various levels of success.

- Be available in student-friendly language.

- Include only those aspects of a performance or product that are most valued.

- Include what is valued most as major parts of the rubric.

- Align with standards.

- Have a user-friendly format.

- Provide directions for use.

- Make language consistent across levels.

- Make levels distinguishable.

- Use no "fudge words," such as *adequate* or *sometimes*.

- Have models to illustrate what is meant.

- Contain descriptive detail.

- Define terms.

- Have visuals to reinforce definitions.

- Use non-value-based adjectives.

- Don't be negative at the low end.

- Be age appropriate.

- Match important goals.

- Include information on what the student did right at each level.

- Make it clear how to differentiate between score points.

Obviously, this list is way too long to be useful, so we looked for logical groupings of ideas and noticed that they seemed to fit nicely into four categories. We call these categories *traits*, and they are shown in Figure 7.3. Note that at this point in our rubric development, we have not yet described levels of quality for each trait. Figure 7.3 merely shows the traits with some definitions. The whole Metarubric, with scoring levels defined, can be found on the CD in the file, "Metarubric."

The Metarubric can look a bit daunting at first, so we will ease into it by just using the trait summary in Figure 7.3 to critique the oral presentation rubric in Table 7.3.

Content

Take a look at the content of the oral presentation rubric in Table 7.3 and answer the following question: "Does it cover everything of importance and does it leave out unimportant things?" (Remember, think analytically, and put aside any comments about clarity or practicality or fairness and focus just on the trait of *Content*. We will look at the other traits in a moment.)

On the positive side, the rubric includes much that is important—delivery, language, and organization. On the negative side, did you notice that there is no place to rate the quality of the oral presentation's content? You may also have noticed that aspects of good delivery and good language choice are missing. We would say this rubric is a little more than halfway there in terms of content.

Clarity

Analyze the clarity of the rubric in Table 7.3 using the Metarubric summary in Figure 7.3. What questions do you have? On the positive side, the various levels of the rubric are defined and are fairly descriptive, and there are samples of student performance that illustrate the various score points on each trait. On the negative side, people frequently ask about the score scale—why there are two scores in each range and how you differentiate between them. Others note words that students would not understand and point out the lack of definition of each trait. So, for the trait of *Clarity*, this rubric is about halfway there.

Practicality

Analyze the rubric in Table 7.3 on the trait of *Practicality* in Figure 7.3. How easy would it be to use? On the positive side, it would be easy for teachers and students to internalize the number of traits and number of score points if a few other details were cleared up, such as how to handle the two score points in each box. It would also be useful as a diagnostic tool

Figure 7.3 Metarubric Summary

The Metarubric contains criteria for judging the quality of rubrics—a rubric for rubrics. There are four traits: *Content, Clarity, Practicality,* and *Technical Quality/Fairness.* The Metarubric summary defines each trait. The complete Metarubric (found on the CD) defines three levels of quality for each trait.

1. **Content:** What counts? What users see is what you'll get.
   - Does it cover everything of importance—doesn't leave important things out?
   - Does it leave out unimportant things?

2. **Clarity:** Does everyone understand what is meant?
   - Are terms defined?
   - Are various levels of quality defined?
   - Are there samples of work to illustrate levels of quality?

3. **Practicality:** Is it easy to use by teachers and students?
   - Will students understand what is meant? Is there a student-friendly version?
   - Can students use it to self-assess and set specific goals?
   - Is the information provided useful for planning instruction?
   - Is the rubric manageable?

4. **Technical Quality/Fairness:** Is it reliable and valid?
   - Is it reliable? Will different raters give the same score?
   - Is it valid? Do the ratings actually represent what students can do?
   - Is it fair? Does the language adequately describe quality for all students? Are there racial, cultural, or gender biases?

to plan instruction, although additional detail in the traits would assist in planning specific lessons and in giving descriptive feedback. We judge the rubric to be about halfway home on this trait, as well.

Technical Quality/Fairness

Finally, examine the rubric in Table 7.3 using the Metarubric trait of *Technical Quality/ Fairness* in Figure 7.3. It does include information about rater agreement, but there is no information about how the rubric functions with different groups of students, how easy it is to achieve high levels of rater agreement, or how it works to score oral presentations with nonnative speakers of English. Some features in the wording might disadvantage

Table 7.3   Sample Rubric for Oral Presentation

Score	Language	Delivery	Organization
A = 5	Correct grammar and pronunciation are used. Word choice is interesting and appropriate. Unfamiliar terms are defined in the context of the speech.	The voice demonstrates control with few distractions. The presentation holds the listener's attention. The volume and rate are at acceptable levels. Eye contact with the audience is maintained. The message is organized.	The speaker sticks to the topic. The main points are developed. It is easy to summarize the content of the speech.
B = 4 **C = 3**	Correct grammar and pronunciation are used. Word choice is adequate and understandable. Unfamiliar terms are not explained in the context of the speech. There is a heavy reliance on the listener's prior knowledge.	The voice is generally under control. The speaker can be heard and understood. The speaker generally maintains eye contact with the audience.	The organization is understandable. Main points may be underdeveloped. The speaker may shift unexpectedly from one point to another, but the message remains comprehensible. The speech can be summarized.
D = 2 **F = 1**	Errors in grammar and pronunciation occur. Word choice lacks clarity. The speaker puts the responsibility for understanding on the listener.	The student's voice is poor. The volume may be too low and the rate too fast. There may be frequent pauses. Nonverbal behaviors tend to interfere with the message.	Ideas are listed without logical sequence. The relationships between ideas are not clear. The student strays from the stated topic. It is difficult to summarize the speech.
Samples of student work illustrating levels of quality are available. Research information on technical quality: Exact agreement rate on scores is about 70%.			

Source: Unknown.

certain groups of students. For example, consider the requirement of "correct pronunciation." Correct for whom? What about nonnative speakers or those who speak a dialect of English? Consider also the phrase, "The message is organized." Different cultures value different organizational patterns. What will we hold students accountable for? This rubric is about halfway home on the trait of *Technical Quality*.

Common Problems with Instructional Rubrics

In our experience, there are a few problems that crop up frequently in rubrics. Most of these problems relate to the Metarubric trait of *Content*. One relates to the trait of *Clarity*.

Counting, When Quality Is More Important Than Quantity

In an attempt to increase the objectivity of scoring guides, it is tempting to count things—the number of spelling errors, the number of references, the number of topics covered, and so on. But, most often this backfires: aren't 2 really good references better than 5 bad ones? Aren't spelling errors on 10 different words more of a problem than 10 spelling errors all on the same word? Couldn't a thorough coverage of a single topic be more impressive than cursory coverage of several topics?

Figure 7.4 shows a writing rubric based on counts.

What message does this rubric send to students about what is important in writing? How well does it define quality? What assistance does it provide on instructional decisions? If I, as a student, understood the rubric, might I be able to write a nonsensical essay and still get a good score?

The bottom line: For classroom uses, don't use counts to indicate quality unless there is compelling evidence that a count actually is the important criterion, that it does define quality.

Important Details Left Out

Let's say that I play the violin and that I'm in a contest. Let's further say that, although I feel my bowing is strong, bowing is not included in the criteria, which evaluate intonation, rhythm, and interpretation. What message does this send me about bowing? At the very least it sends the message that bowing is unimportant. But, more of a problem is that I get no feedback on an important part of my skill so that I know what improvements I need to make.

Three unfortunate things happen when we leave important things out of a rubric: (1) we send the message that what is left out is unimportant; (2) we generate incomplete infor-

Figure 7.4   Rubrics with Problems—Writing Rubric Based on Counts

Introduction

3   Introduces the topic and includes 4 to 5 sentences

2   Introduces the topic and includes 2 to 3 sentences

1   Does not relate to the topic, or includes 1 sentence

Body Paragraph 1

3   Has a topic sentence and at least 3 supporting details

2   Has a topic sentence and 2 supporting details

1   Has no topic sentence or only 1 supporting detail

Body Paragraph 2

3   Has a topic sentence and at least 3 supporting details

2   Has a topic sentence and 2 supporting details

1   Has no topic sentence or only 1 supporting detail

Body Paragraph 3

3   Has a topic sentence and at least 3 supporting details

2   Has a topic sentence and 2 supporting details

1   Has no topic sentence or only 1 supporting detail

Conclusion

3   Summarizes the main points and includes 4 to 5 sentences

2   Summarizes the main points and includes 2 to 3 sentences

1   Does not summarize the main points, or includes 1 sentence

mation on which to plan future instruction; and (3) we provide no feedback to students on the quality of valued elements. For example, let's assume that a state leaves "voice" and "word choice" out of its rubric for writing; it includes only main idea, support, consistent focus, organization, sentence construction, and mechanics. Leaving out important aspects of quality might be done for the very best of reasons—state developers might be afraid that they will not get consistent scores on these traits. But, what do you think might happen to writing instruction if such a rubric were used on the statewide assessment? What message does use of such a rubric send to students about the nature of quality writing? What diagnostic benefit is lost to teachers?

Making sure that the correct information is in rubrics is not just an intellectual exercise; it is personal for students. For example, read the student essay, "Junk Food," in Figure 7.5. The paper certainly has weaknesses. The ideas are incorrect, the organization rambles, grammar and spelling are weak, and sentences don't flow. But, there is one big strength—voice. You want to read the paper because the voice draws you in. What if this student lived in the state where voice was not scored as part of the state assessment? The student would receive the message that his writing has no redeemable value, when actually the student has one huge strength to build on—compelling voice. What impact might this omission have on the student? Similarly, the teacher would receive no feedback about the student's biggest strength, so she might not take it into consideration when planning instruction for this student.

The bottom line: Always include everything of importance on a rubric, even if it is difficult to define. The things most difficult to define are actually those that *most* need definitions, and developing a descriptive rubric is a fine way to proceed. Unless we can define important learning targets so that everyone knows what they mean, how will we ever be able to help students achieve those goals? If we leave important things out of a rubric, what incorrect messages might we send to students about the nature of quality?

Irrelevant Details in a Rubric

The flip side of ensuring that important features of performance are included in a rubric is ensuring that irrelevant details are left out. Imagine a scoring guide for a poster that illustrates knowledge of dinosaurs, for which one criterion is, "Must have three colors." Why does a poster have to have three colors? Can a black-and-white poster be highly effective in communicating information? What message does the requirement of three colors on a poster send to students about the nature of quality? What is our real reason for requiring three colors? If our goal is to teach students to create posters that capture people's attention and enhance the message, the criterion might be better phrased, "The design of the poster draws people in and supports the message." Then the teacher can show students how effective use of color can help accomplish this.

The bottom line: Go for importance. Of course importance implies that we understand the target well enough to know what *is* important. Developing a rubric for "presentation" is harder than checking off "three colors." But it is more useful in teaching students the true nature of quality and in planning instruction toward that end.

Figure 7.5   Junk Food (Student Essay)

Everything in the world has to have food may it be good food or junk food. Junck food is one of the more populare food. Most people like soda pops, hambriger, popcorn, shakes itc. Some of the places you can get these at is at 7 eleven stores, Mcdonalds, Dariy Queen etc.

Some Health food nut say that you will get fat if you eat hamburgere. You will but if you just at health food al the time, your body will get to meny vitimens and you can die. Health food is a food that will give your vitemans and cleans out yore iners.

Eny whay you nead junk food to get your adrental gland working. Junk food like hamburger is good food. Some people say that it is bad for you or is it. I don't think it is so bad for you because you get tomatos, lettice, musterd, relish and meat. Shakes. Shakes are made out of mile, ice, and aritvial flaver and suger.

Some people say that fried chiken is good for you but is it. the chiken is fried in nothing but oil. It is one of my favorit food so I don't care what eny one thinkes. If it is food it is food.

If you just had a candy bare out in the desert would you just throw it a way hec no. If you were out on the dessert you would take one bite of it and keep it in your mouth for days.

If you don't eat eny food you will die in 63 days of what is called starvation. Starvaison ocures wen you don't get enough food and you don't get eny oxegen to your bones.

Source: Anonymous student work.

Why Are We Using Rubrics Anyway?

What's the purpose of our rubrics—to enable students to get a good score or to teach them the nature of quality? If the goal is just to enable students to get a good score, we can put anything on a scoring guide: five references, three colors, fill the page with writing, three paragraphs on each topic, has a picture on the cover. But, if our goal is to define quality, then we need to be much more careful about what we include in our rubrics.

The bottom line: The goal of using scoring guides should be to define quality, and not just to provide a scoring mechanism or justification for giving a grade.

Student-Developed Rubrics Where Anything Goes

We are in favor of involving students in developing the criteria by which their work will be judged. Students can help us refine our thinking and help us spread out the work. Involving students helps them internalize the criteria and bring them to bear on their own work. But, we're also in favor of leading students toward good criteria—criteria that define quality. Most often, we, as teachers, know more about the criteria for quality than students do.

If students come up with criteria along the lines of "three colors" for a quality poster, we need to be prepared to broaden their thinking by showing them examples of effective posters with fewer (or more) than three colors. If they say that work has to be two pages long, we need to be ready to show them effective work that is only one page long, or that is six pages long.

The bottom line: Student involvement in developing criteria is a powerful strategy if done well, but it can lead to misunderstandings about the nature of quality if not done well. Anything does not go. Be prepared to assist your students in their discovery of good criteria through use of thoughtfully chosen examples.

Skimpy Scoring Guides

The previous problems have related to the Metarubric trait of *Content*. This problem relates to the Metarubric trait of *Clarity*. Have you ever seen a rubric like the one in Table 7.4? Sometimes the categories are more clearly fleshed out, but the details for how to assign the number of points are meager or nonexistent. We call these "skimpy rubrics" because there is little help with defining what is meant, or determining levels of quality. Will different teachers be likely to give the same scores to the same papers using this rubric? Will this help a single teacher be consistent in scoring over time and across assignments? Will this kind of rubric help students understand what their score means and will they be able to use the rubric to self-assess and set goals for improvement? We think not.

Compare the rubric in Table 7.4 to the "Central Kitsap Student-Friendly Math Scoring Guide" in the CD file, "Rubric Sampler." Notice that the Central Kitsap rubric defines each trait and provides descriptors that help teachers and students find the correct level of performance. The scoring guide also is illustrated with student work at each level of quality at each grade level. Although imperfect, the Central Kitsap guide is definitely headed in the right direction.

The bottom line: Definitions, descriptive language, and examples are what make rubrics clear. Look for other skimpy and well-defined scoring guides in the CD file "Rubric Sampler."

Table 7.4   Skimpy Mathematics Scoring Guide

	5	4	3	2	1
Understands the problem					
Problem solving					
Correct calculations					
Communication					

5 is high and 1 is low

Developing General Holistic and Analytical-Trait Rubrics

There are different types of rubrics. In Chapter 6, we recommended using *task-specific* scoring for extended written response exercises—that is, scoring guides developed for each individual task, assigning points to specific information contained in the response. If the intent is to assess knowledge, as is the case with many extended written response questions, then the scoring guide needs to reflect the specific information expected, and a task-specific rubric is appropriate.

We don't recommend task-specific rubrics for the types of learning targets described in this chapter—reasoning, skills, and products. For a longer discussion of this point, please see Chapter 2 in *Scoring Rubrics in the Classroom,* the book accompanying ETS's video, *Student-Involved Performance Assessment.* All we will say here is that if we want students to generalize from task to task what they are learning about quality problem solving, making inferences, giving oral presentations, working in a group, or designing experiments, then we need to develop and use general rubrics—those that can be used across tasks. "The influencing of instructional practices to date has been served most powerfully by generic rubrics" (Khattri, Reeve, & Adamson, 1997, p. 4).

Because we are most interested in the instructional aspects of rubrics, from this point on we will concentrate on how to develop general, not task-specific, rubrics.

What "counts" in a performance? What distinguishes levels of quality? What does it look like when a student has reached different levels of competency? What are the essential characteristics that define quality? In the following subsections we discuss the steps we use to clarify the nature of quality and to develop rubrics ourselves, using as our example first-year foreign language studies. As we go, consider how you might apply the process to develop a rubric for one of the learning targets you listed in Activity 7.1. These same steps can be used to develop rubrics for any product or performance, such as group collaboration, oral presentations, lab reports, self-reflection, reading fluency, critical thinking, art criticism, or writing.

Steps in Rubric Development

Step 1   Establish a knowledge base.

Step 2   Gather samples of student performance.

Step 3   Sort student work by level of quality.

Step 4   Cluster the reasons into traits.

Step 5   Identify sample performances that illustrate each level.

Step 6   Make it better.

Rubric Development Step 1: Establish a Knowledge Base

Determine your prior knowledge about quality and begin in one of the following ways. If you're an expert in creating the product or performance yourself, merely write down the features that distinguish levels of performance and refine them through looking at samples of student work. If you feel as if you know what quality work looks like when you see it, but you have difficulty writing it down off the top of your head, engage in the entire process given here.

Sometimes you have no idea where to begin. "What the heck is critical thinking?" "What in the world do they mean by 'lifelong' learner?" In this case, you must talk to others, examine state standards or curricula, and read what experts in the field have written. How do they define quality? Pursue these steps in conjunction with the following process.

In all cases, it is to your advantage to review as many existing rubrics as you can. Why recreate the wheel? Depending on your level of expertise, you can use sample rubrics ahead of time to help you understand what others mean, you can use sample rubrics to corroborate or extend your own thinking, or you can use them as you finish to help you refine your work.

Rubric Development Step 2: Gather Samples of Student Performance

Gather a range of student performances on the reasoning proficiency, skill, or product under consideration. For example, foreign language teachers wanted to develop a rubric for the following learning target: "comprehends and uses spoken language to satisfy social demands." They wanted a rubric to use across languages—French, Spanish, German, and Japanese. So they audio- and videotaped students conversing in the target languages about everyday topics: their families, the area in which they grew up, the weather, their school experiences, and so forth.

Rubric Development Step 3: Sort Student Work by Level of Quality

At this step, sort the samples into three stacks according to level of quality—strong, middle, and weak. Ask yourself, "What makes the strong stack different from the middle stack? What makes it different from the weak stack?" Use the samples to create a list of descriptors of quality at various levels. We recommend trying to come up with as broad and long a list as possible. The foreign language teachers labeled their stacks *proficient*, *mid-range*, and *emergent* because those terms are more positive at the low end of achievement. As they sorted, they wrote down their reasons for placing each student performance in its chosen pile. They kept sorting until they were not adding anything new to their list. Table 7.5 shows what the foreign language teachers came up with.

Table 7.5   Foreign Language Teachers' Brainstormed List of Features Defining Quality

Proficient	Bows and excuses self on approach and leaving (Japanese)
	Speaks in paragraphs
	Offers additional information
	Responds immediately and appropriately to both rehearsed and unrehearsed questions
	Combines several sentences
	Uses confirmational questions naturally
	Responds to novel questions/may ask for clarification
	Speech is approaching natural speed
	Initiates conversation
	Pronunciation is accurate
	Uses a full range of first-year grammar structures correctly
	Elaborates
	Uses complete sentences when appropriate
	Expands response in order to respond to implied questions
	Asks questions of the examiner
	Vocabulary is broad enough to sound natural

Table 7.5   (Continued)

Mid-Range	Bows and excuses self when approaching the teacher (Japanese), but not when leaving Combines learned phrases with interjectives Responds rapidly to rehearsed questions, but few unrehearsed questions Responds appropriately to rehearsed questions, but not to unrehearsed questions Pronunciation causes no confusion Verbs and endings are generally in place; the student can correct if necessary Relationals are generally in place; the student can correct if necessary Asks for clarification in the foreign language Sometimes repeats a question in English before answering Speech speed is slow, but causes no discomfort Speaks in full sentences, but not paragraphs Responds to questions, but doesn't ask any of her own Sometimes has to come up with awkward phraseology to compensate for a moderate vocabulary Anglicizes word order, but the message is communicated Gives desired information, but no more Self-corrects Frequently asks for rephrasing
Emergent	No sign of deference to the teacher (Japanese) Replies in single word utterances or fragmentary speech Responds inappropriately to rehearsed questions Speech is slow and causes confusion and discomfort Pronunciation is anglicized and causes confusion Intonation causes discomfort Hesitates before answering, causing discomfort Rehearsed expressions are confused or misapplied Verbs and endings are confused or misapplied Relationals are misapplied, causing confusion Vocabulary is limited Pronunciation confuses phonemes Misuses of grammar interfere with communication Uses random word order Hesitates excessively Understands few questions Needs frequent repetition and/or clarification of questions in English

When creating your list, include as much detail as you can. Go beyond general terms typically used. Students may not understand "lacks fluency," but they will understand "speaks slowly with hesitation." To generate detail, ask yourself questions such as these: "What specific features made me judge that the speech lacks fluency?" "What am I saying to myself as I categorize the performance?" "What descriptive feedback might I give to this student?" If you want the rubric to provide descriptive feedback and to function as a self-assessment and goal-setting tool for students, it is to your advantage to include those descriptive phrases from the outset.

Rubric Development Step 4: Cluster the Descriptors into Traits

Your sorting and describing will result in a hodgepodge of descriptors at each level of performance. Some invariably will overlap or cluster together into the same category of performance. Invariably, someone will say, "Wait a minute. 'Speaks in paragraphs' is the same as 'Combines several sentences. Why not delete one?" Or, "Wait a minute. We have a whole lot of statements that refer to fluency. Why not group them together?" Or, "I had trouble placing a student performance in a single category because it was strong in fluency but weak in pronunciation. Let's score performance on those two dimensions separately." That's exactly the purpose of Step 4—to determine what major categories, dimensions, or traits seem to be emerging from the sorting process, eliminating redundancies and including descriptors from the brainstormed list that best describe the traits at each achievement level.

The foreign language teachers identified four traits that seemed to cover everything in their lists: pronunciation, grammar, fluency and content, and social skills. They built a draft rubric by deleting redundant descriptors and sorting the remaining statements at each level of quality into these four traits. Table 7.6 shows their draft rubric.

During this process you might find that you need more than three levels of quality because you encounter examples that fall between levels. That is fine as long as you can find descriptors and/or sample performances that differentiate the levels. You can assign the numbers 5, 3, and 1 to the levels and allow 2s and 4s to represent those examples demonstrating characteristics of the two adjoining score points. As long as you get consistent scoring and you and students can differentiate performance levels, identify however many performance levels you need.

Rubric Development Step 5: Identify Sample Performances That Illustrate Each Level

Return to the samples categorized as strong, middle, and weak and select examples that illustrate well what is meant by each trait at each achievement level. These samples—also

Table 7.6   Draft Foreign Language Rubric

Score	Pronunciation	Grammar	Fluency and Content	Social Skills
3	Sounds natural Causes no confusion Accurate Accurate intonation	Verbs, endings, and relationals are accurate Uses the full range of first-year structures	Speaks in paragraphs Offers additional information Response is immediate and appropriate Responds to novel questions without hesitation Speech approaches normal speed Initiates conversation	Bows and excuses self on approach and leaving
2	Beginning to sound accurate; doesn't interfere with communication Can self-correct	Verbs, endings, and relationals are sometimes correct and sometimes incorrect Can self-correct if requested Word order is anglicized but the message is communicated Only simple structures are used well	Tends to hesitate, but responds appropriately to most rehearsed questions Responds rapidly to rehearsed questions, but hesitates with novel questions Tends to repeat the question in English before answering Asks for clarification in foreign language Gives the desired information, no more	Bows and excuses self only when approaching or leaving the teacher, but not both
1	Mostly anglicized Phonemes are confused Interferes with communication Causes discomfort Can't self correct	Uses random word order Verbs, endings, and relationals are mostly confused or misapplied Grammar problems cause confusion in communication Can't self-correct even with prompting Not even the simplest structures are used correctly	Uses single-word utterances Tends to respond inappropriately to rehearsed questions Speech is slow and causes confusion and discomfort Hesitates a lot Rehearsed expressions are confused or misapplied	Does not show deference to the teacher

called *models, exemplars, examples,* and *anchors*—help teachers attain consistency with each other and within their own scoring across time, students, and assignments. Samples also help students understand what each achievement level looks like in concrete terms. As an added benefit, identifying the best performances to illustrate each trait and level can suggest refinements to the rubric.

Be sure to have more than one sample to illustrate each level. If you show students only one example of good performance, all performances might come out looking the same. Rather, show several performances that illustrate each level and trait.

Rubric Development Step 6: Make It Better

Rubrics are always works in progress. As you use rubrics, all of the following can happen:

- Traits are added, deleted or merged. For example, the foreign language teachers noticed that the trait of *Fluency* also included accuracy of the information presented, so they considered splitting *Fluency* into two traits: *Fluency* and *Accurate Content*. They ultimately settled on a single trait under the collective term, *Fluency and Content*.

- Traits and descriptors are refined. For example, in the Six-Trait Model writing rubric (see the CD file, "Rubric Sampler") the trait *Sentence Fluency* was once called *Sentence Correctness*. To be strong on this trait, students had to use complete sentences. Then raters discovered that some good writing had to be scored lower because it contained incomplete sentences, even through the sentence fragments were used to good effect in enhancing the meaning. So the meaning of the trait was changed. What we really want to accomplish with students is not only complete sentences, but control of sentence structure—complete sentences or fragments used consciously to create a feel to the writing, or to support the meaning in the most effective way, given the audience, purpose and format for the writing. So the trait has become *Sentence Fluency*.

- The number of levels increases as raters feel the need to differentiate levels of quality further. Or, the number decreases as raters realize they cannot distinguish accurately between two levels.

- Developers notice that some characteristics are included at one level of the rubric but are not represented, either as a strength or a weakness, at other levels, so they revise the rubric to achieve parallel content.

- A state rubric that works well for the purpose of collecting achievement status information on students may not be as useful for classroom use because it is too skimpy—it does not have enough description to define the levels for students. In this case, teachers might make a descriptive, analytical-trait classroom rubric that parallels the state rubric. For example, the writing rubric in one state has only two traits: *Conventions* to evaluate capitalization, usage, punctuation, and spelling, and *Content, Organization, and Style*, which includes everything else—focus, details, organization, rhetorical style, and so on. At the classroom level, many teachers clarify the "everything else" by using the Six-Trait Model, which covers the same characteristics of good writing as does the state rubric, but is written to meet teachers' and students' needs for more detailed information. Improving student performance through use of the Six-Trait Model therefore directly transfers to higher performance on the state assessment.

Activity 7.3 gives you the opportunity to develop your own rubric using the steps given in this chapter.

TRY THIS

Activity 7.3 Develop a Rubric

Select one of the learning targets you identified in Activity 7.1 as high priority for performance assessment. Develop a general rubric for that target by looking at the rubrics of others, sorting student work, and devising a draft, following the steps given in this chapter. You can find more detailed instructions for rubric development in the CD file, "Rubric Development."

To reduce the amount of time this takes, try the following:

- Work with other teachers on a rubric that everyone can use. It might be a lot of work at first, but once it's finished, you have it forever.

- Get students to help.

- Save your scarce development time for those learning targets that truly need definition. Select the ones you are most fuzzy about, ones that many students have trouble understanding, or ones that state assessment data indicate need attention.

Stage 3: Critique the Assessment—Rubrics

With a performance assessment, we critique the rubric and the task separately. At this point in performance assessment development, we focus on determining the quality of the rubric by using the Metarubric, summarized in Figure 7.3 and found in its entirety in the CD file, "Metarubric." Activity 7.4 provides practice in analyzing your own rubrics for quality with the Metarubric.

DEEPEN UNDERSTANDING

Activity 7.4   Analyze Your Own Rubrics

Choose your favorite scoring guides. Analyze them using either the Metarubric summary in Figure 7.3 or the full Metarubric on the CD in the file, "Metarubric." Analyze them for each Metarubric trait. What do you conclude about how well your rubric scores on the four traits? If you are working with a learning team, you may want to discuss observations and conclusions at your next meeting.

For additional practice using the Metarubric to identify rubrics useful for instruction in the classroom, work through Segments 3 and 4 on the video, *Student-Involved Performance Assessment,* or turn to Chapter 4 in the book packaged with the video, *Scoring Rubrics in the Classroom.* You also may wish to critique the rubrics in the CD file, "Rubric Sampler."

Stage 2: Develop the Assessment—Performance Tasks

Now we turn to developing performance tasks. In this section, as in the section on developing rubrics, we will explore what good tasks look like and describe how to develop tasks that accomplish what they are intended to.

Dimensions of Good Tasks

Although much of the emphasis in performance assessment is on performance criteria, the quality of the task must receive equal attention. The purpose of the task is to elicit the correct behavior on the part of the student so that it can be assessed by the scoring guide.

Thus, there must be alignment between the task and the rubric, and both must reflect the learning target accurately.

Here's an example of a time when the task did *not* elicit the correct performance. A number of years ago, a group of assessment developers were creating fifth-grade prompts for a statewide writing assessment. One they wrote to assess narrative writing went something like this: "You have all heard stories of how the elephant got its trunk or how the camel got its hump. Think of something in nature and make up a story about how it got that way." Many students produced not narrative, but expository writing—why elephants have trunks and why camels have humps. The prompt did not elicit narrative writing, so they couldn't evaluate the students' level of achievement in narrative writing. The tricky part with performance tasks is that if we don't elicit the right performance we can't use the results (if we can even assess the performance at all) as evidence of level of achievement.

To avoid this problem as well as others, we have developed a rubric for judging the quality of performance tasks. Using the rubric development process as outlined previously, we identified five traits: *Content, Clarity, Feasibility, Fairness and Accuracy*, and *Sampling*. These traits are summarized in Figure 7.6.

Content

The job of the performance task is to elicit the right performance from students so that proficiency can be judged accurately. Thus, the performance task, the performance criteria, and the student learning targets to be assessed must match up. If the learning target to be assessed is "Understands how the past affects our private lives and society in general" (Kendall & Marzano, 1997, p. 114), then the task must call forth a product or performance that directly demonstrates that understanding.

Our definition of sound content in a performance task differs somewhat from those you may find in other task development guidelines. Some tend to emphasize authenticity and stress such criteria as *open, active, collaborative, fosters persistence, challenging,* and *rich*. While these might, indeed, be relevant for many of the tasks we design to assess complex targets, they are not criteria for all performance tasks. It is possible to have simpler performance tasks that assess simpler targets. Consider, for example, reading rate. The task is very simple: Ask students to read aloud and calculate the number of words read per minute. *Open, collaborative,* and *rich* are not task requirements in this case. Indeed, were they present, they could compromise the results. Our rule of thumb is this: Simple target, simple task; complex target, complex task.

Figure 7.6   Task Rubric Summary

Content: What are students asked to do?

- The task elicits the right performance; it fits the target and performance criteria.
- Simple target → simple task; complex target → complex task.
- Worth the time spent on it; students will learn from the task.
- The amount of scaffolding supports the task without compromising it.
- Task is engaging/interesting to students.

Clarity: How clear are the instructions?

- Instructions tell students clearly what to do.
- Students are reminded of the performance criteria.

Feasibility: How practical is the task?

- Students have enough time.
- Proper materials and equipment are available.
- Rating can be accomplished within the time allowed.

Fairness and Accuracy: How fair is the task?

- There is nothing in the task that will give an inaccurate picture of student achievement.
- All students have a chance to shine.

Sampling: How well does the task represent the breadth and depth of the target being assessed?

- The task(s) adequately cover all dimensions of the learning target being assessed.

OR

- The task is part of a larger plan to cover all relevant dimensions over time.

There are just enough tasks to show students' level of proficiency; not too few, not too many.

The important consideration is that the task elicit the intended performance so we can observe and evaluate it. Since many targets evaluated with a performance assessment are complex, performance tasks tend to be complex, open, active, and challenging. However, they don't have to have all these characteristics to be sound.

Clarity

Tasks are stated in such a way that students know exactly what to do. A good task also includes the criteria that will be used to evaluate the quality of the performance or product. This helps students focus on the most important aspects to include.

Feasibility

The task can be completed successfully given the time and materials available in the classroom. It is "do-able." Additionally, *Feasibility* refers to scoring—are adequate time and resources available to observe performances and/or evaluate the quality of products?

Fairness and Accuracy

There is nothing in the task that will compromise students' ability to show what they can do. All students have an equal chance to shine. Examples of threats to fairness include the following:

- Exercises and tasks using a context (sewing, baseball) not familiar to some students

- Extensive reading or writing requirements when the achievement to be demonstrated does not relate to reading or writing learning targets

- Exercises or tasks incorporating components irrelevant to the target(s) to be assessed; e.g., oral presentation or group discussion components when the learning target is not oral presentation or group discussion skills

- Anything else that might interfere with students accurately demonstrating their levels of achievement; e.g., successful completion of the task relies on personality traits or cultural background

Sampling

The task or tasks adequately cover all dimensions of the learning target to be assessed, as described in the previous section in this chapter on assessment planning.

Plan the Performance Task

To develop a performance assessment task, we follow the same procedure used in developing an extended written response exercise as described in Chapter 6:

- Specify the learning to be demonstrated.

- Specify the materials and constraints within which achievement is to be demonstrated.

- Remind students of the criteria that will be used to evaluate their performance or product.

Here is an example: "Using a stopwatch and a measuring tape, you are to use your knowledge of the physics of motion to determine the percentage of vehicles that exceed the speed limit as they pass the school. Then you are to write a report in which you explain your experimental design and share your results. Your report will be scored on experimental design, understanding of physics equations, and collection and presentation of results. Rubrics are attached."

Tasks can vary along several key dimensions. Think carefully about the following options as you select or create tasks.

One Right Answer or More than One?

Here's a math problem that has one correct answer: "A group of 8 people are all going camping for 3 days and need to carry their own water. They read in a guidebook that 12.5 liters are needed for a party of 5 people for 1 day. Based on this guidebook, what is the minimum amount of water the 8 people should carry?" Here's a sample math problem with more than one right answer: "Estimate the amount of television advertising the typical American fifth grader will see in a year." Both are good tasks; which option you choose depends on which is better suited to the learning target. Open-ended tasks (those with more than one right answer) often encourage more diversity in solution strategies, but the "how much water" problem, a one-right-answer problem, also lends itself to a number of possible solution strategies.

Written, Oral, or Visual Instructions, Activities, and Responses?

Selecting from among these options requires consideration of who and what you are assessing. When demonstrating a performance skill, students will be performing in front of one or more raters. However, the instructions can be written, oral, or visual, depending on students' needs.

When assessing writing in English, the response will, of course, be a written product. But again, the instructions can be written or oral. When assessing young children's ability to construct a story, the instructions will be oral and the product may very well be visual—a series of pictures that tell a story.

Reasoning is usually assessed by means of a written product, but if student needs or other context factors so dictate, you can have students describe their reasoning orally.

Choice or No Choice?

This is a trickier one. Student choice can increase student motivation. Yet, giving students a choice of tasks to perform only makes sense if all the options are of equal level of difficulty and each adequately samples performance for the intended learning target. If, instead of completing several tasks, students are allowed to choose one, they may select the topic with which they are most familiar, in which case you will be unable to determine their performance across the range of tasks that represent the target in question. Or, students might choose to respond only to narrative writing prompts and not to persuasive writing prompts and you will be unable to obtain a good estimate of ability to write for a variety of purposes. Or, students might choose to read aloud only passages with which they are already familiar and you will not get a good estimate of reading fluency.

For these reasons, standardized tests rarely offer students a choice of tasks to perform. There is more leeway in the classroom. Give students no choice if you need to determine whether they can do a specific thing. Give students choice if you will be giving them several opportunities to perform on a range of topics of similar difficulty.

The answer is different if all students are given the same task and they can choose how to respond. For example, if the target is a reasoning proficiency, students might demonstrate their reasoning through writing, an oral presentation, or a visual display.

Individual Work or Group Work?

In an attempt to make assessments as realistic as possible, teachers often have students work in a group. This is fine if one of your targets is to determine how well students work in a group. But, if your target is to ascertain individual achievement, a group product or presentation will not suffice. To get around this problem, some test developers have students work in groups to make sure everyone is beginning the task with a similar knowledge base. Then students work alone to create the product or perform the skill. In general, though, when assessing individual student reasoning proficiency, skill level, or product development capabilities, the task must be completed by each individual.

Spontaneously Occurring or Separate Event?

In a spontaneously occurring event, you evaluate the learning in the course of regular activities. For example, you may look for students' mastery of subject-verb agreement in writing done for other purposes. Sometimes, however, a separate, planned assignment is easier to control. It might take a long time to determine whether individual students can use subject and object pronouns correctly in their writing without an assignment designed to call forth evidence of that learning target.

Timed or Untimed?

Ideally, you would give students as long as they need to complete a task, but obviously there are some upper limits. You can allocate a certain amount of class time to get started and then students can choose to spend as much time completing the task as needed outside of school. Or, you can specify enough time so that almost all students will finish with no problem, and then offer options as needed for the remaining few who don't.

Figure 7.7 represents a worksheet for planning performance tasks. It is also on the CD in the file, "Performance Task Plan."

Figure 7.7   Plan for a Performance Assessment Task

What learning target(s) will I assess?

What will students do?
- What knowledge are they to use?
- What are they to perform or create?
- What conditions are they to adhere to?
- How much time will they have?

How many tasks will I need to sample well? How should these tasks differ to cover the breadth and depth of what I am assessing?

By what criteria will I judge the performance or product?

TRY THIS

Activity 7.5 Develop a Performance Task

Using Figure 7.7 as a guide, develop a performance task for one of the learning targets you listed in Activity 7.1. If you are working as a part of a learning team, share your task with the team and ask them to critique it using either the Task Rubric summary in Figure 7.6 or the complete task rubric found in the CD file, "Performance Task Rubric." Note any suggestions for revision.

Creating Tasks to Elicit Good Writing

Writer Donald Murray tells us that "a principal cause of poor writing received from students is the assignment . . . they have to be well prepared so that the students know the purpose of the assignment and how to fulfill it. Far too many teachers blame the students for poor writing when the fault lies with the teacher's instructions—or lack of instructions" (Murray, 2004, pp. 98). If the goal of the task is to create a written product, it can be helpful to answer the questions that writers must ask to write well:

- What is my role?

- Who is my audience?

- What is the format?

- What is the topic?

- What is the purpose?

These questions are represented by the acronym RAFTS and are illustrated in Figure 7.8. Figure 7.9 shows how we might use these questions to plan the ingredients for a written task in a content area.

Role

Sometimes we ask students simply to write as themselves, as students, but we can often increase their motivation and the relevance of a task if we ask them to assume a role. Think about these questions to devise student roles: Who might be writing about this topic? If it is a content-area topic (social studies, science, mathematics, health, art, and so on), who in the practice of this content area might be writing about this topic? What job might they have?

Audience

When we don't specify an audience, students are writing to us, their teachers, by default. Yet they don't often know how to envision their audience's needs when they write, even if it is us. For writers to make good decisions about what information to include, what terminology to use, and what tone to adopt, they need to think about to whom they are writing. When we ask students to write thorough explanations, it is helpful if we specify an audience who is not familiar with the topic. If we are the audience, either stated or unstated, students often conclude that we know plenty about the topic already. It is hard to write about something to someone who knows more about it that you do, and that particular circumstance doesn't occur in life beyond school very often. In life beyond school, when we are writing to inform, generally, the audience doesn't have the same level of expertise as the writer does. So, in tasks calling for informational writing, consider specifying an audience who might need to know the information and who doesn't already know it.

Figure 7.8   RAFTS Task Design

R ole (Writers must imagine themselves as fulfilling specific roles—for example, as tour guides or scientists or critics—when they write.)

A udience (Writers must always visualize their audiences clearly and consistently throughout the writing process. If they don't, the writing will fail.)

F ormat (Writers must see clearly the format that the finished writing should have, whether brochure, memo, letter to the editor, or article in a magazine.)

T opic (Writers have to select and narrow their topics to manageable proportions, given their audiences and formats.)

S trong verb (words like "cajole," "tempt," "discourage," when serving as definers of the predominant tone of a piece of writing, will guide writers in innumerable choices of words.)

Source: From "Why Grade Student Writing?" by E. Smith, 1990, *Washington English Journal, 13*(1), p. 26. Reprinted by permission.

Figure 7.9   Content-Area Writing Planning Form

Each of the content areas we teach has beyond-school applications. Specifically, people use the knowledge and skills while working, engaging in hobbies, and performing everyday living tasks.

Think of one subject area you teach. Then think of a few jobs/careers that require extensive knowledge and skill in your subject area. Fill in the chart to help you think about "authentic" applications of writing in your field.

My subject area: _____

What job/career requires use of this subject? (ROLE)	What might this person be writing about? (TOPIC)	To accomplish what purpose? (STRONG VERB)	Who might be the audience for this writing? (AUDIENCE)	What format would the writing take? (FORMAT)

Format

This is a simple component of the task. If a beyond-school application of the writing would take the form of a report or an essay, then by all means specify that format. Decisions about format are driven by three considerations: audience, topic, and purpose. If our audience is primary students, our topic is insects, and our purpose is to inform, a report may not be the best format. We can convey interesting and important information about insects in an alphabet book, on a poster, in a sticker book, or on playing cards. If, on the other hand, our audience is a politician, our topic is water quality (as measured by the number and diversity of stream bugs found in water samples), and our purpose is to persuade the politician to take an action, a combination of a letter and a report will be more suited to the task.

Topic

We rarely leave this out of a task or assignment. However, even this aspect can cause student writing to be better or worse, depending on how it is crafted. When we specify the topic for students, we must exercise caution in how we state it. The question here is, are we going to narrow the topic for students or are we going to expect students to narrow it for themselves? If we have been studying the foundations of the U.S. economic system and we want students to write about the Industrial Revolution, we will have to narrow the topic considerably for them to handle it successfully. Or, we can teach students how to narrow topics and let them determine the aspect they will focus on. Considerations in narrowing topics include who the audience is and how much time the writer will have. Generally, the less time, the narrower the topic. We can write all about the topic of friendship if we have a year or two and want to produce a book, but if we have only a week or so, we may wish to write a simple set of instructions for how to be a friend.

Strong Verb

This does not refer to strong verbs in the students' writing. Rather, in this context, *strong verb* refers to the verb we use in the task itself. What is the *purpose* for the writing? Most often writing tasks in school are set to accomplish one of three purposes—to narrate, to inform, or to persuade—and the forms of writing produced are often referred to as narrative, expository, and persuasive. In narrative writing, the purpose is to tell a story, either real (personal narrative or anecdote) or imagined (fictional narrative). In expository writing, the controlling purpose is to inform. In persuasive writing, we may have one of four purposes: to initiate thought, to change thought, to initiate action, or to change action. We may use both narrative and expository writing in service of persuasion, but the ultimate purpose for the writing is to cause something different to happen. Table 7.7 gives examples of verbs that help students understand what kind of writing they are to produce.

Table 7.7   Verbs Matched to Purpose for Writing

Purpose	Sample Verbs and Phrases	
To narrate	Describe an experience Entertain	Tell the story of Tell about a time when
To inform	Clarify Compare Define Discuss	Describe Explain Inform Teach
To persuade	Challenge Convince Defend	Incite Justify Persuade

So, what does it look like when these ingredients come together? Here is a short assignment (in which the student's role is simply to be an informed student): "Explain the mathematics formula we studied today in a memo to a student who was absent." Here is another short assignment: "Teach younger students how to read a contour map by creating a list of instructions accompanied by diagrams and/or illustrations." Figure 7.10 shows an example of a longer assignment following the RAFTS planning design. (Note that we use the word *purpose* in place of *strong verb* when calling out these elements for students.)

Figure 7.10   Example of RAFTS Task

To Your Health

Imagine that a fifth-grade teacher from the elementary school you attended has asked for your help. She is worried that her students don't understand how healthy childhood habits lead to becoming healthy adults. Because she knows that younger children look up to teenagers, she has asked you to teach her students about how to become healthy adults.

> Your assignment:
>
> In a report to be read by fifth-graders, explain the habits they can establish now to help them become healthy adults.

In framing your report, consider the following questions:
* What are healthy childhood habits?
* What does good health involve beyond healthy eating habits?
* What should a child do, and what should a child avoid?

Role	Well-informed older student
Audience	Fifth-graders
Format	Report
Topic	Health habits
Purpose	To teach (inform)

Your report will be judged on the basis of the attached criteria.

Stage 3: Critique the Assessment—Performance Tasks

At this point in performance assessment development, we focus on determining the quality of the task by using the rubric for tasks, summarized in Figure 7.4 and found in its entirety in the CD file, "Performance Task Rubric." The CD file, "Performance Task Sampler," contains sample performance tasks to critique. Activity 7.6 provides practice using the rubric to analyze your own tasks for quality.

DEEPEN UNDERSTANDING

Activity 7.6   Critique Performance Tasks

Gather one or more performance tasks you have used recently with students. Critique them for quality using either the Task Rubric Summary in Figure 7.6 or the whole rubric on the CD in the file, "Performance Task Rubric." Note the revisions you think they need.

Stages 4 and 5: Administer the Assessment, Watch for Problems, and Revise As Needed

As we noted before, problems can still crop up in assessments, even with the best planning, so it is a good idea to keep notes on any facets of a performance task or rubric that may compromise students' ability to show what they know and can do. Figure 7.11 lists potential sources of mismeasurement peculiar to performance assessment. If something appears to have gone awry, and you can't identify the problem from this list, you may want to use the Performance Task Rubric and the Metarubric to troubleshoot your performance assessment.

Figure 7.11   Potential Sources of Bias and Distortion with Performance Assessment

- Lack of reading skills
- Inappropriate or nonexistent scoring criteria
- Evaluator untrained in applying scoring criteria
- Bias due to stereotypic thinking
- Insufficient time or patience to observe and score carefully
- Student doesn't feel safe
- Unfocused or unclear tasks
- Tasks that don't elicit the correct performance
- Biased tasks
- Students don't know the criteria by which they'll be judged

Seven Strategies for Using Rubrics as Instructional Tools in the Classroom

You're all set with a great scoring guide/rubric for evaluating a skill or product in your discipline. But how do you get students to understand and internalize your standards of quality? Performance assessment is a prime context for using assessment to help students learn. The instructional power here resides in using high-quality performance criteria to help students answer the three questions introduced in Chapter 2 to define assessment *for* learning: "Where am I going?"; "Where am I now?"; and "How can I close the gap?" Try out these seven strategies for using a scoring guide as a teaching tool and watch as students become competent, confident self-assessors and improve their performance in any subject.

Activity 7.7   Watch DVD Segment "Teachers on Rubrics"

Think back to rubrics you have used with students and the effects they have had on student learning. Then go to the accompanying DVD segment, "Teachers on Rubrics" for clips of teachers discussing the use of various rubrics in the classroom.

Where Am I Going?

Strategy 1: Provide a Clear and Understandable Vision of the Learning Target

Student-Friendly Versions of Rubrics

Rubrics are a great way to offer students a clear and understandable vision of the learning target. When we are using a rubric to define or clarify the target, sharing it with students at the outset makes sense. Many of our rubrics, unfortunately, are not yet written in language that makes sense to most of our students, in which case we will have to do a little work before sharing them. For example, a rubric to evaluate the characteristic "self-directed learner" designed for use with middle school students has the following statement in the "Accomplished" column for the first trait: "Takes pride in own work: constantly strives for excellence, works hard, aims to exceed standards, and fulfills all commitments in a timely manner."

What is meant by all these words? We used the process from Chapter 3 to clarify the terms. First we identified the words to be defined, looked them up in a dictionary, wrote out their formal definitions, and then converted the formal definitions into student-friendly terms.

Words to be defined: *Exceed standards*—to go beyond a specified level of quality

Student-friendly language: I work to exceed standards. This means I understand what good quality work looks like and I try hard to make sure all my work is at least that good.

Words to be defined: *Fulfill commitments*—to pledge to a certain course of action

Student-friendly language: I fulfill commitments in a timely manner. This means I can keep track of what I have promised to do and make sure it all gets done on time.

TRY THIS

Activity 7.8 Student-Friendly Rubric Language

Look again at the foreign language draft rubric in Table 7.6. Identify two words that students might not understand. Look these up in a dictionary and covert the definitions into student-friendly language.

Next, look at the rubrics you use in your classroom. Identify one to convert into student-friendly language. Rework the rubric so that students would understand the terms, using the procedures given here.

Introducing the Rubric to Students

Before we hand a rubric out, we may want to introduce the concept of *quality* to students, so they have a better understanding of what they will be seeing in the rubric. In Chapter 2 we described the process we would follow in general terms. Here we use a specific example, illustrating how we would introduce a rubric for writing:

1. Ask students what is important in good writing and record whatever they say on chart paper. Don't try to get them to say certain words or phrases, and don't reword their responses. At this initial stage, we want to hear the words they use to describe quality as they understand it.

2. Read aloud a sample of writing having strengths they may not have thought of. (It can also have weaknesses, but the initial sample should be strong overall. We tend to choose a piece written by a student a little older than the group, selecting an example that will illustrate strong *Content* and *Voice*, two traits students often don't mention right away.) Ask students to think about their list of what is important in good writing. What might they like to add based on the piece they are listening to? You can repeat this with several samples over time and create a multipage list, or you can proceed to the next step after sharing one sample.

3. Tell students, "You have come up with a good list. Many of the things you have identified are also on the list that teachers and strong writers have created. Their list was also long—too long to remember everything—so they decided to see if they could group ideas into categories. They came up with X categories [where X equals the number of

traits in your rubric], which we call traits." Then share the names of the traits in your rubric. If for example, you are using a six-trait writing rubric, you would show a poster or overhead transparency with the six traits listed.

4. Next, share your own definitions of the traits in your scoring guide. (We like to use bulleted lists for each trait, with phrases in student-friendly language as much as possible. Figure 7.12 shows a poster we would use to introduce the trait of *Ideas and Content* to upper elementary and middle school students.) Share definitions one trait at a time and ask students to identify similarities between their list and those you are sharing. "Did we say something about *Ideas and Content* on our list? Where?"

5. Pass out copies of your student-friendly scoring guide. Let students know that as a class, they will be using this scoring guide to examine and assess writing of all kinds—first the work of others, like the samples you have used, and then their own. (A student-friendly version of the six-trait writing scoring guide is on the CD in the file, "Rubric Sampler.")

Figure 7.12   Sample Poster Introducing the Trait of Ideas and Content

Ideas and Content . . . a clear message

- Narrow, manageable focus
- Rich, relevant detail
- Details are interesting, important, and informative!

Strategy 2: Use Examples and Models of Strong and Weak Work

Teaching Students to Use the Rubric to Evaluate Examples

First, gather models of strong and weak work—anonymous strong and weak student work, published strong (and weak, if available) work, and your own work. Share anonymous student samples that model both good work and problems students commonly experience, especially the perennial, pervasive problems. Here is an application of this strategy specific to mathematics. (Strong and weak samples of student work are on the CD in the files, "Samples of Student Writing" and "Student Math Problem Solving.")

1. Choose one trait to focus on at a time. Find a mathematics problem that has anchor papers for each score point on your rubric.

2. Ask students to solve the problem. If you are working with younger students, you may wish to guide students through it using the following procedure:

   - Read the problem together. What is it asking you to do?

   - Underline important information in the problem.

   - Think about how you could solve this problem. What strategies could you use? What procedure will you follow?

   - As you solve the problem, show and tell your thinking. Show with pictures, charts, graphs, or diagrams. Tell using mathematical language to describe your reasoning, the strategies you used, and the procedure you followed.

3. Show an overhead transparency of a strong anonymous response to the problem. Have students score the response (don't tell them it's a strong response), for one trait using the student-friendly scoring guide. To do this (using a five-point scoring guide as the example), ask students to first decide independently whether the response is strong or weak. If they think it's a strong response, they read the scoring guide description of a "5;" if they think it's a weak response, they read the description of a "1." If the extreme ("5" or "1") description doesn't fit the response, students read the "3" description. If the response has some of "1" and some of "3," it's a "2." If it has some of "5" and some of "3," it's a "4." You may ask students to underline the statements in the scoring guide that describe the work they are examining.

4. Once students have settled on a score independently, have them talk in small groups to share their scores, using the language of the scoring guide to explain their reasoning.

5. Ask the class to vote and tally their scores on an overhead transparency. Then ask for volunteers to share their scores and their reasons. Listen for, and encourage, use of the language of the scoring guide.

6. Repeat this process with a weak anonymous sample student response, focusing on the same trait. Do this several times, mixing up strong and weak papers, until students are able to distinguish between strong and weak and give rationales reflecting the concepts in the scoring guide.

Thoughts on Strategies 1 and 2

Remember, when we say "score" in the context of formative assessment, we do not mean "giving a grade for the gradebook." We mean evaluating anonymous student work to help students differentiate levels of quality. No grade is needed for this.

TRY THIS

Activity 7.9   Adapt Strategies 1 and 2

Think about how Strategies 1 and 2 would play out in your classroom. Translate their steps into one or more lessons you could use with your students to refine their vision of quality. Try the lessons out with your class. If you are working with a learning team, share what you did and how it worked.

Where Am I Now?

Strategy 3: Offer Regular Descriptive Feedback

Descriptive feedback points out to students their work's strengths and weaknesses before it is too late—before the final grade—and models the kind of thinking we want them to do themselves about their work. If students have become familiar with the language of the rubric, we can use that language as the basis for descriptive feedback. If we are focusing on one trait at a time, we only need give descriptive feedback on that one trait. This has the effect of narrowing the scope of work for both the teacher and the student. With struggling students, we can show them they do indeed know some things and we can limit the things they need to work on at one time to a less daunting, more manageable number. Our feedback may be verbal, such as that given in a brief student-teacher conference, or we may choose to offer written feedback.[1]

The Three-Minute Conference

If you confer with students as a way to offer feedback on their work, consider asking them to do some thinking prior to meeting with you. This causes the conference to take less time and your feedback to be more meaningful. For this activity, you can have students complete the form in Figure 7.13 (also available on the CD in the file, "Using Feedback to Set Goals").

1. Identify a focus for the feedback—narrow it, if needed. Have them focus only on a few aspects of quality—either you choose the aspects of quality based on what you have been teaching them to do or let them choose, depending on their level of sophistication. (For example, in writing, a teacher may be focusing on how to include details that are interesting, important, and informative, which is part of the trait of *Ideas and Content* in her scoring guide. So she may ask students to think about the quality of their details.)

2. Before meeting with you (or submitting their work for your feedback) have students use the scoring guide to identify what aspects of quality are present in a particular piece of their work. Encourage them to use the language of the scoring guide.

3. Have them follow the same procedure to identify one or two aspects of quality they think need work.

4. Offer your feedback. If you agree, it's simple. If you can, point out a strength the student overlooked. Add to or modify what the student needs to work on, if needed.

5. Ask students to take their own and your opinions into account and decide what to do next. At first students may set large, unmanageable, or nonspecific goals. Help them, if needed, focus their plan on what is doable in the short term.

6. If your students have practiced giving formative feedback, encourage students to use each other as feedback providers.

Offering Written Feedback

You can also use the form in Figure 7.13 as a vehicle for offering written feedback. The student completes the top information and "My Opinion" and turns it in with the work. You fill out the teacher portion as you are reviewing the work, hand it back, and then the student fills in the plan. You may wish to meet with those students whose opinions differ sharply from yours.

Highlighting the Scoring Guide

This idea, from Shannon Thompson (personal communication, 2001), a curriculum specialist in the Central Kitsap School District, is another quick way to offer descriptive feedback, while also getting students to think in terms of their work's strengths and weaknesses. First, students self-assess by highlighting words and phrases on the scoring guide that describe their work. Let's say they use a yellow highlighter. You collect the work with highlighted scoring guides attached and review it. You mark your own judgment of the work's

Figure 7.13   Using Feedback to Set Goals

TRAIT(S): _____   NAME: _____

NAME OF PAPER: _____   DATE: _____

MY OPINION
My strengths are_____

_____

What I think I need to work on is _____

_____

MY TEACHER'S OPINION
Strengths:_____

_____

Work on:_____

_____

MY PLAN
What I will do now:_____

_____

Next time I'll ask for feedback from: _____

_____

Source: Adapted from *Assessment* FOR *Learning: An Action Guide for School Leaders* (p. 193), by S. Chappuis, R. J. Stiggins, J. Arter, and J. Chappuis, 2004, Portland, OR: Assessment Training Institute. Copyright © 2006, 2004 Educational Testing Service. Adapted by permission.

strengths and weaknesses using another color highlighter, let's say blue. Areas where the two colors merge, turning green, represent agreement. Words and phrases where the two colors remain separate represent additional feedback. You may wish to meet with those students whose scoring guides have a significant number of phrases remaining yellow and blue to clarify their understanding of quality. This strategy will work well only if students have had enough practice evaluating anonymous samples to understand the language of the scoring guide.

How Do These Activities Benefit You and Your Students?

Engaging in self-assessment prior to receiving feedback and in action planning afterwards shifts the primary responsibility for improving the work to the student, where it belongs. If you use this as part of your formative conferences with students, you will notice that gradually you will have fewer students to meet with and more students thinking about how the elements of quality you are teaching relate to their own work. In either written or verbal feedback situations, if you are going to the trouble of providing feedback, you want it to be used. Students are more likely to understand and act on your suggestions because you have asked them to access prior knowledge, which provides a mental "hook" for new information.

Strategy 4: Teach Students to Self-Assess and Set Goals

If students have had experience using rubrics following the first three strategies, when it comes time for them to self-assess, they will be prepared to do the kind of in-depth objective thinking about the quality of their work. All we as teachers have to do is provide the time and the opportunity to do so. (We discuss self-assessment and goal setting in depth in Chapter 12.)

How Can I Close the Gap?

Strategy 5: Design Lessons to Focus on One Aspect of Quality at a Time

Sometimes students must master numerous or complex elements of quality and cannot attend to all the elements at one time. So, our fifth strategy suggests that we zero in selectively in our daily teaching. One of the added benefits of creating a bulleted list to represent each trait in a rubric is that, if well crafted, the list defines relatively narrow components of quality that lend themselves to individual teaching and practice. Consider a science rubric consisting of three traits—designing the experiment, collecting and reporting data, and drawing conclusions—where the first trait includes the quality of the hypothesis. We can teach focused lessons on how to create a high-quality hypothesis, and students can focus on just this aspect of quality until they understand it.

Strategy 6: Teach Students Focused Revision

A logical outgrowth of students learning about how to create high-quality hypotheses is that they will be able to turn to previous hypotheses they have written and revise them. Strategy 6 gives students practice at revising their own and others' work.

For example, in a writing class, after students evaluate a piece of their own work they can create a revision plan, telling how they would make their paper stronger for a particular trait. In a mathematics class, students may evaluate an anonymous work sample and work in pairs to write a letter to the (anonymous) author describing how to strengthen the solution for a given trait.

Students' revisions are based on their understanding of the scoring guide, based on our descriptive feedback, based on their self-evaluation, and based on the tips we have offered through direct instruction. They are not stuck, hands waving in the air, waiting until we can get to them, and then mumbling the mantra, "I don't get it."

Strategy 7: Engage Students in Self-Reflection, and Let Them Keep Track of and Share Their Learning

The language of the rubric becomes the language of self-reflection as well. In reflecting on how they have grown in achievement, students can use the concepts, terms, and phrases representing levels of quality to describe their journey as a reader, writer, math problem solver, social studier, and so forth. Portfolios, as we describe in Chapter 11, are an effective vehicle for collecting and sharing evidence of growth, or achievement, and of accomplishments to celebrate.

Table 7.8 presents a summary of the seven strategies and their rationales.

Table 7.8   Assessment *for* Learning—A Practical Performance Assessment Application

	Strategy	Rationale
1	Provide an understandable vision of the learning target. Teach students the concepts underpinning quality in your scoring guide by asking them what they already know (What makes a good ___?), then show how their prior knowledge links to your definition of quality.	Showing the connection between new information and knowledge students already have helps it all make sense and provides a link to long-term memory. It also lays the foundation for students understanding the upcoming learning.
2	Use models of strong and weak work. • Share anonymous strong and weak student work. Have students use the scoring guide to evaluate the samples, then share their reasons, using the language of the scoring guide. • Share published strong (and weak, if available) work. Let students comment on the quality of published examples and your own work, using the language of the scoring guide. • Share your own work. Model the "messy underside" of creating the performance or product for students.	Student performances improve when they understand the meaning of quality. This strategy teaches students to distinguish between strong and weak products or performances, and to articulate the differences. It also encourages teachers to share aspects of the beauty of their discipline. What does it look/sound/feel like when it's done especially well? Modeling the messy underside for students reassures them that high-quality work doesn't always start out looking like high-quality work. As teachers, we tend to smooth over this part, so when the going gets messy for students, they may infer they are "doing it wrong." What does high-quality work look like at its beginning stages? Model it.
3	Offer descriptive feedback instead of grades on practice work, pointing out what students are doing right as well as what they need to work on, using the language of the scoring guide.	Students need descriptive feedback while they're learning. It tells them how close they are to reaching the target, and it models the kind of thinking we want them to be able to do, ultimately, when self-assessing.

Table 7.8   (Continued)

4	Teach students to self-assess and set goals. Ask them to identify their own strengths and areas for improvement, using the language of the scoring guide.	Periodic articulation about their understanding of quality and about their own strengths and weaknesses is essential to students' ability to improve. Self-assessment is a necessary part of learning, not an add-on that we do if we have time or the "right" students. Struggling students *are* the right students.
5	Design lessons around the elements of quality in the scoring guide. Reorganize what you already teach and find or create lessons to fill in the gaps. Focus on one aspect of quality at a time.	Novice learners cannot improve simultaneously all elements of quality of a complex skill or product. If your scoring guide represents a complex skill or product, students will benefit from a "mini-lesson" approach, wherein they are allowed to learn and master a portion at a time.
6	Teach students focused revision. Let students work in pairs to revise anonymous samples. Once they have evaluated a weak sample, ask them to use their reasons to go further: What could you do to make this receive a higher score?	Students need the opportunity to practice using the scoring guide as a guide to revision. That way, they, not their teachers, are doing the thinking about revision and the learning.
7	Engage students in self-reflection. Let them keep track of and share what they know.	Any activity that requires students to reflect on what they are learning and to share their progress with an audience both reinforces the learning and helps them develop insights into themselves as learners. By reflecting on their learning, students are learning more deeply and will remember it longer.

TRY THIS

Activity 7.10 Create a Student-Involved Performance Assessment Plan

Select a rubric as the basis for your plan. It can be one of your state rubrics, another one you currently use, or one you plan to use. The rubric should be a general one, that is, it should apply to more than one task—ideally to a constellation of tasks representing an important reasoning, skill, or product learning target in your content area.

Plan how you would use this rubric as a teaching tool. Begin with Strategy 1 and decide which of the recommendations would fit your subject, rubric, and student needs. Proceed through the strategies, making modifications as needed. Planning forms for this activity can be found on the CD in the file, "AFL Plan."

If you are working as a part of a learning team, you may wish to share your plans with each other. Suggestions for how to facilitate a sharing session are also included on the CD in the file, "AFL Plan."

DEEPEN UNDERSTANDING

Activity 7.11 Watch Video, *Designing Performance Assessments* for *Learning*

Judy Arter and Jan Chappuis show how to evaluate rubrics and performance tasks for quality. This video also includes a segment on how to develop a rubric, with examples taken from the work of a team of science teachers. If you are working with a learning team, watch the video, do the activities, and evaluate one or more of your own tasks and rubrics together.

Summary

Performance assessment is assessment based on observation and judgment—we observe or review a performance or product and make a judgment about its quality. The challenge with this type of essentially subjective assessment is to make it as objective as possible. Performance assessments consist of two parts: a task—what we ask the students to do—and criteria—the basis for judging quality. Much of the work in making performance assessment as objective as possible comes in the area of refining the criteria to maximize rater agreement.

Performance assessment is well suited to evaluating reasoning, skill, and product learning targets.

To select high-quality performance criteria, we look at four dimensions of quality: *Content, Clarity, Practicality,* and *Technical Quality/Fairness.* Do the criteria cover features of work that really define quality? Are each one of these features defined clearly and illustrated with models at all levels of quality? Is the rubric practical for teachers and students to use? Is there anything in the criteria that might disadvantage any group of students?

The steps in developing rubrics and performance criteria that have maximal usefulness in the classroom are (1) establish our knowledge base, (2) gather samples of student performance, (3) sort the samples by level of quality and describe the features of the work at each level, (4) cluster the features into traits, (5) identify good examples to illustrate each level, and (6) revise the rubric as it is used.

To select high-quality performance tasks, examine them for five dimensions of quality: *Content, Clarity, Feasibility, Fairness and Accuracy,* and *Sampling.* Does the content of the task match our learning targets and performance criteria? Is it clear to students what they are supposed to do? Can the task be carried out within the time allowed given the materials at hand? Is there anything in the task that might disadvantage any particular student or group of students? Do we have enough tasks that cover enough dimensions of the targets to ensure that we will be able to infer overall level of student mastery of the target?

To develop performance tasks, we follow the steps we used in creating extended response exercises: specify the learning to be demonstrated, specify the conditions—materials and constraints, and include the criteria by which student work will be judged. We make a series of design decisions along the way: One right answer or more than one? Written, oral and/or visual instructions, activities, and responses? Student choice or no student choice? Individual work or group work? Spontaneously occurring event or separate event? Timed or untimed? Our answers to each of these questions are dependent on the nature of the learning target to be assessed, how we intend to use the information, and the needs of our students.

The rubrics associated with performance assessments provide the classic example of how to involve students in assessment. Rubrics can be used to help students understand where they are going, where they are now, and how to close the gap. With respect to understanding where they are going, good rubrics define quality so that students can see it. They provide a vocabulary for talking about features of quality work. Using models of anonymous strong and weak performance not only helps students deepen their understanding of the features of a quality performance or product, but also allows students to become accurate raters of performance. This accuracy is essential before students begin to self-assess.

Rubrics are also very helpful in allowing students to know where they are now and how to improve. Teachers can use them to provide descriptive feedback to students. They can also be used by students for self-assessment, goal setting, and self-reflection. This chapter presented extensive examples of each of these uses.

Tracking Your Learning—Possible Portfolio Entries

Any of the activities included in Chapter 7 can be used as portfolio entries. Remember, the learning targets for this book are outlined in Figure 7.1, listed in Table 1.2, and described in detail in Chapter 1. The portfolio entry cover sheet provided on the CD in the file, "Portfolio Entry Cover Sheet," will prompt you to think about how each item you select reflects your learning with respect to one or more of these learning targets.

DEEPEN UNDERSTANDING

Activity 7.12   Term Paper Assignment

Read the term paper assignment case study in Figure 7.14. Think about the following questions and discuss them with your team:

1. If you were a student who worked this hard to receive this feedback, how would you react?

2. What went wrong here?

3. Which problems could have been avoided? How?

TRY THIS

Activity 7.13   Help Students Understand Performance Criteria

We can use examples from everyday life to help students understand the concept of levels of quality in preparation for helping them understand the use of rubrics to self-assess. This example uses pizza. Specifically, students must answer the following questions: "What makes a great pizza?"; "What makes a good pizza?"; "What makes a minimum pizza?"; and "What makes a pizza that is below standard?"

The pizza rubric drawn by a first-grade student is shown in Figure 7.15. Think about or discuss the following questions:

1. What evidence in the rubric indicates that this student understands the concept of levels of quality?

2. What questions would you ask to help students distinguish between levels of quality of pizza if you were to ask them to build a scoring guide for pizza?

3. If you were to engage your students in a similar rubric-building activity, what food, familiar item, or process would be appropriate in your setting? The key here is to use something that students have experience with and know well so that all can contribute their ideas.

4. How might you build on this activity to take students into an academic learning target? What might be a good starting academic learning target for your students?

Figure 7.14   Term Paper Assignment Case Study

Mr. Jones, an experienced high school English teacher, gave his class the following assignment: "Read four novels by the same author and write a literary term paper arising from that experience. Develop a guiding thesis and use insights derived from your reading to defend your thesis." He had been covering American literature for decades and had been assigning term papers in this way for as long. It always worked well.

Marissa, an avid reader, had no trouble finding a socially conscious author and searching out and reading four compelling novels about the justices and injustices of our culture. The author was a woman and her stories focused on the female experience in United States history—the roles, challenges, and triumphs of women. However, Marissa had no confidence as a writer, even though her parents had told her that her writing showed talent. She wasn't buying it.

The assignment contained no information about the attributes of a good term paper. "Just apply what you've already learned," said Marissa's teacher. "Think of it as a term paper like all the others." The problem, however, was that Marissa had received almost no prior instruction in how to organize, let alone compose, such a piece. Nevertheless, she picked a prominent character from each novel and structured her paper around a comparative analysis of these women. She established the standards of comparison up front and examined key similarities and differences between and among them. To conclude, she used her comparison to speculate about the character and experience of the author.

She had to turn the draft in by a specified date or have her grade for the project reduced. She met the deadline only to discover that she wouldn't get it back—after all how could one teacher review 180 drafts! (A valid point—especially when there would be another 180 final versions to read and evaluate later.) But the teacher assured the class that as the final deadline approached, they would thank him for requiring the preliminary version.

Over the next two weeks, Marissa worked to polish her paper. She revised and edited slightly—reading paragraphs to her parents and worrying that it just wasn't good enough. Finally the due date arrived and Marissa turned her paper in.

Two weeks later the paper was returned. On the cover, Mr. Jones had written two things: "B+" (certainly a very good grade by most standards, especially for a first big paper) and a single comment: "You used the word 'she' entirely too many times in this paper." There was no other feedback.

When Marissa showed the paper to her parents, they asked what she herself thought of her efforts. She dropped the paper in the waste basket, wondered aloud what the teacher really thought of her work, said she needn't have wasted so much time worrying or working, and left the room. For Marissa, this product-based performance assessment was a frustrating and unfulfilling experience.

Source: Adapted from *Practice with Student-Involved Classroom Assessment* (pp. 156–157), by J. A. Arter & K. U. Busick, 2001, Portland, OR: Assessment Training Institute. Copyright © 2006, 2001 Educational Testing Service. Adapted by permission.

Figure 7.15   First-Draft Pizza Rubric

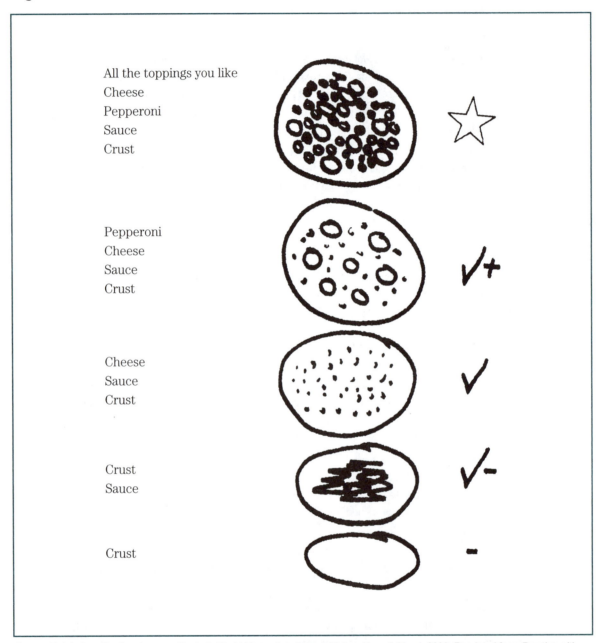

All the toppings you like
Cheese
Pepperoni
Sauce
Crust

Pepperoni
Cheese
Sauce
Crust

Cheese
Sauce
Crust

Crust
Sauce

Crust

Notes

1. The following subsections are adapted from pp. 194–195 of S. Chappuis, R. J. Stiggins, J. Arter, & J. Chappuis, *Assessment FOR learning: An Action Guide for School Leaders*, 2004, Portland, OR: Assessment Training Institute. Copyright © 2006, 2004 Educational Testing Service. Adapted by permission.

CHAPTER

Personal Communication
as Assessment

[**"W**] ho remembers what a noun is?" "How would you describe the workings of a food web to someone who had never heard of one?" "What patterns do you notice in this sequence of numbers?" "What are the defining characteristics of a free-market economy?" We use personal communication as a form of assessment constantly in the classroom. Most often it serves as assessment *for* learning—to introduce a topic or to probe students' depth of understanding, for example—but with careful attention to specific rules of evidence, we can get valuable information in service of assessment *of* learning, as well. To promote accurate and effective use of personal communication, in this chapter we address the following topics:[1]

- When to use personal communication assessment.

- The types of personal communication assessment—instructional questions and answers, class discussions, conferences and interviews, oral exams, conversations with others about students, and student journals.

- How to avoid possible sources of bias that can distort results.

- How to use personal communication as assessment *for* learning.

Chapter 8 focuses on the shaded portions of Figures 8.1 and 8.2.

Figure 8.1   Keys to Quality Classroom Assessment

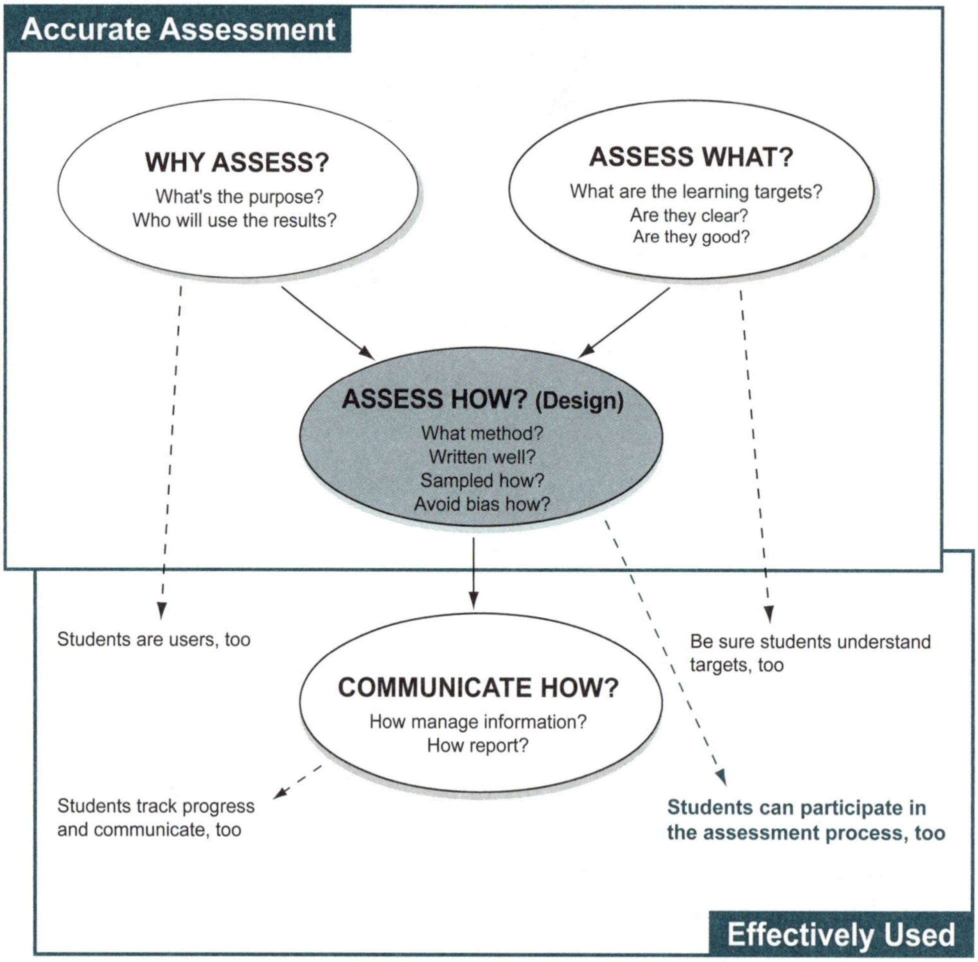

Accurate Assessment

WHY ASSESS?
What's the purpose?
Who will use the results?

ASSESS WHAT?
What are the learning targets?
Are they clear?
Are they good?

ASSESS HOW? (Design)
What method?
Written well?
Sampled how?
Avoid bias how?

Students are users, too

Be sure students understand targets, too

COMMUNICATE HOW?
How manage information?
How report?

Students track progress and communicate, too

Students can participate in the assessment process, too

Effectively Used

Figure 8.2   A Plan for Matching Assessment Methods with Achievement Targets

Target to Be Assessed	Assessment Method			
	Selected Response	Extended Written Response	Performance Assessment	Personal Communication
Knowledge Mastery				
Reasoning Proficiency				
Performance Skills				
Ability to Create Products				

Source: Adapted from *Student-Involved Assessment* for *Learning*, 4th ed. (p. 178), by R. J. Stiggins, 2005, Upper Saddle River, NJ: Merrill/Prentice Hall. Copyright © 2005 by Pearson Education, Inc. Adapted by permission of Pearson Education, Inc.

This chapter does not follow the same format as the three previous chapters on assessment methods, where we systematically went through five stages of assessment planning and development—planning, developing, critiquing, administering, and revising. Personal communication tends to be more informal. Therefore, our focus is more on what to keep in mind to make results from this assessment method as informative as possible.

When to Use Personal Communication Assessment

There are several conditions to keep in mind when deciding whether personal communication will yield accurate and useful information.

Matching Method to Target

The first consideration for using personal communication assessment is the type of learning target to be assessed, as described in the target–method match section of Chapter 4. Personal communication assessment is good for assessing knowledge, reasoning, and those skill targets requiring oral communication, such as speaking a foreign language, participating in group discussion, and giving oral presentations.

TRY THIS

Activity 8.1 Learning Targets Best Assessed with Personal Communication

To begin applying the content of this chapter to your own context, please find five or so knowledge, reasoning, and/or oral language skills targets in the curriculum materials or standards documents you use. Label each as knowledge, reasoning, and/or oral language skills and save them for later use.

Other Contextual Conditions

Several other considerations influence the choice of personal communication assessment:

- The teacher and the student must share a common language. We don't just mean a shared vocabulary and grammar, although these obviously are critical to sound assessment. We also mean a common sense of the manner in which a culture shares meaning through verbal and nonverbal cues.

- Shy or withdrawn students may not perform well in this kind of assessment context, regardless of their real achievement. To make this method work, two people must connect in an open, communicative manner. For some students, this simply is too risky, often for reasons beyond the teacher's control. There also is the danger that students with very outgoing, confident personalities will try to lay down a "smoke screen" to misrepresent their real achievement.

- Personal communication works best as assessment when students feel they are in a safe learning environment. We create safe learning environments when we make it clear to our students that it is okay to grow at different rates. We promote safety when we permit students to succeed or fail in private, without an embarrassing public spotlight. Establishing safety for students requires establishing a humane peer environment sensitive to the plight of those who perform less well and supportive of their attempts to grow. In addition, we help students feel safe enough to risk learning when they have the opportunity to improve and perform again later to demonstrate their higher level of success.

- Personal communication works best as assessment when students understand that sometimes as their teachers we need an honest answer, not their attempt at a best possible answer or the answer they think will please us. Students must know that if they give us what they deem to be the socially desirable response to a question, a response that misrepresents the truth about their achievement or feelings, then we will be less able to help them.

- Because there are sometimes no tangible results, such as a grade or a score, from assessments conducted via personal communication, records of achievement must be managed carefully. When the information is to be used only over a span of a few moments or hours on narrow targets for a few students, extended record keeping is unnecessary. When the context includes many students, complex targets, and a requirement of later use, we must absolutely keep track of results. This process is helped by high-quality rubrics for the reasoning or skills being observed or discussed.

- Use personal communication assessment only when it is certain to generate enough information to make an adequate inference about student performance. This is a sampling issue. If a teacher wants to determine if students have understood the geometry concept just taught he might ask a few oral questions. If he only calls on students who raise their hands, he may not obtain a representative sample from which to make an accurate generalization about the whole class's level of understanding.

  Sampling problems can also arise when a teacher asks the wrong questions. For example, if a teacher intends to determine how well students can problem solve using a geometry concept, she will not be able to make a sound inference if questions require recall only.

Types of Personal Communication Assessment

As with the other assessment methods, personal communication includes a variety of assessment formats: questioning, conferences and interviews, class discussions, oral examinations, and journals and logs. Some of these formats are face-to-face communication, while some are written communication. We group them all into the category of personal communication because their central intent is to create a dialogue between student and teacher.

Instructional Questions and Answers

You are no doubt intimately acquainted with this format. As instruction proceeds, we pose questions for students to answer, or we ask students to question each other. We use this practice to encourage thinking and deepen learning, and also to provide information about the learning. We listen to answers, interpret them (either by means of internally held standards or a written rubric), infer the student's level of attainment or misconceptions, and act accordingly. In this section we first discuss questioning used to assess students' level of understanding or misconceptions. We then look at questioning strategies that encourage thinking and deepen learning.

Assessing Level of Understanding

The following are keys to successful use of oral questioning as an assessment device:

- Plan key questions in advance of instruction to ensure proper alignment with the target and with students' capabilities.

- Ask clear, brief questions that help students focus on a relatively narrow range of acceptable responses.

- Probe various kinds of reasoning, as appropriate. Figure 8.3 shows question stems and key words that elicit various types of reasoning.

- Ask the question first and then call on someone to respond. This keeps all students on their toes.

- Call on both volunteers and nonvolunteers. This, too, keeps all students in the game.

- After posing a question, wait five seconds for a response. Giving students time to think before answering increases desirable outcomes—the number and length of responses, the quality of responses, student confidence, and student and teacher attitudes and expectations (Rowe, 1972; 1987).

Questioning Strategies That Promote Reasoning

When we use personal communication in this manner, we are engaging in assessment *for* learning; we are using the assessment itself to teach and deepen reasoning proficiencies. We present some suggestions here. For more detail see Clarke (2001), Hunkins (1995), Knight (2000), National Literacy Strategy (1998), and Rowe (1972, 1987).

- Use questions that go beyond recall. Label the type of reasoning that you are looking for—comparing, analyzing, evaluating, and so forth—and include the specific reasoning verb in the question.

- Ask a question in different ways to maximize student understanding of what is being asked.

- Use questions to summarize or emphasize key points for learning.

- Wait at least five seconds after asking a question before selecting a student to respond.

- Ask students to discuss their thinking in pairs or small groups. A reporter speaks on behalf of the group.

- Ask all students to write down an answer, then collect responses and read out a selection.

- Give students a choice among different possible answers and ask them all to vote on the options.

- Ask students to paraphrase each other's questions and responses.

- Invite students to elaborate. For example, "Say a little more about . . ." This encourages students to develop more complex contributions. Pursue a line of questioning with individuals to understand their thinking.

- Echo what students say. For example, "So you think that . . ." This helps students clarify their own thinking, and communicates that you value their response.

- Ask clarifying questions. For example, "What do you mean by that?" This sets the expectation that vague answers are unacceptable, and encourages thoughtful, precise answers.

- Let students observe and comment on responses; don't do all the responding yourself.

- Model the response patterns that you'd like to see from students. For example:

  1. Speculate on a given topic. This encourages students to explore ideas and understand that uncertainty is a normal stage in the thinking process.

  2. Reflect on topics. For example, "Yes, I sometimes think that . . ." This encourages students to explore the topic rather than seeking a single answer.

  3. Don't be afraid to say that you don't know the answer to a question. Follow "I don't know the answer" with "How could we find an answer?"

Assessment for Learning with Questioning Strategies

Just as with written selected response, short answer, and extended response assessments, oral questions need not always flow from teacher to student. Students can be taught various question stems that elicit different patterns of reasoning for whatever content they are studying. Students can learn to use question stems, such as those in Figure 8.3. They can also learn to provide descriptive feedback to peers or to self-assess using the rubrics you will be using to evaluate their performances, as described in Chapters 2 and 7.

Figure 8.3   Question Stems and Verbs That Elicit Different Types of Reasoning

---

Words that elicit recall of information:

Explain, understand, describe, identify, tell, name, list, give examples, define, label, match, choose, recall, recognize, select

Question stems that elicit various patterns of reasoning:

Analyze:

- What are the important components, parts, or ingredients of _____?
- What is the order in which _____ happened? What are the steps?
- What is the main idea of what you read or saw? What are the details that support this main idea?
- What familiar pattern do you notice? (Examples include familiar story structure and numerical sequence.)
- What is this question asking?
- What information do you need to solve this problem or approach this task?

Figure 8.3   (Continued)

Compare/contrast:

- Discriminate (or distinguish) between _____ and _____.
- How are _____ and _____ alike and/or different?
- Think of an analogy for _____.
- Can you think of something else that is similar? (For example, what other stories have similar openings, characters, plots, or themes?)

Synthesize:

- What do you conclude from _____ and _____?
- How would you combine, blend, or organize _____ and _____?
- How might you adapt or modify _____ to fit _____?
- How would you describe _____ to someone else?
- How might you formulate a response or answer to _____?

Classify:

- Find an example of _____.
- What is _____ an example of?
- How might you sort_____ into groups or categories?

Infer/deduce:

- Predict what will happen next.
- Why did the author do _____?
- What are the implications of _____?
- What can you conclude from the evidence or pieces of information? (For example, "What does that tell us about numbers that end in five or zero?")

Evaluate:

- Take a position on _____ and justify, support, defend, or prove your position.
- What is your opinion on _____? What evidence do you have to support your opinion?
- Appraise, critique, judge, or evaluate _____. Support your appraisal, critique, judgment, or evaluation with evidence.
- Dispute or judge this position. Is it defendable or not? Why or why not?
- Is this _____ successful? What evidence do you have to support your opinion?
- Could _____ be better? Why or why not?
- Which is better? Why?

TRY THIS

Activity 8.2   Generate Oral Questions

Refer to the list of learning targets that you created in Activity 8.1. Choose one and list several questions you could ask to determine students' preexisting knowledge of the topic, and/or generate different levels of reasoning about the topic. If you are working with a learning team, share your questions and refine them. Try them out and report your observations and conclusions.

TRY THIS

Activity 8.3   Practice Questioning Strategies

In this chapter, we have suggested various questioning strategies—use of wait time, ways to encourage all students to respond to questions, and modeling the types of responses we want from students. Individually, or with your learning team, make a checklist of one or more of these strategies you want to practice in the classroom. Videotape or watch each other during a questioning session. Analyze the videotapes for instances when the targeted questioning strategies were used well and when an opportunity for a questioning strategy was missed.

This activity can be expanded to include students as questioners and as observers and evaluators of questioning strategies.

Conferences and Interviews

Some student-teacher conferences serve as structured or unstructured audits of student achievement in which the objective is to talk about what students have learned and have yet to learn. We converse with students about their levels of achievement; levels of comfort with the material they are to master; specific needs, interests, and desires; or any other achievement-related topics that contribute to an effective teaching and learning environment.

It is helpful to remember that interviews or conferences need not be conceived as every-pupil, standardized affairs, with each event a carbon copy of the others. We might meet with only one student or vary the focus of the conference with students who have different needs. The following are keys to successful use of conference and interview assessment formats:

- Carefully think out and plan questions in advance. Remember, students can share in their preparation.

- Focus on particular learning targets.

- Plan for enough uninterrupted time to conduct the entire interview or conference.

- Be sure to conclude each meeting with a summary of the lessons learned and their implications for how you and the student will work together in the future. Let the student summarize, if appropriate.

One important strength of the interview or conference as a mode of assessment lies in the impact it can have on our relationships with students. When conducted in a context where we have been up front about expectations, students understand the achievement target, and all involved are invested in student success, conferences have the effect of empowering students to take responsibility for at least part of the assessment of their own progress. As an example of how this can work, remember the description of the three-minute conference in Chapter 7. We offer more information about options for structuring student-teacher conferences in Chapter 12.

Class Discussions

When students participate in class discussions, their contributions can reveal a great deal about their levels of understanding and their achievements. Class discussions have the simultaneous effect of enhancing both student learning and their ability to use what they know.

To take advantage of the strengths of this method of assessment while minimizing the impact of potential weaknesses, think about the following:

- Prepare questions or discussion issues in advance to focus on the intended achievement target.

- Be sure students are aware of your focus in evaluating their contributions. Are you judging the content of students' contributions or the form of their contribution—how they communicate? Be clear about what it means to be good at each. Consider using a rubric to help establish clarity. An example, "Group Discussion Rubric," appears on the CD in the file, "Rubric Sampler."

- Keep in mind that the public display of achievement or lack thereof is risky for some students. Provide those students with other, more private means of demonstrating achievement.

- In contexts where achievement information derived from participation in discussion is used to influence high-stakes decisions—assessments *of* learning—keep dependable records of performance. Rely on more than your memory of their contributions. Again, a rubric can be helpful.

As an example of how this can play out in a classroom context, consider this group discussion task set before a group of 10 high school students to assess their analytical and comparison reasoning abilities, understanding of complex ideas, and ability to engage in a discussion with peers. Students prepared by reading *Good and Evil Reconsidered*, by Friedrich Nietzsche, and "The Greatest Man in the World," by James Thurber. The task consisted of engaging in a discussion about the following question: "How does the classification of men described by Nietzsche compare to Thurber's main character?" Two teachers served as raters using the rubric, "Group Discussion Rubric," with three traits: *Content Understanding*, *Reasoning* (in this case analysis and comparison), and *Interaction with Others*. At the end the two raters compared their ratings. Additionally, in case any students were too shy to jump into the middle of the discussion, students wrote up their analyses.

To view a class discussion and hear the teacher explain what she does, please watch the accompanying DVD segment, "Personal Communication."

Student Involvement in Assessing Group Discussions

Assessing student ability to engage in productive group discussions requires a rubric. If group discussion skill is an important learning outcome in your classroom, you can teach students to self-assess with the rubric (using the strategies introduced in Chapter 2 and expanded on in Chapter 7), as described in the following activity.

TRY THIS

Activity 8.4   Scored Discussion

Part 1: Refine the rubric for group discussion.

1. Individually or with your team review the "Student-Friendly Guide to Group Discussions" rubric on the CD in the file, "Rubric Sampler." Determine if there is anything you feel is missing from the rubric. Add it. (Especially attend to state content standards in communication. Make sure the rubric aligns.) If the wording in the rubric is not clear enough for your students, revise it. (Note that, as written, the rubric includes both interaction skills and understanding/reasoning surrounding the topic being discussed.)

2. Videotape students during a group discussion.

3. Practice analyzing the group discussion proficiency of individual students using the rubric. Do this either individually or with your learning team. Discuss possible sources of bias and distortion that might interfere with obtaining an adequate picture of individual students' group discussion proficiency. Discuss how to minimize these problems.

4. Refine the rubric and assessment procedures.

Part 2: Use the rubric to help students understand what it looks like when they are performing well in a group discussion.

1. Ask students what it looks like when people are working well together in a group discussion. What would people be doing? What would they not be doing?

2. (Optional.) Show a video of students having a group discussion. Ask students if there is anything else they would like to add to their list of features of a quality group discussion. (Note: Be sure to obtain the written permission of all students being videotaped. Also, we recommend that those on the videotape be anonymous—i.e., unknown—to those critiquing it.)

3. Ask students to compare their brainstormed list to the group discussion rubric. At what points do their list and the rubric overlap? Where do they not overlap?

4. Have students use the rubric to practice scoring anonymous individual students on a videotape, for one trait at a time. Be sure to have students justify their scores using wording from the rubric. Keep going until students get pretty good at evaluating performance.

Activity 8.4 (Continued)

5. Ask students to work in pairs to give advice to individual students on the videotape regarding how to improve their performance.

6. Provide students with descriptive feedback regarding their own performances based on the rubric for group discussions. Then ask them to self-assess their next performance using the rubric.

Share what you are trying in the classroom and your observations with your learning team. Consider reflecting on questions such as these:

- Could students score the discussions successfully? If not, why not? What will they need to learn to do so?

- Did students generate the same list of features of quality as the teachers? What were the discrepancies? What can you conclude from this?

- Was this engaging for students? Why or why not? What might you do differently to increase engagement?

- What would you need to do before using this task and rubric as an assessment *of* learning to ensure that results for individual students are accurate?

Source: Adapted from *Practice with Student-Involved Classroom Assessment* (pp. 181–182), by J. A. Arter & K. U. Busick, 2001, Portland, OR: Assessment Training Institute. Copyright © 2006, 2001 Educational Testing Service. Adapted by permission.

Oral Examinations

In this case, we plan and pose questions for students, who reflect and provide oral responses. We listen to and interpret the responses, evaluating quality and inferring levels of achievement. This is similar to an extended written response assessment, but with the added benefit of being able to ask followup questions. Oral examination has great potential for use, especially given the increasing complexity of our valued educational targets, the increased diversity of students, and the complexity and cost of setting up performance assessments.

Quality control guidelines for oral examination include those listed in Chapter 6 for extended written response assessments as well as some guidelines particular to this form of assessment, as follows:

- Develop brief exercises that focus on the desired target.

- Rely on exercises that identify the knowledge to be brought to bear, specify the kind of reasoning students are to use, and identify the standards you will apply in evaluating responses.

- Ask questions using the easiest possible vocabulary and grammatical construction. Don't let language get in the way of allowing students to show what they know.

- Present one set of questions to all students; don't offer choices of questions to answer.

- Develop written scoring criteria or a checklist of desirable features of a response in advance of the assessment. Be sure that qualified experts in the field would agree with the features of a sound response.

- Be sure criteria separate content and reasoning targets from facility with verbal expression.

- Prepare in advance to accommodate the needs of any students who may confront language proficiency barriers.

- Have a checklist, rating scale, or other method of recording results ready to use at the time of the assessment.

- If necessary, audiotape responses for later reevaluation.

For an example of how an oral examination might be used to contribute to a final grade, consider this test developed by a foreign language teacher for her first-year students. One of the important goals for the term was the ability to engage in short social conversations. She specified the contexts in which students were to learn to converse, (e.g., meeting someone for the first time, talking about your school, talking about your family, asking directions), and students practiced such discussions with each other over the course of the term. As part of the final exam, the teacher drew one of the topics at random for each student, who then was responsible for conducting the conversation.

Running Records

A common form of reading assessment in primary grades is what is known as a *running record*. This part performance assessment, part personal communication is a direct observation of oral reading skills, which can be used as either a summative assessment *of* learning or, more commonly, a diagnostic or an ongoing formative assessment. In early grades it can be used to identify which students do not have the basic reading skills needed for a successful school experience and who therefore need additional time and intervention.

In one version, teachers use an oral reading rubric to determine proficiency in accuracy, rate, and fluency. They administer the assessment individually to students, which typically takes no more than 10 minutes per student. The teacher introduces a task and passage, then asks students to read aloud. While students are reading, the teacher evaluates one or more of the following characteristics:

- *Rate*—How many words read aloud in a specified time or how long it takes the student to read the passage aloud

- *Accuracy*—How many errors the student makes in word recognition

- *Phrasing/fluency*—The ability to read the passage with awareness of syntax and expression

In addition, sometimes teachers assess student comprehension by asking readers to recall, organize, or summarize what they read.

Clearly, a major drawback to this format of assessment is the amount of time it takes to administer oral exams. The foreign language teacher mentioned found a way to minimize the time by engaging in only one conversation per student, still a significant time commitment, but the only way to measure the learning target accurately. If the purpose of the assessment is formative rather than summative, students can question, or in the foreign language example, converse with, each other. Of course this requires a good rubric, one that students have been taught how to use.

Journals and Logs

Sometimes personal interactions take a written form. Students can share views, experiences, insights, and information about important learnings by describing them to their teacher in a written form—by using journals. This can be especially helpful if teachers assign writing tasks that cause students to center on particularly important achievement targets. Further, teachers can then provide students with written feedback. In addition, because these written records accumulate over time, students can use them to reflect on their improvement as learners—the heart of assessment *for* learning.

Four particular forms bear consideration: response journals, personal writing journals or diaries, dialog journals, and learning logs.

Response Journals

Response journals are most useful in situations where we ask students to read and construct meaning from literature, such as in the context of reading and English instruction. As they read, students write about their reactions. Typically, we provide structured assignments to guide them, including such tasks as the following:

- Analyze characters in terms of key attributes or contribution to the story.

- Analyze evolving story lines, plots, or story events.

- Compare one piece of literature or character to another.

- Anticipate or predict upcoming events.

- Evaluate either the piece as a whole or specific parts in terms of appropriate criteria.

- Suggest ways to change or improve character, plot, or setting, defending your suggestions.

Assessment *for* Learning with Response Journals

One interesting example of the use of a response journal to help students learn more deeply comes from Janice Knight: "Most students' initial efforts at writing journal entries were lengthy, literal accounts about what was read. These boring responses, displaying a lack of critical thinking, filled page after page in their journals. It seemed that demonstration lessons on how to [think more deeply] were needed." So, she taught students how to use a system for coding their journal entries for the types of thinking displayed. She taught the codes one at a time, using teacher modeling and having students practice writing about what they read showing a specific type of thinking. She saw a dramatic increase in the depth of thinking displayed in journal entries. By having the students code their responses, "not only does the teacher have a record of the type of thinking that went into their creation, so do the students. They can readily self-evaluate and work independently towards improving their responses. The students are also more motivated to include different kinds of thinking in their entries" (Knight, 1990, p. 42).

Table 8.1 shows a set of symbols we devised for coding response journal entries according to the various patterns of reasoning discussed in Chapter 3—recall, analysis, synthesis, classifying, comparing, contrasting, inference, and evaluation.

Table 8.1 Icons for Student Self-Assessment of Response Journal Entries

R	**Recall**—Facts, plot design, sequence, details, summary. Tell the sequence of events in *The Ransom of Red Chief.*	*	**Analysis**—Ingredients, component parts, internal functioning. How did the author create a mood of happiness?
	**Synthesis**—Pool or integrate information to reach a new insight. What do you conclude from the two authors' visions of leadership?		**Classify**—Organize into categories. What types of stories did we read this year?
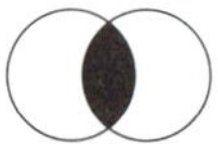	**Compare**—Comparison, similarity. How are the main characters in X and Y alike?		**Contrast**—Contrast, difference, distinction, discrimination, differentiation. How are the styles of A and B different?
	**Idea to Example**—Analogy, categorization, deduction, prediction, consequence. In our list of stories, find some examples of friendship.		**Example to Idea**—Induction, conclusion, generalization, finding essence, hypothesis. What is the main theme of this story?
	**Evaluation**—Value, judgment, rating. Was Ahab right to chase the whale? Why or why not? Did you like the plot? Why or why not?		

Source: Adapted by permission from Lyman, F. (1987). "The Thinktrix: A Classroom Tool for Thinking in Response to Reading." In *Reading: Issues and Practices. Yearbook of the State of Maryland International Reading Association Council.* Vol. 4. pp. 15–18.

TRY THIS

Activity 8.5   Journal Icons

Part 1: Refine the journal icons.

1. If you are keeping a learning log, use the icons in Table 8.1 to classify the types of entries you have made.

2. Review the procedures for Part 2. Discuss any questions or issues you might have. Revise the icon list or descriptors as needed.

3. Look at Figure 2.2, "Seven Strategies of Assessment *for* Learning," in Chapter 2. Identify which strategies Part 2 employs.

Part 2: Use the journal icons to help students understand how to incorporate various patterns of reasoning into their response journal writing.

1. Prepare a bulletin board displaying the journal icons.

2. Find examples from journal entries that show the type of reasoning you want to encourage.

3. Prepare a lesson that teaches students one of the cues. Plan how you'll introduce the usefulness of icons to students, how you'll model the particular pattern of reasoning you want students to practice, how you'll use the sample journal entries to give students practice at recognizing instances of the pattern of reasoning, and how you'll ask students to generate their own journal entries that illustrate the desired reasoning pattern.

4. Try out the lesson(s) and share the results with your learning team.

Personal Writing Journals

Personal writing journals or diaries represent the least structured of the journal options. In this case, we give students time during each instructional day to write in their journals. The focus of their writing is up to them, as is the amount they write. Sometimes we look at the writing to gain information, while at other times the writing is solely for the student's use. It is important to establish a clear purpose and audience for the personal writing journal at the outset. If it is to be used for student practice, then, while we may read it, our comments will provide descriptive rather than evaluative feedback. If the journal is purely for the student's use, then if we read it, we comment only at the invitation of the student. When the personal writing journal is to be evaluated, either we or the student, or both, make judgments. Often we encourage novice writers to experiment in their journals with new forms of writing, such as dramatic dialogue, poetry, or some other art form. Sometimes students use their journals as a place to store ideas or questions, as a seedbed for future writing topics. Personal journals offer students the opportunity to write for personal enjoyment and still provide both themselves and us with evidence over time of their improvement as writers.

Dialogue Journals

Dialogue journals capture conversations between students and teachers in the truest sense of that idea. As teaching and learning proceed, students write messages to us conveying thoughts and ideas about the achievement expected, self-evaluations of progress, points of confusion, or important new insights, and periodically turn in their journals. We read the messages and reply, clarifying as needed, evaluating an idea, or amplifying a key point, then return the journals to the students. They read what we wrote, sometimes responding, and other times moving on to a new topic. This process links us with each student in a personal communication partnership.

Learning Logs

Learning logs ask students to keep ongoing written records of the following aspects of their studies:

- Achievement targets they have mastered

- Targets they have found useful and important

- Targets they are having difficulty mastering

- Learning experiences (instructional strategies) that worked particularly well for them

- Experiences that did not work for them

- Questions that have come up along the way that they want help with

- Ideas for important study topics or learning strategies that they might like to try in the future

The goal in the case of learning logs is to have students reflect on, analyze, describe, and evaluate their learning experiences, successes, and challenges, writing about the conclusions they draw.

Possible Sources of Bias That Can Distort Results

There are several potential sources of bias that might distort the results of personal communication assessment. Since personal communication overlaps with performance assessment when assessing oral skills such as second-language fluency and oral presentations, it can fall prey to the same sorts of problems as performance assessment—tasks that don't elicit the needed performance, poor or nonexistent performance criteria and rubrics, lack of consistency in using rubrics, and tasks that don't match rubrics.

Also, because personal communication overlaps with extended written response when assessing knowledge and reasoning, it can fall into the same traps, such as unclear questions, poor or nonexistent scoring guides and rubrics, lack of the English skills needed to show what is known, and exercises that don't make clear the knowledge to be brought to bear, the kind of reasoning to use, or the standards to be used in evaluating responses.

There are also some potential pitfalls that apply only to personal communication:

- Trying to remember everything without writing it down. Keeping good written records is important.

- Unconscious personal and professional filters, developed over years of experience, through which we hear and process student responses. Such filters allow us to interpret and act on the achievement information that comes to us through observation and personal communication. We develop such filters as efficient ways to process large quantities of information. However, sometimes they backfire. For example, if we have come to expect excellent work from a student, we might overlook a lapse in understanding by inferring that the student actually had the understanding but unintentionally left the information out of an explanation. These same filters may cause us to provide more clues to some students than to others without realizing it, thereby causing the assessment task to vary in level of difficulty unintentionally.

  Also, unexamined stereotypes might come into play. If we're not expecting a person to be good at spatial reasoning, we might underrate what we actually hear. If a student looks unkempt, we might unintentionally shade our judgment of the quality of the student's contribution to a group discussion.

- Personal communication can result in inaccurate results due to inadequacies in sampling. If we are observing students during small-group discussions, we might miss a student's finest moment or not see typical performance because there are too many students to watch or too many things to watch for. Our sample may be too small to make a good inference about student achievement.

- Group discussion can also fall prey to sources of bias due to personality. A shy person who knows the material might be too uncomfortable to speak up in a group. If the goal of the discussion is to assess understanding of the material, we may make an incorrect inference.

Summary

Personal communication assessment is an efficient and effective way to both gather information about students to plan next instructional steps, and to involve students in their own assessment. Personal communication can be used to collect information about knowledge, reasoning, and level of certain skills such as ability to speak a foreign language.

There are several different ways to collect information through interpersonal communication—instructional questions and answers, conferences and interviews, classroom discussions, oral examinations, and journals and logs. Some of these are oral and some are written.

Personal communication forms of assessment must adhere to standards of sound assessment practice. Teachers must base them on a clear idea of which learning targets are to be the focus, have a clear purpose for gathering the information, and attend to possible sources of bias that could lead to misinterpretation of student learning. Such sources of bias include the following:

- Sampling procedures that don't allow gathering enough or the right information to make a needed inference.

- Trying to keep mental records.

- Students who, for reasons of language or personality, don't or can't show what they know or can do.

- Asking the wrong type of question to get at a learning target. For example, asking recall questions when trying to get at reasoning.

- Not checking for personal filters that might create subjective interpretations of student performance.

- Not having enough proficiency with a topic to identify indicators of understanding or not understanding.

As with other forms of assessment, personal communication can be used as a platform for formative assessment and student involvement. Because of the similarities between short oral answers and selected response written questions, extended oral responses and extended written response, and personal communication and performance assessment, strategies for student involvement outlined in Chapters 5, 6, and 7 can also be used with personal communication. In this chapter we provided activities to involve students in the oral questioning of each other, using journal icons to deepen thinking, and using a group discussion rubric to promote better group discussions.

■ *Tracking Your Learning—Possible Portfolio Entries*

Chapter 8 marks the end of Part 2 of this book. This is a good time to add portfolio entries and/or reflect on your learning as documented in your growth portfolio. Each portfolio entry that you choose should show some dimension of what you know and are able to do with respect to the learning targets illustrated in Figure 8.1 and described in Table 1.2. Be sure to include a portfolio entry cover sheet with each new entry. Such a form, provided on the CD in the file, "Portfolio Entry Cover Sheet," will prompt you to think about how each item you select for your portfolio reflects what you have learned.

■ *Additional Portfolio Entries to Represent Learning from Parts 1 and 2[2]*

1. Make a list of assessments that do and don't meet standards of quality as outlined in Figure 4.4, "Potential Sources of Bias and Distortion." Briefly describe your rationale for including each on the list.

2. Write an explanation of a student-involvement strategy you have tried with your class. Give an account of what you and your students did, what worked well, whether you would try it again, and what you would do differently, if anything.

3. Construct a concept map that shows your current understanding of how the following topics link:

Selected Response	Essay	Assessment Methods
Performance Assessment	Products	Fill in the Blank
Constructed Response	Dispositions	True/False
Reasoning	Learning Targets	Personal Communication
Skills	Matching	Knowledge/ Understanding
Sampling	Unclear Tasks	Sources of Bias & Distortion
Quality Assessment	Unclear Criteria	Problems with Test Administration

4. Outline the major learnings in Part 2 of this book. Include a statement of which major points might need to be the focus of future learning in your building or district.

5. Take another look at the previous assessments in your portfolio. Amend your commentary on their quality. (Do not remove your original commentary.) Use the quality assessment rubrics on the CD in the file, "Assessment Quality Rubrics," to help direct your commentary. What difference do you find in the content and depth of your original commentary versus your amended commentaries?

6. Select a new assessment (test, quiz, essay test, or performance assessment) that you have recently used or taken. This can be one that someone else developed or it can be one that you developed yourself. Using the quality assessment rubrics on the CD in the file, "Assessment Quality Rubrics," reflect on the quality of this assessment and write a brief analysis. What are its strengths? What parts might be improved?

7. Write a brief comparison of the quality of the three assessments you have evaluated. Is the quality improving over time? How do you know?

8. Take the "Confidence Questionnaire" (on the CD) again. How is your classroom assessment confidence changing over time?

9. Analyze the content of your assessment growth portfolio for sampling and potential sources of bias and distortion. Would a reader of your portfolio get an accurate view of your confidence and competence in classroom assessment? Would a reader get an accurate picture of (1) your knowledge of quality and ability to apply this knowledge in developing and selecting assessments for use, or (2) your knowledge of assessment *for* learning and application of that knowledge in the classroom? Consult Figure 4.4 for a summary of potential sources of bias and distortion. What should you do to avoid or correct these potential problems?

10. Review previous portfolio entries and note your progress in confidence and competence. For example:

    *   How has your thinking about assessment changed over time?

    *   What are you doing differently in the classroom as the result of what you've learned so far?

    *   What impact have you noticed on students? Colleagues? What evidence do you have for this impact?

    *   What questions from the beginning of your study can you now answer? What new questions do you have?

Notes

1. Portions of this chapter have been reprinted and adapted from Chapter 7, pp. 177–198, of R. J. Stiggins, *Student-Involved Assessment* for *Learning*, 4th ed., 2005, Upper Saddle River, NJ: Merrill/Prentice Hall. Copyright © 2005 by Pearson Education, Inc. Reprinted and adapted by permission of Pearson Education, Inc.

2. The following portfolio entries have been adapted from pp. 198 and 200–201 of J. A. Arter & K. U. Busick, *Practice with Student-Involved Classroom Assessment*, 2001, Portland, OR: Assessment Training Institute. Copyright © 2006, 2001 Educational Testing Service. Adapted by permission.

Communicating Assessment Results

Communicating About Student Learning

We have been asked several times by teachers, "What makes for good feedback?—
a question to which, at first, we had no good answer. Over the course of
two or three years, we have evolved a simple answer—
good feedback causes thinking. (Paul Black, 2003c, p. 7)

[I] n our discussion of communicating about student learning we want to keep front and center the student as primary audience for assessment information, for if the student decides on the basis of assessment information not to continue trying to learn, no learning will take place. Beyond the student, however, we know there are other audiences whose information needs the classroom teacher must also meet. In this chapter, we begin by planning for balance in assessments *for* and *of* learning in any given unit or period of instruction. We next examine managing information generated from assessments *for* and *of* learning as a prelude to effective communication. Then we conclude with an in-depth discussion of principles of effective communication about student learning.

This chapter introduces topics that are explored in depth in subsequent chapters— report card grading in Chapter 10, portfolios in Chapter 11, student-involved conferences in Chapter 12, and standardized testing in Chapter 13.

This chapter concentrates on the shaded portions of Figure 9.1:

Figure 9.1   Keys to Quality Classroom Assessment

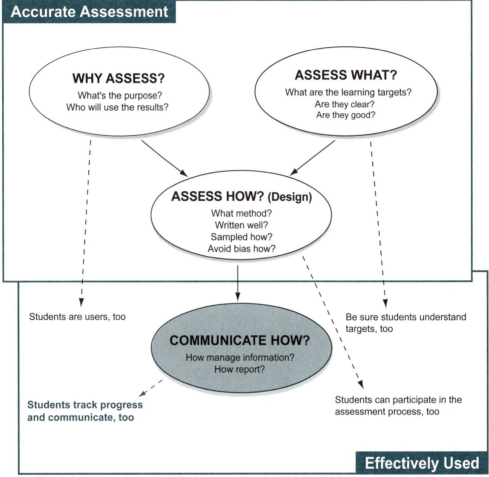

Balancing Assessments *for* and *of* Learning

We do not have a clear differentiation between assessment *for* and *of* learning when everything that moves—homework, practice activities, projects, papers, labs, quizzes, and tests—results in a score that contributes to the final grade. All assessments that result in a grade become assessments *of* learning, with associated motivational effects, whether or not we have intended them to be. When this is the case, it is not necessarily because we believe it is the best option; it has traditionally been the only option many of us have known.

What might we do instead? There are two parts to this question. The first is, How do we synchronize assessments *for* and *of* learning in actual practice? The second relates to motivation: How do we encourage students to do practice work if the score is not figured into the final grade?

Synchronizing Assessments *for* and *of* Learning

We can plan assessments *for* and *of* learning in several ways. We can separate them entirely so formative assessments *never* contribute to a grade. Or, under certain circumstances, we can use assessments originally intended to be formative as part of our summing up. We also can use assessments originally intended to be summative as sources of formative information and motivation to further learning. Let's examine each in turn.

First, we can entirely separate assessments *for* and *of* learning. We can structure assessments wherein the purpose is to offer descriptive feedback to the learner—assessments *for* learning—leading up to a final, separate, assessment *of* learning, such as a midterm or a culminating performance. In some situations, this works well. In classes where knowledge and reasoning targets make up the bulk of instruction, assessments *for* learning may take the form of activities such as homework assignments, practice with drafting assessment questions, or self-assessment and goal setting on the basis of learning targets represented in assessment plans. Although work generated through these activities is assessed to give students information about strengths and areas of further learning, the assessment information will not be used in calculating a final grade.

Then, there may be periodic assessments *of* learning (e.g., midterms and final examinations) to document levels of individual student achievement. These may be planned so that each assessment covers different learning targets, with the final grade calculated by combining information across assessments. Or, the periodic assessments *of* learning might be planned so that later tests cover the material from earlier tests. That way, if students demonstrate additional learning of earlier concepts, summative judgments of level of achievement can be updated. In this case, the more current information replaces the out-of-date information.

But complete separation of assessments *for* and *of* learning doesn't always make sense (Black, 2003a, b, c). For example, consider an elementary teacher who has taught his students to self-assess their writing systematically using a scoring guide. Students draft papers, give each other suggestions for improvement based on the scoring guide, get descriptive feedback from the teacher based on the scoring guide, revise their writing, track their progress in writing over time, and so forth, as Emily did in the vignette that opened this book. The goal is improvement, not grading, so all of this is assessment *for* learning.

At some point, this teacher will need to make a summative judgment of writing quality—he will need an assessment *of* learning. He can ask students to write a separate paper (or three to four to get a large enough sample) for this final assessment. Or, he can use some of the papers written during the course of instruction and improved using assessment *for* learning strategies as evidence of student achievement at that point in time. In this case, some formative assessments—assessments primarily designed to promote learning—will eventually be used to inform the final grade.

This scenario might play out in the primary grades, especially for reading and writing learning targets. The Juneau (Alaska) Borough School District has developmental continua for reading and writing that track student achievement through a series of levels designed to span grades K–5. Each stage in each continuum is defined and illustrated with student work. Teachers and/or students select work at predetermined times during the school year to reflect the student's current level of achievement on the continuum. This evidence is used to report progress to parents and to summarize student standing for the district; no separate assessment is required.

Any learning target at any grade level where proficiency develops over time is a potential candidate for judicious overlapping of assessments *for* and *of* learning. These include reasoning, skill, and product targets—problem solving or communication in mathematics, creating research reports, displaying data, giving oral presentations, planning and carrying out experiments, or playing a musical instrument. Reasoning, skill, and product targets tend to be taught throughout content units; they develop over time in many content contexts.

As we have seen in Chapters 5 through 8, summative assessment *of* learning can be used formatively (Black, 2003a, b, c), as when students analyze the results of a test to see which ideas they have mastered and which need more work, or when teachers use information from final tests to plan revisions to instruction.

Motivating Practice Without Grading Everything

A common question is: "How will I motivate students to do the practice work needed to improve performance if I don't make everything count toward a grade?" This question is based on an underlying assumption that the promise of As or the threat of Fs functions well as a tool for motivating students. Again, research and probably your own experience show that this system of motivation does *not* work well for all students; most noticeably it does not work for those who are performing marginally or those who are failing. As we have seen, scores of studies, many cited throughout this book, advocate reducing evaluative feedback and increasing descriptive feedback to affect motivation and achievement. Letting go of figuring practice work into the grade requires careful thought and planning, for if no other solution to the motivation problem is in place, trouble will surely result, just as predicted. If, however, this change is supported by the use of the other principles of assessment *for* learning, the set of practices you put into place will act to develop an internal sense of motivation in students. This is precisely why these principles are associated in the research with such large achievement gains.

Consider an example from a chemistry teacher, who has created a computer program that generates practice exercises (and instruction, as needed) for students. Students are assessed on every exercise, but the information is not figured into the final grade. The assessment is purely for students' information. The system reports current success rate, how much assistance the student needed to obtain correct answers, and how performance has improved over time. Students can aim for whatever summative grade they want. To get an "A" on the assignment, a student needs to obtain a specific number of correct answers in a row without assistance from the computer. A "B" is a different mix, and so forth. Students are in complete control of their learning because the learning and the grade are directly connected; they can keep practicing with immediate feedback and assistance as long as it takes to attain the desired grade. When students are ready for a summative grade, they signify they are finished. Later, they can raise their grades without penalty through additional practice to demonstrate higher levels of achievement.

In this example, students know the learning target, constantly receive feedback about where they are in relationship to the target, and are able to practice, without penalty and with as much assistance as they need, until they feel they are ready for the final assessment *of* learning. What would you predict the motivational and learning consequences of this protocol would be as compared to a series of homework assignments, each of which generates a score for the final grade? This teacher reports that student performance on computation is much higher than in previous years, and not a single student this term has requested extra help with computational questions.

Acclimating Students to Descriptive Feedback

In some situations, a short transition period may be in order in which students get used to receiving descriptive rather than evaluative feedback. Consider one teacher who feels that homework is essential to learning the material. Saying that homework is purely formative and won't figure in the final grade could make homework in her class a lower priority than homework in other classes—students might do it last and only if they have time. So she tells students that homework will count for 10 percent of the final grade, which is just enough to encourage students to complete it. But, she also tells students that homework is practice work and the most important information is from tests. So, if the information from tests indicates that students have improved their performance since completing their homework, the scores on homework will not be used in calculating the final grade. On the other hand, if the homework provides additional reliable information about student learning, as with borderline grades, she might very well count it in the grade. In this situation, the mere completion of homework is not enough—the scores on the assignments must reflect level of achievement for them to be used as data for the grade.

DEEPEN UNDERSTANDING

Activity 9.1   Synergy Between Assessments *for* and *of* Learning in Your Classroom

How might you achieve synergy between assessments *for* and *of* learning in your classroom? Will you completely separate the two? Will you use some formative assessment episodes to contribute to the final grade? Which protocols will work best with your students and your subject area(s)? If you are working with a learning team, consider discussing these questions.

TRY THIS

Activity 9.2 Auditing for Balance

Identify a unit of instruction for which you have assessments already assembled. Use the form found on the CD in the file, "Auditing for Balance," to check your balance between assessments *for* and *of* learning. Discuss your results with your learning team.

Information Management Decisions

Once you have mapped out which assessments serve which purposes, planned, and written or selected the assessments, the information begins to accumulate. How do you keep track of it? We recommend separating information generated from assessments *for* and *of* learning because they will be used for fundamentally different decisions. Table 9.1 shows the information management decisions required in each context.

What Evidence Will I Gather? Who Will Gather It?

The decision about what evidence to gather—the learning targets—has already been made. Obviously evidence can be gathered on any type of learning target—knowledge, reasoning, skills or products—by selecting an appropriate assessment method—selected response, extended written response, performance assessment, or personal communication.

If the purpose is assessment *for* learning, students and perhaps others such as parents will be partners in collecting evidence. If the purpose is assessment *of* learning, such as assigning a report card grade or recommending students for special services, we believe that teachers should gather the evidence. The more high-stakes the decision, the more important it is that the teacher coordinate the evidence.

Table 9.1   Information Management Decisions

Decisions to Be Made	Assessment *for* Learning	Assessment *of* Learning
What evidence will I gather? Who will gather it?		
• What learning targets am I going to keep track of?	Enabling classroom targets	Standards or benchmarks
• Who gathers the samples—teacher, students, or both in partnership?	Student involved	Teacher
Where will the evidence go? How will I store it?		
• Will I retain descriptive detail for each assessment or will I record a summary score for each entry?	Store descriptions of ongoing performance target by target	Store final judgments, at some point in time, of proficiency
• Where will I store information—gradebook, portfolios?	May include actual work samples, for example, in a portfolio	Probably won't include work samples, so a gradebook will work
• Who will store the information—teacher, students, or both in partnership?	Student involved	Teacher
How, if at all, will I summarize information?		
• Will I summarize across assessment occasions to come up with a composite score?	No, maintain the details in evidence; but, some summary to see improvement over time	Don't maintain detail
• Who will summarize the information—teacher, students, or both in partnership?	Student involved	Teacher

Source: Adapted from *Student-Involved Assessment* for *Learning*, 4th ed. (pp. 229, 236), by R. J. Stiggins, 2005, Upper Saddle River, NJ: Merrill/Prentice Hall. Copyright © 2005 by Pearson Education, Inc. Adapted by permission of Pearson Education, Inc.

Where Will the Evidence Go? How Will I Store It?

When the purpose is assessment *for* learning, more detail is required so that you can plan instruction, keep track of learning on each achievement target, and provide descriptive feedback. If the learning targets lend themselves to practice with selected response or short answer assessments, you can record information learning target by learning target, or even question by question, for diagnostic and feedback purposes. In the case of performance assessments, you may want to maintain a working folder or other collection of work samples, either in hard copy or electronic format, along with rubrics or developmental continua descriptive of the work included. In the case of evidence gathered through personal communication, you may have anecdotal records keyed to standards of quality represented on a rubric for specific learning targets.

When the purpose is assessment *of* learning and you intend to make a summative statement about level of achievement, you may want to dispense with much of the detail and keep just a numerical score.

Keeping the Records Separate

We advocate adopting record-keeping practices that provide a clear delineation between assessments *for* and *of* learning. Here are some possibilities:

- Separate record books, or separate sections in a book, one for detailed information organized by target or rubric rating area, and the other for summary information, also organized by learning target

- Different colors in the same record book, where only one color is used to determine the final grade

- Computer programs in which you can create separate categories for formative and summative information

- Collections of student work (with the intended learning targets identified) for the detailed formative assessment information and a record book or computer program for the summative information

Creating the Categories

For both assessments *for* and *of* learning, information needs to be stored according to what learning it assesses. Traditionally, we have recorded assessment information by event—homework, quiz, lab, test, written assignment, and so on—rather than by learning target. In many cases, this system does not record what students have mastered and what they need to work on.

To use the results of assessments to provide descriptive feedback, to plan instruction, to track student progress toward important content standards, or to provide summative standards-based report card grades, both our formative and summative recording systems must organize the information by learning target or by target clusters. For formative records, we want to capture the details about specific learning targets, whereas for summative records we can combine separate learning target information into the content standards they contribute to, or even into strands representing several content standards.

For example, a record book for third-grade mathematics could show learning targets such as "adds three-digit numbers in columns," "subtracts with borrowing," and "learns multiplication facts through 10" as separate categories in the formative portion and then combine those learning targets into one category, "Computation," or strand, "Number Sense," in the summative portion of the record book. As you can see, organizing records in this fashion requires that we know exactly which learning targets each piece of information represents. Or, both formative and summative information can be recorded on the same page. Table 9.2 shows an elementary-level example, with information organized by learning target. Table 9.3 shows an example of a gradebook page set up to record both summative and formative information, organized by strand.

The same holds true for portfolios. We need some means of keeping track of student performance by the parts of each learning target. It is not sufficient simply to deposit work into a portfolio without designating what information it provides. Descriptive detail about the achievement represented can be recorded as comments on a cover sheet or as phrases from a rubric.

Storing the Information

If the purpose is assessment *for* learning, we recommend that the record-keeping task fall to the student, with teacher supervision. The more involved with keeping track of achievement students are, the more in touch with their own progress they can be. "How'm I doing?" ought to be a question they can answer themselves at any point in the grading period. If the purpose is assessment *of* learning, the teacher does the keeping track.

Table 9.2   Elementary Gradebook Arranged by Learning Target

Number Sense																							
	Identifies place value to 10,000s					Reads, writes common fractions					Reads whole numbers through 4 digits					Writes whole numbers through 4 digits				Orders and compares whole numbers through 4 digits			
Date																								
Task																								
F/S																								
Students																								
1.																								
2.																								
3.																								

Computation								
	Addition	Subtraction	Multiplication		Division		Uses calculator to + or – 4 or more digits	Estimation Skills
	+ with 3 or more digits	– with 3 or more digits	Facts to 10	Fact Families	Facts to 10	Fact families		
Date								
Task								
F/S								
Students								
1.								
2.								
3.								

Task: SR = Selected Response; PA = Performance Assessment; O = Oral; HA = Homework Assignment; Q = Quiz

F/S: F = Formative; S = Summative

Source: Adapted from the work of Ken O'Connor, Scarborough, Ontario. Personal communication, June 1, 2004. Adapted by permission.

Table 9.3   Standards-Based Gradebook for Mathematics

Standard	Math Process					G R A D E	Number Ops & Rels				G R A D E	Geometry					G R A D E	Measure-ment				G R A D E	Stats & Prob				G R A D E	Algebraic Rels				
Date																																		
Task																																		
F/S																																		
Students																																		
1.																																		
2.																																		
3.																																		
4.																																		
5.																																		
6.																																		
7.																																		
8.																																		
9.																																		
10.																																		
11.																																		
12.																																		
13.																																		
14.																																		
15.																																		
16.																																		
17.																																		
18.																																		
19.																																		
20.																																		
21.																																		
22.																																		
23.																																		

Task: SR = Selected Response; PA = Performance Assessment; O = Oral; HA = Homework Assignment; Q = Quiz

F/S: F = Formative; S = Summative

Source: Adapted from the work of Ken O'Connor, Scarborough, Ontario. Personal communication, June 1, 2004. Adapted by permission.

To view an extension of these ideas focusing on how to record formative and summative data, please watch the accompanying DVD segment, "Record Keeping."

How, if at All, Will I Summarize Information?

Not all information needs to be summarized. Assessment *for* learning information might be discussed with students in the greatest possible detail to reveal what they can do well and the next steps in learning. Such information might not be used to track progress over time or to sum up status. But, sometimes assessment *for* learning information requires summary. When students report on their own progress or status, part of their report often requires that they summarize their achievement, accompanied by work samples or other evidence. Assessment *of* learning information generally is summarized.

When creating a summary, we answer a series of questions (Stiggins, 2005):

- Will the information be summarized as a single score or as a group of scores, such as a profile of analytical performance ratings?

- Will the information be converted to a letter grade, a percentage, or a proficiency level?

- Who will do the summarizing—teacher, student, gradebook software, parents, or someone else? If the purpose is assessment *of* learning, teachers do the summarizing. If the purpose is assessment *for* learning, students and others can assume some or all of this responsibility.

DEEPEN UNDERSTANDING

Activity 9.3 Managing Achievement Information for Emily's Classroom

Reread the story in Chapter 1 about Emily at the school board meeting. Using the questions in Table 9.1 as a guide, describe the information management system that would have to be in place in Ms. Weathersby's classroom to support both her students' and her own uses of assessment.

Conditions for Effective Communication

Imagine that your district has recently revised its report card so that it is now standards based, and the new grading key looks like this (Arter & Busick, 2001):

4 – Exceeds standard for this grade

3 – Meets standard for this grade/proficient

2 – Does not meet standard but making progress

1 – Does not meet standards/not progressing

X – Not covered this reporting period

What would need to be in place for the new grading key to communicate clearly to all who will read the report card?

Whether we communicate about student learning by means of a report card, a written summary, a developmental continuum, or a personal conference, certain conditions are required for effective communication: a shared understanding of the learning targets, accurate information, clearly defined symbols, and communication tailored to the audience (Figure 9.2).

Shared Understanding of the Targets

Everyone who is part of the conversation—parents, students, and any others—must understand which learning targets underpin the information. This understanding goes beyond just agreeing that reading or writing is the topic of discussion; we need clarity with a capital *C*. What specific aspects of reading proficiency are we assessing and communicating about?

For example, mathematics learning targets for the grading period include computation, algebraic thinking, problem solving, and communication in mathematics; all of these underpin the grade on the report card. If parents think the grade reflects only computation, the intended message will be misunderstood. Or, if the report card category for a grade in a physical education class is "PE," but the course includes knowledge and application of health information as well as physical fitness, parents may understandably assume the grade reflects only the physical fitness part of the learning.

Figure 9.2   Conditions for Effective Communication

1. ***Targets Are Clear.*** Everyone understands the learning targets in question.

    a. The particular learning targets to be discussed

    b. What those learning targets mean

2. ***Information Is Accurate.*** The information to be communicated is based on accurate assessments—appropriate method for the target, sampled well, with nothing to bias or distort the results. Information known to be inaccurate is not used.

3. ***Symbols Are Clear.*** Everyone understands the meaning of summary symbols.

4. ***Communication Is Tailored.*** The communication is tailored to the audience (parents, students, or others)—What does the audience need to know and when do they need to know it?

    a. *Timing*—When does the audience need the information?

    b. *Level of detail*—Information can be descriptive or judgmental, depending on the needs of the audience. The communication method—report card grades, mastery judgments, narratives, rubric scores, portfolios, standardized test scores, etc.—is chosen with needed level of descriptive detail in mind.

    c. *Unintended negative side effects*—How will all involved anticipate and avoid potential unintended consequences and negative side effects?

We can clarify learning targets for parents as well as for students in any of the ways discussed in previous chapters: sharing work samples; using definitions; sharing rubrics; or detailing the specific knowledge, reasoning, skills, and/or products that comprise a learning target. Many districts and schools choose to write a parent-friendly version of their curriculum. They share it by making parent-friendly curriculum guides available for teachers to distribute at open house or curriculum night, sending them home with every student, and/or posting them on the district or school website.

Accurate Information

Our communication is only as good as the assessments on which it is based. If assessment information is not accurate, communication will be meaningless, at best, with the potential to do damage in all other instances. Accuracy, as we have seen, depends on beginning with clear targets, identifying the purpose for the assessment, matching assessment methods to learning targets, gathering enough information to make a stable estimate of student learning, and avoiding practices that might bias or distort the true picture of student learning. It goes without saying, but we will say it anyway, that no one should use information known to be inaccurate in *any* form of communication about student learning.

Clearly Defined Symbols

Especially in communication situations involving symbols, such as grades, it is helpful to think of the teacher as the message sender and of the audience—students, parents, grandparents, colleges and universities, scholarship programs—as message receivers. The goal of communication is for the message sent by the teacher to be received intact by the audience. Therefore, everyone involved must have *the same understanding* of the symbols used to convey learning. Whether they are letter grades, ratings, check marks, percentages, or smiley faces, the symbols must be defined, and the definitions must be clear to the intended audience(s). Think back to the new report card grading key at the beginning of this section. The symbols shown, even with their definitions, stand a good chance of being interpreted differently by message senders and receivers. Without further definition, teachers may find it difficult to agree among themselves, as well. When this happens, we have confounded meaning, and all the work invested in creating grade reports does not result in shared understanding of student achievement.

Communication Tailored to the Audience

One size does not fit all when it comes to communication. Some audiences need detail to assist them to make needed decisions to help students learn. Others do not. Some audiences need frequent information, others do not.

Timing

The frequency of information depends on the nature of the decisions to be made with it. Students and teachers make decisions about teaching and learning that require information on a continuous basis. Parents generally need information frequently, but not necessarily continuously, to make decisions in support of their children's learning. Administrators and school boards need less frequent information on which to base decisions, as those decisions involve more long-range and large-group planning and resource allocation. Effective communication systems are built with these differences in mind.

Level of Detail

As discussed, the level of detail needed depends on the decision to be made. Teachers and students need detail about specific standards and enabling learning targets because they are making specific decisions about what has been learned and what should come next. Parents need highly descriptive information at times, especially when we request their intervention. At other times they need to know only that learning is progressing on track. This is true of others as well. For example, instructional support personnel may need very detailed information, while administrators may require general summaries of student achievement to meet their decision needs.

Different reporting formats supply different levels of detail. The ways of communicating about student achievement are varied, and we can group them into several categories: test scores, grades, narratives, portfolios, and conferences. They provide different levels of detail for decision makers with different decisions to make. We introduce the options briefly here, and expand on each in the following chapters.

Test Scores and Grades

A single test score, whether from a standardized test or a classroom assessment, can work well for certain decisions, especially for summative purposes, as we have seen. Yet, it can also mask specific detail. Think back to Claire's math test described in Chapter 3. The symbols summarizing achievement were a smiley face, a "–3," and an "M." Those symbols, although intended as standards-based reporting, did not provide any information on which standards were assessed. Without knowing that information, the teacher, Claire, and Claire's parents will not know which standards Claire is proficient with and which standards need additional work.

Written Narrative Feedback

This mode of communication can take one of two forms: comments written on (or attached to) student work, or narrative reports written about student achievement. In either case, we include specific, detailed information about students' levels of achievement on valued learning targets. Some schools and districts use a narrative form of reporting in conjunction with, or instead of, a symbol-based report card to provide a more precise and individualized account of learning.

Portfolios of Student Work

Portfolios can be structured to tell a variety of stories, ranging from tracking a trajectory of improvement to certifying competence. The amount of detail is controlled by the purpose for the portfolio and the learning targets represented.

Conferences About Student Achievement

We turn to the conference format when we have lots of detail to share. Although conferences are time consuming, they can be the most effective communication method when we need to make certain our message is understood. They are also used to provide supplementary detail to written forms of communication. They are typically conducted between student and teacher, between two students, between teacher and parent, between student and parent, or with student, teacher, and parents together. Conferences can be led by any one of the participants. In assessment *for* learning contexts, often it is the student who takes the leadership role.

Meeting Student and Parent Needs

What Students Need

- An understanding of the purpose of the assessment—how the results are to be used

- Frequent, timely information that promotes ongoing dialogue to keep them informed of where they are with respect to intended learning targets

- Descriptive rather than evaluative statements or judgments (e.g., grades or statements of mastery) on practice work

- Descriptive feedback that delineates what students can do and the next steps in learning, not just what they can't do

What Parents Need

In addition to a clear understanding of the symbols, parents generally find the following helpful:

- Detail beyond the grade: What learning targets underpin the level of achievement demonstrated? Which ones did the student do well on? Which ones need work? What can parents do at home to support the learning?

- Evidence of level of achievement: This evidence should be more than grades in a gradebook. For example, it can consist of models of work at different developmental levels or levels of mastery, samples of the child's work for comparison purposes, and so on.

- Clarity regarding how grades are assigned: What standard or scale is student work measured against?

- Information about the context: For grading, this means that the teacher should be prepared to discuss the strengths and limitations of the assessments on which the grade is based, how and why a single piece of information is weighted as compared to other information, and how information is combined to arrive at the grade. For portfolios and parent conferences this means that the teacher and student should be prepared to talk about how well the samples of work in the portfolio represent current learning or growth.

- Input: Parents have insights into their children's learning that can be of great value in planning next steps. Teachers should seek parental input; communication should not be only one way.

DEEPEN UNDERSTANDING

Activity 9.4 Revisit Grading Key—4, 3, 2, 1, X

Reread the grading key for the revised report card that appeared earlier in this chapter. Which conditions for effective communication from Figure 9.2 did the school district violate? What might the district do to rectify the situation? If you are working with a learning team, be prepared to discuss your thoughts on these questions.

Summary

Both assessments *for* and *of* learning have a place in the classroom, and both play a crucial role in communicating about student learning. Teachers have developed various protocols to attain synergy between the two (Black, 2003a, b, c). The possibilities are (1) separate the two totally, (2) use a carefully chosen sample of formative assessments to contribute to the final grade, (3) use summative assessments formatively for the next round of learning, and (4) use transition strategies when shifting from evaluative to descriptive feedback on the practice work. When we use assessments to meet students' informational needs while there is still time for them to act on the information to influence the final grade, we increase students' motivation to achieve.

Balancing assessments *for* and *of* learning in the classroom does not need to consume a lot of time. Often it is simply a matter of identifying which of the assessments already scheduled will serve formative needs and which will serve summative needs. If our classroom assessments are of high quality, we will be able to calculate a justifiable grade with fewer assessment scores than may be in place in many gradebooks now.

Tracking Your Learning—Possible Portfolio Entries

Any of the activities in this chapter can be used as portfolio entries. Once again, the learning targets for this book are outlined in Figure 9.1, listed in Table 1.2, and described in detail in Chapter 1. The portfolio entry cover sheet provided on the CD in the file, "Portfolio Entry Cover Sheet," will prompt you to think about how each item you choose for your portfolio reflects your learning with respect to one or more of these learning targets.

TRY THIS

Activity 9.5 Critique an Assessment for Good Communication

We suggest that you critique sample assessments this time for the trait of Good Communication. You will find the Good Communication rubric on the CD in the file, "Assessment Quality Rubrics." Once again, we recommend that you rate the quality of your selected assessments by using the following procedure:

1. Individually, read the strong level of the Good Communication rubric—"fast tracked." Then read the beginning level—"side tracked"—and finally the middle level—"on track." Mark the words and phrases that jump out at you as those really describing each level of quality.

2. Discuss with your colleagues any questions you have about the rubric.

3. Individually, look at your first sample assessment. If you think it is strong for the trait of Good Communication, begin reading the rubric at the "fast tracked" level. If you think it is weak, begin reading at the "side tracked" level. If you think it's strong, but "fast tracked" doesn't quite match what you see in the assessment, read "on track." Conversely, if you think it's weak, but what you read in "side tracked" doesn't quite describe it, read "on track."

4. There is no such thing as a "right" score, only a justifiable score. Justify your score using the words and phrases from the rubric that you felt described the assessment.

5. Compare your scores to those of your colleagues. Discuss discrepancies and attempt to come to a resolution.

You may wish to use your own assessments or to select from several sample assessments on the CD in the file, "Assessments to Evaluate." Our analyses of each of these samples using the Classroom Assessment Quality Rubrics are also on the CD in the file, "Assessment Critiques."

Assessment *of* Learning: Report Cards

[L] earning and teaching can take place just fine without grades. As we have seen, student learning benefits from feedback, but it seldom benefits directly from grading. So why do we grade? The simplest reason, other than that we've always done it, is that some instructional decision makers need summary information about student learning. Parents consistently indicate their desire to see the familiar, periodic report card grades so they know how their children are doing. Employers, other schools, athletic coaches and school advisors, scholarship committees, automobile insurance companies—the list goes on—want learning summarized in the shorthand that grades afford in order to make decisions about student eligibility for various programs.

Once teachers assign summary grades, they are used for many purposes, few of which are within the teacher's control. As we have noted in previous chapters, assessments *of* learning that contribute to a report card grade can affect students' motivation to learn, for better or worse. Our job as teachers, therefore, is first to ensure that grades are sound: they are built on assessments of high quality; they are accurate; and they mean what they are intended to mean. Secondly, our job is to avoid or control their unintended negative impact on learning.

In this chapter we look at the purposes for grading, explore some of the challenges inherent in assigning report card grades, and suggest what can be done to use grading to support learning. We examine a set of guidelines for grading and outline steps in the process that can be used to arrive at fair and accurate report card grades. Finally, we offer a rubric for reviewing grading practices.

The focus of this chapter is indicated by the shaded portions of Figure 10.1.

Figure 10.1   Keys to Quality Classroom Assessment

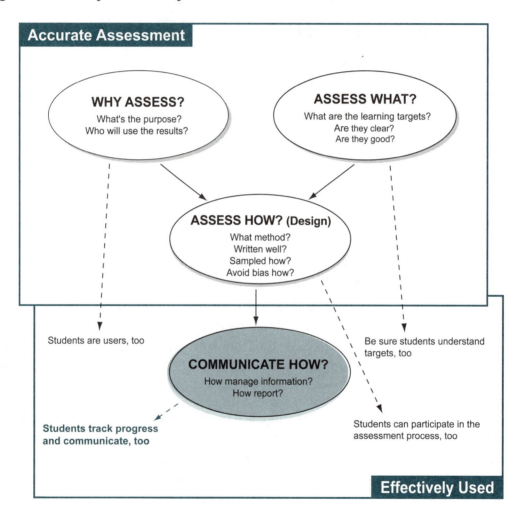

REFLECT ON YOUR LEARNING

Activity 10.1   Reflect on Current Practice

To start our discussion about grading with a practical dimension, let's look at one teacher's experience. While reading her description of her early years as a teacher, think about whether it parallels any of your own experiences with grading, or what you might know and do in your classroom that this teacher did not.

"As a young teacher, I never had a student or parent seriously question a report card grade that I assigned. As a result, I never really had to open my gradebook to others to show all of the different colored symbols and markings, numbers and letter grades, comments and codes that I somehow massaged (calculated is too strong a description) into a final grade. I was lucky, because had they done so, I would have been hard pressed to explain or defend a nonsystem, or my procedures for grade calculation. Although I didn't realize it fully at the time, I had no real guide for ensuring my grades were accurate, consistent, or fair; and in the end the grades I assigned were far more intuitive, subjective, and emotional than they were rational. It never occurred to me then that those grades might serve to either hinder or help someone to be a better learner. So although I never wanted to have grades be harmful, I frequently and subjectively included in the final grade all kinds of things—perpetual tardiness, a lack of effort on the part of a student whom I thought should be doing better, and good behavior are just a few examples.

"Further, I used one grading scheme for low performers and another for 'smart' kids, and more often than not, everything, no matter when it happened in the semester, counted toward the final grade. I didn't think about the relative importance of the test or assignment, and I didn't differentiate between practice and final exercises or assignments. I had no set curriculum, which may be one reason why in my mind grading was divorced entirely from teaching and learning. And because of that separation, it didn't bother me in the slightest that a student aide evaluated a large portion of student work, entered the data, and helped in figuring the grades."

Answer these questions and save your responses for a future activity: What, if anything, in this teacher's description of her grading practices matches your own? Conversely, what can you identify in your practice that differs from what this teacher did?

The Challenges of Report Card Grading

Unfortunately, the teacher in Activity 10.1 did not have the opportunity to learn what we call *sound grading practices* in her preservice education. Therefore, she had no standards of quality or fairness to guide her. As is the case with many teachers, she was left to develop her own system for arriving at report card grades.

And yet, of all the things we do as teachers, few have the potential for creating more problems and miscommunication than grading. All it takes to realize this is to be the teacher on the explaining end in a conference with a parent who is challenging her child's grade. We can experience friction at report card preparation time as we struggle to assign the grade of a student who worked hard during the semester, but who achieved at a low level, resulting in what is sure to be a disappointing grade. At times like this we can be emotionally torn, valuing our relationship with the student and drawn to a solution that considers the student's individual circumstances while forsaking objectivity and accuracy.

We confront even more challenges inherent in grading, especially the amount of time it takes, when we set about trying to manage the wealth of information we collect through assessments *of* learning. We sort through it, prioritize it, and assign weights to certain evidence, all in an attempt to get a clear picture of student performance. And yet in the end, like the teacher in Activity 10.1, many of us funnel the information through a process of our own making, from which emerges a single letter or number grade.

And finally, there is the challenge of changing report card grading practices to reflect standards-based instruction. In a standards-driven environment, the goal is to provide students and their parents with specific information that communicates about student progress toward the standards. Yet many grading systems in today's schools continue to communicate about student learning using a traditional letter/number grading system that fails to provide specific information about (or in some cases, is not even based on) student mastery of content-area academic standards.

Why Do We Grade? The Purpose of Grades

Most would agree that we grade to communicate about student achievement. But in many classrooms, grades have been used as a tool to communicate about factors other than student achievement. Often attendance, effort, participation, and behavior have been folded into a report card grade, as teachers reward behavior likely to result in learning or punish behavior that is unlikely to help. In so doing, these teachers use grades as motivators. In that same sense, it's not uncommon to see grades used at the school level to sort and order students from highest to lowest for purposes of determining each student's rank in class. Instill a sense of competition, some believe, even with an artificial creation of winners and losers, and students will work harder and learn more. In this case, grades are assigned on a curve to spread students out on a long continuum of achievement. If some or all of these purposes factor into the determination of a single report card grade, who can possibly interpret the true meaning of that grade in terms of student achievement?

And as we saw with the young teacher in Activity 10.1, often we lack a consistent set of guidelines for calculating grades. Many of us calculate grades by adhering to our own unique procedures and formulae. Some of us have no articulated process other than to record, average, and convert to a grade, while others use elaborate mathematical systems to "crunch" the grade. Electronic gradebook programs offer little or no guidance in how to use their features to ensure fairness and accuracy. Even with school and district policies in place, there can be as many different grading systems in a school as there are teachers.

REFLECT ON YOUR LEARNING

Activity 10.2   What Are Your Purposes for Grades?

Think about the purposes behind the grades you assign. What are you trying to communicate through the use of report card grades? To what extent are your learning goals the basis for the grades you assign? What in your grading practices are aligned with the ideas presented in this chapter so far? What, if anything, seems to be in opposition? In framing your responses, take into account your notes from Activity 10.1. If you are working with a learning team, consider discussing these questions as a group.

So, what can be done to meet the challenges? First, it is helpful to remember that there is a difference between the *purpose* we have for giving the grades, and the subsequent *uses* of the grades given. At the outset, our purpose is to communicate, but after we give grades, others use them for a variety of their own purposes.

School administrators, guidance counselors, college admissions offices, prospective employers, and others use those grades to make decisions such as planning academic and career pathways, placing students in classes, selecting students for special programs, determining eligibility for a team, school, or college admissions, evaluating school programs, and for instructional planning and improvement. How parents use grades is based in part on their perceptions of what their purpose is. Some believe they are provided so they know how their student is performing relative to others in the class. Some believe grades are a tool to gauge improvement over time, although the focus of improvement varies based on what the parent sees as most important: mastery of the learning targets, effort, preparing for the future, and so forth. Other parents believe grades are primarily a motivational tool, and use them as the basis for rewards or punishments (Munk & Bursuck, 2003). Students use grades to decide whether they are capable in a subject, whether they will continue to put forth effort, and what will or won't be part of their future education and career, among many other things.

Three Grading Principles

Each decision maker counts on grades to be accurate; major decisions that affect students' well-being are made on their basis. We teachers are in charge of ensuring their accuracy. *Our responsibility is to provide as accurate a picture of learning as possible.* This requires that we carefully answer three questions—one we've already seen, and two others that follow it: "What is our purpose for grading?"; "What factors should we include in the grade?"; and "How do we combine those factors to give the truest picture possible of student achievement?"

We offer answers to those questions in the form of three *grading principles*—three statements that serve as the foundation for an accurate and defensible grading system: "The purpose of grades is to communicate"; "Grades communicate about achievement"; and "Grades reflect current level of achievement."

DEEPEN UNDERSTANDING

Activity 10.3   The Dilemma of Late Work

Imagine that your seventh-grade daughter's midterm progress report in social studies says she is getting a C, yet the only tests and assignments you have seen have had As or Bs on them. Your daughter tells you she's done all the required work and can't explain where the C came from.

You meet with the teacher, who checks your daughter's records on the computer. The printout shows the following list of entries leading to an average of 76 percent.

> Unit 1 Test: 95%
>
> "Effects of Migration" Report: 85%
>
> Unit 2 Test: 85%
>
> "Effects of Trade" Report: 40%

The teacher tells you that your daughter's last report was one week late. Her policy is to subtract 10 points for each day an assignment is late, so had your daughter's "Effects of Trade" report been on time, she would have received a score of 90 percent. But, you point out, your daughter seems to be grasping the concepts very well. "Well, this is how we figure grades," the teacher replies.

With your learning team or another group of colleagues, discuss the following questions:

1. What does a C communicate to others?

2. What problems does the practice of reducing the grade for late work solve?

3. What problems does it cause?

4. What are the teacher's options for dealing with late work?

Principle 1: The Purpose of Grades Is to Communicate

We may all agree that a grade's purpose is to convey information about student learning. But we all know of grading practices that are intended also to serve the purpose of motivating students to be better or more responsible learners. While these are important aims in education, grades are not the best way to accomplish them. Indeed, grades cannot function both as communicators and motivators. Consider these two scenarios:

> *John is a very capable student who, in the teacher's opinion, is not perform-*
> *ing at the level he should. His end-of-term grade is a borderline B/C. His teacher*
> *gives a C to help John see that he needs to put forth more effort; in other words,*
> *to punish him for not doing more, in the hopes that he will wake up and work*
> *harder.*

> *Sarah is a hardworking student who always turns everything in. Her end-of-*
> *term grade is a borderline C/D. Her teacher raises her grade to a C to build up her*
> *self-esteem; in other words, to reward her for her hard work, in hopes that this will*
> *keep her from being discouraged.*

Grades, in these two examples and in the scenario in Activity 10.3, are figured with the intent of motivating the student—the desire is to change behavior. When we do this, we are on shaky ground, for several important reasons.

First, the motivational effects of grades are unpredictable, as we have no way of knowing whether the student gets the message. Tinkering with grades to cause a change in behavior is not a reliable way to effect the desired change. In John's case, his lack of attention to the quality of his work can and should be addressed directly, well in advance of report card grading time.

Second, altering grades to encourage students to keep trying can hide a more important issue. Why is Sarah's effort not resulting in achievement? Raising the grade does nothing to address this real problem, which must be addressed head on if the teacher is to serve Sarah well.

Third, no studies support the use of low grades or marks as punishments. Instead of prompting greater effort, low grades more often cause students to withdraw from learning (Guskey & Bailey, 2001).

Fourth, the practice of assigning grades to shape behavior is not consistent with a standards-based educational system. When we alter grades in hopes of encouraging certain behaviors or punishing others, we miscommunicate about students' real levels of achievement. John, Sarah, and your daughter all received Cs in our scenarios, yet all had very different levels of achievement. When the grade leaves the teacher's hand, it needs to stand alone as communication. The motivation effect is fleeting, if it exists at all, yet the grade is permanent. When we allow motivational intent to alter grades, we cripple the grade's ability to communicate.

Principle 2: Grades Communicate About Achievement

Once we have accepted that grades should be assigned for the purpose of communicating, we must ask ourselves, "Communicate about what?" We know that grades *can* include evidence of academic achievement, effort, aptitude, attitude, group participation, homework completion, and compliance with rules, among other things. This principle requires that subject area grades include only evidence of academic achievement as defined by our learning targets, and that all other factors, if reported, be reported separately. Few would argue that achievement should *not* be included in the grade, but there are plausible arguments for including other factors. Let's look at arguments for including those factors and examine the problems their inclusion creates.

Including Effort

Effort is highly valued both in and beyond school. It is a necessary ingredient in achievement for many students. Students who put forth effort are easier to teach and to manage. When students are trying hard to learn, our jobs as teachers are much easier because the students are meeting us at least halfway. Many classroom teachers see effort as inseparable from achievement. Also, employers value people who work hard, who demonstrate persistence, who take initiative, and who go beyond what is required of them to make the business successful. These are all arguments for including evidence of effort in the report card grade.

But on the other hand, John's and Sarah's Cs tell us nothing about their very different levels of effort. If information about their effort would assist us in interpreting the grade they were assigned, then evidence of that effort should be reported separately from the achievement grade. Rarely are there explicit criteria the teacher can use to judge effort. The task is made even harder by the fact that students, through their physical appearance or behavior, may appear either to be engaged or totally out of it, when in fact, just the opposite maby be true (Brookhart, 2004). If we wish to communicate about level of effort, we will need to define what we mean by "effort," determine how best to evaluate it, determine what symbols we will use and what they will mean, and then create a separate space on the report card for our judgment. This implies additional work for the teacher, but if effort is worth gathering data about and worth communicating, then we can see no other way to make meaning clear.

Including Aptitude

What about aptitude? If a student is not capable of doing grade-level work, but we assign it anyway, should we not adjust the grading scale to take into account our estimation of that student's reduced ability? Conversely, if the work assigned is too easy for a student's ability, should we lower the grade to reflect the difference between the quality of work and what the student is capable of? In both cases, the answer has to be no, for two reasons.

First, there is great debate in the fields of psychology and measurement about what constitutes *intelligence* and how to gauge it. In the classroom we are not equipped with the kinds of background or tests needed to be accurate in our judgments of intelligence. We can do students great harm if we act on an inaccurate perception of their ability. But, in fact, we don't determine students' instructional needs on the basis of evidence of intelligence. Instead, we use evidence of past performance as a guide in determining which learning targets are most appropriate for a given student, and then we adjust the targets, if needed, so that the student encounters work at the right level of difficulty. If we were simply to adjust the grading scale, we would mask not only the student's true level of achievement, but also a learning problem that we should address.

The second reason for not adjusting the grading scale for aptitude is that it confuses the meaning of the grade. As with effort, when a teacher raises or lowers a grade based on any information other than achievement data, the grade becomes uninterpretable. It cannot stand alone as a communicator about student learning.

Including Other Factors

And so it is for all other factors we might wish to take into account in figuring final grades—attendance, homework completion, turning work in on time, group participation, attitude, and the like. The same three issues recur: (1) using the grade as a way to motivate better performance is not generally effective; (2) it is difficult to measure many of the other factors accurately; and (3) their hidden inclusion makes the subject area grade uninterpretable. If we decide that factors beyond level of achievement are important to report, we must decide what data to collect, then collect and report it separately.

Principle 3: Grades Reflect Current Level of Achievement

In a standards-based environment, grades must reflect our best estimate of student achievement at the time the grade is given. If more recent information about student achievement shows a new level of attainment, thereby making previous evidence outdated, then the grade should be based on the newer evidence. Anything else provides an incorrect picture of student achievement and can lead to ill-informed instructional and support decisions, to say nothing of misleading the student.

Grading Guidelines

We can combine the three grading principles into one sentence: *Grades communicate about current status of achievement.* This statement guides all grading decisions. It translates into a series of actions, summarized in Figure 10.2 as grading guidelines. We discuss each guideline in turn in the following subsections.

Guideline 1: Organizing the Gradebook

Arrange achievement data according to achievement target, not according to type or source of information such as tests, quizzes, labs, or homework, as described in Chapter 9. This guideline is purely practical. When instruction and assessment are planned according to learning target, it only makes sense to record that information by learning target, or by cluster or strand. It makes even more sense when the report card format itself is standards based. Organizing a gradebook this way also can help you track your instruction and assessment as you progress through the standards you are responsible for teaching.

Guideline 2: Including Factors in the Final Grade

Achievement and Other Factors

Record evidence of subject area achievement separately from evidence of student characteristics such as effort, class participation, compliance with rules, attitude, neatness/sloppiness of a paper, timeliness of turning in assignments, attendance, interactions and cooperation with classmates, and classroom attention and/or inattention. Keeping these valuable pieces of information separate facilitates instructional planning and communicating about problems.

Figure 10.2   ETS Grading Guidelines

1. **Organizing the gradebook**
   - Arrange gradebook entries according to achievement target.

2. **Including factors in the final grade**
   - Report and summarize achievement evidence separately from other student characteristics.
   - Use extra credit work only if it supplies additional evidence of achievement.
   - Record a score of zero only if that is the score on the work.
   - Handle borderline cases by collecting additional evidence of student learning.

3. **Considering assessment purpose**
   - Use assessments *for* learning as the basis for providing students with descriptive feedback they can use to see how to improve; do not factor them into report card grades without a compelling rationale.

4. **Considering most recent information**
   - Base grades on the most current evidence of the student's level of achievement.

5. **Summarizing information and determining the final grade**
   - Make final grades criterion referenced.
   - Convert, weight, and combine information with care.
   - Convert rubric scores to grades using a decision rule.
   - Select the best measure of central tendency to use in combining assessment information into a final grade.

6. **Verifying assessment quality**
   - Base all grades on verifiably accurate assessments of student achievement.

7. **Involving students**
   - Keep students apprised of their current level of achievement.

Extra Credit Work

Evaluate and record extra credit work in the same way that you would evaluate and record any other evidence of achievement. Do not record points for mere completion of extra credit work and consider it achievement information. Without an evaluation of quality, the information does not reflect student learning. When just having done extra credit work factors into the grade, we are mixing effort with achievement.

Zeroes

Do not enter missing or invalid evidence of achievement into grade books as zero. *Zero* implies the total absence of learning. Missed tests, scores attained by cheating, or assignments not handed in do not offer data about level of learning.

Averaging zeros with other scores to calculate a final grade skews the score and results in an inaccurate picture of student achievement. Consider the case of a student who has taken three of four tests and attained scores of 100, 90, and 95 percent. The student missed one test and the score was entered as a zero, due to an unexcused absence. Her average is 71 percent, usually a C but sometimes a D. This grade clearly does not reflect her level of achievement. A more fair solution to the problem of missing work is to gather or use other information about student learning to fill in the gap. This student could, for instance, take the test before or after school. If we can't get other information in time, we may have to use an "Incomplete" to stand in for the grade until we can get enough information to make a stable generalization about the student's level of achievement on the course learning targets.

If we wish to punish irresponsible behavior, that punishment must take a form that does not distort the student's actual record of academic achievement. That record is too important for informing subsequent instructional decisions in a standards-driven environment to permit its distortion. We encourage you to work with your colleagues and your school to identify other solutions to and consequences for the problems for which zeroes have been the consequence in the past.

Guideline 3: Considering Assessment Purpose

As recommended in Chapters 2 through 9, differentiate between assessments *for* and *of* learning. Use assessments *for* learning as the basis for providing students with descriptive feedback they can use to see how to improve. Keep track of them separately, and do not factor information from assessments *for* learning into report card grades indiscriminately or without a compelling rationale.

Guideline 4: Considering Most Recent Information

Base grades on the most current evidence of the student's level of achievement on the intended learning targets. The practice of averaging over an entire grading period does not yield a summary of current level of achievement for learning targets that reflect continuous growth—reasoning, skills, and products, such as writing, oral presentation, experimental skills in science, or speaking a foreign language, for example. However, there are cases when averaging from various points in the grading period makes sense. If we divide the content to be learned in a social studies course into several equal segments, each lasting about two weeks of the grading period, we might give a summative assessment at the end of each segment. Averaging makes sense here, because each summative assessment provides information on different learning targets. No content has been repeated, so every score represents the most current information on the targets covered.

Guideline 5: Summarizing Information and Determining the Final Grade

Make Final Grades Criterion Referenced, Not Norm Referenced

Assessments, achievement records, and grades should reflect student attainment of established achievement targets, rather than the students' place in the rank order of the class. If a student receives a grade of B, the interpreter must understand that the B reflects attainment of a certain level of mastery of the learning targets for that subject.

Guskey (1996) advises against normative grading with the following argument: "Grading on a curve makes learning a highly competitive activity in which students compete against one another for the few scarce rewards (high grades) distributed by the teacher. Under these conditions, students readily see that helping others become successful threatens their own chances for success. As a result, learning becomes a game of winners and losers; and because the number of rewards is kept arbitrarily small, most students are forced to be losers" (p. 21).

All students could get an A, or "Exceeds the standard," if they prove that they have learned the material at the corresponding level of mastery.

Make Modifications for Special-Needs Students with Care

Part of our responsibility and challenge in standards-based schools is to expose all students to an appropriate and rigorous curriculum. How we grade students with special needs should reflect both that goal and their individual progress toward the standards as specified in their IEP (Munk & Bursuck, 2003). For these students, as with all students, we need to make final grades criterion referenced, and have the grade indicate the level of learning attained relative to the learning goals documented in the IEP. In this context, report card grades should be accompanied by some narrative description or rating system that clearly communicates student progress toward the IEP goals (O'Connor, 2002). When such modified learning targets are the basis of grades, ensure this is clear to all parties and is incorporated into the IEP. A special needs student can receive an A for attainment of different learning targets than other students in the same classroom, if such targets are specified in advance through an IEP. We simply must be sure that everyone understands that either the learning targets have been modified or a specialized grading plan within the IEP is being applied (Brookhart, 2004).

Converting, Weighting, and Combining Information

Some of the assessment information to be combined into a grade might be percentages or number correct on a test or assignment, while others might be ratings using rubric numbers or letters, smiley faces, checkmarks, or other evaluative marks. We'll examine each separately—first percentage or numbers and then converting rubric scores to grades.

Having gradebook entries that are all raw scores (number correct out of number possible) or percentages (percent correct) is the typical, traditional situation. It is acceptable to record information in that manner as long as the numbers adequately represent level of mastery of specific learning targets. If this is so, then we recommend two traditional combination procedures. You can convert all scores to percentages, combine the percentages, and then convert the final percentage to a grade using a predetermined scale (A = 90–100%, B = 80–89%, etc.). Or, you can convert all entries to raw scores, add up the total number of points and set a numerical cutoff for each grade. In either case, remember to use only the most current body of information and sample the learning targets adequately.

If you wish to give greater weight to some assessment results than to others, you can accomplish this by multiplying those scores by their weight before adding them into the overall computation. For instance, if some are to count twice as much as others, simply multiply their percentages by two (count them twice) when averaging. Let's say you administer three tests during a grading period, all of which contribute to the grade. But one test (number 3) covers a much broader segment of the curriculum than do the other two. So you weigh it at twice the value of the other tests. The calculation would be as follows:

$$[(\% \text{ test } 1) + (\% \text{ test } 2) + 2(\% \text{ test } 3)] \div 4 = \text{Average } \%$$

Figure 10.3 shows the process translated to real data for one student, Robert.

Figure 10.3   A Weighted Assessment Example

Robert's scores:

Test 1: 79%   Test 2: 84%   Test 3: 82%

[79% + 84% + (2 x 82%)] 4 = Average %

(79 + 84 + 164)/4 = Average %

327/4 = Average %

81.75 = Average %

Reporting the final percentage score on the report card has the benefit of preserving some detail about a student's level of achievement. But most districts require teachers to convert the academic achievement average or point total to a letter or number grade, from A to F or from 4.0 to 0 or from "Exceeds the standard" to "Does not meet the standard."

Just remember that cutoffs vary from district to district, school to school, and even teacher to teacher. The range for an A in some places may be 94 to 100 percent, for example, and in other places it may be 80 to 100 percent. Although these differences cannot be eliminated, we can acknowledge the lack of precision they carry.

Converting Rubric Scores to Grades

If the objective is to communicate thoroughly about student achievement, then don't convert rubric scores to letter grades at all if you can help it. Rather, communicate using the points on the rubric. The description of the performance corresponding to the score provides clear, focused feedback.

When a grade is absolutely necessary, as it sometimes is, you must formulate a plan for converting ratings to grades. First we'll consider the situation where an entire grade is based on ratings, then we'll discuss how to determine a final grade when you need to combine ratings with percentage scores from assessments such as tests and quizzes. We'll proceed by outlining the issues through an example and then pose our solutions.

DEEPEN UNDERSTANDING

Activity 10.4   Agatha's Writing Grade

Look at Agatha's scores in Table 10.1 on eight writing samples over a grading period. These scores were based on a writing rubric that covers six dimensions, or traits, of a good paper: ideas, organization, voice, word choice, sentence fluency, and conventions. (For the sake of illustration, assume that all pieces of writing went through the whole writing process and were used formatively to help guide next steps in instruction. Also, although all writing in reality may not necessarily be assessed on all six traits, for this example we have scores on each trait for each paper.)

Decide two things: First, if you had to give a grade on paper number 4, what grade would you give? Why? What concerns do you have? Second, if you had to give a writing grade for the grading period, what would it be? Why? What concerns do you have?

Table 10.1   Agatha's Scores for Six Weeks

Agatha's Six-Trait Scores on Eight Papers							
Paper no. & Date	Ideas	Organization	Voice	Word Choice	Sentence Fluency	Conventions	Total	Percent
1–9/5	2	2	2	2	3	3	14	14/30 = 47%
2–9/9	3	3	2	2	3	2	15	15/30 = 50%
3–9/13	3	3	3	3	3	3	18	18/30 = 60%
4–9/17	4	3	3	3	4	3	20	20/30 = 67%
5–9/21	3	4	4	4	3	4	22	22/30 = 73%
6–9/25	4	3	4	3	4	4	22	22/30 = 73%
7–9/29	5	5	5	4	4	3	26	26/30 = 87%
8–10/4	5	5	5	5	4	4	28	28/30 = 93%
Total	29	28	28	26	28	26	165	Average of percentages = 69% 165/240 = 69%

Source: Adapted from *Scoring Rubrics in the Classroom: Using Performance Criteria for Assessing and Improving Student Performance* (p. 79), by J. A. Arter & J. McTighe, 2001, Thousand Oaks, CA: Corwin. Adapted by permission.

Paper Number 4

Most teachers say that, if required, they would give Agatha a C on paper 4 in Activity 10.4 because she received four "3s" and two "4s." In other words, teachers tend to average the scores to get a 3.3 (20 divided by 6) and convert this to a grade using a conversion rule that A equals 5, B equals 4, and so on. This works as long as everyone agrees that the description behind a score of, say, "4" indicates B work. But, what happens if the description of "4" indicates A work? Or, if your rating scale consists of only 4 points and you have to convert it to a five-point grade scale, A–F, what do you do then?

Before attacking these issues, we want to look at what *not* to do. For this example, we will adopt the percent-to-grade conversion rule shown in Figure 10.4.

Figure 10.4 Sample District Percent-to-Grade Conversion Rule

A+ = 97 – 100%	C = 73 – 76%
A = 93 – 96%	C– = 70 – 72%
A– = 90 – 92%	D+ = 67 – 69%
B+ = 87 – 89%	D = 63 – 66%
B = 83 – 86%	D– = 60 – 62%
B– = 80 – 82%	F = 59% and below
C+ = 77 – 79%	

Notice that Agatha received 20 out of 30 possible points for the paper. This converts to 67 percent, a D+. But, the wording of the "3" scores on the rubric ("6 + 1 Traits: Analytical Writing Scoring Guide," found on the CD in the file, "Rubric Sampler") doesn't describe D work. Therefore, it usually doesn't work to convert total rubric points to a percentage and then to a grade.

Here is another example that illustrates how direct conversion of rubric scores to percent correct doesn't work. On a five-point scale, a student could only get 5 = 100, 4 = 80, 3 = 60, 2 = 40, and 1 = 20 percent, which converts to A, B–, D–, F, and F. Is it true that a score of "3" represents D– work, or that a score of "2" represents failing work? Probably not.

Consider a score of "1," which would convert to 20 percent. While a 20 percent might denote failing work, assigning such a percentage would unfairly weight the low score when combining it with other scores. For example, what if Agatha got scores of "5," "4," "4," "4," "5," and "1" on paper number 4? The average percentage would be 100 + 80 + 80 + 80 + 100 + 20 divided by 6, or 77 percent, a C+. Does a C+ adequately represent her performance on paper 4? Maybe yes, maybe no. We can't automatically decide that based on the math calculation alone.

Instead of converting rubric scores to percentages and then to grades, it is better to convert the rubric score directly to the grade, but not necessarily using the conversion of "5 equals A, 4 equals B," and so on. Rather, we recommend using professional judgment to determine what grade is associated with which pattern of rubric scores. It might be that, looking at the descriptions of performance underlying each score point, a "5" indicates A+ work, a "4" is an A, a "3" is a B, a "2" is a C, a "1.5" is a D, and a "1" is an F.

Or, it might be that each grade corresponds to a pattern of scores. To do this, based on your understanding of the nature of the performance being evaluated, determine what constitutes "excellent work," what constitutes "very good" work, and so on. Map this kind of thinking onto a set of profiles of ratings that then become connected to each letter grade. A decision rule that illustrates this logic is shown in Table 10.2. Consider again Agatha's paper number 4. She has four "3s" and two "4s." This means that 40 percent of the scores are "4s" and 60 percent of the scores are "3s." Using the decision rule in Table 10.2, this would convert to a high C, or a C+.

Table 10.2   Sample Decision Rule for Converting Ratings to Grades

If the student's profile of ratings (on a five-point scale) is	The grade is
At least 50% of the ratings are 5s and the rest are 4s	A
75% of the ratings are 4s or better and the other 25% are not lower than 3	B
40% of the ratings are 3s or better and the other 60% are not lower than 2	C
At least 50% of the ratings are 2s or above	D
More than 50% of the ratings are 2s or below	F

Final Grade on All Papers

Using the average of the percentages earned on all papers (in Agatha's case, 69%) doesn't appear to be accurate. Sixty-nine percent would convert to a D+, which misrepresents Agatha's current performance, as evidenced by her later work. Even averaging the final four papers (the most recent work) to determine a percentage (98 ÷ 120 = 82%) might not work, because 82 percent in our example converts to a B−, which may not accurately represent her current level of achievement either. The solution is, again, a decision rule, such as the ones discussed.

Most of you probably also would recommend using the final papers because of Guideline 4—use the most recent information. But, how many of the final papers would be appropriate? The single final paper might not be enough because it might not sample a broad enough range of audiences and purposes. Again, there is no strict number; sampling is a matter of professional judgment. For the sake of this example, we will use the final four papers.

Using these papers and our decision rule, Agatha's final grade in writing would be 33 percent "5s," 50 percent "4s," and 17 percent "3s," yielding 83 percent "4s" or better and the remaining 17 percent "3" or higher—a B.

Of course, decision rules can be either more complicated *or* simpler. A more complicated, yet perhaps even more accurate, decision rule might have A as being at least 50 percent of scores are "5s," 45 percent are "4s," and the other 5 percent are at least "3s," and so on. This provides some leeway for the odd weak score. The point is that professional judgment is required when converting rubric scores to grades. There's no way to get around it.

Combining Rubric Scores with Percentage Scores to Get a Final Grade

Rarely are all scores in a grading period based on rating scales. Most frequently the gradebook is a mixture of percent correct on tests and ratings. For example, in social studies, a teacher might have a series of percent correct on selected response and extended written response tests and a series of ratings on such skills as research and oral presentation. Or, in Agatha's case, in addition to the ratings on eight papers, there might be a series of percentage scores on tests of grammar, punctuation, and spelling. Since it makes no sense to find a percent correct on rubrics and other rating scales, how should information from the two sources be combined?

We suggest two possible ways. Procedure 1 is as follows:

- Convert both the percentage and rating portions to independent final grades. The percentage portion, for example, would be found by averaging the relevant percentages and using the percent-to-grade conversion scale adopted by your district. The rating portion would be calculated by a decision rule using the most recent work.

- Combine the final grades. For example, you may create this rule: Two As would get an A. An A/B split would get an A–. Two Bs would get a B. A B/C split would get a B–, and so on.

- One part of the final grade could be weighted more than the other. In the social studies example, the percentage score part of the grade might be twice as important as the rating part. Thus, if the percentage part of the grade is an A and the rating part is a B, the teacher might assign the following grade: (2 x A) + B = A.

Procedure 2 is as follows:

- Convert the rating portion to a final grade using your preferred decision rule. Leave the percentage portion as a percentage.

- Use the district's percent-to-grade conversion rule to convert the grade of the rating portion into a percentage. For example, assume the district's conversion rule is as shown in Figure 10.4, and the student earned a B. This would translate to somewhere between 80 and 89 percent. Using the decision rule in Table 10.3, you might convert this B into the percentage at the midpoint of the range (85%).

- Average the converted percentage on the rating portion with that from the percentage portion. For example, if the percentage portion were 93, then 85 + 93 ÷ 2 = 86 percent. This converts to an overall grade of B.

Table 10.3   Sample Decision Rule for Converting Grades to Percentages

Grade	Percentage
A	90 – 100% Midpoint = 95%
B	80 – 89% Midpoint = 85%
C	70 – 79% Midpoint = 75%
D	60 – 69% Midpoint = 65%
F	0 – 59% Midpoint = 30% Compromise = 50%

DEEPEN UNDERSTANDING

Activity 10.5   Assigning a Final Grade

Pretend that you are a biology teacher. You have given two midterms and a final exam covering knowledge of the content. Additionally, you have kept track of performance on laboratory work for the term. The scores you have recorded for one student are shown in Table 10.4. You have told the students that one half of their final grade comes from tests and the other half from labs. What final grade would you give this student? Why?

Table 10.4   Sample Biology Scores for One Student

Tests (knowledge targets) count one-half the grade and labs (skill and product targets) count one-half the grade.

TESTS

Knowledge Targets	Test 1	Test 2	Test 3
1–4	80%		95%
5–8		75%	85%
9–12			80%

LABS

Skill/Product Targets	Lab 1	Lab 2	Lab 3	Lab 4
Proper use of equipment	2	2	3	4
Observation and recording information	4	3	5	4
Lab Report:				
Format	1	3	3	4
Content	4	3	4	5
Communication	4	4	3	4

We would give the student in Activity 10.5 a B. We would replace the score on Test 1 with 95 percent and the score on Test 2 with 85 percent because we want to use the most current information on each set of learning targets. Therefore, the average of 95, 85, and 80 is 87 for the percent portion of the grade.

We would use only the scores from the final two labs because we want to use the most current information. Using the decision rule in Table 10.2 we would assign a grade of B to the rating portion—30 percent of the ratings are "3," 50 percent are "4," and 20 percent are "5." Following procedure 2 as described previously, this converts to an 85 percent (using Table 10.3). Each of the two portions counts one-half toward the grade, so the average of the two portions is 87 + 85 ÷ 2 = 86 percent. This converts to a B using the conversion rule in Figure 10.4.

Summary of Converting Rubric Scores to Grades

Our guidelines for converting rubric scores to grades are summarized in Figure 10.5.

Figure 10.5   Summary—Converting Rubric Scores to Grades

1. *Don't convert rubric scores to letter grades at all if you can help it.* The descriptions associated with each score point give a clearer picture of the students' level of achievement.

2. *Use a decision rule to convert a set of rubric scores to a final grade.* Look at the rubric and decide what level on the rubric describes "excellent work," "good work," "fair work," and "poor work." Then come up with a decision rule for combining the rubric scores.

3. *Replace out-of-date evidence with more recent evidence.* Keep in mind, however, that you still need a large enough sample of work to provide a stable estimate of achievement.

4. *Be careful when combining rubric scores with percentage information to form a final grade.* Decide how much weight the percentage and rating portions of the grade will get. Combine letter grades directly using these weights. Or, use a decision rule to convert the resulting rubric grade back to a percentage and then combine the percentage with other percentage scores using your weighting scheme.

Select Measure of Central Tendency Thoughtfully

Combine assessment information from various assessments into a final grade using the best measure of central tendency—average, median, or mode—for the type of data.

We traditionally combine individual pieces of achievement evidence into a final summary by averaging them. But there is a danger here. Averages are influenced strongly by extreme scores. We addressed this problem earlier in our discussion of entering zeroes into the gradebook. Not only might such an entry misrepresent the truth of a student's achievement on that one assessment, but when combined with other scores it will exert an inordinately strong downward force on the average. Recall from the earlier discussion that scores of 100, 90, 95, and 0 average to 71, a C– on many scales. This clearly does not fairly represent achievement in this case. To counter this problem, some have advocated using median scores rather than mean (average) scores to summarize achievement. Space limitations do not permit us to explore these issues in depth. We recommend that you consult O'Connor (2002), especially page 141, for a fuller discussion.

Decide Borderline Cases with Extra Evidence

In those instances when a student's academic average lies right on the borderline between two grades, we recommend that the decision about which way to go be based not on consideration of nonachievement factors such as effort, but on additional evidence of learning. Some teachers keep one assessment or assignment reflective of important learning in reserve to administer for such instances. Others review the record to determine how the student performed on some of the most important assessments. Others take a look at extra credit that provides evidence of learning. Whatever you do, base your judgment on the most current evidence of achievement you have.

Guideline 6: Verifying Assessment Quality

When assigning grades, use the most accurate body of evidence available. Base all grades on verifiably accurate assessments of student achievement. Discard any inaccurate information from grading records. No one has yet developed an information management and communication system that can convert inaccurate information—misinformation about a student's achievement—into accurate evidence. To communicate effectively and accurately, we need to meet the standards of sound assessment practice described in previous chapters. ETS's training video, *Evaluating Assessment Quality: Hands-on Practice,* also provides experience in auditing classroom assessment for quality.

Guideline 7: Involving Students

At any time during the grading period, be sure students know how their current level of achievement compares to the standards they are expected to master.

Whenever students interpret their performance to be below what they want in their record of achievement, they can be given the opportunity to study more, learn more, and retake that assessment. This is especially crucial when the material in question is prerequisite for later learning. If the objective is to bring all students to appropriate levels of mastery of standards, anything we can do to keep students learning and wanting to succeed is worth doing.

Activity 10.6   Your Own Grading Process

It is the beginning of the semester. You're going to send report cards home in nine weeks. How do you get there from here? What are the steps in your personal process? List them and then mark each one to indicate your level of satisfaction with each: + = works fine; > = could be better; # = needs work or unsure what to do. Then compare your process to the one outlined in Figure 10.6. Where does your practice align? Where does it diverge?

Steps in Report Card Grading

To put the grading guidelines into practice and to obtain accurate, justifiable grades, we suggest following the six steps shown in Figure 10.6.

Figure 10.6   Steps in Report Card Grading

1. Start with the learning targets. Create a plan for what learning you will assess for grading purposes during the quarter.

2. Make an assessment plan to lay out how you will regularly find out what your students are learning.

3. Create, choose, and/or modify assessments.

4. Record information from assessments as you give them.

5. Summarize the achievement information into one score.

6. Turn the score into a grade.

Steps 1 and 2: Start with learning targets and make an assessment plan. Create a list of what learning you will assess for grading purposes during the quarter, as described in Chapter 9. Make an assessment plan to lay out how you will regularly find out how well your students are doing on these learning targets. For each assessment in your plan, you may want to list the learning targets it addresses, when the assessment is to take place, and the method(s) of assessment, as described in Chapter 4. Sampling is an important consideration at this stage: "How can I gather the fewest possible number of assessments for grading and still make an accurate estimate of a student's level of achievement?" Your plan must represent a reasonable workload for you and your students.

Step 3: Create, choose, and/or modify assessments. Devise, select, or modify assessments, either in advance of instruction or along the way, as instruction unfolds.

Step 4: Record information from assessments as you give them. Record scores according to the learning target(s) they represent. Don't convert detailed information to a summary grade yet; keep analytical rubric scores intact in the gradebook.

Step 5: Summarize the achievement information into one score. Convert each score to a common scale, multiply any scores to be weighted by their weighting factor, and then apply the appropriate measure of central tendency to get one summary score.

Step 6: Turn the summary score into a grade. Use preset criterion-based standards, rather than norm-referenced standards, to convert the summary score into a grade.

DEEPEN UNDERSTANDING

Activity 10.7   Video: *Grading and Reporting in Standards-based Schools (60:00)*

Rick Stiggins and Ken O'Connor guide viewers through a discussion of the most compelling issues related to collecting evidence of student achievement and lay out a process to develop more effective grading practices. Individually or as a team, watch the video to reflect on your own grading practices and to discuss changes you may want to make.

Rubric for Grading Practices

Table 10.5 presents a rubric showing each of the previous seven grading guidelines as a performance continuum that you can use to think about your own grading beliefs and practices.

Table 10.5   Rubric for Evaluating Grading Practices

Criterion	Beginning	Developing	Fluent
1. Organizing the gradebook	The evidence of learning (e.g., a gradebook) is entirely organized by sources of information (e.g., tests, quizzes, homework, labs, etc.).	The evidence of learning (e.g., a gradebook) is organized by sources of information mixed with specific content standards.	The evidence of learning (e.g., a gradebook) is completely organized by student learning outcomes (e.g., content standards, benchmarks, grade level indicators, curriculum expectations, etc.).
2. Including factors in the grade	Overall summary grades are based on a mix of achievement and nonachievement factors (e.g., timeliness of work, attitude, effort, cheating). Non-achievement factors have a major impact on grades.	Overall summary grades are based on a mix of achievement and nonachievement factors, but achievement counts a lot more.	Overall summary grades are based on achievement only.
	Extra credit points are given for extra work completed, without connection to extra learning.	Some extra credit points are given for extra work completed; some extra credit work is used to provide extra evidence of student learning.	Extra credit work is evaluated for quality and is only used to provide extra evidence of learning. Credit is not awarded merely for completion of work.
	Cheating, late work, and missing work result in a zero (or a radically lower score) in the gradebook. There is no opportunity to make up such work, except in a few cases.	Cheating, late work, and missing work result in a zero (or lower score) in the gradebook. But, there is an opportunity to make up work and replace the zero or raise the lower score.	Cheating, late work, and missing work is recorded as "incomplete" or "not enough information" rather than as zero. There is an opportunity to replace an "incomplete" with a score without penalty.
	Borderline grade cases are handled by considering non-achievement factors.	Borderline cases are handled by considering a combination of nonachievement factors and collecting additional evidence of student learning.	Borderline grade cases are handled by collecting additional evidence of student achievement, not by counting non-achievement factors.
3. Considering assessment purpose	Everything each student does is given a score and every score goes into the final grade. There is no distinction between "scores" on practice work (formative assessment or many types of homework) and scores on work to demonstrate level of achievement (summative assessment).	Some distinctions are made between formative (practice such as homework) and summative assessment, but practice work still constitutes a significant part of the grade.	Student work is assessed frequently (formative assessment) and graded occasionally (summative assessment). "Scores" on formative assessments and other practice work (e.g., homework) are used descriptively to inform teachers and students of what has been learned and the next steps in learning. Grades are based only on summative assessments.

Table 10.5   (Continued)

4. Considering most recent information	All assessment data are cumulative and used in calculating a final summative grade. No consideration is given to identifying or using the most current information.	More current evidence is given consideration at times, but does not entirely replace out-of-date evidence.	Most recent evidence completely replaces out-of-date evidence when it is reasonable to do so.
5. Summarizing information and determining final grade	The gradebook has a mixture of ABC, percentages, + √ –, and/or rubric scores, etc., with no explanation of how they are to be combined into a final summary grade.	The gradebook may or may not have a mixture of symbols, but there is some attempt, even if incomplete, to explain how to combine them.	The gradebook may or may not have a mix of symbol types, but there is a sound explanation of how to combine them.
	Rubric scores are converted to percentages when averaged with other scores; or, there is no provision for combining rubric and percentage scores.	Rubric scores are not directly converted to percentages; some type of decision rule is used, the final grade many times does not best depict level of student achievement.	Rubric scores are converted to a final grade using a decision rule that results in an accurate depiction of the level of student attainment of the learning targets.
	Final summary grades are based on a curve—a student's place in the rank order of student achievement.	Final grades are criterion referenced, not norm referenced. They are based on preset standards such as A = 90–100% and B = 80–89%. But, there is no indication of the necessity to ensure shared meaning of symbols—i.e., there is no definition of each standard.	Final grades are criterion referenced, not norm referenced. They are based on preset standards with clear descriptions of what each symbol means. These descriptions go beyond A = 90–100% and B = 80–89%; they describe what A, B, etc. performance looks like.
	Final grades for special needs students are not based on learning targets as specified in the IEP.	There is an attempt to base final grades for special needs students on learning targets in the IEP, but the attempt is not always successful; or, it is not clear to all parties that modified learning targets are used to assign a grade.	Final grades for special needs students are criterion referenced, and indicate level of attainment of the learning goals as specified in the IEP. The targets on which grades are based are clear to all parties.
	Final summary grades are based on calculation of mean (average) only.	The teacher understands various measures of central tendency, but may not always choose the best one to accurately describe student achievement.	The teacher selects among measures of central tendency (average, median, mode) as appropriate.

Table 10.5   (Continued)

6. Verifying assessment quality	There is little evidence of consideration of the accuracy/ quality of the individual assessments on which grades are based. Quality standards for classroom assessment are not considered and the teacher has trouble articulating standards for quality. Assessments are rarely modified for special needs students when such modifications would provide more accurate information about student learning.	The teacher tries to base grades on accurate assessment results only, but may not consciously understand all the features of a sound assessment. Some standards of quality are adhered to in judging the accuracy of the assessment results on which grades are based. The teacher can articulate some of these standards; or, uses standards for quality assessment intuitively, but has trouble articulating why an assessment is sound. Assessments are modified for special needs students, but the procedures used may not result in accurate information and/or match provisions in the IEP.	Grades are based only on accurate assessment results. Questionable results are not included. The teacher can articulate standards of quality, and can show evidence of consideration of these standards in classroom assessments. Assessments are modified for special needs students in ways that match instructional modifications described in IEPs. Such modifications result in generating accurate information on student achievement.
7. Involving students	Grades are a surprise to students because (1) students don't understand the bases on which they are determined, (2) students have not been involved in their own assessment (learning targets are not clear to them, and/or they do not self-assess and track progress toward the targets); or (3) teacher feedback is only evaluative (a judgment of level of quality) and includes no descriptive component.	Grades are somewhat of a surprise to students because student-involvement practices and descriptive feedback are too limited to give them insights into the nature of the learning targets being pursued and their own performance.	Grades are not a surprise to students because (1) students understand the basis for the grades received, (2) students have been involved in their own assessment (they understand the learning targets they are to hit, self-assess in relation to the targets, track their own progress toward the targets, and talk about their progress), and/or (3) teacher communication to students is frequent, descriptive, and focuses on what they have learned as well as the next steps in learning. Descriptive feedback is related directly to specific and clear learning targets.

Summary

We may think at times that the pursuit of grades dominates the lives of far too many students, and that the focus on grades still adversely affects the environment of too many classrooms. However grades are used once they are given, we must be dedicated to ensuring that they communicate as clearly and accurately as possible when we create them. The issue is not whether something needs to be done about grades; the issue is what to do. The grading guidelines in this chapter reflect current research and opinion on what grading practices should look like if they are to promote learning.

We also believe that there is a role for professional judgment in grading. In fact, it is impossible in any grading context to leave professional judgment out of the equation. Each teacher brings to their grading practices specific knowledge about individual students and their progress toward the standards. We exercise professional judgment when deciding what content to test. We exercise professional judgment when deciding how best to convert rubric scores to grades. The goal of the guidelines in this chapter is to make an essentially subjective system as objective and defensible as possible.

One of our messages throughout this book is about the power of a classroom with an aligned system of curriculum, instruction, assessment, and reporting. By now you know it begins with clear curriculum targets aligned to standards. Teachers then clarify those targets for students and transform them into accurate assessments. Along the way students are involved in their own assessment, record keeping, and communication about their progress toward those targets, and student learning is documented and organized in gradebooks according to learning target and standard. Finally, student achievement is reported to parents and students relative to those same standards. This system, we know, improves student achievement.

This chapter has focused largely on assigning report card grades by subject in a traditional letter- or number-based system. Often parents expect, if not demand, this form of reporting, and yet they also value the specific information that can be provided through a standards-based reporting form (Guskey, 2002). We have established here that the purpose of grades is to communicate about student achievement. The next two chapters will explore other forms of communication. As you proceed, keep the goal of standards-based education in mind: to teach, assess, improve, and communicate about student learning in relation to academic learning standards. We can focus less of our time on providing subject area grades and still accomplish our goal if we move toward the use of rich, descriptive performance statements that provide specific information about where the student is relative to each standard. In the chapters that follow, we will provide more detail about how to gather and communicate that detail. When we do it well, the payoff is worth it for us and for our students.

■ *Tracking Your Learning—Possible Portfolio Entries*

Any of the activities included in Chapter 10 can be used as portfolio entries. Remember, the learning targets for this book are outlined in Figure 10.1, and listed in Table 1.2 and described in detail in Chapter 1. The portfolio entry cover sheet provided on the CD in the file, "Portfolio Entry Cover Sheet," will prompt you to think about how each item you choose for your portfolio reflects your learning with respect to one or more of these learning targets.

Specific recommendations for portfolio content follow.

TRY THIS

Activity 10.8   Analyzing Your Own Grading Practices

Review the grading rubric in Table 10.5. Then analyze your grading practices. Discuss both the rubric and your self-ratings with your learning team. What implications might this have for what you do?

DEEPEN UNDERSTANDING

Activity 10.9   Your Friend's Gradebook

Imagine that Table 10.6 represents your friend's gradebook for the first grading period. She has not read this text, but she knows you pay careful attention to making sure your grades are sound and defensible, so she asks your help in straightening out her gradebook. Show her how to get a defensible grade for Abe and Sal. What questions would you ask your friend? What suggestions would you make for record keeping for the next grading period? If you are working with a learning team, you may wish to discuss these questions as a group.

Table 10.6   Your Friend's Language Arts Gradebook

	Ideas	Org.	Word Choice	Conventions	Conventions Test	Spell Test	Oral Presentation	% Total	Grade
Abe	3	2	3	5	8/10	85%	12/15		
Sal	4	4	5	3	9/10	65%	15/15		

TRY THIS

Activity 10.10   Converting Your Own Rating Scales to Grades

Individually or with your learning team choose a common rating scale or rubric that you use frequently with students.

1. How will you address the recommendation to use the most recent information? Will you give separate assignments and tasks? If so, how many and of what kind? Will you choose the final several pieces of work generated during the grading period? If so, how many and of what kind?

2. What decision rule will you use to convert rubric scores to grades? What is your justification for this rule?

3. How will you combine rubric scores with percentage scores to determine final grades?

CHAPTER

Portfolios

[**T**] he desire to capture and communicate the depth of student learning has been at the heart of portfolio use for years. A report card grade summarizes the story of achievement in one word at the same level of detail that a topic summarizes the story of a book: "prejudice" is a topic of *To Kill a Mockingbird*, but that one word does not begin to tell the story. A *portfolio* is a collection of artifacts put together to get at the full story, to help students, teachers, and others understand in depth one or more aspects of student learning.

Sometimes you will encounter the term *portfolio assessment*, as though it were an assessment method, such as performance assessment. It is not. A portfolio's contents, and the collection as a whole, can be assessed, but we do not advocate using the term *portfolio assessment* because, as we hope we make clear, portfolios are collecting and communicating devices.

We often associate portfolios with artists, who use them to communicate visually about their talent, style, and range of work, or with writers, who put them together to illustrate their writing capabilities. The contents are selected to offer a rich and detailed view of their subjects' characteristics or qualities. As you have proceeded through this book, we have encouraged you to follow a series of portfolio development suggestions to reflect on and document your own classroom assessment learning path.

Beyond their potential as a rich source of information, portfolios play a significant role in learning. Many times the responsibility for collecting, interpreting, and sharing portfolio contents falls to the teacher. However, we pass by a powerful learning experience when the *subject* of the portfolio (the student) is not also the *author*, for when students assemble and share portfolios, they perform acts of metacognition that deepen their ability to learn, their desire to learn, and the learning itself.

Involving students in this work provides an ideal venue for getting them to take notice of, keep track of, and celebrate their learning. Collecting, organizing, and reflecting on their own work builds an understanding of themselves as learners and nurtures a sense of accomplishment. Becoming reflective learners, developing an internal feedback loop, learning to set goals, and noticing new competencies and new challenges are all habits of thought we can cultivate in students through the use of portfolios.

Portfolios can tell lots of different stories; the keys to using them well lie in knowing which story you intend to tell, maximizing the students' role, and managing the variables accordingly. In this chapter we will explore the kinds of portfolios commonly used today, purposes for each, and keys to their successful use, including options in the following areas:

- Portfolio contents

- The role of the teacher and the role of the student

- Managing portfolios

- Student self-reflection

Chapter 11 addresses the shaded portions of Figure 11.1. Figure 11.2 shows the series of decisions that will frame this chapter.

Figure 11.1 Keys to Quality Classroom Assessment

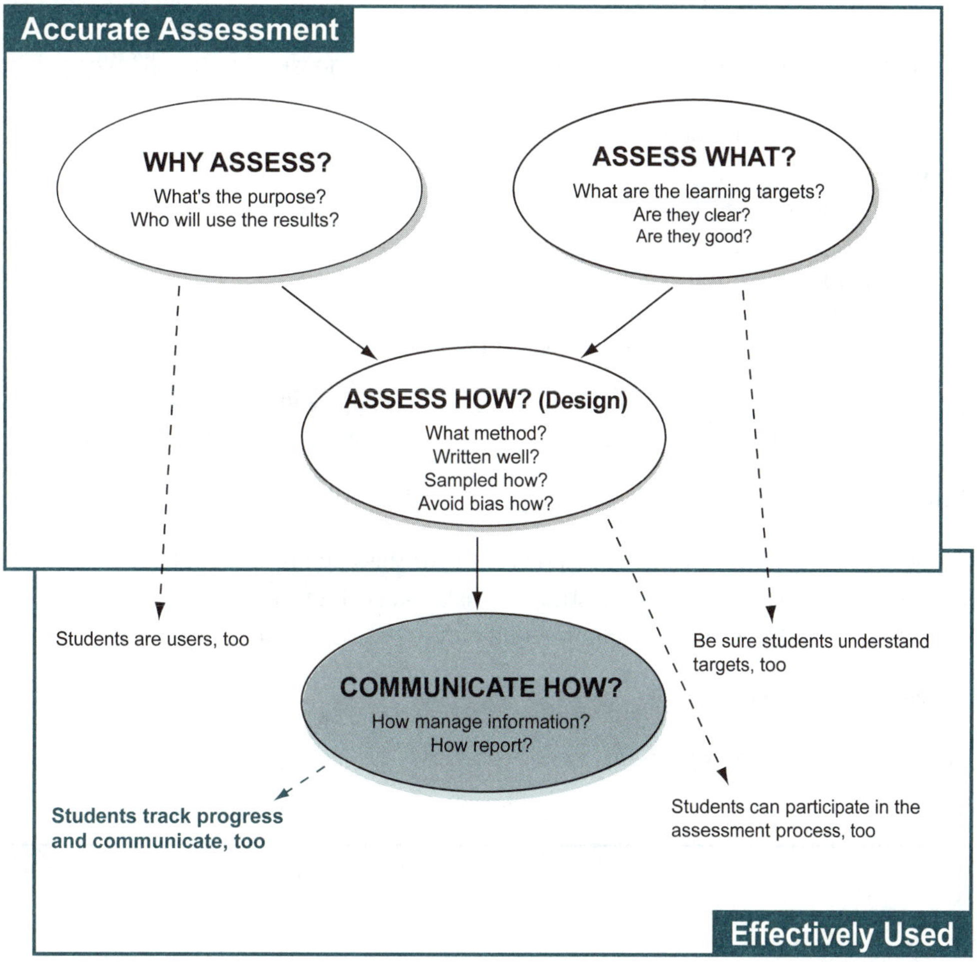

Accurate Assessment

WHY ASSESS?
What's the purpose?
Who will use the results?

ASSESS WHAT?
What are the learning targets?
Are they clear?
Are they good?

ASSESS HOW? (Design)
What method?
Written well?
Sampled how?
Avoid bias how?

Students are users, too

COMMUNICATE HOW?
How manage information?
How report?

Be sure students understand targets, too

Students track progress and communicate, too

Students can participate in the assessment process, too

Effectively Used

Figure 11.2   Portfolio Decision Flow

1. What kind(s) of portfolios will we assemble? What story do we want to tell? Who will be our audience?
   a. Project documentation
   b. Growth
   c. Achievement
   d. Competence
   e. Celebration

2. Which learning target(s) will be the focus of our portfolios?

3. Based on purpose and target(s), which pieces of evidence will we include? What are our guidelines for inclusion? How will we ensure a representative sample of student work?

4. How will the quality of portfolios be judged, if at all? Who will do the judging, if anyone?

5. Student involvement: How much responsibility for this can my students take?
   a. What kinds of annotations will students make on each piece?
   b. What will be the focus of students' culminating self-reflection?

6. How will we manage the artifacts?

7. When and with whom will we share our portfolios?

DEEPEN UNDERSTANDING

Activity 11.1   Job Interview Simulation

Imagine you are applying for a new teaching position. Instead of a regular application form, the selection committee has asked you to submit a portfolio that illustrates who you are as an educator right now.

1. What would you include in the portfolio? Why?

2. Would your portfolio include different items depending on the job? Why or why not?

3. What input from others would help you assemble your job application portfolio?

4. What are the implications of this exercise for the role of *purpose* when designing portfolios?

Kinds of Portfolios—Focus on Purpose

What goes into a portfolio? All of a student's work? Only the best? "Before" and "after" samples? Whatever the student selects? Before we make that decision, we must think about what story we want the portfolio to tell. As a collection of evidence, the portfolio itself is only an organizing tool. The *artifacts* (the individual items) in an artist's, an author's, or your own assessment portfolio require more than physical existence in a folder to hang together as a story. They need a theme—struggle, achievement, competence, celebration—to guide the selection of ingredients. What is the storyline—Here is how this person completed each step of a project? See how this person has grown? Here is a picture of this person's level of achievement now? This person has attained these competencies? Here is what this person is proud of?

With the importance of storyline in mind, we will look at five basic purposes for portfolios: project documentation, growth, achievement, competence, and celebration. The portfolios you are familiar with most likely will fall into one or more of these categories.

Project Portfolios

Project portfolios are, as the name suggests, focused on the work from an individual project. Their purpose is to document the steps taken, often to show evidence of having satisfactorily completed intermediary steps along the way to the finished product. Sometimes their purpose is to show competence, such as with writing processes or scientific processes. They also can document such things as time management capabilities.

Artifacts are chosen to provide evidence suited to the project to be documented. In the case of a research paper, students might show their progression of work from initial question to finished product, including those pieces of evidence that best illustrate the major steps they took. Each piece of evidence is accompanied by an explanation of what step or steps it is intended to show and how it does that. Students may write a comprehensive "process paper" or they may annotate each artifact. In either case, students will learn more from the process and remember it better if they also write a reflection on what they learned from completing the steps involved in the project.

Growth Portfolios

Growth portfolios show progress toward competence on one or more learning targets. They document increasing levels of achievement. Students select evidence related to a given learning target at two or more points in time, and their annotations explain the level of achievement each artifact represents. The selection may represent best work as of a point in time or typical work. The sampling challenge is to ensure that the samples chosen really do represent best *or* typical work, and not anomalous work from which to judge growth (e.g., selecting a piece of poor quality at the beginning that under-represents the student's true level of achievement at that time). The student writes a self-reflection to summarize growth: "Here's how far I've come and here's what I know and can do now that I couldn't do before."

Achievement Portfolios

Achievement portfolios document the level of student achievement at a point in time. They are comprised of best, most recent work organized by the learning target each represents. In the case of achievement portfolios, it is important to attend to the number of samples collected. Certain learning targets will call for multiple samples to demonstrate level of achievement while other achievement targets may need only one. Student annotations refer to the learning target and level of competence each sample shows. These are often used as the basis for discussion and goal setting at conference time.

Competence Portfolios

Competence portfolios offer evidence in support of a claim to have attained an acceptable or exemplary level of achievement. They sometimes take the form of "exhibition of mastery" portfolios or "school-to-work" portfolios. As with achievement portfolios, competence portfolios require that we attend to sampling issues. It is crucial to their success to determine in advance the number of pieces of evidence needed to support an assertion of competence for each learning target addressed. We want to show that a high level of achievement has been sustained and is not just the result of chance.

Celebration Portfolios

Celebration portfolios give students the opportunity to decide what accomplishments or achievement they are most proud of. In this case, students decide what to put in and why. The elementary teacher may choose to leave the subject of the celebration open ended— "anything you're proud of"—or focus it more narrowly—"your work in science" or "things that show you are a reader." Secondary teachers using celebration portfolios generally narrow the focus to the subject they teach.

Working Folders

Working folders are not portfolios. They function as holding bins, sometimes for every scrap of paper related to a project, sometimes as an idea file, sometimes as a collection of works in progress, and other times as an undifferentiated collection of finished pieces. Working files are often used as the place to go to review work that might be included in the portfolio, the collection of all possible artifacts from which to make selections. Portfolios serving more than one purpose can be developed from a single working folder. Similarly, the same piece of student work can be selected for portfolios having different purposes.

Portfolio Contents—Focus on Targets

While portfolios lend themselves naturally to the types of targets assessed best by performance assessments, we are not limited to the evidence produced by that one assessment method. All five kinds of learning targets—knowledge, reasoning, skill, product, and disposition—can be the focus of evidence gathering for portfolios. Thus, all forms of assessment can be included: tests and quizzes, pretests, extended-response assessments, performance assessments, and documentation of the results of personal communication. Although all work in a portfolio should have some form of commentary present, each entry does not have to consist of a formal assessment.

Portfolios can reflect a single learning target, a series of learning targets, or all learning targets in a given subject. They can also cross subject areas. As an example of the latter, consider the middle school portfolio project in which students were to demonstrate their achievement of oral communication skills across subject matter areas.

Artifacts

The artifacts in a portfolio should not consist simply as proof of direction-following (unless that is the intended learning). They must be aimed at telling a story about specific, intended learning. It might seem to be a simple point, but it bears emphasizing: Clearly identify the learning targets about which the portfolio is intended to communicate. *Do not skip this step.* Many common portfolio problems can be avoided entirely right here. You have identified the purpose (to document project work, growth, achievement, or competence, or to celebrate), and now you must be clear about what learning targets are the focus of the project, growth, achievement, competence, or celebration.

Let's say your students will assemble a project portfolio. The project consists of a task: to design and conduct a scientific investigation, to document the work and the results, and to prepare a written report. What learning targets are the focus of this project? What aspects of the learning will the portfolio document? You may be focusing on "designs and conducts a scientific investigation." You might choose to have the students document the steps of their investigations, in which case, they might collect artifacts to show how they formulated the question, how they came up with the investigation design, what they did at each step, the thinking behind their data interpretation, and the options they considered in settling on an explanation. In this case, how would the portfolio assignment differ from a written report, which may include the question, a description of the investigation, presentation of data, and conclusions? For one, the portfolio contents are chosen to illustrate the thinking behind the steps of a scientific investigation, not just to document that they were done. The goal of this kind of portfolio is not to show that students completed each step—the report can do that—but to show how they thought through and implemented each step.

Sampling

Sampling is an important issue for various kinds of portfolios. For example, if the purpose is to demonstrate level of achievement in a student-led conference and the target is problem solving in geometry, we will have to think about how much evidence is enough to show level of achievement. How many of what types of artifacts would need to be included in the portfolio to be sure that any inference we make about overall student problem-solving competence is accurate? We might need, say, 10 examples from various topics in geometry, some of which may include real-life applications. Therefore, to ensure that students are providing accurate information to their parents, we might specify what types of items must be included in the portfolio, and which learning targets are to be represented. Selection of the sample in this case depends on the kind of learning targets at the focus of the achievement.

Who Decides?

Think about a portfolio not as an object, but as a process. Traditionally, the artifacts have been the student's, but the process may have been conducted largely by the teacher. However, when students assemble the portfolio, reflect on what the evidence says, and prepare to share, they become better learners. Inviting students to help determine what will go into the portfolio offers them an opportunity to practice thinking about what constitutes evidence in a given context. Help them think through the criteria for the selections they will be making. Rather than just telling them the criteria outright, you may want to engage them in the same kind of thinking you had to do about purpose and learning targets. To the extent that your students are able to do it (and even young ones can complete much of this), let the majority of work shift from the teacher to the student, where it belongs. It is to their benefit. Table 11.1 summarizes the extent to which teachers and students make various decisions for each kind of portfolio.

Work Sample Annotations

If a portfolio's contents consist solely of samples of student work, no matter who collects them, it will not function effectively either as a communication tool or as an enhancement to student learning. More is needed to bring the story to life and to be the catalyst for increased achievement.

Work sample annotations are whatever comments students or teachers make about each piece of evidence selected for the portfolio. Generally, they link the work to the intended learning in some way. Creating these comments helps portfolio authors be clear about why they are choosing each artifact and what it shows. They also help the portfolio's

Table 11.1   Who Decides?

Decision	Kind of Portfolio: Teacher Decides				Celebration
	Project	**Growth**	**Achievement**	**Competence**	
Learning Target(s)	Teacher or both	Teacher or both	Teacher or both	Teacher	Student or both
Contents: Number and kind of each type of entry	Student or both	Both	Both	Both	Student
Contents: Specific artifacts	Student or both	Student or both	Student or both	Student or both	Student
Performance Criteria	Teacher or both	Others	Others	Others	Student, if any
Audience	Student or both	Teacher or both	Teacher or both	Teacher or both	Student or both

audience know what to notice; without some form of explanation for each artifact included, the audience is left to infer how it relates to the learning. If students prepare such statements when selecting their artifacts, when the time comes to share their portfolios with others, nervousness or other distractions will not cause them to forget *how* this particular entry demonstrates their learning.

An unstructured form of annotation is the "pause and think" comment. Students use a work sample to reflect in an open-ended way about what they are learning—why the learning is important to them, something they notice about themselves as learners, a key point they have learned from doing the assignment, and so on. ("One important thing I have learned from doing this is _____.")

Annotations can also take the form of statements of the learning target each artifact represents, along with an explanation of how this artifact demonstrates achievement. ("I can summarize stories. I have included the biggest events and main characters. I have left out the details. I have put things in the right order and used my own words.")

Another form of annotation consists of student self-assessment against established criteria. For growth and achievement portfolios, students point out features of the work that match phrases in the criteria and draw conclusions about level of quality, strengths, and areas for improvement. For competence portfolios, students explain why a particular artifact constitutes proof of proficiency, showing how it meets established criteria. ("This work is an example of level _____ on the _____ criteria because _____.")

Frequently, annotations are written on a cover sheet. We have included an example on the CD in the file, "Student Portfolio Cover."

Goal Setting

What better way is there to establish an "I can do it" mindset toward learning than to let students show themselves and others that they are accomplishing their goals? In essence, goal setting involves answering three questions: "What do I need to work on?"; "What is my plan?"; and "Who will I ask to help me?" We recommend that students answer, "What do I need to work on?" only *after* identifying what they are doing well.

In one form of goal setting, the student's annotation for each artifact includes an area or learning target to work on, based on analysis of the artifact's strengths and weaknesses. In another form, students set goals after reviewing the whole portfolio.

Student Self-Reflection

Portfolios frequently also include student self-reflection. It can be tempting to pass over having students reflect on what the portfolio as a whole represents. After all, when students have pointed out what they have learned, justified the claim with evidence, and set goals for future learning, what is left? The answer is, "Plenty!" Success at self-reflection may seem serendipitous at first—somewhat outside our control—in asking such an open-ended question as is required for true self-reflection. But, learning beyond the stated intentions can take place if we allow students to think about themselves as learners and provide opportunities for them to dig a little deeper into what the learning means to them. If they have completed the other steps, they are primed to uncover insights into themselves. Insight requires time to reflect, which is what this part of the portfolio process provides. If we pull up here, however, we have stopped just short of increased learning.

If students have not done reflective thinking before—not fill-in-the-blank thinking, but open-ended, thinking-about-myself-as-a-learner thinking—be prepared to give some class time for helping them learn how to do it. Explain the task, model it, let students discuss it, then set a time limit and wait patiently. Let volunteers read aloud and ask them what doing this has taught them. After they know what is required in this kind of thinking, self-reflection makes a good homework assignment, especially if students discuss their thoughts with their parents before writing. Table 11.2 shows some questions you can use to stimulate student self-reflection, and Table 11.3 offers some phrases to help students get headed in the right direction with annotation, goal setting, and self-reflection.

Table 11.2   Questions That Spark Student Self-Reflection

Questions That Invite Vague Answers	Questions That Invite Insights
Analysis of Skills and Processes: • Why do you like the things in your portfolio? • What's the best? • What's the worst piece here? • Why didn't you include more writing samples? • What will you do next?	*Analysis of Skills and Processes:* • What makes this your best piece? • What makes your best piece different from your least effective piece? • What can you do in math now that you couldn't do before? • How good is your answer? What would make it better? • If you could work further on this piece, what would you do? • How does this relate to what you've learned before? • Of the work we've done recently, what do you feel most confident about? What do you still not understand?
Analysis of Processes: • Why did you do it this way? • Did you like working in a group? • What didn't work?	*Analysis of Processes:* • What steps did you go through in completing this assignment? Did this process work and lead to successful completion or were there problems? What would you change next time? • What are the ways you find working with others useful? Not useful?
How Skills and Processes Have Changed Over Time: • What's different now? • How do you feel about your work now? • What progress have you made?	*How Skills and Processes Have Changed Over Time:* • How is your work at the end of the year different from your work at the beginning? • Has the way you've planned work changed over time? If so, how? • In which area have you noticed the most improvement? How do you know?
Affective and Other Areas: • What's fun to do in school? • Do you like math? • Are you a good learner?	*Affective and Other Areas:* • Do you think you keep going on tasks differently now than in the past? If so, why? • What subject do you like the most? Why? • What type of work do you enjoy doing the most? Least? Why? • What impact has this project had on your interests, attitudes, and views of this area?

Source: Adapted from *Practice with Student-Involved Classroom Assessment* (p. 306), by J. A. Arter & K. U. Busick, 2001, Portland, OR: Assessment Training Institute. Copyright © 2006, 2001 Educational Testing Service. Adapted by permission.

Table 11.3   Student Phrases for Annotations, Goal Setting, and Self-Reflection

Component	Phrases
Annotations regarding intended learning or learning target	This _____ shows that I have learned . . . I can . . .
Annotations to explain how the piece demonstrates the intended learning or learning target	Here is the evidence: As evidence, please notice . . . My work meets these criteria: My strengths in this _____ are _____.
Goal setting	One area that needs work is _____. Next, I would like to learn . . . The next thing I need to learn is . . . Next I will work on . . . The part of quality (trait) I will focus on next is . . .
Reflection on learning	In working on _____, I also learned _____. Here is what doing _____ taught me about myself as a learner: The thing I liked most about doing _____ is . . . The thing I liked least is . . . I have become better at _____. I used to _____, but now I _____.

Another way to help students develop reflective thinking is to find or create a rubric that describes what good quality self-reflection looks like and then use the Seven Strategies, discussed in Chapters 2 and 7, to teach them how to improve.

Judging Quality

For many of the learning targets focused on in portfolios—reasoning, skills, and products—and for some of the processes for portfolios, it is useful to have performance criteria. It is almost impossible for anyone to choose items for a portfolio without knowing what a good-quality performance looks like. Absent such performance criteria, students fall back on their own devices to determine what quality looks like. Maybe the only criterion for quality that a student knows for writing is "length," or "neatness," or "correct spelling." In such cases, student selections and annotations generally do not result in a coherent portfolio story.

There are three possible types of performance criteria that are useful with portfolios: criteria for entries, criteria for self-reflection, and criteria for the portfolio as a product in and of itself.

Criteria for Judging Individual Entries

In some cases, at least a portion of portfolio entries may reflect knowledge targets, and therefore may be represented by selected response tests or other artifacts not requiring rubrics to judge level of achievement. However, each entry, if it is a performance assessment, will have one or more criteria by which to judge its quality, as discussed in Chapter 7. Such rubrics define what various levels of quality look like on whatever reasoning, skill, or product target is the focus of the portfolio. For example, students gathering evidence of their ability to make oral presentations should have a rubric that defines what a high-level oral presentation looks like. It also helps if they understand the rubrics by having gone through the Seven Strategies, as described in Chapters 2 and 7.

Criteria for Self-Reflection

As noted previously, students don't all come to us knowing how to self-reflect. They don't know what it is, why it is important to do, and what good-quality self-reflection looks like. Teaching students how to use a rubric for self-reflection helps the process to be more powerful. One example, "Self-Reflection Rubric," is included on the CD in the file, "Rubric Sampler."

The purpose of such a rubric is formative, not summative: to help students understand what self-reflection is and how to do it, rather than to grade students' efforts at self-reflection (unless, of course, ability to self-reflect is one of the learning targets you report formally). Here are some specific ideas about teaching students how to use self-reflection rubrics, drawn from Strategy 1 of the Seven Strategies described in Chapters 2 and 7.

1. Gather written student reflections from several grade levels. Mix them up and ask students to identify the grade levels and indicate why they think so. This helps students see how sophistication in self-reflection grows.

2. Ask students to select the two or three they think demonstrate the best self-reflection and say why.

3. Have students apply these budding criteria (their responses to "say why") to additional samples and add to their list of characteristics.

4. Show students your draft self-reflection rubric and have them compare it to their list and add and subtract features.

Criteria for the Portfolio as a Whole

Sometimes it is useful to have a rubric for the portfolio as a product in and of itself. For example, your rubric might contain the traits of clear targets, adequate evidence to make a case, good self-reflection, and ease in finding information. This also helps students understand the purpose of a portfolio and what you are looking for in it. Once again, unless the portfolio itself is a graded assignment, the rubric's purpose is not to grade the portfolio overall, but rather to help students understand the nature of quality. A sample portfolio rubric is included on the CD in the file, "Rubric Sampler."

Sharing Options—Communicating with Portfolios

We determine the audience for a portfolio by thinking about the story it has to tell. Who might be interested in this story? Audiences for portfolio sharing include parents, other students, teachers, the principal, central office staff, community members, grandparents, special friends, businesses, review committees, and potential employers. Student-involved conferences, addressed in Chapter 12, often rely on portfolios to focus the discussion.

The audience for a portfolio can also be its creator. After assembling your own classroom assessment portfolio, you may be the only one who sees it. If so, is it a waste of time? We believe not. However, for most students, sharing their work with an interested audience can generate additional learning and insight into themselves as learners, as well as increased motivation to keep going.

Summary of Portfolio Decisions

Table 11.4 summarizes how type of portfolio affects portfolio design—what evidence it contains, who develops performance criteria and judges quality, and the type and degree of student involvement. Table 11.5 outlines student and teacher responsibilities with respect to portfolios.

Table 11.4   How Type of Portfolio Affects Design

Portfolio Type & Purpose	Implications of Purpose for Portfolio Design			
	Targets: What story will the portfolio tell?	Sampling: What kinds of evidence must it contain?	Who develops performance criteria and judges quality?	Student Involvement
Project To show steps in completing a project; to document learning from a project	How did I go about this project? What were the steps? What decisions did I make? What did I learn from this project?	The finished product and items that document the process—e.g., journals, logs, drafts, reviews by others, photos; commentary on what each item shows, or a process paper; student self-reflection	Teacher and students or teacher; performance criteria must relate directly to the specific purpose.	Students analyze their work along the way to understand their own process; students reflect on their learning.
Growth To show progress in learning on given learning targets	How have I grown as a learner? What can I do now that I couldn't do before? Where have I improved?	Periodic dated entries documenting learning for specified targets; student self-reflection on growth	There might not be any outside criteria. Or, students, or teachers, or both could develop criteria and judge quality.	Student-involved record keeping and self-reflection
Achievement Status To document level of achievement on given learning targets at a point in time	Where am I with regard to the learning targets we are studying? What is my level of achievement right now?	Representative samples of current level of achievement, linked to specific learning targets	May have criteria developed by others. Or, students, or teachers, or both could develop criteria and judge quality.	Students may participate in selecting items; students identify which learning targets each represents; students write self-reflections.
Competence To document attainment of level of mastery	I am competent at this learning target.	Sample of evidence for each target represented; annotations and/or an overall explanation to show how the evidence demonstrates competence	May have criteria developed by others, for example when documenting student competence on district or state standards.	Students may participate in selecting evidence. They will explain how the collection supports an assertion of mastery. They may write self-reflections.
Celebration To showcase work or learning students are proud of	What did I like best this year? What do I feel best about?	Anything the student wants, at any time; statements of what each item shows and why it was included	The student. There might not be any outside criteria.	Students make all of the choices. They have to think about what they value and why.

Source: Adapted from *Practice with Student-Involved Classroom Assessment* (p. 302), by J. A. Arter & K. U. Busick, 2001, Portland, OR: Assessment Training Institute. Copyright © 2006, 2001 Educational Testing Service. Adapted by permission.

Table 11.5   Portfolio Responsibilities

	Student Responsibility	**Teacher Responsibility**
Purpose	Can explain process to parents	Determine purpose of portfolio Explain to students why they are collecting artifacts Explain process to parents
Artifacts	Select, date, annotate, and file work samples	Set up organizing system (or offer options for older students) Offer guidance on selection, as needed Provide time to select, annotate, and file work samples (model as needed)
Reflection	Prepare reflection suited to purpose of portfolio	Provide time to prepare reflection (model as needed)
Quality	Can use a rubric to assess the portfolio's quality, if appropriate	Can use a rubric to assess the portfolio's quality, if appropriate
Audience	Can help determine audience Invite audience; prepare to share	Determine audience (can be done with students) Arrange opportunity for sharing

DEEPEN UNDERSTANDING

Activity 11.2   What Type of Portfolio Is This?

In Figure 11.3, match each portfolio example on the right to its major purpose on the left. Add your own examples on the right and classify them. How does this matching help you design portfolios?

Figure 11.3   What Type of Portfolio Is This?

Portfolio Matching Quiz

Instructions: Match each purpose for portfolios on the left to the various examples on the right. Add your own examples on the right. What implications does this have for how the various examples are designed?

Portfolio Purpose	Example
a. Celebration	____ 1. Student-led conferences
b. Growth	____ 2. Certify competency for high school graduation.
c. Project	____ 3. Job interview
d. Competence	____ 4. Personal favorites
e. Achievement	____ 5. Science fair
	____ 6. Tracking student progress toward standards in mathematics.
	____ 7. College entry
	____ 8. Help students see themselves as readers. Students choose anything in their world that documents themselves as readers.
	____ 9. Alternative credit
	____ 10. Identify gifted students using multiple intelligences.
	____ 11.
	____ 12.
	____ 13.

Source: Adapted from *Practice with Student-Involved Classroom Assessment* (p. 303), by J. A. Arter & K. U. Busick, 2001, Portland, OR: Assessment Training Institute. Copyright © 2006, 2001 Educational Testing Service. Adapted by permission.

Keys to Successful Use

Portfolios are a means to an end, not an end in themselves. They are a means to help students learn more deeply and embed learning into long-term memory. They are a means to help students take responsibility for their own learning and engage in the critical thinking needed to make portfolio decisions. They are a means to deepen communication with others about complex student learning targets. If students do the communication, they are a means of practicing communication skills.

Suggestions follow for effectively implementing portfolios, related to four key issues that contribute to success: quality, keeping track, time, and classroom environment.

Quality

A portfolio as a reflection and communication device is only as good as its contents. Each piece must provide credible evidence. Each entry is only as good as the assignment given. For example, a state not too many years ago asked teachers and students to assemble portfolios to demonstrate student problem-solving ability in mathematics. They got back many portfolios filled with worksheets, which did not require the problem solving they were looking for. If you want to assess problem solving you need to give students assignments that require them to problem solve. The underlying assignment that created each artifact must be sound, or the evidence will not be accurate. If this is the case, we either cannot use the information, making it a waste of time, or if we do use the information, we risk muddling our communication to students and their parents.

When portfolios are used as a means of communication, they must adhere to the same conditions of quality communication as other methods: everyone understands the targets communicated about; the assessments and other work underpinning the portfolio are an accurate portrayal of student learning; any symbols used to convey information (e.g., rubric ratings) are clear; and communication is tailored to the audience. Portfolios are an excellent way of tailoring communication to meet parents' information needs, because they are interested in and can use the descriptive detail about their children's work that portfolios provide.

Keeping Track

Periodically schedule time for students to select, date(!), and annotate artifacts. Choose a system for keeping track of everything. Possibilities follow—the key to success here is finding one that fits your organizational style.

1. *Identifying the artifacts*—First, identify the type of artifact you will be keeping: the physical product itself, a photograph of articles or projects that do not lend themselves to storage, a videotape, an audiotape, the artifact on a computer hard drive or disc, or something else.

2. *Organizing the artifacts*—What you choose depends on what type of artifacts you will be collecting. Options include notebooks, file folders, accordion folders, hanging files in a file drawer, clear-view binders, 11 X 17 paper folded in half as dividers (especially for growth portfolios—artifacts can be pasted on each facing page, with flip-up annotations), binders with categories, and binders with envelopes for computer discs.

3. *Storing the collections*—Options include magazine file boxes, cereal boxes, laundry detergent boxes, plastic crates, or file cabinet drawers (with collections organized by period at the secondary level and by table group, row, or subject at the elementary level). If choosing to store artifacts in a computer program, remember that the software is only a place to keep artifacts. Computer programs won't automatically create quality portfolios; you still have to make all of the decisions outlined in this chapter.

Time

Front load the portfolio experience—take time up front to save time later. Teach students the purpose and process for portfolios, criteria for individual entries, criteria for self-reflection, and criteria for the portfolio as a whole. Turn responsibility over to students as soon as possible. In our opinion, portfolios are not worth the time they take if teachers do all the work.

Classroom Environment

Nowhere do respect, dignity, fairness, and compassion play a greater role in nurturing learning than when we are asking students to publicly show what they know. Keeping a portfolio is a risk-taking behavior: risk that someone else's artifacts will be better than mine; risk that mine will be better than everyone else's or than my friend's; risk that I will look clueless, or smug. We make our classrooms safe by what we model and what we allow, by how we treat each student and how we allow each student to treat others.

Summary

Portfolios serve two functions: to improve communication about complex student learning targets, and to promote student learning.

All decisions regarding portfolios, from selecting content to determining the amount of student involvement, depend on the purpose of the portfolio. We examined five types of portfolios—project, growth, achievement, certifying competence, and celebration—and the effect of these purposes on portfolio design decisions, summarized in Tables 11.1 and 11.4.

Involve students in preparing and maintaining portfolios. Why do we prepare portfolios in the first place? It is too much work to use them solely as backup evidence for a grade. Therefore, no matter what kind of portfolio you have, to be worth the investment of time as a learning and communication tool, portfolios must have three elements:

- Student involvement in content selection

- Student commentary on the contents—why they were selected and what they represent

- Self-reflection about what they learned

The real power of portfolios is in opportunities they provide students to analyze, summarize, and reflect on their own learning.

■ *Tracking Your Progress—Possible Portfolio Entries*

Any of the activities in this chapter can be used as portfolio entries. Once again, the learning targets for this book are outlined in Figure 11.1, listed in Table 1.2, and described in detail in Chapter 1. The portfolio entry cover sheet provided on the CD in the file, "Portfolio Entry Cover Sheet," will prompt you to think about how each item you choose for your portfolio reflects your learning with respect to one or more of these learning targets.

Specific recommendations for portfolio content follow.

Activity 11.3   The Dilemma of Student Selection and Clear Communication

Read the case study in Figure 11.4, in which teachers are dismayed by the shallowness of young students' portfolio selections and reflections. Think about or discuss with your learning teams the following questions:

1. What contributed to the weaknesses of these portfolios?

2. What advice would you give the teachers about preparing learners for self-assessment?

Figure 11.4   The Dilemma of Student Selection and Clear Communication

It's almost time for quarterly reporting. The teachers in this elementary school have enthusiastically embraced the notion of using portfolios as part of their assessment system. They've attended a portfolio workshop, and have spent time brainstorming and agreeing on portfolio purposes (showing growth over time, involving students in self-assessment, communicating more richly about student learning with parents, and having students involved in selecting and reflecting on their work.) The PTA helped buy colorful folders for storing student products, and the staff developed sets of criteria for looking at certain kinds of work (problem solving, reading, and mathematics). But now that it's time to send the portfolios home, the results of the first round of student selection seem to be revealing some serious weaknesses:

"How can I send these portfolios home?" says one teacher, face to face with what she views as disaster. "Yesterday, I asked my students to make selections from their working folders. It seemed to go okay. Then I had them write brief reflections on why each piece was chosen. When I looked them over, I was horrified. They've chosen things that I never would have. Some of the most important work we've done all quarter isn't there. Parents will get a really poor picture of what we've been doing and what their children are learning. They're going to think we're not doing our jobs. And the reflections! The reasons are so trivial. 'I like it.' 'It got the best grade.' 'The colors are my favorites.' Where are their insights? They don't know what to say. I thought this portfolio idea was going to be the answer for us. Now I'm wondering if there's any way to salvage this mess."

Figure 11.4   (Continued)

"My students don't know how to make good selections," says another teacher. "I'm really not sure what to do now. Their thinking is very unsophisticated. I thought I had done a good job of helping them understand what a portfolio is all about, but it's obvious they don't have the same criteria in their heads that I have in mine. I value their involvement in the process, and want them to feel ownership, but these portfolios just don't do the job."

A second-grade teacher adds her thoughts: "I really did a lot to help them select portfolio pieces. I even set up some that had to be included—especially their unit books. We put together booklets that students make covers for and include the things they've done related to the unit. So everyone's portfolio includes some of the same stuff. Then they get to choose some other pieces. They're still not very good at reflection, but I'm a little bit more secure about sending things home now. Still, there are things that are really important that I don't know how to deal with, like group projects and things they construct. I'm also starting to worry about whether we're going to need a whole new building to house the portfolios at the end of the year—never mind next year!"

In frustration and with worries about changes in their own thinking about portfolios, the group asks for a chunk of time on the next faculty meeting agenda. There are questions inside of questions that need to be examined: Should we all send home portfolios? Can we individually choose not to? Since we've spent so much time on portfolios, how will we come up with other information for parents if we don't use them? Formal reporting is just around the corner and something has to be decided.

Source: Adapted from *Practice with Student-Involved Classroom Assessment* (p. 303), by J. A. Arter & K. U. Busick, 2001, Portland, OR: Assessment Training Institute. Copyright © 2006, 2001 Educational Testing Service. Adapted by permission.

REFLECT ON YOUR LEARNING

Activity 11.4   Analyze Your Own Growth Portfolio

Using Figure 9.2, "Conditions for Effective Communication" from Chapter 9, analyze how well your assessment growth portfolio meets the listed conditions. Consider the following:

1. Is it clear which learning targets are the focus of your portfolio?

2. Is the purpose for your portfolio clear?

3. Have you been able to use information in the chapters thus far as guidance in selecting items to communicate accurately about your learning?

4. What performance criteria are you using to track your growth in learning about assessment?

5. How have you been involved as both the subject and the author of the portfolio?

Source: Adapted from *Practice with Student-Involved Classroom Assessment* (p. 309), by J. A. Arter & K. U. Busick, 2001, Portland, OR: Assessment Training Institute. Copyright © 2006, 2001 Educational Testing Service. Adapted by permission.

TRY THIS

Activity 11.5   Plan for Students

From your experience developing your own growth portfolio, how might your students benefit by doing portfolios? How might you answer the following questions in planning to use portfolios with your students?

1. For what purpose?

2. Addressing what learning targets?

3. What content? Who decides? When are items added? What cover sheet will be used for entries? How will you ensure adequate sampling of the learning targets the portfolio will cover? How will students be involved?

4. What performance criteria will you use and who will develop them?

5. Who will be the audience for the portfolio? How will students share their portfolios with others? When?

Source: Adapted from *Practice with Student-Involved Classroom Assessment* (pp. 309–310), by J. A. Arter & K. U. Busick, 2001, Portland, OR: Assessment Training Institute. Copyright © 2006, 2001 Educational Testing Service. Adapted by permission.

Conferences About
and with Students

[A] *conference* occurs when two or more people meet to discuss a predetermined topic to satisfy an information need. We have all participated in conferences at some level—as teachers, as parents, and in some cases, as students. Conferences with students as participants are a natural extension of learning when students have previously self-assessed and set goals. They provide the opportunity for students to reflect on and share what they know about themselves as learners.

In this chapter we will explore the purposes for conferences, the formats to meet those purposes, and how to conduct successful conferences to meet the information needs of students, teachers, and parents. We concentrate on the shaded portions of Figure 12.1.

Figure 12.1   Keys to Quality Classroom Assessment

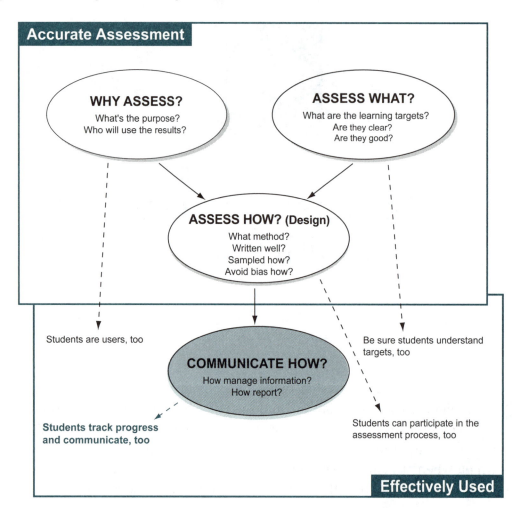

REFLECT ON YOUR PRACTICE

Activity 12.1   Your Experiences with Conferences

Note the kinds of conferences you have participated in. Choose two specific experiences to think about further. What was the context? What was the purpose? What was your role? What was the role of the student, if any? What was the focus of the conversation? Record your responses on the form found on the CD in the file, "Experience with Conferences." Keep this form handy and refer to it as you progress through the chapter.

Purposes for Conferences

Conferences can be used to communicate in both assessment *for* and *of* learning contexts. All conferences involve sharing information; whether they are formative or summative in nature hinges on whether they occur during or after the learning. We would consider conferences formative when the purpose is to give or receive feedback, to help students formulate goals, or to create with colleagues or parents an individualized program or other intervention for a student. Conferences are summative in nature when the purpose is to share information about learning that has already occurred.

To understand the options, think of conferences as falling into five general categories according to their purposes: offering feedback, setting goals, planning an intervention, demonstrating growth, and communicating achievement. Table 12.1 summarizes how topics, participants, and formats can be combined to create a variety of conference options to meet differing information needs.

The Feedback Conference

As described in Chapters 2 and 7, in a feedback conference, students receive another's opinion about the strengths and weaknesses of their work. The purpose is to offer information that will provide them insight so they can continue to improve the work. A secondary purpose is to model the kind of thinking we want them to do when they self-assess.

Table 12.1   Conference Options

Purpose	Topic	Focus	Participants	Location
Feedback	Strengths and areas for improvement	Single work sample or small number of work samples	Two students	School
			Small group of students	School
			Student and teacher	School
Goal setting	Long- or short-term achievement goals	Single work sample, multiple work samples, or growth or achievement portfolio	Student and parent	Home
			Two students	School
			Student and teacher	School
Intervention	Area of concern	Body of evidence illustrating a problem or issue to resolve	Teacher and parent	School
			Teacher and student	School
			Teacher, parent, and student	School
			Teacher and other staff members	School
			Teacher, other staff members, and parent	School
			Teacher, other staff members, parent, and student	School
Demonstration of Growth	Improvement on one learning target	Two or more work samples ("before & after")	Student and parent	Home
			Two students	School
	Growth over time	Growth portfolio	Student and teacher	School
			Student and significant adult	School or home
Communicating Achievement	Level of achievement	Achievement portfolio	Two students	School
	Demonstration of competence	Grade reports	Student and significant adult	Home, school, or other site
	Evidence of meeting goals	Other teacher- or student-maintained records	Parent and teacher	School
			Parent and student	School or home
		Portfolio containing evidence of setting and meeting goals	Parent, student, and teacher	School
			Parent, student, teacher, other significant adults, community members	School

Participants

Although we most often think of teachers as the people giving the feedback, students who have had practice in discussing the quality of anonymous work can become quite good at offering useful insights into one another's work. For example, when students meet in writing groups, the purpose of the discussion is to offer formative feedback to each member. In any context, students can confer with a partner, or with a small group. Conferences can be scheduled so that everyone is engaged in one at the same time, or students may be encouraged to schedule a conference with a partner whenever they need it or within a set time frame (as in the case of a project). Many teachers find it effective to allow students to choose whether they receive feedback from them or from a peer.

Keys to Success

Do the following to maximize the success of the conference:

- Prior to the conference, make sure students understand the learning targets at the focus of the discussion.

- Prior to the conference, give students practice with assessing work representing the learning targets they are to master.

- During the conference, focus the feedback on the learning targets.

- Limit the number of learning targets to be discussed at one sitting.

The Time Issue

Whether students are meeting in pairs, in groups, or with you, there are time issues to consider. Obviously, it is a time saver for you whenever students offer useful feedback to each other. Your role then is to manage the time so everyone who needs or wants it has opportunity to receive feedback. Perhaps the most significant time problem arises in a student-teacher conference, when the student needs extensive teaching in order to act on the feedback. For example, you may discover the student is not yet clear about standards of quality, and that you need to spend time explaining them. This conference leaves the realm of feedback and enters the realm of private tutorial, which can cause it to take much more time than anticipated or practical. When you need to limit the time a feedback conference takes, there are several things you can do:

- Consider having students assess their own work prior to the conference. As noted in Chapter 7, students who do some initial thinking about their work prior to receiving feedback are more likely to understand and act on your suggestions.

- Take note of what feedback students don't understand or can't act on, and rather than reteach extensively at each conference, plan further large- or small-group instruction with those needs in mind.

- Limit the focus of the feedback to one or only a few aspects of quality per session.

- Schedule student-teacher conferences only with those who want or need one. Plan time for student-to-student conferences for the others.

The Fine Line Between Offering Feedback and Doing the Work for the Student

Doing the revising for students not only creates time crunches, it tends to negate the purpose for descriptive feedback in the first place. Again, let's think about how this works in the context of writing. If a student clearly does not understand what to do next based on your feedback, you might choose to demonstrate. If this showing includes reworking some aspect of the student's work, you must exercise caution. Is your goal to create a better writer, or to create a better piece of writing? If it is to create a better piece of writing, then theoretically, you can dispense with the student and do it yourself. If your goal is to create a better writer, then doing the writing for the student will, in most cases, not work. The person who does the writing and the revising does the learning.

Parents can benefit from understanding this distinction, as well. Have you ever received a student's homework and noticed signs of parents crossing the line between helping and coauthoring? In either case, we recommend that if the student can't do what you expect, then step back and teach rather than overstep and do it for them.

The Goal-Setting Conference

In a goal-setting conference students confer with another person to set long- or short-term goals for learning. The purpose generally is to guide them to the next steps in their learning within the framework of the content standards, not necessarily to let students define their own standards.

Working with students to set goals can occur informally without a scheduled conference, it can be the focus of a conference discussion, it can be the end result of a feedback conference (as described in Chapter 7), or it can be part of an improvement or achievement conference. Students can set short-term or long-term goals. We address goal setting as a process separately from other conferences to highlight important keys to success.

Keys to Success

Goal setting is a straightforward next step in student-involved assessment. When students regularly identify their strengths and areas for improvement, they are primed to describe the next steps in their learning. These are generally short-term goals, aimed at improving achievement one step at a time. A plethora of books has been written on the topic of how to craft goals; we are going to keep it simple here and focus on components most important to students and their work at school. We recommend that students take the following steps:

- Examine evidence to determine an area of focus.

- Formulate a goal statement.

- Make an action plan.

- Identify assistance needed, if any.

- Determine a time frame.

For example, Maria-Teresa looks through her corrected math test and realizes that several of her errors are due to problems with zeroes in multiplying. She sets a goal for herself: "I will get better at multiplying when the numbers end in zero. I will ask the teacher for an explanation of what to do, and then I will ask for a sheet of problems to practice at home. If I get stuck, I will ask for help from my mom. Next Friday, I will take another test on multiplying."

As another example, you have a student, George, review a collection of his writing and he notices that he misses points consistently due to incorrect spelling. What happens when his thinking about his work stops here? Chances are, his responsibility for learning will also stop; the job of planning what to do and taking action will land on you. If you give George an opportunity to continue thinking, you teach him to take ownership of improving. He sets a goal for himself: "From now on, I will circle words I am unsure of when I am editing and then I will look them up in the dictionary."

Then, by setting up a simple system, such as a "goals" folder, Maria-Teresa and George can each keep track of their goals and their progress toward meeting them.

Goals That Work

Goals that work include a statement of what the student will learn or get better at, and a plan of action stating what the student will do. The process can be as simple as including a line on a self-assessment form that reads, "Next time I will _____" (Gregory, Cameron, & Davies, 2000, p. 40), or it may require more structured thought. Because in some cases the student will need outside assistance, goals may include a statement about who will help. And insofar as students have knowledge about the pacing of their learning, goals statements are most effective when they include a time element. Although not required, a goal statement can also include reference to the evidence they use to choose the goal. When you put this in, students can remember the "before" picture of their achievement and compare it to their "after" picture to show themselves and others how far they have come, even if they have not yet fully attained their stated goals.

Figure 12.2 shows an 11th-grade health goal statement example. Figure 12.3 shows a goal statement frame for older students, and Figure 12.4 shows a frame for younger students. (Figure 7.13 in Chapter 7 also has space for goal setting, and Figure 5.15 in Chapter 5 shows another goal-setting frame that students could use after self-assessing on a selected response test.)

Clear Statement of the Intended Learning

In general, students need access to their work to set attainable goals. They can set goals by reviewing a single piece of work or a collection. It is important that they review the work itself, and not just a list of scores or grades. A grade report alone usually does not provide enough detail for student goal setting to be meaningful and it can lead to fuzzy or too-general statements, such as "I will get better at math," which is too broad a goal to fuel an action plan. Without a clear statement of the intended learning—Are there some par-

Figure 12.2   Example of 11th-Grade Student's Health Goal

Name: _John Jurjevich_   **Date:** _February 20, 2004_

What I need to learn:

I will learn to diagram how the immune system works.

Evidence of current level of achievement:

Test on communicable diseases 2/18/04

Plan of action:

I will study the pages on pathogens and the immune system in the book and will practice creating a picture of how the immune system works, with all parts labeled.

Help needed—what and who:

My book and me

Time frame:

I will be ready to be retested on Feb. 26

Evidence of achieving my goal:

Test on Feb. 26

ticular concepts or standards that the student wants to work on? One or more underlying achievement targets?—you cannot identify the most productive course of action. Level of goal attainment is also easier to track with a goal stated in terms of the intended learning target: "I will learn how to create good inferences" leads directly to action and to sources of evidence, whereas "I will get better at reading" does not. To produce such goals, students need access to the intended learning and evidence of their strengths and weaknesses—the diagnostic assessment *for* learning information, not just the summative assessment *of* learning information.

Figure 12.3   Goal Statement Frame for Older Students

Name: _____   Date: _____

What I need to learn:
Evidence of current level of achievement:
Plan of action:
Help needed—what and who:
Time frame:
Evidence of achieving my goal:

Figure 12.4   Goal Statement Frame for Younger Students

Name: _____   **Date:** _____

I will learn _____

_____

My "before" picture—evidence I used to choose my goal:_____

_____

My plan is to _____

_____

I need these materials: _____

_____

I will ask for help from _____

I will be ready to show my learning on this day: _____

My "after" picture—I will show my learning by _____

_____

The Action Plan

The second part of a goal statement answers the question, "How will I do this?" It specifies the action the student will take, which may involve reviewing material learned previously, reworking a product or performance until it meets a certain level of quality, or learning something the student missed in the course of instruction.

Even students who independently can identify what they need to work on sometimes need outside advice on how to go about getting better. At such times, a short conference may be needed, during which giving advice on a plan of action consists of helping students understand what their options are. For example, David may have reviewed his three previous lab reports and decided he needs to improve in writing hypotheses. He may have no idea how to do this, in which case his teacher can confer with him to explain what resources or opportunities are available.

The Role of Homework in the Action Plan

Homework completion as a plan of action is tricky, because lots of learning problems *would* be solved if students would only do the practice work. All students *should* do their homework, and in all likelihood their achievement will improve when they attain this habit. However, a general action plan, "Do my homework," is not precise enough in most instances, and may not be the solution at all.

Consider this plan: "I will get better at double-digit division by doing my homework every night." We are tempted to praise this plan and run with it. But, what if the specific problem does not flow directly from lack of practice? It is similar to an adult who says, "I will improve my health by getting exercise every day." If, however, this person creates an exercise plan to solve the specific problem of too much sodium in his diet, it will not correct the problem. Doing homework, like getting exercise, is almost always a good idea, but it may not go far enough in accomplishing the desired result. Specific action beyond the regular work may be needed, and it may be accomplished in school or at home. When students create their action plans, they need to understand what role, if any, homework plays in attaining their specific goal.

Identifying Assistance

If every student needs assistance and they all need it from you, the teacher, this process will choke on its own rope. When Maria-Teresa knows what her goal is and needs help remembering the math procedure, she does need assistance. She may need it from you, or she may not. Could someone else in the room be her "go-to-girl" for multiplying with zeroes? When you help students see their best hope is *not* always you, their teacher, you make the process more manageable and deepen your students' learning in the bargain. As the saying goes, "She who helps another learns it twice."

Determining Time Frame

Asking students to set themselves a time limit, or specifying one, helps students both make a realistic plan and get motivated to start working. It also lets them decide or know when they will demonstrate their level of achievement of the goal.

The "Before" and "After" Pictures

Goal setting is most satisfying when we see real progress toward the desired outcome. Part of the motivational hook for students and the key to re-engaging marginally interested students is tangible, hard evidence of progress. A system that lets students keep track of where they started and what they have accomplished increases accountability for follow through. It can be as simple as a manila envelope with the goal statement stapled to the outside and evidence of the beginning point, progress toward the goal, and goal attainment tucked inside.

To make this work, students need time periodically to reflect on their progress toward their goals and to collect evidence. If the goal is a small one, as Maria-Teresa's is, the "before" picture—the test—and the "after" picture—the retest—can suffice as evidence. It is important to not let the action plan peter out, as happens with many New Year's resolutions, or students may conclude they are not good at follow through. Instituting a simple procedure for students to collect "before" and "after" evidence contributes to developing a sense that "I can set goals and carry them through to completion."

Student-Selected Long-Term Goals

In some classrooms, students set long-term goals in response to open-ended questions such as those suggested by Gregory, Cameron, and Davies: "'What do you want to be able to do in this class by the end of the term?' 'What skill do you want to improve?' 'What's the one thing you'd like to try doing in this course that you've never done before?'" (2001, p. 17). To set and carry through with these goals, students may not need to examine evidence of previous achievement. In this instance, the process requires that students do the following:

- Set the goal.
- Determine what evidence demonstrating progress toward the goal to collect.
- Collect and keep track of the evidence.
- Share their progress with an audience—another student, or a parent, for example.

Your job becomes one of setting up, modeling, and monitoring the process. This type of long-term goal setting is a perfect context for portfolio use.

Activity 12.2   Set a Goal for Learning

Using the form in either Figure 12.3 or 12.4, work through this process for a goal you, yourself, might like to accomplish. A printable version of the frames appears on the CD in the file, "Goal-Setting Frames."

Setting Goals Together

Once you have modeled goal setting and helped students understand what they are to do at each step, many students will be able to proceed on their own. There are times, however, when students will benefit from discussing their ideas with another person. Students may be able to confer with each other or with their parents, or they may need you to help them, especially with their action plan. The conference itself can be formal or informal; you can set aside a time when all students participate in a goal-setting conference, they can conduct one with a parent at home, it can be a part of an ongoing process that students engage in when they reach certain checkpoints in their learning, or it can be up to the student to select when it will occur.

To make the process work, remember, students will need to understand three things: what the intended learning is, where they are now with respect to the intended learning, and what their options are for closing the gap.

The Intervention Conference

Planning an intervention with others can occur any time a student is having difficulty. As a teacher, you meet with parents to discuss a problem with behavior, work habits, or achievement and make a plan for improvement. You meet with other teachers and specialists when a student's work is significantly above or below expectations to modify instruction or to recommend placement in a specialized program. Generally, the student is not present in these conferences, although in some cases, especially the parent-teacher discussion of a problem, the student's perspective and participation can help you craft a solution.

Central to the effectiveness of these conferences is the quality of records you keep. This context requires separate records for level of achievement, work habits, effort, attendance, and the like, as well as records that allow you to determine the student's strengths and weaknesses relative to the learning targets to be mastered. With such records, you are able to pinpoint problems and participate in recommending suitable solutions. Without them, you may lack credible data from which to draw conclusions about the best course of action.

The Demonstration of Growth Conference

These conferences can focus on improvement on one learning target or on growth over time spanning a number of learning targets within one subject or across subjects. If your students have self-assessed and set goals, they will have selected one or more specific learning targets to work on. Asking them to share the evidence of their improvement with another person can help them notice and take pride in their accomplishment, even if the accomplishment represents a small step.

Improvement on One Learning Target

This is a simple, narrowly focused conference topic, generally conducted between two people. Struggling learners especially benefit from noticing that they have been successful in achieving a short-term goal in a short period of time. The conference can take place with a parent or other adult at home, with another student at school, or with you or another staff member at school. You can specify the audience or you can let students choose with whom they wish to share.

Growth over Time

In this conference, the purpose is to show progress toward competence on predetermined learning targets. Participants can include the student and one or more of the following: another student, parent, teacher, other significant adult, or another staff member at the school. Generally, these conferences take place at school.

Preparation

Whether the focus of growth is one learning target or a whole constellation of them, you will want to help students prepare by guiding their choice of artifacts to use as evidence of improvement. Portfolios and working folders come in handy here, as it can be quite powerful for students to assemble work samples showing a clear "before" and "after" picture of their learning. (Refer to Chapter 11 for more information on growth portfolios and working folders.) Students also should be prepared to explain the learning target or targets, talk briefly about what they did to improve, and summarize what they can do now that they couldn't do before. Others involved in the conference also need to be prepared to participate. You can prepare them by writing a short note explaining the intent of the conference and their role in it, perhaps also asking them to view and comment on the evidence in advance. You may instead wish to have students write the notes.

Figure 12.5 shows a form that can be used in preparation for and during the conference. You also will find this form on the CD in the file, "Growth Conference."

Followup

It is important to find out how the experience went for all involved. Followup can be as simple as asking students to complete a conference evaluation form, such as the one in Figure 12.6, reading the comments from participants, and debriefing the conference experience with the class as a whole. (A printable version of Figure 12.6 appears on the CD in the file, "Conference Evaluation Form.") In rare instances, you may have to address a less-than-positive outcome for a student or a parent, in which case, you may want to schedule a followup conference.

Figure 12.5   Form for Demonstration of Growth Conference

Name: _____   **Date:** _____

Learning Target(s)	
Evidence of where I started	
Evidence of where I am now	
What I did to improve	
What I can do now that I couldn't do before	
What to notice about my work	

Date of conference:

Start and end times:

Participant(s):

Comments from participant(s):

Figure 12.6   Conference Evaluation Form

Name: _____	**Date:** _____

What I learned from this conference	
What I liked about it	
What I would change about the conference	
Other comments	

The Achievement Conference

An achievement conference occurs any time you want to share information about a student's current status. One format most of us are familiar with is the parent-teacher conference scheduled at the end of the first grading period to elaborate on information from the report card. When the student is present, these conferences are referred to as "student-involved" or "student-led" conferences. Because of their effectiveness in creating and sustaining student motivation, we believe that achievement conferences can and should involve students.

Several of the portfolios described in Chapter 11 can function as the basis for an achievement conference. The topic of discussion might be the student's level of achievement, demonstration of student competence with respect to specified learning targets, or evidence of having met goals.

Participants

The participants can vary to suit the topics. In a *two-way conference*, the student can meet with another student, the teacher, a parent, or another significant adult. In a *three-way conference*, participants can include the student, the teacher, and a parent or significant adult. In a *showcase conference*, the student can meet with a group of any number of adults, from parents and significant adults to community members.

Sometimes the audience, purpose, and context are specified, as when the audience is parents, the purpose is to discuss students' performance in school, and the context is afterschool conferences at the end of a reporting period. In this case, you might be most likely to focus on level of achievement with respect to the major learning targets taught. When the topic is demonstration of competence, teachers sometimes choose a showcase conference. These are often more formal events than the conferences described previously. As mentioned in Chapter 11, when the focus of the discussion is a portfolio, you can determine which audience to invite by asking, "Who might be interested in the story this portfolio has to tell?" Whichever decisions you make, the conference plan must be chosen to meet both your and the students' needs.

Preparation

For many students and parents, it is a novel idea to have the student present during a conversation about the student's learning. Some initial preparation is required to make two-way, three-way, and showcase student-involved conferences run smoothly. Students will need a clear understanding of the learning targets and work samples that show what they have learned. They must be able to discuss strengths, areas needing improvement or areas of challenge, and goals they have set for themselves. They will need time to rehearse the conference with others in the classroom.

We recommend that you set the conference agenda together with students and that students, if they are able to, write the invitation to parents and/or other participants. Either in the invitation or in a separate communication, parents and other participants will need to be informed of what to expect and what their role will be. Some teachers send work samples that will be the focus of the discussion home in advance for parents to think about in preparation for the conference.

When the format is a three-way conference, especially when it replaces the traditional parent-teacher conference, as a part of your explanation to parents, we recommend that you offer them the option of scheduling an additional meeting, without the student present, to discuss any concerns that they may not want to raise in the three-way setting.

During the Two-Way Conference

You may have several two-way (student and parents) conferences scheduled at the same time during the day. Your role is to assure parents that you will be available to clarify information as needed. Before the conference begins, each student introduces their parents to you. Then they all go to the conference area (for example, student's desks or tables set up for that purpose). Students begin by sharing the conference agenda with their parents. They then explain the learning targets and show samples of their work illustrating level of achievement, attainment of competence, or evidence of having met goals—whatever the topic of the conference is. Parents listen carefully, ask clarifying questions, and offer comments about students' work and learning. Students may have already set goals and created action plans for future work, which they would discuss at this time, or students and parents may do that together as a part of the conference.

During the Three-Way Conference

The three-way conference is similar to the two-way conference, in that students introduce their parents to you and begin the conference by sharing the agenda. It differs in that, because you are a participant, you schedule only one at a time. Students explain the learning targets and proceed as described previously. The parents' role is also much the same. Your role as teacher is to help students clarify their comments, if needed, and to add to their descriptions of strengths and areas needing improvement, again if needed. We recommend that you end each conference with a summary of the student's strengths and positive contributions to the class.

During the Showcase Conference

The student's role in a showcase conference is to share the agenda with the participants, explain the learning targets that are the focus of the achievement, and present and discuss how the work samples presented illustrate whatever is the topic of the conference—level of achievement, competence on specified learning targets, or attainment of goals—focusing on strengths and areas needing improvement, if appropriate to the topic. The student also answers any of the participants' questions. The participants in a showcase conference listen carefully, ask questions, and make comments about the work. Your role is to be prepared to facilitate, encourage, and clarify, as needed.

Preparing for and Conducting a Conference Focused on Evidence of Meeting Goals

Sometimes the topic of a conference is not the learning per se, but rather students' ability to set learning goals and meet them. As with the "Improvement on One Learning Target" conference, asking students to share evidence of having set and met goals can help them notice and take pride in their accomplishments.

You can structure these as two- or three-way conferences. Students can share with you or with another student at school, a parent or other significant adult at home or at school, or with you and a parent at school.

Help students prepare for this conference by providing a structured way for them to keep track of the goals they have set and the progress they have made toward each one. Suggestions for how to do this appear earlier in the section, "Goal-Setting Conferences." Students should prepare to explain the learning targets that are the subject of their goals and to talk briefly about what they did to improve. As with all other conference formats, the other participant or participants need to understand the intent of the conference and their role in it. Again, either you or the students can communicate this. Figure 12.7 shows a form students can use while preparing for and conducting the conference. (This form also appears on the CD in the file, "Evidence of Meeting Goals.")

Followup

In any one of these conference formats, conducting followup is key to their success. We recommend that all participants, including students, complete a conference evaluation form (see Figure 12.6) so that you can obtain information about what worked well and what didn't (if anything), identify any problems you need to deal with, and gather ideas for

Figure 12.7   Form for "Evidence of Meeting Goals" Conference

Name: _____   Date: _____

Goal I have met	Evidence of where I started	Evidence of where I am now	What I did to improve

Date of conference:

Start and end times:

Participant(s):

Comments from participant(s):

what you might do next time. Summarize and share comments with students, parents, and any other participants. Also, give students the opportunity to debrief the experience as a group.

To view a classroom teacher participate with her students in conferences and hear her thoughts on the experience, please watch on the accompanying DVD the segment entitled "Student-Involved Portfolio Conferences."

REFLECT ON YOUR LEARNING

Activity 12.3   Comparing Conference Experiences to Ideas in the Chapter

Refer back to the form you completed for Activity 12.1. Identify the similarities and differences between the kinds of conferences we describe and those you have experienced. What changes, if any, might you make in the conferences you currently hold?

DEEPEN UNDERSTANDING

Activity 12.4   Video: *Student-Involved Conferences*

Individually or as a team, watch the ETS video, *Student-Involved Conferences*, and work through the activities, which include participating in a simulated student-involved conference. Featuring Anne Davies, an internationally recognized expert in all aspects of formative assessment, the video includes segments of students conducting two-way, three-way, and showcase conferences and offers more detailed information about how to set up, conduct, and follow up student-involved conferences.

Summary

In the majority of instances, conferences about students can include students to the benefit of all involved. They can participate in and even lead them, but only with the proper preparation throughout the year. To comment accurately and in detail about their work, students must have been involved all along in their learning and in assessment; they must be prepared to discuss what the intended learning is, where they are now with respect to it, and what they might do next to continue as learners.

In this chapter, we have looked at conferences that function in assessment *for* and *of* learning contexts: conferences whose purposes are to offer feedback, to set goals, to plan an intervention, to share improvement, and to communicate about achievement. We have offered suggestions for whom to include in each type of conference, what preparation will maximize success for all involved, and what followup is needed. In addition, we have explained what happens in a two-way, a three-way, and a showcase conference.

We encourage you to select carefully from the conference options available to meet your needs and the information needs of parents, but most especially to think about how students can be involved in conferences to take responsibility for their learning and to show what they have accomplished.

■ *Tracking Your Learning—Possible Portfolio Entries*

Any of the activities included in Chapter 12 can be used as portfolio entries. Remember, the learning targets for this book are outlined in Figure 12.1, and listed in Table 1.2 and described in detail in Chapter 1. The portfolio entry cover sheet provided on the CD in the file, "Portfolio Entry Cover Sheet," will prompt you to think about how each item you choose for your portfolio reflects your learning with respect to one or more of these learning targets.

In addition, you could include a summary of your responses to the following activity.

DEEPEN UNDERSTANDING

Activity 12.5 The High School Faculty Debate on Student-Led Conferences

Read the case study in Figure 12.8 in which teachers discuss their experiences with student-led conferences. Think about or discuss with your learning team the following questions:

1. What could the first teacher have done to create a more successful experience?

2. What contributed to the second teacher's success?

3. How good is the celebration idea in the principal's proposal from the teachers', students', parents', and community members' points of view?

4. What would it take for the "School Success Celebration" to be successful?

Source: Adapted from *Practice with Student-Involved Classroom Assessment* (p. 320), by J. A. Arter & K. U. Busick, 2001, Portland, OR: Assessment Training Institute. Copyright © 2006, 2001 Educational Testing Service. Adapted by permission.

Figure 12.8 The High School Faculty Debate on Student-Led Conferences

A high school principal recently returned from a national conference on assessment full of excitement about an innovative new idea—student-led parent conferences—and he put the topic on the agenda for the next faculty meeting. After introducing it and discussing some of its positive aspects, the principal invited the faculty to comment.

One teacher was negative about the idea based on his experience at a previous school. There, students assembled portfolios that included all subjects and met with their parents in home room at year's end to review their achievement. Conferences were 20 minutes, so it took a long day and evening to complete them all.

For this teacher, such conferences just didn't work. First, 20 minutes was not enough to cover six different subjects. Further, students didn't know what work to place in their portfolios or how to share it, so the meetings turned out to be very brief discussions of

Figure 12.8   (Continued)

the report card grades—completely from the student's point of view. Finally, homeroom teachers were not equipped to answer parents' questions in subjects other than their own, so parents' needs were not satisfied. All in all, it was a disaster and was abandoned after one try.

Another teacher offered a different experience. She had one student who seemed full of academic potential but didn't seem to care about school. The student's only comment was, "If my parents don't care, why should I?" When the teacher called the parents it became obvious that there had been a severe breakdown in communication in the family.

In a risky move, the teacher bet the student that her parents did care and that she could prove it. During the next grading period, the two of them assembled a growth portfolio showing the student's improvement. Further, the teacher asked her to think about how she might present herself as an improving student and to write biweekly self-reflections about the work in her portfolio. As the term ended, the teacher asked the student to invite her parents in for a special student-parent-teacher conference. The conference was a success for all.

In response to these comments, the principal made a proposal: The faculty could institute student-led conferences to bolster three initiatives already in place. First, twelfth graders are required to complete special senior projects. Second, the guidance staff has all college-bound students assemble "college admissions portfolios." Finally, students are required to complete a certain number of community service hours and assemble evidence of the productivity of their work. All three might provide an excellent basis for a school and community-wide, end-of-year acknowledgement of a productive school year.

Specifically, he proposed a three-day "School Success Celebration." Senior projects might culminate in "showcase" student-led conferences in which students presented their work for review and discussion. College admissions portfolios might be shared with parents or review boards. Community service portfolios might be presented in a group session.

The principal asked for volunteers to see if this idea was both feasible and useful.

Source: Reprinted from *Practice with Student-Involved Classroom Assessment* (pp. 321–322), by J. A. Arter & K. U. Busick, 2001, Portland, OR: Assessment Training Institute. Copyright © 2006, 2001 Educational Testing Service. Reprinted by permission.

CHAPTER

13

Practical Help
with Standardized Tests

 t's tempting as a teacher to ignore or downplay standardized tests because they offer little specific help with day-to-day instruction. But standardized tests form a part of our lives, from the driver's test to the state proficiency test.

Standardized tests represent one way to gather and communicate information about student achievement. These tests meet the information needs of policy makers and curriculum and program planners, decision makers who need accurate information once a year to make appropriate programmatic decisions on behalf of students. In other words, these are assessments *of* learning intended to help adult decision makers, rather than student decision makers, as is the case in assessments *for* learning.

In this chapter, we treat standardized tests as a communication tool. We emphasize what educators need to know to use them most productively to communicate about student achievement and to support student learning. This chapter covers following topics:

- What standardized tests are and are not; what they are designed to do and what they cannot do, including common misconceptions about them.

- How to interpret various standardized test scores.

- How to use the materials and results from standardized tests to promote student learning.

- Legitimate ways to prepare students for standardized tests.

- How to communicate standardized test results to others.

- Educators' responsibilities with respect to standardized tests—providing accurate information as well as protecting student well-being.

We concentrate on the shaded portion of Figure 13.1.

Figure 13.1   Keys to Quality Classroom Assessment

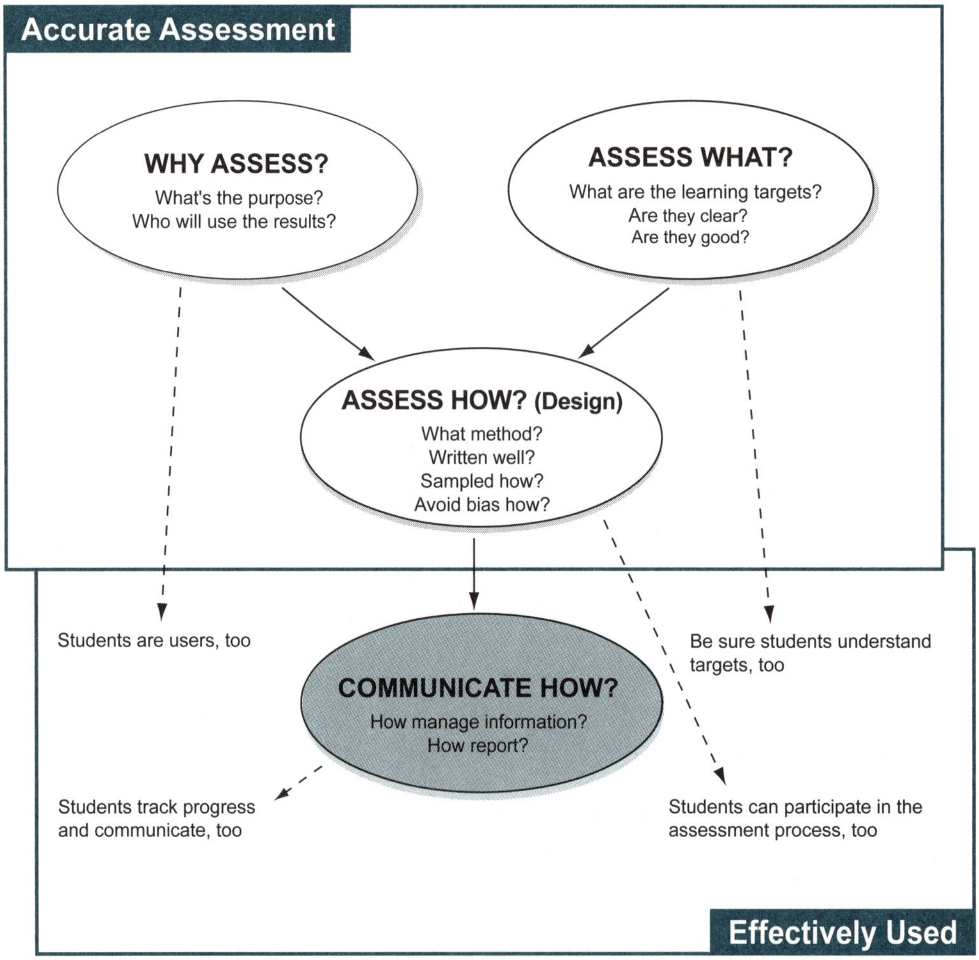

Information Every Educator Needs

All educators should know the basics about the standardized tests used in their school district, especially the state test, for several reasons. First, we might be called upon at any moment to explain a test to someone else, such as a parent. Second, a good understanding of the test helps us know if it is possible to use the results to make modifications to instruction. Finally, we need this information to be informed users of tests and results, and to be able to advocate for the well-being of our students when it comes to the use of these tests.

TRY THIS

Activity 13.1   Standardized Tests Used in Your District

Think about a major standardized test used in your district. These days, for most teachers this will be your state proficiency test, a published standardized test, or a test developed locally to match state or district content standards. Answer as many of the following questions as you can. (A printable version of this questionnaire appears on the CD in the file, "Standardized Test Inventory.") When you have finished, keep your answers and refer to them as you read through the chapter.

1. What is the title of the assessment?

2. What terms are used to refer to the learning targets assessed?
    _____ content standards _____ benchmarks _____ indicators
    _____ curriculum intentions _____ learning expectations
    _____ other

3. What is the stated purpose for the assessment? Check all that apply:
    _____ accountability _____ graduation requirement _____ program planning
    _____ identifying schools "in need of assistance" _____ other

4. At what grade levels is the test is given? In what content areas for each grade? When is the test is given? When are the results made available?

5. What students must be included in the assessment? Who is exempt, if anyone?

6. What criterion-referenced or norm-referenced scores are reported? Check all that apply: _____ raw score _____ percent correct _____ percentile
    _____ grade equivalent _____ mastery (competency) scores
    _____ other

Activity 13.1 (Continued)

7. What labels are given to different levels of student performance? What does it mean in score terms to have "passed"?

8. Are scores reported with error bands, margins for score error, or confidence intervals? If so, what does this mean?

9. What are legitimate (ethical) ways to prepare students for taking the assessment and what preparation strategies should you avoid?

10. If a student's test scores vary significantly from his or her grade on the report card, how should you address the discrepancy?

11. List the content standards covered, the number of test questions for each standard, and the method of assessing each standard for the grade level or content area closest to your current assignment.

12. How can you use materials from the testing program, such as rubrics, released sets of test questions, and released sets of student constructed responses, to help students understand the nature of quality performance to increase their level of achievement?

Much of this information can be found on your state's website or obtained from your district/school test coordinator. The content of this chapter is also designed to help you answer these questions. We will revisit this activity later and ask you to refine your responses, as needed.

DEEPEN UNDERSTANDING

Activity 13.2 A Definitions Pretest

In Figure 13.2, match the "measurement-ese" word on the left to the descriptions on the right. More than one description can match to a single word. Some descriptions will not match to any word. Then use the answer key found on the CD in the file, "Measurement-ese Answers" to see how well you scored. Save your answers, as we will revisit this test at the end of the chapter. If you get all of these correct, you may wish to skip the section on definitions.

Figure 13.2   Make Measurement-ese* Understandable

Measurement-ese	Matching Letters (one or more)	Descriptions
1. Standardized 2. Content standards 3. Performance standards 4. Norm-referenced test 5. Criterion-referenced test 6. Standards-based assessment 7. Raw score 8. Percent correct score 9. Percentile score 10. Grade equivalent score 11. Stanine score 12. Mastery scores		a. Assessments that are given across classrooms. b. Only applies to selected response assessments; does not apply to performance assessments. c. Questions on the assessment are selected to cover important content. d. Assessment and scoring procedures are uniform—students take the test at the same time in the same way so that results can be compared across test takers. e. Questions on the assessment are selected to "spread" students out on a continuum of achievement so that relative standing can be determined. f. Questions on the assessment are selected to match state or local content standards. g. Student performance is compared to other students to identify relative standing. h. Statements that relate level of performance on an assessment to various levels of proficiency. i. Student performance is compared to a desired level of performance on the content. j. Statements of what we want students to know and be able to do. k. Total number of points scored on an assessment. l. The percent of students scoring at or below a given score. m. A statement of levels of proficiency on an assessment. n. Average score obtained by students in various grade levels. o. Number of points scored divided by number possible. p. Same as a "normal curve equivalent." q. Broad indicator of student standing in relationship to other students. r. A criterion-referenced score. s. A norm-referenced score. t. Scores go from K.0 to 12.9. u. Scores go from 0 to 1. v. Scores go from 0 to total possible. w. Scores go from "way below competence" to "advanced competence" or similar terminology. x. Scores go from 0 to 100. y. Scores go from 1 to 9. z. Scores go from 1 to 99.

* *Measurement-ese* = jargon used by those whose profession is to measure educational achievement.

The Nuts and Bolts of Standardized Tests

Important Definitions

It is important that you first understand the meaning of the following key terms: *standardized test, norm-referenced test, criterion-referenced test,* and *large-scale assessment.*

Standardized Test

Standardized means that all students take the same test under the same conditions with the same instructions and scoring. Test administration and scoring are thereby "standard" for all students. This results in scores that can be compared across students, classrooms, buildings, and districts, which is useful for certain decision makers. For example, district staff want answers to many questions: "How are we doing overall?"; "Which subject areas or schools need more resources or professional development?"; "Which students have mastered the learning targets?"; "Which students need more help?"

When we think of standardized tests, we usually think of the required tests from the state or district. But given our definition, some classroom assessments, such as final examinations administered to all students in the same grade or course, can also be called standardized tests.

Norm-Referenced Tests

Some standardized tests are norm referenced. This means that they are set up to compare student achievement to that of other similar students. *Norm referenced* literally means that student scores are referenced (compared) to a norm group (a group of similar students). Selected norm-referenced scores, including percentiles and grade equivalents, are described later in this chapter.

"Norm referenced" also has a parallel in the classroom: grading on the curve. Such grades do not reflect what each student has learned, but rather how much each student has learned (as reflected in their computed scores) compared to all other students in the class.

Criterion-Referenced Tests

The purpose of *criterion-referenced* tests is to show how learning compares to a preset criterion of acceptable performance on specified learning targets, rather than to compare students to one another. Such scores help users understand the extent to which students have mastered specific bodies of knowledge and skills. When these come from local or state content standards, a criterion-referenced assessment might also be called *standards aligned* or *standards based*. Selected criterion-referenced scores, including percent correct and level of mastery, are described later in this chapter.

Classroom assessments are usually criterion referenced. Teachers place on the assessment exercises that students must know and be able to do. Then teachers determine the degree to which this material and these skills are actually attained—either through a rating or percent correct.

Large-Scale Assessment

Another frequently used term is large-scale assessment. A *large-scale assessment* is simply that—one that is given to a large number of students across classrooms and schools at more or less the same time—given on a large scale. Any kind of assessment can be large scale, but the term usually refers to standardized tests, both norm and criterion referenced.

Common Misconceptions

There are three important misconceptions about standardized tests that you must avoid to use these tests effectively: (1) only multiple-choice, norm-referenced tests can be standardized; (2) the same tests cannot yield both norm-referenced and criterion-referenced scores; and (3) multiple-choice standardized tests can assess only content mastery; they can't assess reasoning or problem solving. We discuss each in turn.

Misconception 1

Only multiple-choice, norm-referenced tests can be standardized. Actually, any type of assessment—multiple-choice to performance assessment, norm-referenced to criterion-referenced, and large-scale to classroom assessment—can be standardized. Sometimes "standardized" is used synonymously with "multiple-choice, norm-referenced," but that use is incorrect. It is possible to standardize, for example, a writing assessment—all students receive the same prompt, have the same time frame in which to write, are given the same instructions and amount of help, and receive scores back that were all produced the same way. In fact, most standardized tests—from commercially published to state assessments—have selected response as well as constructed response questions. A few have also included performance assessments; these tend to be expensive to give and score and so are used less frequently on large-scale assessments.

Misconception 2

The same tests cannot yield both norm-referenced and criterion-referenced scores. Assessments can in fact be both norm referenced and criterion referenced. Not only do you get information about how students' performance compares to other similar students, but you also get information about mastery of individual competencies. In fact, most current norm-referenced tests include criterion-referenced features such as a report of the percent correct on test questions covering individual learning targets.

Misconception 3

Multiple-choice standardized tests can assess only content mastery; they can't assess reasoning or problem solving. As we've seen before, some kinds of reasoning and problem solving can be assessed in selected response format. For example:

1. Which of the following is the main idea of the story? (analysis)

2. Which of the following is most likely to happen next? (inference)

3. Which of the following theories best explains the given data? (induction)

4. Which of the following phyla is least likely to contain examples of animals that have fur? (classification)

The catch is that not all types of reasoning can be assessed in this fashion. Asking students to evaluate the quality of something requires an explanation, which calls for the use of extended written response. In this same sense, to assess students' ability to use their knowledge productively to solve complex, multipart problems requiring the application of several patterns of reasoning used in combination, you will need an extended written response or performance assessment.

Test Development

Those who develop standardized tests go through the same development steps as listed for classroom assessments in Chapter 4—clarify targets, clarify purposes, decide on numbers of questions and assessment methods, develop a test plan, write questions and exercises, assemble the test, try it out, and revise to improve the test. They also adhere to the same standards of quality—select clear and important targets, identify clear and appropriate purposes, use appropriate methods, adhere to proper sampling techniques, and avoid sources of bias and distortion.

Initial Test Development

As mentioned previously, the purpose of many tests is to measure proficiency on those state standards deemed most important. Commercial test publishers developing tests for use in many states generally study the most common state standards, curriculum documents, and textbooks. Thus, many commercially produced standardized tests base their tests on the most common elements across states so they stand the best chance of aligning with as many states' standards as possible.

Once they have selected the learning targets, test developers determine the method to be used to assess each target, decide on the relative importance of each target, and develop a test plan. Items and exercises for the test come from item banks written by people hired for just that purpose. They generally produce two to three times the number of items to be on the final test (1) to ensure that sufficient qualifying items are available and (2) to create alternative versions of the text when required.

Resulting item pools are reviewed by many groups, from content area specialists to minority group representatives, to eliminate any items with unsound or biased content. After items that don't pass the reviews are deleted, the remaining items are pilot-tested to determine if students interpret exercises as intended, the percent of students getting each question correct, how well each question distinguishes between students who know the material and those who don't, which questions are redundant, and which are confusing.

Sometimes the items passing the pilot test go through additional review for quality and bias before final selection.

Establishing Norms

Once the test is drafted, if it is to yield norm-referenced (comparative) scores, it is given to large numbers of students (known as the *norm group*) across the range of achievement levels. The resulting "norms" permit users to determine how each student's score compares to other students who took the same test under the same conditions (during the norming phase). Norm-referenced scores do not reflect how each student compares with others who took the test at the same time; they reflect how each student compares to the norm group. For example, if a test was normed in 2001, students' scores are derived by comparing their performances to those of the 2001 norm group.

Establishing Competency Levels

Criterion-referenced scores, on the other hand, compare each student's score to a preset standard—not to the scores of other students. Such scores are intended to determine who has attained competence and who has not. So the development of this kind of test raises the questions, "What is the standard?" "How good is good enough?" How high a score on the test is good enough to be categorized as "exceeds the standard," "meets the standard," "approaches the standard," or "does not meet the standard"? Typically, a team of qualified judges is convened to make these decisions.

There are various procedures for doing this; one common method is known as a "bookmark" procedure. All questions on a test (say, the math test) are rank ordered from the easiest to the hardest. Individual judges (teachers, community members, etc.) answer the question, "At what point would I expect that students at this level of competency would begin having difficulty answering the questions correctly?"

If, for example, the judges decide that students who meet the standard will begin to have trouble answering questions at about the difficulty of question 35, the *cut score* (or lower boundary) for "exceeds the standard" should be about 35. Similarly, cut scores are identified for "meets the standard," and "approaches the standard." Everyone's judgments are averaged to obtain an initial set of cut scores.

There are other procedures, too numerous and technical to describe here. What you need to know is what procedure your state has used and what issues, if any, arose, during the process.

Some Surprises to Consider

Some of the specifics of developing standardized tests lead to surprising results. These surprising turns may cause controversies, misuses, and misunderstandings about what various standardized tests can and can't do. We present some examples in this section.

Targets Broad in Scope

Developers of standardized tests generally have to cover a lot of ground in a relatively short amount of time, and therefore can't assess any single learning objective in a lot of detail. As a result, diagnostic information—specific information about exactly what students are strong and weak on—often is missing from results. Test results might indicate that students are doing better on measurement than geometric sense, but may not indicate specifically what knowledge and skills need improving.

Some tests (more often commercial, norm-referenced tests than state-developed standards-based tests) might include several grades' worth of content in a single 40-item test. The intent is to cover a broad sweep so that students can be easily spread out and ranked. This means the coverage of any single topic may be very shallow. It's easy to see why in this context the majority of material covered in any textbook or local curriculum will not be tested, even though the test is capable of providing a dependable rank order of students.

Because of their broad scope, commercial tests sometimes are unable to track small changes in learning. So, it is not possible to use them to track short-term student progress.

This is a perfect example of how test purpose influences design. It is not that the norm-referenced test is bad; just that it was designed to do one thing—spread students out for ranking—and not another—provide detailed diagnostic information. We don't wish to indict norm-referenced tests, but to point out some of the compromises test developers must make to accommodate purpose, amount of material to cover, and who is taking the test.

Assessment Methods Chosen for Reasons Other Than Optimum Accuracy

Assessment methods are sometimes chosen because of cost rather than considerations of accuracy. For example, performance assessments are expensive to score, and have been deleted from some standardized tests because it takes several exercises to sample a performance adequately, which becomes cost prohibitive on a large scale.

The unfortunate result is that some states are returning to testing only learning targets that can be assessed with multiple-choice questions. Although test developers are very clever at tweaking multiple-choice to assess lots of important learning targets, there is still a limit to what such items are capable of assessing.

It's important to know the details of assessment methods used on your standardized tests and why they were chosen. Does your assessment include extended written response and performance assessment? If not, why not? Which valued learning targets in your discipline are *not* represented on your standardized tests?

Questions That Are too Easy or too Hard Are Deleted

When the standardized test is norm referenced, in addition to covering the most important things that students need to know and be able to do, test questions are chosen to spread students out. Questions that everyone gets right or wrong don't distinguish among students, so these aren't used regardless of the importance of the content. One implication of deleting questions that are too hard or too easy is that material considered critical may not be covered.

This is another example of how test purpose influences design. The criteria for selecting test questions can be quite different if the primary purpose of the test is to rank order students than if it is to assess student mastery of essential material.

Criterion-referenced assessments are more like classroom assessments in this regard—they are designed to assess important content, regardless of how many students answer the question correctly. So, sometimes difficult or easy questions are left on the test because they reflect valued learning targets.

Consequences of Assessment

The purpose of standardized tests (whether norm or criterion referenced) is to obtain accurate information about student achievement so that important decisions can be made well. But if we are not careful, unintended negative side effects can crop up, such as narrowing the curriculum.

Here's how this can happen. Tests are designed to sample a broader curriculum than what is tested. The idea is that, if instruction covers the curriculum well, students' performance on test items that cover a random subset of material should be representative of their performance had they been assessed on everything. The problem arises when focus is placed only on the material on the assessment and not on the broader curriculum it samples. Instead of being a set of questions that samples the curriculum, the assessment *becomes* the curriculum. Therefore, assessment results only provide information on how well students do on *what happens to be assessed*. You can no longer generalize about how students would do if everything had been covered.

Other potential negative side effects of assessments can arise from impact of the pressure to obtain higher scores on high-stakes tests. This can lead to the temptation to help floundering students in inappropriate ways, thereby artificially inflating scores. Unethical or inappropriate help can distort results, thus rendering scores useless for any decisions.

On the other hand, large-scale standardized assessments can improve learning if they focus teachers on the most important content to teach or encourage teaching in specific ways that promote student thinking.

Activity 13.3   Hills' Handy Hints

Here is a quiz that covers your understanding of how to interpret various test scores. In Figure 13.3, identify each question as being either true or false. The answers are in Figure 13.4.

Test Scores and What They Mean

Raw Scores

What They Mean

When students take a test, the number of questions they answer right, or the total number of points they score, is called their *raw score* (Stiggins, 2005).

How to Use Them

Raw scores underpin the determination of all other scores on standardized tests. The total possible raw score can help us see how detailed the coverage is on a test. For example, if there is a reading comprehension test with only 10 questions, you know either that the coverage is not deep or it is not broad. If a mathematics assessment on addition with carrying has 30 items, you know the topic is covered more deeply.

Percent Correct

What They Mean

Percent correct is just what you expect: raw score divided by total possible—the percentage of all items of the test answered correctly.

How to Use Them

Percent correct is a criterion-referenced score. It is the most frequently used score type in classroom assessment. It also underpins criterion-referenced score reports (such as many state assessments), where percent correct will determine which standards are mastered and which are not. Percent correct scores indicate student mastery of the individual learning targets covered by the test. On a mastery test, students are judged to have mastered the target if they answer correctly a certain percentage of the questions covering that target (Stiggins, 2005).

Figure 13.3   Appropriate Uses of Test Scores—Quiz

T   F   1. Tim is a sixth grader. He obtained a grade equivalent score of 9.2 in reading. This means that Tim scored well above average sixth graders in reading.

T   F   2. Tim's grade equivalent score of 9.2 in reading means that Tim could well be put in a class of ninth graders for material in which reading skills were important.

T   F   3. Tim obtained a grade equivalent score of 7.3 in arithmetic on the same test battery from which his reading grade equivalent score is 9.2. This means that in reading Tim is nearly two years ahead of his performance in arithmetic.

T   F   4. Juanita is a sixth grader. She got a percentile score of 70 in reading on a published standardized test. This means that Juanita got 70 percent of the items correct.

T   F   5. The principal at Hartford Elementary set a goal of getting every pupil up to the 50th percentile within four years. This is a reasonable goal for most modern schools.

T   F   6. Susie, a third-grade student, scored at the 30th percentile in arithmetic at the end of the school year. Scores this low are regarded as failing, and therefore Susie should be retained for another year in arithmetic instruction so that she will not be handicapped in the future.

T   F   7. Mr. Rivera noticed that most of his students received the same stanine score each year. This means that they are not making much progress in school.

T   F   8. Patricia went down from the fifth stanine last year to the fourth stanine this year. Her teacher should be concerned about this.

T   F   9. Mr. Rivera wondered about his student, Elena, whose stanine score in reading comprehension went up from the fourth stanine to the sixth stanine. That big a difference is important.

Source: Adapted from *All of Hills' Handy Hints*, by J. R. Hills, 1986, Upper Saddle River, NJ: Merrill/Prentice Hall. (A compilation of articles that originally appeared in *Educational Measurement: Issues and Practice*, September 1983, Vol. 2, No. 1, to Fall 1984, Vol. 3, No. 3.) Copyright 1983 by the National Council on Measurement in Education. Adapted by permission of the publisher.

Figure 13.4   Test Score Quiz—Answers

1. **True.** A grade equivalent score is the average performance of students on the test at each of several grade levels. A sixth grader who has gotten a grade equivalent of 9.2 has performed like a ninth-grade student on the sixth-grade test. Therefore, he has performed above average for students in his grade.

2. **False.** A grade equivalent of 9.2 means that Tim does as well as ninth graders on sixth-grade work. It does not necessarily mean that he can do ninth-grade work.

3. **False.** Tim's score of 9.2 on reading and 7.3 on arithmetic could be equal scores if one used another score scale such as percentiles. The difference between the two grade equivalent scores may be due to the fact that students tend to differ less within a grade on arithmetic than on reading. In addition, grade equivalent scores above a student's grade do not necessarily mean that he or she has really mastered skills beyond his own grade level.

4. **False.** Percentile scores indicate the relative standing in a group, not the percent of items that are correct.

5. **False.** The 50th percentile is defined as being the average score. To be the average, some scores must be below it and some above. It is unrealistic to try to get everyone up to the average. If everyone does improve, or if only the bottom half improves, the 50th percentile also increases. While the change in the 50th percentile will not appear on the form of the test now being used, the next time the test is normed, the 50th percentile will move up.

6. **False.** Scores at the 30th percentile are really not far below average. The 30th percentile means that the student has scored better than 30% of similar students taking the test. Usually no more than a few percent of a class are failed, say 3 or 4 percent, not anywhere near 30 percent. Besides, a nationally standardized test may not accurately sample the arithmetic skills covered in Susie's class.

7. **False.** Students who receive the same stanine each year are maintaining their relative position in the group; they are learning just the amount that would be expected of someone with this standing. If, however, the stanine jumps substantially, then they are learning more than would be expected of someone with their beginning level of performance.

8. **This depends.** Sometimes the change from one stanine to another can result from getting a single extra question right or wrong. In that case there's probably nothing to be worried about! However, if the student goes from high in the range of stanine five to low in the range of stanine four, there might be something to worry about.

9. **True.** When scores differ by two stanines, we tend to think of there being a real difference, not an error of measurement. A difference that large is unlikely to be an accident so it deserves further investigation. Perhaps Elena has benefited from some effective teaching, or she may have become more motivated, or she may have found more time to read, or something in her life that was impeding her progress may have been removed.

Source: Adapted from *All of Hills' Handy Hints*, by J. R. Hills, 1986, Upper Saddle River, NJ: Merrill/Prentice Hall. (A compilation of articles that originally appeared in *Educational Measurement: Issues and Practice*, September 1983, Vol. 2, No. 1, to Fall 1984, Vol. 3, No. 3.) Copyright 1983 by the National Council on Measurement in Education. Adapted by permission of the publisher.

Percentile Score

What They Mean

Percentiles are norm-referenced scores—comparing students with one another in ways that rank students. They tell you what percentage of the norm group a student outscores. For example, a student with a percentile score of 55 performed better than 55 percent of the students in the test's norm group.

Test publishers sometimes also provide percentile norms that compare an individual student's score to students from the norm group that are similar in geographic region, of the same gender, or of like ethnicity. This allows users to determine how their students perform in comparison to other students who are like them in these particular ways.

It is easy to confuse percentiles and percent correct. Percent correct tells you merely how well a student performed on a given set of test items. Percentiles tell you how well a student performed compared to students in the norm group.

How to Use Them

The question percentiles answer is, "How is each student doing compared to all similar students?" Students can maintain their relative standing in relationship to each other over time, so staying at approximately the same percentile over time is not necessarily a problem. It doesn't mean that students have stopped learning. It simply means that they are learning enough to maintain their relative standing in the group. A declining percentile doesn't mean that a student has forgotten some of what she or he knew before. It only means that student didn't learn enough compared to the norm group to maintain a consistent place in the rank order.

Here are four recommendations for appropriate use of percentiles:

1. Try not to overinterpret percentile jumps! Because of the nature of the score scale, a gain of 10 percentile points in the midrange (say, from the 50th to the 60th percentile) doesn't represent the same amount of learning as a gain of 10 points at the extremes (say from the 90th to the 99th percentile). A single additional item answered correctly (that is, one extra point on the test) might jump a student from the 50th to the 60th percentile. However, it might take six extra points to jump from the 90th to the 99th percentile.

2. Resist any attempts to use norm-referenced test scores, especially percentiles, to assign course grades. The coverage of such tests is too broad to align well with the requirements of a single course of study.

3. Resist all attempts to use norm-referenced test scores, especially percentiles, to retain students in a grade or keep them from graduating from high school. They say little about what students actually know and can do relative to state or local achievement standards.

4. In summarizing student achievement, do not average percentile scores. We won't go into why, but trust us, if you need to summarize over a number of students, compute an average raw score and then convert that to a percentile.

Stanines

What They Mean

A stanine is a norm-referenced score. Table 13.1 shows a table of stanines. Stanines are similar to percentiles but are less precise. There are 99 levels of percentile rankings, but only 9 levels of stanines (the term is an abbreviation of "standard nine"). They describe in general terms how a student compares to other, similar students. For example, a stanine of 5 means that a student is "average" as compared to the norm group.

How to Use Them

As with percentiles, the way to use stanines is as a general indicator of how a student's performance on the test compares to other similar students and as a general green or red flag. They can't really be used to track student progress because the range of scores in any single stanine is too broad. A student could make a lot of progress, even compared to other students, and still stay in the same stanine.

As we saw with percentiles, students tend to maintain their relative standing in relationship to the norm group over time, so, once again, staying in the same stanine over time is not necessarily a problem. It doesn't mean that a student has learned nothing. It means that the student is learning just enough to maintain her relative standing in the group. It's when students jump stanines that we need to take notice. Since stanines are so broad, a stanine jump could mean a significant gain or loss in achievement.

Once again, a stanine says nothing about what, specifically, a student knows and can do. Therefore, they are of limited value in planning instruction.

Grade Equivalent Scores

What They Mean

Grade equivalents are the trickiest scores of all because they don't mean what it looks like they mean. Grade equivalents are norm-referenced scores, not criterion-referenced scores.

Table 13.1   Understanding Stanine Scores

Stanine	Percent of Scores	Percentile Range	Descriptor
9	4	96–99	Well above average
8	7	89–95	Above average
7	12	77–88	
6	17	60–76	Average
5	20	40–59	
4	17	23–39	
3	12	11–22	Below average
2	7	4–10	
1	4	1–3	Well below average

Source: Reprinted from *Student-Involved Assessment* for *Learning*, 4th ed. (p. 262), by R. J. Stiggins, 2005, Upper Saddle River, NJ: Merrill/Prentice Hall. Copyright © 2005 by Pearson Education, Inc. Reprinted by permission of Pearson Education, Inc.

This means that they describe relative standing in a group (as do percentile and stanine); they have nothing to say about the actual level of work students are able to do.

During norming, if students in the second month of third grade get an average raw score of 25 correct on the new tests, from then on, whenever that test is administered all students who get 25 right will be assigned a grade equivalent of 3.2. However, it's way too expensive to retest students in every grade level every month. Instead, test publishers estimate grade equivalents by actually giving the test to students, say, in the first month of the third and fourth grades. They plot these two points on a graph of grade levels by test scores, then draw a line between them; monthly grade equivalents are estimated by reading them right from the graph. To estimate grade equivalents before grade 3 or after grade 4, developers just extend the line and read other grade equivalents from the points represented on the line.

How to Use Them

Use grade equivalents as only a rough measure of how students compare to their peers. You can't compare grade equivalents across tests. For example, if a third grader gets a grade equivalent of 6.2 on a math test and a 5.0 on a reading test, you can't say that the student is three years ahead in math, two years ahead in reading, and one additional year ahead in math than reading. All the grade equivalents tell you is that the student did very well on the third-grade test in both reading and math, as compared to the norm group.

Competency and Mastery Scores

What They Mean

Competency scores (also called proficiency level, performance level, objective proficiency score, mastery level, or achievement level) are criterion referenced; they relate student performance to preset levels of mastery of the content. For example, if a test includes 10 items covering a particular standard and a score of 7 out of 10 is required to be judged competent, then the student's score must meet or exceed that number correct to be judged to have passed that standard.

How to Use Them

Competency scores tell you how well students have mastered important knowledge and skills. You can compare them across content and subject areas—for example, you can say "Martha meets the standard in math, but not in reading."

Sometimes statements of competency are made based on very few test items. For example, a standardized test might only have 3 questions that cover the target, "reading a bar graph." If a student gets 2 right out of 3, the skill is marked as mastered. But according to your classroom standards, you may not judge that this student has mastered reading bar graphs. Be sure you know the number of items on which statements of mastery are based.

Summary of Test Score Types

Table 13.2 presents a summary of the score types we have discussed in this section.

Table 13.2   Test Score Summary

Score	Meaning	Strengths	Cautions
Raw	Number of questions answered correctly or number of points earned. The range goes from zero to the total possible.	Provides the basis of all other scores.	Difficult to interpret by themselves. Can't be used to compare across tests.
Percent Correct	Total points earned divided by the total possible. The range goes from 0 to 100%.	Easy to understand. Can communicate level of mastery of specific learning targets.	Small numbers of test questions don't provide very good estimates of mastery.
Percentile	The percent of students in a norm group that score below any particular raw score. The range goes from 0 to 99.	Permits clear comparison to other similar students. Can compare scores across tests in a battery.	Often confused with percent correct. Cannot be averaged. Provides no information about the actual content learned.
Stanine	Divides scores into 9 broad categories based on percentiles. The range goes from 1 to 9.	Provides a broad take on the relative performance of a student compared to others. Can be averaged.	Too broad to detect small differences in achievement.
Grade Equivalent	Compares performance on the test to that of various other grade levels who took the same test. The range goes from K.0 to 12.9.	Provides a general picture of how well a student did compared to others.	Not a criterion-referenced score. Does not indicate the level of work a student is capable of doing.
Competency Level	The level of mastery of content. Levels are set by panels of experts.	Allows statements of what students know and can do. Can be compared across learning targets to come up with a profile of strengths and weaknesses.	Sometimes based on very few questions. Sometimes not fine grained enough to identify specific strengths and weaknesses.

Source: Adapted from *Student-Involved Assessment* for *Learning*, 4th ed. (p. 265), by R. J. Stiggins, 2005, Upper Saddle River, NJ: Merrill/Prentice Hall. Copyright © 2005 by Pearson Education, Inc. Adapted by permission of Pearson Education, Inc.

Fine Tuning Your Sense of Scores

Now that we have considered various types of scores, we offer additional insights into their interpretation.

Oddities About Norms

One surprise about norms is how they compare between an older and newer version of the test. As you know, test publishers regularly update their tests. Sometimes they update just the norms; sometimes both content coverage (new items) and norms. When norms are updated, test publishers equate the tests so that scores between the two editions can be directly compared. This provides a way of predicting what students' scores would be on one edition of the test if they actually took the other edition.

When a new version of a test comes out, percentile scores can go down at first. That is, students who were scoring in the 75th percentile on the old version might only be at the 65th percentile on the new, which can cause concern all around. The score dip with new norms can come from the fact that, over time, districts align their curricula to the content of the test. If the test content changes, even if the intention is to assess the very same learning targets, the test might no longer match precisely what is taught, and scores go down.

The score dip can also come when students in the same grade level are learning more and more over time. So, the average score (the 50th percentile) keeps going up. If a student got a 50th percentile on the old test (better than 50% of students in the norm group), that might correspond, for example, to the 45th percentile on the new norms. It's not that the student suddenly knew less, it's that everyone else knows more. The competition is suddenly harder.

Oddities About Competency Levels

It appears that competency levels are very likely not comparable across states, across grades in the same state, and across content areas in the same state (Kingsbury, Olson, Cronin, Hauser, & Hauser, 2003). Speculations on the reasons include the fact that states developed their competencies to represent different things. Some states set high standards as ideals to shoot for. Others set them to represent minimum competency. This means that schools that are "failing" in one state might be doing just fine if they were in another.

Another issue with competency levels revolves around the technical adequacy of standards-settings procedures. As we saw before, setting standards is an exercise in professional judgment. Different groups on different occasions in the same state could come up with different cut scores. What this says is that we need to use competency indicators with our eyes open. We need to know how competency levels were set in our state or district and the issues that arose during the process.

Measurement Error

Test scores are imprecise. They contain errors that could cause them to be a little high or low relative to a student's true level of achievement. Because of student guessing, poorly written questions or exercises, poorly trained human raters, and, in fact, anything else on the list of potential sources of bias and distortion in Chapter 4, Figure 4.4, sometimes tests over- or underestimate achievement. The error can be larger or smaller depending on how carefully all potential problems have been addressed.

We rarely attain perfect precision. There will always be some level of error—of unreliability. Therefore, as assessment users, we must always take that imprecision into account in interpreting test scores.

Let's look at an example: Some percentage of students must meet state standards for a district to meet adequate yearly progress requirements. Each student takes a test on those standards and is judged to have passed or not based on a predetermined score. One student, Lynn, scores 29, one point below the cutoff score of 30 required to pass. The test score carries a standard error of 2 points. So on retake, Lynn might well score over 30 or just below. Has Lynn mastered the standards or not? No one can say for sure. But a score this close deserves a very close look and perhaps retesting to be certain of her level of mastery.

The better the quality of the test and the conditions under which it is administered, the narrower the margin of error will be, leading to more precise scores. This is why we need to adhere to standards of assessment quality—to prevent bad decisions due to errors of measurement. Always ask the test developer for information about the margin of error of scores, so you can make cautious interpretations and help others do the same.

Activity 13.4   Interpret Your Own Standardized Test Report

Attempt to identify examples of each of the following test report elements on a selected individual student standardized test score report that you use in your district or state. If your report does not include that score, write "doesn't apply." Then answer the questions that follow. (A printable version of the list and questions appears on the CD in the file, "Standardized Test Reports.")

- Number correct/raw score

- National percentile

- National stanine

- Grade equivalent

- Competency or mastery levels

- Performance on individual content standards or learning targets

1. How big are the error bands around each type of score? What does this mean?

2. On mastery scores, above which scores are you certain students have met mastery and below which scores are you sure that students have not met mastery? For those in the gray area, what additional information might you collect to help determine proficiency level?

3. What are the possible implications for instruction of the results on this test? Look for relative strengths and weaknesses—error bands that overlap the least with each other or with the "proficient" level.

4. What don't you understand about this report? How are you going to find answers?

Using Standardized Tests to Promote Student Learning

Summative assessments can be used formatively. Most standardized tests arise from lists of specific standards or test blueprints that are readily available. In addition, their developers offer released test items, rubrics, and samples of student-constructed responses. These can be used just like any other blueprint, sample item, rubric, or sample of student work to promote learning as described in Chapters 5–8. Here are two specific ideas that we have discussed previously, applied to the context of standardized tests.

Make Learning Targets Clear to Students Using Released Test Questions

Use released test questions or item specifications from your state or district assessment if you want to know how instruction might be tweaked in the areas for which you are not satisfied with student performance. Figure 13.5 presents an activity using sample standards and test item specifications to determine how much experience students have had answering questions aimed at a specific learning target or standard.

Notice that the questions are "formulas" into which specific information can be placed. If they are available, they are likely to be part of the blueprint (specifications) for the assessment. If they are not made available, you will have to infer the formulas yourself based on examination of test questions.

Deconstruct the Standards

Remember the idea suggested in Chapter 3 of starting with standards and deconstructing them into the building blocks of student success? This is an excellent way to think about improving student performance on the knowledge and reasoning targets measured by high-stakes tests. Begin with a content standard on which you would like achievement to improve, and then ask the following questions:

- What must my students know and understand when the time comes to perform well on a test of this standard? Plan instruction and classroom assessment to put this building block in place.

- What patterns of reasoning must my students be masters of when the time comes to score well on a test of these priorities? Provide lots of guided practice, with student involvement in to take them there.

- What performance skills or product development capabilities must be in place when the time comes for my students to shine on a test of these standards? Proceed to set them up for success.

Figure 13.5 Sample State Grade 10 Standards and Relative Test Questions

Content Standard: Summarize text

Example of multiple-choice item:

Which sentence below summarizes what this [selection] is about?

a. The correct response is the best summary.

b. An incorrect response may contain an idea not included in the passage.

c. An incorrect response may contain an idea from the passage that is too narrow to be acceptable as a summary.

Example of a short-answer item:

Write a paragraph in your own words to summarize what happens in this story.

During the year, my students generally have the following practice answering questions aimed at this learning target:

Extensive	Some	None

⟵――――――――――――――――――――⟶

Source: Adapted from *Washington State Essential Academic Learning Requirements: Reading*. 2004. Olympia, WA: Office of Superintendent of Public Instruction. Retrieved July 2004 from the World Wide Web: http://www.k12.wa.us/assessment/WASL/reading7rdspecs.aspx. Adapted by permission.

TRY THIS

Activity 13.5   Use Item Formulas to Help Students Learn

1. Choose a learning target from your standardized test report for which you want to improve results.

2. For the level of the test your students took, find a released sets of test questions.

3. Each released question will identify the target it is intended to cover. If the target is not specifically listed next to the question, you might have to find the test specifications for your test level that list which questions cover each learning target.

4. Gather a number of test questions intended to cover the learning target so that you can get a broad view of the target. Keep in mind the possibility of narrowing the curriculum if you base instruction only on a single question from the released items.

5. Think about how frequently you give students the opportunity to respond to questions like these.

6. Generalize about the type of questions you would ask students to have them practice the thinking required to do well on the learning target. Devise questions and "formulas" for questions if they are not already provided.

7. Make a plan for how you might provide students additional practice on the learning covered by the test questions.

Does this look like a lot of work? Then, get help from students. What might be the benefits to students of engaging them in such an analysis? You might also conduct these analyses with your learning team.

Ethical Test Preparation Practices

The goal of test preparation (sometimes called *testwiseness*) training for students is to ensure that test scores are accurate; that nothing in the testing situation will cause students' learning to be mismeasured. *The goal is not to maximize test scores regardless of what students know and can do.* The following are considered to be ethical test preparation practices:

- Have students practice filling out information asked for on the answer sheet—name, date, grade, etc.

- Practice answering easy questions using directions from and the format of the test, especially for younger students. This includes practice marking answers on a separate answer sheet.

- Focus instruction on the overall content areas you know to be on the test.

- Give students information about the test: what will be tested, how results will be used, how long it is, when it will be given, the materials they should bring, and who will be giving the test.

- Teach students how to pace themselves on the test: practice timed exercises during instruction; have older students practice noting the time they have to answer the questions and where they need to be when time is halfway up; have younger students practice working alone for up to 30 minutes.

- Instruct students to answer all the questions first, and then check answers if there is time (students do the checking).

- Teach students how to make educated guesses by ruling out any choices known to be wrong and guessing among those that remain.

- Have students practice on released test questions from previous test administrations, especially if you use a set of questions that samples well from what students know.

The following set of practices are not considered to be ethical and should be avoided:

- Focusing instruction directly on content questions you know to be on the test

- Providing students with extended practice on old or parallel forms of the test without guided practice on how to improve

TRY THIS

Activity 13.6   Translate Standardized Test Jargon into Student-Friendly Language

With your learning team or with students, identify the specific information on your standardized test that students need to know: test purpose, content, length, dates, penalties for guessing, test scores reported, information on student reports, and implications for instruction. Identify the words and ideas that need to be translated into student-friendly language and complete that translation.

Might involving students in this process aid their learning? If you judge the amount of learning to be worth the time, plan how you will involve students in understanding standardized tests for themselves.

To decide which of the legitimate test preparation activities to use, you can use the form in Table 13.3 to diagnose your students' test preparation needs. You can use the quiz, "What Would You Do?" in Figure 13.6, and Figure 13.7, "What Testwise Students Do," with students. (Printable copies of each of these appear on the CD in the files of the same names.)

Table 13.4 summarizes what can and can't be done during test administration. For more information about this topic, view on the accompanying DVD the segment, "Ethical Test Preparation."

Table 13.3   Possible Test-Taking Problems Students Might Have and What to Do About Them

Problems and Solutions	% of Students with This Problem
1. Spending too much time on difficult questions or not finishing the test. *Solution: Teach students to skip difficult questions and come back to them later; practice pacing themselves; practice making educated guesses; and practice skimming and scanning.*	
2. Not guessing. *Solution: Teach students how to make educated guesses and tell them that guessing is acceptable.*	
3. Not understanding directions or not listening to instructions. *Solution: Use the directions to take classroom quizzes; define words in the directions students might not know; give students longer and longer directions to follow.*	
4. Not using answer sheets correctly or not knowing how to fill in the bubbles on the answer sheet. *Solution: Practice using a similar answer sheet during instruction.*	
5. Not knowing how to organize test materials on the desk, how to handle a test booklet and separate answer sheet, or how to keep track of their place on the answer sheet. *Solution: Practice these skills during classroom quizzes or on simple questions just before the test. Show students how to mark their place with a pencil, eraser, or ruler.*	
6. Experiencing excessive nervousness and anxiety. *Solution: Let students know what to expect (content, length, etc.), what to bring, how to prepare physically, practice positive self-talk, and most importantly, involve students in classroom assessment during instruction so that they understand the learning targets.*	
7. Finishing too early, not checking over answers, or skipping too many questions. *Solution: Let students know it is acceptable to make educated guesses; give students a way to identify questions that they want to go back and check; have students practice using all of a given amount of time to check for skipped questions or questionable answers.*	
8. Exhibiting disruptive behaviors or sharing answers with others. *Solutions: Move students up front; space students out; sometimes have students practice working alone; provide test "barriers" on individual desks.*	
9. Showing up late for the test or not showing up at all. *Solution: Contact parents to identify the underlying problem.*	
10. Lacking motivation to try hard on the test; e.g., making designs on the answer sheet. *Solution: Build student confidence throughout the term by using assessment* for *learning strategies.*	
11. Needing to use the bathroom during testing. *Solution: Provide opportunities before the test. Make sure all students know in advance that the time to use the bathroom is before the test.*	

Figure 13.6 What Would You Do?

Read each statement and decide whether it is true or false. Circle your choice.

T F 1. Test questions should be answered in the order they appear no matter how long it takes for each answer.

T F 2. If there is time left after finishing a test, you shouldn't review your answers.

T F 3. It will save a lot of time if you don't read the directions given within the test.

T F 4. If there is a time limit on the test, you should spend more time on questions you are not sure of.

T F 5. If you're not sure of an answer, it's okay to guess.

T F 6. With a multiple-choice question, you don't need to read all of the possible choices before answering.

T F 7. After answering each question, it's a good idea to make sure you have marked the answer you meant to mark and to make sure the number of the test question matches the number on the answer sheet.

T F 8. If you're not sure of the answer, partial knowledge can sometimes help to eliminate some answer choices.

T F 9. It is good to be nervous while taking a test.

T F 10. After your teacher has explained about taking the test, you should only ask a question if others do.

Answers: 1-F, 2-F, 3-F, 4-F, 5-T, 6-F, 7-T, 8-T, 9-F, 10-F

Figure 13.7   What Testwise Students Do

A. **Prepare yourself**

- Get a good night's rest.
- East breakfast the day of the test, but don't eat too big a meal.
- Get to school early.
- Don't drink a lot of fluids just before the test.

B. **Take the test**

- Concentrate.
- Don't talk.
- Listen carefully.
- Read written instructions carefully before answering questions because instructions can change for different sections.
- Ask questions if you don't understand what you are to do.
- If you don't know an answer, stay calm. Many standardized tests are designed so that very few students know all the answers. Make an educated guess and come back to the question later.
- Pace yourself. Make a note of what the time will be when you'll have five minutes left so you can skim through and answer the rest of the questions as quickly as possible.
- Read each question or problem all the way through and then carefully read all the answer choices before responding.
- Don't puzzle more than a few seconds over any multiple-choice question or problem. On your second pass through the test, change your strategy. Read everything and try to eliminate any of the answer choices.
- Make sure the number of the question in the test booklet matches the number on the answer sheet.

Figure 13.7   (Continued)

C. **Keep a positive attitude; change negative self-talk to positive self-talk**

- If you're thinking, "I'll never get finished," change it to, "I can do it one step at a time."

- If you're thinking, "If I miss this, I've really blown it," change it to, "Some anxiety is inevitable, but I don't have to worry about it."

- If you're thinking, "Why am I so anxious? I hate feeling like this. I know I'm doing a lousy job," change it to, "I really do have confidence in my basic ability. I can show what I know."

- If you're thinking, "I'm behind, I've got to hurry," change it to, "Don't anticipate problems, just keep going."

- If you're thinking, "People will think I'm dumb if they finish before I do," change it to, "Good students take all the test time available to make sure their answers are right."

- If you're thinking, "Help, I don't know the answer and I don't have time to figure it out," change it to, "I'll skip this one and come back to it later."

- If you're thinking, "I hate myself, why try?," change it to, "I can do my best and that's all that's required."

What Parents Need to Know About Standardized Tests

You may have encountered a question from a parent along this line: "Why does there seem to be so much testing these days?" Although federal and state requirements are part of the answer, accountability testing is only a portion of the bigger picture of school testing. At the local level, many districts and schools have also added layers of testing. For example, tests known as common assessments, interim assessments, or short-cycle assessments have been put into place by many schools and districts to help in providing more frequent data about student attainment of content standards. Department tests in high school, grade-level diagnostic reading tests in elementary school, district direct writing assessments: all add to the increasingly larger picture of standardized testing in schools today.

Regardless of the number of standardized tests, we can help parents understand that the tests are a very small percentage of the total assessment picture at school. The vast

Table 13.4   What Can and Can't Be Done During Test Administration

Can Be Done	Can't Be Done
Rereading the directions to students.	Giving hints.
Circulating to make sure that everyone is on the correct section of the test and is handling the answer sheet properly.	Reading questions to students unless the directions tell you to do so.
Suggesting that a student who appears to be struggling reread the directions.	Defining words in the test questions.
Helping a student to keep his place in the test by having him move a pencil, eraser, or ruler down the page, and pointing out if the question and answer numbers do not match.	Timing the test improperly.
Answering questions about logistics—where she should be in the test booklet and the answer sheet; where the instructions are; how long she has to finish, etc.	Paraphrasing the directions.
Arranging the room and materials to be conducive to test taking: place easily distracted students in the front, reduce crowding, have materials ready for easy distribution, make sure lighting and temperature are adequate, test in a familiar place, make sure writing surfaces are large enough.	Answering questions on content.

majority of assessments originate in the classroom and are designed or selected by the teacher—the person in the best position to know and communicate in specific ways the achievement status of each student in the class. Whatever the purpose of the standardized test (accountability, program evaluation, general indicator of short-term group progress), all educators can help parents see that these tests should not be confused with assessments designed to improve daily teaching and learning in the classroom. Our job collectively is to keep an eye on them to see that they don't get out of balance (Chappuis & Chappuis, 2002).

You may already have a sense of what the parents you work with want to know about testing. Anticipating parent interests and communicating with them proactively helps establish a testing environment built on a common foundation of fact. Here are a few general questions parents might ask about testing, followed by examples of topics to communicate to parents before and after testing.

- How much class time will be devoted to testing and test preparation?

- How strong is the link between what my child learns in the classroom and what is asked on the test?

- How are the results of the assessment going to be used? What kinds of decisions will be made about my child?

- What does it mean if my child's test scores don't seem to match the classroom report card grades? Which is more important? Which is more accurate?

Before the Standardized Test

Test Information

Parents ought to know everything we want students to know about tests before they take them:

- The content of the test and how it relates to what students are learning in the classroom

- The purpose(s) of the test and how it might affect students

- The time, location and duration of the test

- How the test will be scored

- What assessment methods are used

- How the information/results of the test will be reported back to students and parents, and when

- What students need to bring, if anything

Might it be worthwhile to have students do some of the explaining to their parents? What might that look like with your students in your classroom?

How to Prepare Their Children

Figure 13.8 presents ideas for what parents can do to prepare their children to take standardized tests. Decide which of these things to discuss with the parents of your students.

Figure 13.8   How Parents Can Help Prepare Students for Standardized Tests

A. Before the Test

1. Reinforce discussions from school. Discuss the following:

    a. The purpose for the test—to help teachers see what students know and to let the community know how much students are learning. This is important, so students need to try their best to show what they know and can do.

    b. What's on the test—the content covered and how it relates to what they've been learning in school.

    c. How to approach hard questions. Don't worry if you can't answer all the questions; many standardized tests are designed so that few students can answer all the questions. Make educated guesses; rule out the choices you know are wrong and guess among the rest. Mark questions you are unsure about and revisit them if you have time. Answer all the questions even if you have to guess on some.

2. Be encouraging. If you say, "You don't do well on these tests," your child will expect failure. Encourage your child just to try her best.

3. The night before the test:

    a. Make sure your child doesn't go to bed angry, and plan ahead to stay away from known problems.

4. The morning of the test:

    a. Have your child get ready early enough to avoid hurrying.

    b. Have your child eat a good breakfast, but not a heavy one.

    c. Have your child dress in something he likes and that is familiar. Being comfortable is important.

    d. Be positive when you send your child to school. Encourage her to try hard and don't worry if she doesn't know everything.

B. After the Test

1. Ask your child to tell you about the test. What questions did he expect? Which were surprises? How hard was it? What did he learn? What could he do differently if the test could be taken over?

2. Talk about the content of the test and what her plans are for revisiting the material before the next test.

3. Acknowledge your child for trying hard on the test. Do not punish a child for doing poorly. This will only hurt future performance; the test itself was punishing enough if he had a hard time.

4. When you get the test results for your child, don't compare her performance with that of other children. Saying something like, "Why aren't you as smart as Jennifer next door?" will not make your child want to try harder; it is more likely to make her stop trying.

5. Talk to your child's teacher about any questions you have.

After the Standardized Test

The conditions for effective communication in Chapter 9, Figure 9.2, apply to standardized tests as well as to every other assessment:

1. Everyone is clear on the learning targets to be communicated about—both what they are and what they mean. Showing parents samples of released test questions and associated student responses help parents understand what was or will be on the test.

2. Communication is based on accurate information obtained from the test. We need to help parents take into account numbers of questions on each learning target, the precision of the scores, errors of measurement, what learning targets, if any, were left off the test because of restrictions in the assessment methods used.

3. Symbols are clear. Parents need to understand what the various test scores represent and how to interpret them. On norm-referenced tests parents are often confused about the different between percent correct and percentiles, and often misinterpret grade equivalents. On criterion-referenced, mastery tests parents need to understand what "mastery level work" looks like and what it means to have "mastered" a target.

4. Communication is tailored to the audience in terms of level of detail. Parents want to know whether or not their child's test performance is okay. Discuss results as evidence of continued or new progress. Be descriptive as much as possible. Talk about differences between once-a-year testing and classroom assessment and what each reveals; norm-referenced and criterion-referenced information and what each reveals; how the results can and will be used for the benefit of the student; and what parents can do to help boost learning.

5. Timing. Parents need to know information as soon as it is available.

6. Avoid negative side effects by keeping communication private, focused on what students can do and their next steps in learning (if the test is designed to provide such information), and making sure parents understand the scores and what they do and don't mean.

Implications for Teachers

Teachers have a pivotal role to play in standardized testing.[1]

Responsibility 1: Protect the Well-Being of Students!

Teachers are the first line of defense in keeping students free from harm that can occur from standardized tests.

Give Students the Opportunity to Learn

Increase student confidence by providing students the opportunity to learn what they need to hit the achievement targets reflected in the standardized tests they take:

- Get test specifications so that you know what's on the test.

- Review content standards so that you understand the learning objectives that test questions are aimed at assessing.

- Deconstruct content standards into the enabling knowledge, reasoning, performance skill, or product development targets so that you are confident that you are laying the foundation for success by concentrating on the building blocks for that success.

- Analyze the test questions that are used to assess each content standard to get a richer idea of how others have defined success on the content standard and the implications this has for instruction.

- Commit to teaching the entire curriculum; don't restrict instruction just to the specifics on the test.

- Help students see the connection between what they will be asked to do on the test and the greater range of ways they will be asked to use their knowledge in school and in the world.

- Engage in assessment *for* learning activities, including student involvement, so that you and they know how they are progressing over time. Keep students in touch with the learning targets they are to hit, where they are in this journey, and what to concentrate on next, so that standardized test results will come as no surprise to anyone.

Build Student Confidence in Other Ways

- Give students information about the test as outlined previously.

- Engage in productive test preparation as described previously.

- Tell students it is important to try as hard as possible to obtain accurate information, but (if this is the case) it's not expected that they get everything right; many tests are not designed for that.

- Remain positive and encouraging.

Advocate for Students

With parents and the community, advocate for the following:

- Balance between assessments *of* and *for* learning, and between large-scale and classroom assessments. Point out the learning targets standardized tests frequently leave out because they cannot be assessed in selected response format.

- Good standardized tests (1) that provide examples of student work, rubrics, and questions that flesh out important learning targets; (2) that are aligned as closely as possible to important student learning targets; (3) that don't provide an overwhelming time load on the educational system; (4) that are reliable and valid; and (5) that have only positive side effects.

- Appropriate test accommodations for those students who need them. Students should not be placed in the position where failure is certain—a test that is too hard, testing in English when students don't understand English, or test conditions that don't meet physical needs. Common test accommodations include location, timing, physical aids, breaks, time of day the test is administered, or tests given in a different order.

- Proper use and interpretation of results. Standardized test results should not be used for course grades. Take error of measurement into account when considering use of results for sanctions. Do not use results as the sole measure for making important decisions about students, teachers, or schools. Standardized tests can only provide a broad picture of performance; many are not detailed enough to promote specific instructional planning.

- Reporting results in sensitive ways. Protect the privacy of all students.

Responsibility 2: Strive for Accurate Results

Accurate results serve students. Inaccurate results harm students.

- Administer tests as instructed—timing, instructions, and so on. This includes instructions for what help we can give students and what help we can't. If you believe any of these procedures might harm a student, advocate for that student ahead of time.

- Don't apologize for giving the test and don't give the opinion that the test is worthless. Teacher stance affects student performance.

- Make sure that testing accommodations and modifications occur for students who need them.

- Only engage in ethical test preparation activities.

Summary

Any assessment given to different groups of students under the same conditions, with the same instructions and scoring procedures, can be considered a standardized test. Such tests can be effective communication tools and can assist in improving learning if we know both how the specific test is designed to be used and its limitations.

In this chapter we have addressed what teachers need to know about standardized tests in order to do the following:

- Fulfill their role in producing accurate standardized test scores.

- Interpret and use standardized test scores wisely and help others do the same.

- Give students the opportunity to learn so that they face standardized testing with confidence.

- Advocate for the well-being of students.

- Use standardized test results and materials as tools for learning to the extent possible.

Standardized tests are developed using the same steps as classroom assessments, and must adhere to the same standards of quality. Unintended negative side effects to guard against include narrowing the curriculum (teaching directly to the content of the standard-ized test) and engaging in practices that artificially inflate scores.

Results can be reported as percentiles, which compare students' performances to those of a norm group; they can be reported as criterion-referenced scores that compare students' performances to a preset standard of acceptable performance on specified learning targets; or they can be reported as both norm- and criterion-referenced scores.

Scores take the form of several of the following on any given test: raw scores, percent correct, percentile, stanine, grade equivalent scores, or competency or mastery scores. Our challenge as educators is to know what each one means and what decisions each is designed to inform. We must also be able to interpret the standard error of measurement for each test.

We also may make standardized tests part of assessment *for* learning. We can make the learning targets clear to students in advance, and structure our preparatory lessons as ongoing formative assessments.

Parents and students need to know the purpose and legitimate, intended use of each standardized test students take, how closely each test links to the curriculum, and how to interpret results if they don't appear to match classroom evidence of achievement. Parents also need to know how to prepare their children for the test and how to talk to them about it afterwards.

As classroom teachers, we can protect students' well-being and improve their perfor-mance by giving them opportunities to learn the achievement targets they are responsible for learning and by building their confidence as test takers. And we can strive for accurate results by adhering to ethical test preparation practices.

◼ *Tracking Your Learning—Possible Portfolio Entries*

Any of the activities included in Chapter 13 can be used as portfolio entries. Remember, the learning targets for this book are outlined in Figure 13.1, and listed in Table 1.2 and described in detail in Chapter 1. The portfolio entry cover sheet provided on the CD in the file, "Portfolio Entry Cover Sheet," will prompt you to think about how each item you select reflects your learning with respect to one or more of these learning targets.

Any of the following activities would also make good portfolio entries. Each could also be used as a learning team activity.

DEEPEN UNDERSTANDING

Activity 13.7   When Grades Don't Match the State Assessment Results

Imagine that a few students in your class who get As don't meet state standards and a few students who get poor grades do meet state standards. Then answer these questions (a set of possible answers follows):

1. Why might the situation be occurring? Consider the extent to which conditions for sound communication are violated (Chapter 9). Might other standards of quality assessment (either in the large-scale or classroom assessment) be violated?

2. What would you do to repair this situation?

Possible Answers:

Question 1: (1) The state assessment only includes achievement, while grades might include factors other than achievement. (2) Class work might not be aligned with priorities in the state assessment, so classroom assessments might measure different things than the state assessment. (3) The classroom assessments underpinning the grades aren't accurate. (4) It is unclear how the state performance standard cut-off relates to teachers' grading cut-offs.

Question 2: (1) Clarify state assessment and classroom learning targets. Do they match? If not, should they? Is instruction aligned? (2) Check classroom assessments for accuracy—do they meet the five standards for quality? (3) Calibrate classroom assessments to the state assessment so that teachers and students know the level needed to perform on classroom assessments to meet state standards.

REFLECT ON YOUR LEARNING

Activity 13.8   A Definitions Posttest

Retake the "Measurement-ese" quiz from Activity 13.2. Then use the answer key found on the CD in the file, "Measurement-ese Answers" to see how well you scored. Compare this score to your first score. What do the results show you have learned? Write a short reflection on how your understanding has changed concerning issues surrounding standardized tests.

Additional Portfolio Entries to Represent Learning from Part 3

If you haven't yet done so, select your responses to activities in Chapters 9–13 to add to your portfolio. As always, each chosen portfolio entry should show some dimension of what you know and are able to do with respect to the learning targets illustrated in Figure 1.2 and described in Table 1.2. Be sure to include a portfolio entry cover sheet with each new entry. Such a form, provided on the CD in the file, "Portfolio Entry Cover Sheet," will prompt you to think about how each item you select for your portfolio reflects what you have learned.

Completing one or more of the following activities will represent a culmination of learning as displayed in your portfolio.

1. Reanalyze at least one of the assessments already in your portfolio. (Do not remove your previous samples or commentaries.) Add commentary about what you see now that you didn't see before. Overall, what differences do you notice in your ability and/or confidence to analyze assessments for quality?

2. Choose a final assessment (selected response test, extended written response test, or performance assessment) that you have recently used. It must be one that you administered, scored, and recorded for use within the context of your teaching. Using the "Assessment Quality Rubrics" found on the CD, briefly analyze the quality of this assessment. What are its strengths? What could be improved?

3. Write a brief analysis of the quality of the assessments overall in your portfolio. Is the quality improving over time? How do you know?

4. Take the "Confidence Questionnaire" found on the CD one final time. Describe how your classroom assessment confidence has changed over this course of study.

5. Write an analysis of changes you have seen in student motivation and achievement that you believe are attributable to changes in your assessment practices. Include examples of student work that shows those changes, if available.

Culminating Portfolio Preparation for Sharing with Peers

Prepare to share your portfolio with your learning team or other audience by doing one or both of the following activities.

1. Write an overall self-reflection on your learning. You may want to use one or more of the questions that follow to focus your reflection. Additionally, you may find that one or more of the forms designed for student portfolio use in Chapter 12 will help guide your reflection.

   • What specific evidence of improvement do you see in your own classroom assessments? Comment on your proficiency in using as many different assessment methods as are relevant in your classroom. What criteria did you use to judge the quality of assessments? Can the reader tell?

   • Did the nature and quality of your critiques change over time? How do you know?

   • What are you doing differently in the classroom as the result of what you have learned? How does this relate to the Five Keys to Quality Assessment? (Refer to Chapter 1 if necessary.)

   • How has your thinking about assessment changed?

   • Did your self-ratings of confidence change over time? In what specific ways?

   • What has been the impact on students of assessment practices you have instituted as a part of this study?

   • What questions did you began this study with that you can now answer? What new questions do you have?

2. Write a "Dear Reader" letter, in which you tell your portfolio audience about yourself as a classroom assessor and point out what you would like your audience to notice about your portfolio. Be sure to include a statement of purpose for your portfolio.

Include a table of contents of all the pieces in your portfolio. Organize your portfolio in a way that makes it easy for the reader to see your growth as a classroom assessor. Date everything, and for each piece state why you included it and what evidence it provides.

Conduct your last team meeting as a celebration of learning by sharing your portfolios with one another. Congratulate each other and thank your team for their commitment to learning!

Notes

1. Portions of this section have been reprinted and adapted from Chapter 10, pp. 267–271, of R. J. Stiggins, *Student-Involved Assessment* for *Learning*, 4th ed., 2005, Upper Saddle River, NJ: Merrill/Prentice Hall. Copyright © 2005 by Pearson Education, Inc. Reprinted and adapted by permission of Pearson Education, Inc.

Closing Comments
from the Authors

As we conclude our journey together through the realm of classroom assessment and its relationship to student success, each of us would like to offer some brief final thoughts for you to consider as you look back at this experience and look forward to what comes next.

Rick

The really big idea here for me is student involvement in assessment, record keeping, and communication. The idea that students might manage their own learning and assessment changes everything. For decades in the United States, school improvement has been based on the belief that it is the adults in the system whose instructional decisions contribute the most to student learning. We now understand that this is wrong. It is as though we have believed that we—the big people in schools—are in charge of the learning. We are not. It's not that we adult teachers, administrators, policy makers, and parents don't contribute immensely to student learning and school effectiveness. We do. But the data-based instructional decisions that students make are far more important. Our students read the assessment results we provide to them and *they* decide whether learning is within reach for them or not, whether the learning is worth the investment required to accomplish it. If they come down on the wrong side of these issues—if they give up in hopelessness—we cannot help them learn. Therefore, we must be merchants of hope. We must help them continue to believe that success is within reach—to believe they can hit the target if they keep trying. This requires an entirely different role for assessment. It requires assessment *for* learning. Please take the idea of student-involved assessment very seriously and make it come alive in your classroom.

As you look to the future, as unusual as this is going to sound, I urge you to consider repeating *this* learning experience. As I have traveled over the years doing presentations on student-involved assessment *for* learning, educators come to me regularly and say, "I heard you present last year (or several years ago) and every time I hear you talk about these ideas, I see and understand something new, some new way to think about student involvement in assessment." The primary reason for this is not that I have added new material to my presentations in the interim, although I do that. It is because, once you have the basic framework of these ideas in your mind and become open to its feasibility—that is, you open an assessment framework in your mind that is fundamentally different from the one we experienced in our youth and careers—it becomes possible to add to this evolving structure of knowledge of sound assessment practice with relative ease. It is almost as though believing permits seeing. For this reason, now that you have completed this initial learning experience, I urge you to repeat it. Now that you see the big picture, go back and begin to fill in the details. You can do this by leading others through the learning team experience you just completed. Please consider this possibility.

But before you go, please do me a favor. Return to the opening of Chapter 1 and reread the story of Emily. She is our "poster child." Make her experience come alive for all of your students.

Jan

I have two final thoughts about classroom assessment, both having to do with students.

The first concerns three essential questions for us as teachers: Where am I headed with my students? Where are my students now? How can I close the gap? Whenever you act to answer one of these questions, ask yourself, "Am I doing something that students could do? Could they do it along with me, or instead of me? Would it be a good use of instructional time—would it enrich their learning to do it?" Any time the answer is "yes," you have a student-involvement activity at your fingertips, an activity with the capability of deepening both the learning and students' commitment to their learning.

The second has to do with the message assessments send to students. When our daughter was small, we taped this sentence to our refrigerator door: "What you think of me, I'll think of me, and what I think of me, I'll be." In the classroom, assessments are a mirror, reflecting to students who they are as learners. Formative or summative, formal or informal, high-stakes or no-stakes assessments, whatever we put on student work—comments, grades, letters, numbers—creates and reinforces their vision of what kind of learners they are. Our greatest challenge is to give students accurate information in a way that reflects what they can do at least as clearly as it shows what they still have to learn.

What does further learning look like? Here are some options for continuing to learn once you have finished this program. You can undertake them individually, as a learning team, or as a whole department or faculty.

1. Select an assessment method you'd like to focus on. Throughout the year, critique all of your assessments employing that method and revise them as necessary.

2. Select an assessment method and revise your teaching to incorporate the assessment *for* learning ideas presented here. Keep track of your students' growth, and let students also keep track of their growth.

3. Select a subject, class, or course to focus on. Throughout the year, critique all of your assessments for that subject, class, or course and revise them as necessary.

4. Select a subject, class, or course to focus on. Revise your teaching to incorporate the assessment *for* learning ideas presented here. Keep track of your students' growth, and let students also keep track of their growth.

5. Revise your grading practices to align with what you believe to be best practice. Initiate a discussion with your colleagues regarding grading practices.

6. Find out who else in your department, building, or district might be interested in learning more about assessment. Help them form a learning team and/or lead it yourself.

7. If you did not watch the videos along with your reading, you may want to make them the focus of your next year's learning.

8. Whatever changes you make in teaching and assessing practices, look for changes in students' motivation, attitudes, and achievement. Help them notice the changes as well.

Judy

My final thoughts can be summarized in two main ideas: clear targets and action research. Over the years I have been impressed again and again with the realization that having clear enough learning targets for students is three quarters of the battle when designing good assessments. When the learning targets are clear the assessments follow naturally. This first became abundantly clear to me while trying to adequately capture the intent of learning outcomes for high school mathematics end-of-course tests. For example, what does "knows the binomial theorem" imply for what students know and are able to do? Surely the assessment items would look different with each of the following interpretations: Can the student choose the binomial theorem from a list, write it out, use it to solve a problem when told to do so, or recognize when using the theorem is the best way to solve a problem?

Another manifestation of the same issue has arisen repeatedly when helping teachers decide how to assess coursework. When teachers ask, "How should we assess science fair projects?" the question really is, "What are we trying to accomplish with students through the science fair project?" We don't assess the science fair project itself, we assess the learning outcomes we want students to achieve. Similarly, when asked, "How do we assess 'ungraded primary'?" the question should really be, "What do we want students to know and be able to do from the experience of being in a ungraded primary classroom?" We assess the learning targets, not the means to attaining them. Instructional activities and settings are the means to an end—the learning we want students to attain from doing the activity.

Knowing specifically what we are trying to accomplish with students is the first, and most important, step in having sound assessments, good record keeping, and useful communication with others about student achievement.

My second final thought relates to action research. The idea is quite simple: Collect information on the impact of one's instructional innovations to determine if the innovation is working, and if not, what to do about it. The claim to evaluate is that implementing high-quality, student-involved assessment *for* learning will improve student achievement. Is it working for you? The goal is to compare the performance of students on the receiving end of such assessment *for* learning with those who are not. Here are some ideas implemented by various teachers: (1) Compare this year's student performance on an assignment including student self-assessment with the performance of last year's students on the same assignment, before student self-assessment was used. (2) At the secondary level, choose one class in which to involve students in assessment. Compare the performance of this class to other classes in the same subject. For example, one teacher compared her class with the most learning problems to her AP class in which she did not implement assessment *for* learning. The initially low-performing students outshone her AP students. (3) Compare the performance of students with teachers on your learning team to the performance of students with teachers not on your learning team. The comparison can be as simple as a particular assignment you have in common or as complicated as standardized test scores for a particular set of learning targets you are emphasizing.

If these two ideas—clear targets and action research—were implemented in all classrooms, I am certain that we would see major gains in student learning and teacher confidence.

Steve

Now that you have completed this program of study, my hope is that you can more clearly see how assessment becomes instruction when it is used *for* learning, and not just for measurement. The principles of assessment *for* learning lead naturally to specific instructional strategies, and classroom teaching takes on a new dimension as a result. When we teach students the language of quality, or help them understand the intended learning by providing student-friendly versions of the targets we want them to hit, or teach them the skills of self assessment, we help change how assessment is viewed and used in the classroom. Further, when we use scoring guides as instructional tools, and involve students in their own assessment through such strategies as test item creation, peer evaluation, and student-led conferences, we teach students to use assessment to understand and improve how and what they are learning.

For us as educators, it can take a while to make the shift from our traditional, somewhat narrow view of assessment as mostly "testing," to one that uses assessment as another form of good teaching. That is understandable; our own experience as students and later as classroom teachers has largely held us to using assessment to produce grades and student achievement data. So making the transition in how we view and use assessment *for* learning is certainly asking us to adopt a different paradigm. For the parents of the students we work with it is no different. In fact, for them it is probably more difficult to break out of a mindset that has a fixed role for testing, grades, and classroom competition. All of us can help parents help their children be better learners by introducing them to the ideas and practices used in a classroom striving to use assessment *for* learning. Just as we engage students as partners and have them assume more responsibility for their own success, so too can we enlist parents. But they must first understand how the process works. We encourage you to open an ongoing dialogue with the parents of your students, communicating with them about what assessment looks like in your classroom, and helping them see what they can do to support student learning through the use of assessment.

Appendix A:
CD Titles by Chapter

Chapter 1
Sample Course Credit Form
Establishing Learning Teams
Establishing Your Portfolio
DVD Table of Contents
Portfolio Entry Cover Sheet
Confidence Questionnaire

Chapter 2
Table 2.1
Portfolio Entry Cover Sheet
Assessment Quality Rubrics
Assessments to Evaluate
Assessment Critiques
Determining Where I Am Now
Student Surveys

Chapter 3
Graphic Organizers
Deconstructing Standards
Portfolio Entry Cover Sheet
Assessment Quality Rubrics
Assessments to Evaluate
Assessment Critiques

Chapter 4
Target–Method Match Chart
Assessments to Evaluate
Analyze for Clear Targets
Test Planning Forms
Portfolio Entry Cover Sheet
Assessment Quality Rubrics
Assessment Critiques

Chapter 5
Test Planning Forms
Analyze for Clear Targets
Test of Franzipanics
Franzipanics—Answers
Reasoning Item Formulas
Goal Setting with Tests
Portfolio Entry Cover Sheet
Assessment Quality Rubrics
Assessments to Evaluate
Assessment Critiques

Chapter 6
Rubric Sampler
Portfolio Entry Cover Sheet

Chapter 7
Metarubric
Rubric Sampler
Rubric Development
Performance Task Plan
Performance Task Rubric
Performance Task Sampler
Samples of Student Writing
Student Math Problem Solving
Using Feedback to Set Goals
AFL Plan
Portfolio Entry Cover Sheet

Chapter 8
Rubric Sampler
Portfolio Entry Cover Sheet
Assessment Quality Rubrics
Confidence Questionnaire

Chapter 9
Rubric Sampler
Auditing for Balance
Portfolio Entry Cover Sheet
Assessment Quality Rubrics
Assessments to Evaluate
Assessment Critiques

Chapter 10
Rubric Sampler
Portfolio Entry Cover Sheet

Chapter 11
Student Portfolio Cover
Rubric Sampler
Portfolio Entry Cover Sheet

Chapter 12
Experiences with Conferences
Goal-Setting Frames
Growth Conference
Conference Evaluation Form
Evidence of Meeting Goals
Portfolio Entry Cover Sheet

Chapter 13
Standardized Test Inventory
Measurement-ese Answers
Standardized Test Reports
Test-Taking Problems
What Would You Do?
What Testwise Students Do
Portfolio Entry Cover Sheet

Appendix B:
DVD Titles by Chapter

Chapter 1
"Program Introduction"
"Learning Teams"
"Interview with Emily"

Chapter 2
"Assessment OF/FOR Learning"
"Impact of Student-Involved Assessment"

Chapter 7
"Teachers on Rubrics"

Chapter 8
"Personal Communication"

Chapter 9
"Record Keeping"

Chapter 12
"Student-Involved Portfolio Conferences"

Chapter 13
"Ethical Test Preparation"

References

Arter, J. A., & K. U. Busick. 2001, *Practice with student-involved classroom assessment*. Portland, OR: Assessment Training Institute.

———, & J. McTighe. 2001. *Scoring rubrics in the classroom: Using performance criteria for assessing and improving student performance*. Thousand Oaks, CA: Corwin.

Assessment Reform Group. 2002. *Testing, motivation and learning*. Cambridge, UK: University of Cambridge, Faculty of Education.

Black, P. 2003a. Formative and summative assessment: Can they serve learning together? Paper presented at the American Educational Research Association annual meeting, Chicago, April 23.

———. 2003b. The nature and value of formative assessment for learning. Paper presented at the American Educational Research Association annual meeting, Chicago, April 23.

———. 2003c. A successful intervention—Why did it work? Paper presented at the American Educational Research Association annual meeting, Chicago, April 23.

Black, P., C. Harrison, C. Lee, B. Marshall, & D. Wiliam. 2002. *Working inside the black box: Assessment for learning in the classroom*. London: King's College Press.

Black, P., & D. Wiliam, 1998. Inside the black box: Raising standards through classroom assessment. *Phi Delta Kappan, 80*(2): 139–148.

Bloom, B. 1984. The search for methods of group instruction as effective as one to one tutoring. *Educational Leadership, 41*(8): 4–17.

Brookhart, S. M. 2004. *Grading.* Upper Saddle River, NJ: Pearson Education.

Butler, R. 1988. Enhancing and undermining intrinsic motivation: The effects of task-involving and ego-involving evaluation on interest and performance. *British Journal of Educational Psychology, 58*: 1–14.

Caine, R. N., & G. Caine. 1997. *Education on the edge of possibility.* Alexandria, VA: ASCD.

California Department of Education. 1994. *A sampler of mathematics assessment: Addendum.* Sacramento, CA: California Department of Education.

Central Kitsap School District. 1999. *Physical education essential learnings.* Silverdale, WA: Author.

———. 2000. *Grades K–6 language essential learnings.* Silverdale, WA: Author.

———. 2000. *Grades 7–10 language essential learnings.* Silverdale, WA: Author.

———. 2001. *Grades K–6 mathematics essential learnings.* Silverdale, WA: Author.

———. 2001. *Science essential learnings.* Silverdale, WA: Author.

———. 2001. *Social studies essential learnings.* Silverdale, WA: Author.

———. 2001. *The student-friendly guide to mathematics problem solving.* Silverdale, WA: Author.

Chappuis, J., & S. Chappuis. 2002. *Understanding school assessment: A parent and community guide to helping students learn.* Portland, OR: Assessment Training Institute.

Chappuis, S., R. Stiggins, J. Arter, & J. Chappuis. 2004. *Assessment FOR learning: An action guide for school leaders.* Portland, OR: Assessment Training Institute.

Clarke, S. 2001. *Unlocking formative assessment.* London, UK: Hodder & Stoughton.

DuFour, R. 2001. In the right context. *Journal of Staff Development, 22*(1): 14–17.

Dweck, C. 2001. *Self theories: Their role in personality, motivation and development.* Philadelphia, PA: Psychology Press.

Ehrenberg, R. E., D. J. Brewer, A. Gamoran, & J. D. Willms. 2001. Does class size matter? *Scientific American, 285*(5): 78–85.

Erickson, L. 2001. *Stirring the head, heart, and soul: Redefining curriculum and instruction*, 2nd ed. Thousand Oaks, CA: Corwin.

Florida Department of Education. n.d. *Grade Level Expectations for the Sunshine State Standards: Mathematics, Grades 6–8*. Miami, FL: Author. Retrieved April 2003 from the World Wide Web: http://www.firn.edu/doe/curric/prek12/pdf/mathgle6.pdf

———. n.d. *Grade Level Expectations for the Sunshine State Standards: Science, Grades 6–8*. Miami, FL: Author. Retrieved April 2003 from the World Wide Web: http://www.firn.edu/doe/curric/prek12/pdf/scigle6.pdf

Fullan, M. 2000. The three stories of education reform. *Phi Delta Kappan, 81*(8): 581–584. Cited in Schmoker, 2002.

Gao, X. 1996. Sampling variability and generalizability of work keys: Listening and writing scores. ACT Research Report Series 996-1. Iowa City, IA: American College Testing.

Glickman, C. 2002. *Leadership for learning: How to help teachers succeed*. Alexandria, VA: Association for Supervision and Curriculum Development. Cited in Schmoker, 2002.

Graves, D. 1983. *Writing: Teacher & children at work*. Portsmouth, NH: Heinemann.

Gregory, K., C. Cameron, & A. Davies. 2000. *Self-Assessment and goal-setting*. Merville, BC: Connections.

———. 2001. *Conferencing and reporting*. Merville, BC: Connections.

Guskey, T. R. (ed.). 1996. *Communicating student learning*. Alexandria, VA: Association for Supervision and Curriculum Development.

Guskey, T. R. 2002. *How's my kid doing?: A parent's guide to grades, marks, and report cards*. San Francisco: Jossey-Bass.

Guskey, T. R., & J. Bailey. 2001. *Developing grading and reporting systems for student learning*. Thousand Oaks, CA: Corwin.

Hibbard, M. (ed.). 1996. On the cutting edge of assessment. Special issue, *Education Update, 38*(4).

Hunkins, F. P. 1995. *Teaching thinking through effective questioning*. Norwood, MA: Christopher-Gordon.

Hunter, M. 1982. *Mastery teaching*. Thousand Oaks, CA: Corwin.

Jensen, E. 1998. *Teaching with the brain in mind*. Alexandria, VA: ASCD.

Jewell, E., & F. Abate. 2001. *The new Oxford American dictionary*. New York: Oxford University Press.

Kendall, J., & R. Marzano. 1997. *Content knowledge: A compendium of standards and benchmarks for K–12 education,* 2nd ed. Aurora, CO: Mid-continent Regional Educational Laboratory.

Khattri, N., A. L. Reeve, & R. J. Adamson. 1997. *Assessment of student performance: Studies of assessment reform*. Washington DC: U.S. Office of Education, Office of Educational Research and Improvement.

Kingsbury, G. G., A. Olson, J. Cronin, C. Hauser, & R. Hauser. 2003. *The state of state standards*. Portland. OR: Northwest Evaluation Association.

Knight, J. E. 1990. Coding journal entries. *Journal of Reading, 34*(1): 42–47.

Knight, S. 2000. Questions: Assessing and developing children's understanding and thinking in literacy. Manchester, UK: Manchester School Improvement Service. Retrieved from the World Wide Web: http://www.aaia.org.uk

LeMahieu, P., D. Gitomer, & J. Eresh, 1995. Portfolios in large-scale assessment: Difficult but not impossible. *Educational Measurement: Issues and Practice, 14*(3): 11–28.

Lucas, C. 1992. *Introduction: Writing portfolios—changes and challenges*. In K. Yancey, *Portfolios in the writing classroom*, pp. 1–11. Reston, VA: NCTM.

Marzano, R., D. Pickering, & J. McTighe. 1993. *Assessing student outcomes: Performance assessment using the dimensions of learning model*. Aurora, CO: Mid-continent Regional Educational Laboratory.

Meisels, S., S. Atkins-Burnett, Y. Xue, D. D. Bickel, & S. H. Son. 2003. Creating a system of accountability: The impact of instructional assessment on elementary children's achievement test scores. *Educational Policy Analysis Archives, 11*(9). Retrieved from the World Wide Web at http://epaa.asu.edu/epaa/v11n9/

Mendel, S. (n.d.). Creating portraits of performance. Aurora, CO: Peakview Elementary School.

Munk, D. D., & W. D. Bursuck. 2003. Grading students with disabilities. *Educational Leadership, 61*(2): 38–43.

Murphy C. U., & D. W. Lick. 2001. *Whole-faculty study groups: Creating student-based professional development*, 2nd ed. Thousand Oaks, CA: Corwin.

Murray, D. 2004. *A writer teaches writing*, 2nd ed., rev. Boston, MA: Thomson/Heinle.

National Literacy Strategy. 1998. *Talking in class*. Reading, UK: National Centre for Literacy and Numeracy.

National Research Council. 1996. *National science education standards*. Washington, DC: National Academy Press.

North Thurston Public Schools. 2001. *K–12 arts curriculum*. Lacey, WA: Author.

O'Connor, K. 2002. *How to grade for learning: Linking grades to standards*, 2nd ed. Arlington Heights, IL: Skylight.

Putnam, R. T., & H. Borko. 2000. What do new views of knowledge and thinking have to say about research on teacher learning? *Educational Researcher, 29*(1): 4–15.

Rodriguiz, M. C. 2004. The role of classroom assessment in student performance on TIMSS. *Applied Measurement in Education, 17*(1): 1–24.

Rowe, M. B. 1972. Wait-time and rewards as instructional variables: Their influence on language, logic, and fate control. Paper presented at the annual meeting of the National Association for Research in Science Teaching, Chicago, April. ERIC ED-061103.

———. 1978. Specific ways to develop better communications. In R. Sund & A. Carin (Eds.), *Creative questioning and sensitivity: Listening techniques*, 2nd ed. Upper Saddle River, NJ: Merrill/Prentice Hall.

———. 1987. Wait time: Slowing down may be a way of speeding up. *American Educator, 11*(1): 38–43, 47.

Sadler, D. R. 1989. Formative assessment and the design of instructional systems. *Instructional Science, 18*: 119–144.

Schmidt, W. H., C. C. McKnight, & S. A. Raizen. 1996. *Splintered vision: An investigation of U.S. science and mathematics education: Executive summary*. Lansing, MI: U.S. National Research Center for the Third International Mathematics and Science Study, Michigan State University. Cited in Schmoker & Marzano, 1999.

Schmoker, M. 2002. The real causes of higher achievement. *SEDLetter, 14*(2). Retrieved 12 May 2004 from the World Wide Web: http://www.sedl.org/pubs/sedletter/v14n02/1.html

Schmoker, M., & R. Marzano. 1999. Realizing the promise of standards-based education. *Educational Leadership, 56*(6): 17–21. Retrieved 14 May 2004 from the World Wide Web: http://www.ascd.org/publications/ed_lead/199903/schmoker.html

Shavelson, R. J., G. P. Baxter, & X Gao. 1993. Sampling variability of performance assessments. *Journal of Educational Measurement, 30*(3): 215–232.

Shavelson, R. J., G. P. Baxter, & J. Pine. 1992. Performance assessments: Political rhetoric and measurement reality. *Educational Researcher, 21*(4): 22–27.

Shutes, R., & S. Peterson. 1994. Seven reasons why a textbook is not a curriculum. *NASSP Bulletin, 78*(565): 11–20.

Smith, E. 1990. Why grade student writing? *Washington English Journal,* Fall: 24–28.

Sparks, D. 1998. "Professional development." *AEA Advocate,* 18–21. Cited in Schmoker, 2002.

Stiggins, R. J. 2005. *Student-involved assessment* for *learning*, 4th ed. Upper Saddle River, NJ: Merrill/Prentice Hall.

Stigler, J. W., & J. Hiebert. 1999. *The teaching gap: Best ideas from the world's teachers for improving education in the classroom.* New York, NY: Free Press. Cited in Schmoker, 2002.

Tierney, R. J., M. A. Carter, & L. E. Desai. 1991. *Portfolio assessment in the reading-writing classroom.* Urbana, IL: National Council of Teachers of English. Norwood, MA: Christopher-Gordon.

Washington state essential academic learning requirements: Arts. 2004. Olympia, WA: Office of Superintendent of Public Instruction. Retrieved 14 May 2004 from the World Wide Web: http://www.k12.wa.us/CurriculumInstruct/Arts/default.aspx

Washington state essential academic learning requirements: Civics. 2004. Olympia, WA: Office of Superintendent of Public Instruction. Retrieved 14 May 2004 from the World Wide Web: http://www.k12.wa.us/CurriculumInstruct/SocStudies/civicsEALRs.aspx

Washington state essential academic learning requirements: Social studies skills. 2004. Olympia, WA: Office of Superintendent of Public Instruction. Retrieved 14 May 2004 from the World Wide Web: http://www.k12.wa.us/CurriculumInstruct/SocStudies/socstudiesskillsEALRs.aspx

Wiggins, G., & J. McTighe. 1998. *Understanding by design.* Alexandria, VA: Association for Supervision and Curriculum Development.

Index

Assessment uses and users, 14-15: needs of, 16, 18, 26, 27 table 1.2

Auditing for Balance, 285 act. 9.2

B

Bias and distortion: in assessment methods, 27 table 1.2, 115-16 fig. 4.4, 118, 180, 193, 271-72, 273, 275, 294, 394, 396, 398, 408, 413, 422, 427 act. 13.7; in rubrics, 203, 205, 220 fig. 7.6, 221

Black, Paul, 38, 40, 279

Borko, H., 20

C

Central Kitsap School District, 209-10, 237

Clarke, Shirley, 58-59

Classification, 67

Class size, 37

Communication, 12, 15, 16: effectiveness of, 17, 26, 27 table 1.2; of learning targets, 292-97, 379; of test results, 388, 410, 422, 424. *See also* conferences.

Conference Evaluation Form, 376

Conferences, 260, 279: achievement, 378-80; demonstration of growth, 375-76, 377 fig. 12.5; feedback, 363, 365-67; follow-up, 376, 377 fig. 12.5, 378 fig. 12.6, 381, 382 fig. 12.7, 383; goal-setting, 367-74, 381; intervention, 374-75; options for, 364 table 12.1; parent-teacher, 45, 296, 304, 374-75; participants in, 365, 378-80; purposes of, 361, 363; student-led, 376, 378-81, 385 act. 12.5. 385 fig. 12.8; time limits of, 236-37, 261, 365-66, 373

Confidence Questionnaire, 28 act, 1.7, 275, 429

Content standards, 54, 75, 80-81, 83, 101, 367: key words, 64 table 3.2; in test development, 112, 133

F

Feedback, 6, 29, 41, 279: descriptive 36-38, 40, 42 fig. 2.2, 93, 154, 197, 203, 214, 236-37, 239, 241 table 7.8, 245, 258, 281, 283-84, 287, 313, 365; evaluative, 38, 283-84; formative, 237, 238 fig. 7.13, 365; negative impact of, 9, 39; "stars and stairs," 43-44; written, 236, 237, 239, 295. *See also* conferences.

Foreign Languages: learning targets in, 63 table 3.1, 97 act. 4.2, 176, 254; rubrics for, 211-16; sample tests, 265

Formative assessment. *See* assessment *for* learning.

"Franzipanics," 139 act. 5.5, 140 fig. 5.6

Franzipanics Answers, 139 act. 5.5

G

Goal setting, 74: frames for, 369 fig. 12.2, 370 fig. 12.3, 371 fig. 12.4; long-term, 373-74; by students, 44, 163 fig. 5.15, 345-47, 367-9, 372, 375

Goal-Setting Frames, 374 act. 12.2

Goal Setting with Tests, 158 act. 5.7

Grading, 3, 13, 27 table 1.2, 33 table 2.2, 38, 40, 46, 117, 332 act. 10.9, 333 table 10.6, 427 act. 13.7: absence of, 282, 283, 301; averaging, 314, 324-25; equivalents, 403-05, 406 table 13.2, 422; final, 281, 283, 321, 324, 329 table 10.5; guidelines for, 302, 305, 311-16, 318-21, 323-28, 331-32; keys, 292, 294, 296; of late work, 307 act. 10.3; limitations of, 39, 43, 304, 310, 314, 368; negative impact of, 301, 308, 310, 324, 331; normative, 314, 392; practices of, 303 act. 10.1; principles of, 306, 308-11; purpose of, 301-02, 304-05; recording of, 285, 286 table 9.1, 287-88, 289 table 9.2, 290 table 9.3; on report cards, 14, 17, 24, 29, 35 table 2.3, 279, 285, 288, 301-32, 378; rubrics for, 33 table 2.2, 316, 318-21, 324 fig. 10.5, 328-30 table 10.5, 331; and sampling, 320, 327; standards-based, 288, 292, 304, 311, 314-15, 331-32; student-involved, 325, 330 table 10.5; summarization in, 291-92; weighted, 315-16. *See also* scoring.

Graphic Organizers, 69

Group work, 105: class discussions, 261-62; in performance assessment, 223, 245, 254, 365; problems with, 272; rubric for, 262, 263-64 act. 263, 273; teacher collaboration, 57, 84

Growth Conference, 376

Guskey, T. R., 314

H

Health class: goal setting in, 368, 369 fig. 12.2

Homework, 38, 281, 284, 372

I

Indicators, 27 table 1.2

Inference: defining of, 65; testing of, 97 act. 4.2, 102, 146, 154 fig. 5.9, 155, 156 fig. 4.10, 170

Intended learning. *See* learning targets.

Intentional teaching, 56

Interpretive exercises, 146

J

Journals, 93: coding in, 267-68, 269 act. 8.5; dialogue, 270; guidelines for, 266-67; learning logs, 44, 93, 270; personal, 269-70; response, 267

Juneau Borough School District, 282

K

Keys to Classroom Assessment, 31 act. 2.1

Knight, Janice, 267-68

Knowledge targets, 61-62, 72-73, 75 table 3.4, 153 fig. 5.8, 164, 170: content standards of, 64 table 3.2; examples of, 63 table 3.1; identification of, 70-71; method matching for, 99, 100 table 4.1, 101-02, 111 table 4.4, 125 fig. 5.2, 129, 169 fig. 6.2; proposition writing for, 134

L

Language Arts: gradebook for, 333 table 10.6; learning targets in, 58, 63 table 3.1, 185 fig. 6.6, 223, 282; program evaluation, 4-6; reasoning in, 68, 69, 70 table 3.3. *See also* writing proficiency.

Learning targets, 10, 12, 13 fig. 1.2, 17, 26, 55 fig. 3.1, 60 fig. 3.2, 75 table 3.4: accountability testing, 3, 6, 56, 77-78, 89; benefits of, 54, 60-61; communication of, 292-97, 379; framing of, 17-18, 27 table 1.2, 33 table 2.2, 42 fig. 2.2, 84, 368-69; language clarity of, 15, 42-43, 58-59, 292-97; in mathematics, 10, 53-54, 292; method matching, 95, 96-98 act. 4.2, 99 fig. 4.2, 105-06, 112-13, 120 act. 4.6, 125, 169 fig. 6.2, 191 fig. 7.2, 253 fig. 8.2; organization of, 76-77, 111, 285, 286 table 9.1, 287-88; and self-assessment, 46, 59; sources of, 75-76; standards in, 56, 80-83, 311, 398; success criteria, 58-59. *See also* dispositional targets; knowledge targets; performance assessment; product targets; reasoning.

Learning teams, 20-22, 26

M

Matching tests, 91, 123, 137, 138 table 5.3: guidelines for, 144-45, 149, 150 fig. 5.7

Mathematics: goal setting, 367; learning targets in, 44, 57-58, 63 table 3.1, 68, 106, 130, 170, 183 fig. 6.6, 282; rubrics for, 234-35; standards in, 10, 53-54; test plans, 130 table 5.1, 222

"Measurement-ese," 390-91 act. 13.2, 428 act. 13.8

Measurement-ese Answers, 390 act. 13.2, 428 act. 13.8

Metarubric, 218 act. 7.4

Modeling, 152, 241 table 7.8, 245, 258, 267, 363, 374. *See also* sampling.

Motivation, 3, 27, 223, 225, 298: and assessment, 19 act. 1.6, 25 fig. 1.4, 27 table 1.2, 29, 36-38, 40, 41 act. 2.2, 46, 51 fig. 2.3, 429; and conferences, 373, 378; and grading, 281, 301, 304-06, 308-09, 310; lack of, 39, 103, 115, 283, 415 table 13.3; in self-assessment, 4, 6, 152, 157, 185, 268

Multiple-choice tests, 15, 91, 123, 138 table 5.3, 393-94, 397: examples of, 136, 137 fig. 5.5, 139, 140 fig. 5.6, 141-43; guidelines for, 142-44, 146, 149, 150 fig. 5.7, 155; limitations of, 115 table 4.4

Classroom Assessment *for* Student Learning
Doing It Right — Using It Well

Rick Stiggins, Judith Arter, Jan Chappuis and Steve Chappuis

The concepts, skills and instructional strategies needed to apply assessment *for* learning in your classroom.

Classroom Assessment for *Student Learning: Doing It Right — Using It Well* is the core of a larger, comprehensive professional development program that comes in either a Professional Development Package for staff development specialists or in a School Package for school-wide implementation. These packages also include the following interactive training videos on DVD:

- *Assessment* for *Student Motivation*
- *Evaluating Assessment Quality: Hands-On Practice*
- *Assessing Reasoning in the Classroom*
- *Commonsense Paper and Pencil Assessments*
- *Designing Performance Assessments* for *Learning*
- *Grading & Reporting in Standards-Based Schools*
- *Student-Involved Conferences*

Jan Chappuis   Steve Chappuis   Rick Stiggins   Judy Arter

www.assessmentinst.com/resources/ati-study-guides/

ISBN-13: 978-0-13-254876-2
ISBN-10:   0-13-254876-3

EAN

9 780132 548762

90000